THE OXFORD CENTRE FOR
HEBREW AND JEWISH STUDIES

The Oxford Centre for Hebrew and Jewish Studies, established in 1972 as the Oxford Centre for Postgraduate Hebrew Studies (and known by that name until the end of 1993), is one of the world's leading institutes for academic research and teaching in Jewish studies. It is an autonomous academic institution enjoying very close links with the University of Oxford; the work of its Fellows, most of whom hold University lectureships in their various fields of scholarly specialization, is fully integrated into that of the University. Its courses are open to graduates and undergraduates, and several hundred students have participated in them. In addition, leading scholars from all over the world have accepted invitations to come to the Centre, either as Visiting Fellows or to participate in conferences, seminars, and symposia.

THE LITTMAN LIBRARY OF JEWISH CIVILIZATION

EDITORS
Philip Alexander
Nicholas de Lange
Jonathan Israel

MANAGING EDITOR
Connie Wilsack

Dedicated to the memory of
LOUIS THOMAS SIDNEY LITTMAN
who founded the Littman Library
for the love of God
and in memory of his father
JOSEPH AARON LITTMAN
יהא זכרם ברוך

'Get wisdom, get understanding:
Forsake her not and she shall preserve thee'
PROV. 4: 5

Jewish Identities in the New Europe

EDITED BY

JONATHAN WEBBER

PUBLISHED FOR

**THE OXFORD CENTRE FOR
HEBREW AND JEWISH STUDIES**

London · Washington
Littman Library of Jewish Civilization
1994

The Littman Library of Jewish Civilization
74 Addison Road, London W14 8DJ, UK

1640 Rhode Island Avenue, NW
Washington DC 20036–3278, USA

© The Oxford Centre for Hebrew and Jewish Studies 1994

A catalogue record for this book is available from the British Library

Library of Congress Cataloging-in-Publication Data
Jewish identities in the new Europe / edited by Jonathan Webber
p.   cm.
Includes bibliographical references and index.
1. Jews—Europe—Identity—Congresses.
2. Jews—Europe—History—20th century—Congresses.
3. Holocaust, Jewish (1939–1945)—Influence—Congresses.
I. Webber, Jonathan.
DS 135.E83J5 1994
940'.04924—dc20   93-47335 CIP
ISBN 1–874774–15–3

Copy-editing: Connie Wilsack
Proof-reading: Connie Wilsack and Janet Moth
Design by Pete Russell, Faringdon, Oxon
Typeset by Footnote Graphics, Warminster, Wiltshire
Printed and bound in Great Britain by
Biddles Ltd., Guildford and King's Lynn

'Be fruitful and multiply;
a nation and a company of nations shall be of thee.'

Foreword

THE collection of essays presented in this volume derives from a symposium held in Oxford in 1992—the year when the 'new Europe' came
into being. Soon after the beginning of the symposium, we became aware
that we were moving into a new cognitive dimension: not only because
many of the facts presented were new, but because it soon became apparent
that the contemporary Jewish condition—in Europe, and in terms of the
relationship between the Jewish communities of Europe and those outside
it—warranted new criteria of interpretation.

The invited group that attended the symposium comprised Jewish and
non-Jewish scholars and Jewish intellectuals. Most had been involved for
many years with the problems of contemporary Jewish life. They included
people from western Europe, Israel, and the United States, and also people
from the former Communist countries, who brought their own preoccupations to the deliberations.

The integrated effort of all present established an intellectual atmosphere
in which the new information delivered was not merely absorbed but was
shifted through the lens of the diverse approaches and academic disciplines
represented around the table. Significantly, one of the participants said at the
concluding session that he was leaving in chastened mood, aware that he
would have to re-evaluate concepts and refocus approaches. He expressed a
feeling that was widely shared.

The symposium dealt not only with the more familiar, internal dimensions
of Jewish life, but also with the external ones, meaning the consequences
for Jews of developments within the wider society. Such developments can
be broadly categorized under three headings: political and economic; religious; and ideological.

The external development most urgently affecting Jews is unquestionably
the political and economic upheaval in most former Communist states. The
remaining Jewish communities of these countries, now only shadows of the
powerful east European Jewries of the pre-Holocaust years, are striving to
reorganize themselves. The pictures drawn by participants from those countries were bewildering in their complexity.

On the external religious front, discussions focused on the efforts that
have been going on in the last two generations towards a theological
redefinition of the Christian–Jewish relationship. The main element of this

is the recognition by the Protestant and Catholic churches that their negative attitude towards Jews and Judaism was one of the elements that facilitated the Nazi destruction of European Jewry. This recognition is only a first step in a long spiritual elaboration of the theological problem that Judaism poses to contemporary Christianity; its final resolution is likely to take a long time, requiring as it does a series of involved and difficult decisions. The Protestant Church seems to be more incisive in this regard than the Catholic Church, whose pace has faltered somewhat since the promising start made by Vatican II in 1965.

The main ideological aspect of the external Jewish condition to be considered was antisemitism. Here again, a chequered picture emerged. In most west European countries, relations between Jews and non-Jews are good; in the former Communist countries the situation is less reassuring, particularly since economic hardship and ideological turmoil are reviving old antisemitic slogans. In this respect, little seems to have changed since the 1920s and 1930s. It remains to be seen what new ideological and spiritual attitudes towards Jews will unfold in the Muslim states of the former Soviet Union. Fuelled by the ongoing Arab–Israeli conflict, Islamic fundamentalism in the Middle East is developing new antisemitic attitudes that are spreading to Muslim countries elsewhere, and even to the increasing Muslim population in western Europe.

But Muslim antisemitism is not the only new ideological development with which Jews are now confronted: in western Europe, as in the United States, the New Age movement, which now has many millions of followers, poses an increasing threat. Antisemitism and anti-Zionism are central components of the New Age ideology. While in some respects that ideology appears illogical and inconsistent, historical experience should make Jews aware of the possible consequences.

In discussing the internal Jewish scene, it became clear that Jews have conflicting perceptions of their fellow Jews in other countries as both 'self' and 'other', and that this is a major element in the shaping of Jewish attitudes to the Jews and Jewish communities of other countries. Interestingly, the unfolding of the Jewish existence in Europe seems on some levels to be a replay of the formulations and controversies of an earlier age—the confrontations between religious and secular (now also called ethnic) conceptions of the Jewish people, or between diverse religious positions, such as Progressive Judaism versus Orthodox Judaism.

Much consideration is also being given to the contemporary significance of the Zionist idea. None among the participants was indifferent to the Zionist idea, but attitudes varied about what role it might now fulfil. In the background was the obvious presence of the State of Israel—as alternatively a source of support, a country in need of support, a challenge, or a possible place of refuge in time of need—but the sentiment that emerged was far from clear on whether the ideological significance of Zionism and the communal and political significance of the Jewish state are necessarily related. On the one hand, classical Zionist ideology has developed a diaspora-oriented agenda: Zionist organizations, and foremost the Jewish Agency, are now supporting Jewish endeavours in diaspora countries even if they are not related to *aliyah*. On the other hand, some of the participants related how Zionist institutions had been reluctant to assist efforts to reorganize Jewish communities in the former Soviet Union. The majority of the participants saw this opposition as negative.

Last but not least, several contributions dealt with the Holocaust and its consequences. There was a general awareness that the after-effects of the destruction of such a large part of European Jewry are still being felt— although it must be said that the Jewish response to the shock has not been one of despair, but rather a sense of responsibility for the living and an awareness of the need to rebuild the basis of Jewish existence.

Most of the internal and external issues of Jewish life considered at the conference found their reflections in the discussions about present-day Jewish demography. It became evident that there are still large segments of the Jewish people who, as in the past, are 'sitting on packed suitcases', ready to leave the countries where they are living. For the Jewish people, it seems, the age of large-scale migration is not yet over.

One particular demographic consideration emerged very clearly: in counting Jews today, conventional Jewish demographic categories are no longer relevant. Jewish demographers are now talking about 'core' and 'enlarged' Jewries. Participants were quick to confirm the growing relevance of these categories, although there was some debate about the criteria for definition and the relative size of both categories. Recent American Jewish censuses have suggested that using the more inclusive definition would increase the estimated size of the American Jewish community by nearly 50 per cent.

Core Jewry is easy to define: those Jews who define themselves as such, are recognized as Jews by their Jewish environment, and conform in a relatively broad sense with traditionally accepted criteria of Jewishness. The difficulties start with the enlarged category: non-Jews living in Jewish households and participating in Jewish patterns of life; Jews who do not consider themselves Jewish; Jews (and also non-Jews) who participate in Jewish *and* non-Jewish religious activities (like attending both church and synagogue); and non-Jews of Jewish ancestry seeking a way back to Judaism.

A central process in twentieth-century Jewish society has been that cultural and social integration in the general environment has often been accompanied by a loss of Jewish identity. While this process continues to be common, especially in the Americas and in western Europe, the reverse trajectory is also appearing: de-assimilation. People with some Jewish family connections, sometimes two or more generations back, are increasingly looking for ways to return to the fold. Sometimes the motivation is intellectual or emotional, but in many cases there appears to be genuine subjectivization of the ways of defining who is a Jew. The lack of clarity in how to cope with this new demographic and sociological situation is causing sharp debate among Jews and Jewish institutions, particularly with the opening up of eastern Europe.

Systematic description of the internal and external components that together comprise the current Jewish reality is important to understanding contemporary Jewish identities, but cannot convey the sense of wonder about the dynamics and complexities of contemporary Jewish life that comes across so strongly in these essays. Even the definition of Europe is not at all self-evident in this context: for some, 'Europe' means the European community (i.e. western Europe, but excluding Switzerland, Austria, and the other non-member countries); for others, 'Europe' extends from Gibraltar to Russia—and thus even as far as Vladivostok on the Sea of Japan.

One of the fascinating things that emerges from this volume is the extent to which each of the major Jewish centres in Europe (however defined), the United States, and Israel experiences centrifugal and centripetal forces in their attitudes towards the other centres. The diverse models of religious behaviour rooted in this or that Jewish centre may be accepted or rejected by Jews from other centres, depending on their ideological or religious orientation. In the final debate of the symposium, one of the speakers accused the participants from some of the western European Jewries of indifference to what was going on in other Jewish centres. There was criticism of what was seen as Israeli ambivalence towards the efforts of the Jews of the former Soviet Union to organize communities and organizations *in situ*. It became clear that there are circumstances in which the influence of Israel is seen as beneficial, and circumstances in which it is resented.

Historical experience indicates how old these claims and counter-claims are, and that the inherent dilemmas cannot easily be completely resolved. But our symposium saw the debate itself as significant. From the very beginning an unformulated question influenced the deliberations: given that the diverse segments of contemporary Jewry are so extremely different in their characteristics and problems, what do they in fact have in common? Indeed, what was it that had brought two dozen eminent, busy people to undertake long journeys from far-away countries in order to spend three days discussing the condition of contemporary European Jewry?

The most rational answer is that the deliberations were inspired by an overall idea: in spite of the geographical and the spiritual differences that had come up or flared up during the deliberations, there was an underlying awareness of shared interest, common belonging, and even of mutual commitment. The underlying ideology was rarely explicitly mentioned; apparently it was simply taken for granted. Its classical name would be the *kelal yisrael* concept: the age-old principle of the mutual responsibility of one Jew for the other, and of one Jewish community for the next one.

E.F.

Preface and Acknowledgements

THE idea for this book came from a conference on Jewish Identities in the New Europe held in July 1992 in Yarnton Manor, the home of the Oxford Centre for Postgraduate Hebrew Studies. The conference, and this resulting publication, was sponsored by Mr Frank Green, a private Anglo-Jewish benefactor, as part of a wider programme under his sponsorship established in the 1980s to assess key issues in the contemporary Jewish world. The programme, which provides for co-operation between the Oxford Centre for Postgraduate Hebrew Studies and the Hebrew University of Jerusalem, has supported academic posts, young researchers, international academic symposia, and publishing. The Frank Green Programme has thus come to represent a most fruitful initiative and among other things continues to bring together scholars concerned with contemporary Jewish life.

The subject of Jewish identities in the new Europe can be approached in a variety of ways, and the range of essays in this volume attests to the fact. In considering how best to represent this graphically on the front cover, I worked together with the managing editor of the Littman Library, Connie Wilsack, and the Library's designer, Pete Russell, to find a series of images that would together evoke something of the range of identities being discussed. By way of a preface, then, it seems appropriate to identify them.

First, the photographs of the individuals; they all have English connections, but the biographies are very different. The young boy in the uniform of the Hasmonean Jewish Primary School in London, Robert Lederman, graduated from City University and the B'nei Akiva youth movement and then left England for Israel, to study at the yeshivah in Efrat in the West Bank. Mrs Colette Littman, director of the Littman Library, was born and educated in Egypt but now divides her time between London and Dorset, in the heart of the English countryside; her late husband, Louis Littman, founder of the Littman Library, was born in London to Polish Jewish parents and educated in America and Cambridge. Many will recognize the photograph of the British chief rabbi, Jonathan Sacks, the first occupant of that post to have studied at both the University of Cambridge and the University of Oxford. There is a photograph of my mother, Carmel Webber, probably the first Jewish woman to have been born in Golders Green in London, today one of Europe's most important Jewish centres. Her own mother was Romana Goodman, one of the founders of Wizo, the Women's International Zionist Organization, and her father was Paul Goodman, author of a history of the Jewish people and executive secretary for fifty years to the Spanish and Portuguese Jews' Congregation in London. The four Hasidim, members of the Lehrer and Strassman families, today live in Antwerp; Mr Strassman senior was born and educated in Golders Green, but his father-in-law, Mr Lehrer senior, is a survivor of Auschwitz, having been born in Nowy Sacz in Poland. The photograph was taken outside the Remuh Synagogue in Cracow when the family returned recently to Poland to visit their place of origin and pray at the tombs of revered Hasidic rabbis.

The other photographs on the front cover represent a different set of Jewish identities. The French flag, for instance, carries an inscription in Yiddish identifying it as the standard of the French Communist Jewish resistance during the Second World War; the photograph was taken at a rally held outside the town hall of Cannes in April 1992 to protest the release from a French prison of a Nazi war criminal. There is a wall-painting from the *beis hamidrash* of the main synagogue of Piotrków Trybunalski in central Poland, the holes made by Nazi bullets still clearly visible in the simple representation of the ten commandments. The photographs of other Jewish monuments in eastern Europe show something of the magnificence of Jewish art in these long-established communities: the floral decorations and the picture of the hands of a *kohen* raised in priestly blessing are elements of the baroque splendour of the synagogue in Łancut, Poland, while the turrets belong to the building that housed the Burial Society of Prague. Finally, for a collection of this kind we could not resist a section of text from the Book of Esther, a tale about the destiny of Jews scattered across 127 provinces of an ancient empire.

It is with much pleasure that I record my warm thanks to a number of people who not only made this book possible but also assisted in a variety of ways. First to Mr Frank Green, for sponsoring the Fellowship in Jewish Social Studies that I hold at the Oxford Centre for Postgraduate Hebrew Studies. I am most grateful to Dr David Patterson, founder president of the Oxford Centre, through whose encouragement my academic interest in the field of modern Jewish society first came about, and to his successor, Professor Philip Alexander. The conference on which this book is based was organized together with Professor Evyatar Friesel and Professor Robert Wistrich, and needless to say it would not have come about at all had it not been for their energy, imagination, and commitment to the topic; it was their input from the outset that assured the quality of that meeting. Everyone present at the conference was unanimous in their praise of Priscilla Frost, conference manager and administrator extraordinaire. She often worked late into the night—as subsequently did Mary Aldworth in typing the edited papers. The copy-editing was undertaken by Connie Wilsack with loving care. I am grateful to her for permitting me to spell 'east Europe' with a lower-case 'e' (to reflect a 'new Europe' approach to a united Europe, where geography is no longer politics). My thanks go also to Ludo Craddock and Janet Moth for their patience in dealing with a slow and preoccupied editor; their understanding and co-operation were much appreciated.

A briefcase full of these typescripts has accompanied me round a series of travels and research visits in a number of European countries, both east and west; it is almost with regret that I realize that I shall no longer be shuffling them about in the restaurant cars of trans-European express trains. My final thanks, therefore, are to Professor Detlef Hoffman and his colleagues at the Kulturwissenschaftliches Institut in Essen, whose generous invitation to a Fellowship enabled me to finish my work on this book in a supremely serene and civilized atmosphere.

Essen   J.W.
November 1993

Contents

Introduction

JONATHAN WEBBER

CONTINUITY AND DISCONTINUITY IN JEWISH IDENTITY

T HE meaning and purpose of Jewish identity has all been explained long, long ago. The early books of the Hebrew Bible first described the outlook of the ancestors of the Jewish people, provided the text of the divine revelation at Mount Sinai, and narrated the details of the journey—both physical and spiritual—towards a homeland. Later books of the Bible, followed successively by the Mishnah and Talmud, and then by subsequent rabbinic literature, established a chain of tradition that in effect provides a continuous link between the ancient Hebrews and the Jews of our own day. The technical specifications governing the nature of Jewish identity have thus been worked on for millennia. Anyone interested in this or that aspect needs merely to consult these learned texts; for the benefit of those untrained in interpreting the technicalities, specialists have usually been available in each generation to transmit an explanation, elaboration, or commentary. Indeed, Jewish history in this sense is little more than the constant reworking and remodelling of the ancient vision according to the local circumstances of the day.

Have the Jews lost sight of their ancient vision because of the enormously long series of transmissions from generation to generation? Has the chain of tradition become so long that the original biblical imagination has become garbled and perhaps even unrecognizable in the process? Until modern times, the Jews mainly resisted formulating a heresy of this kind, but over the past couple of centuries or so the European enlightenment has slowly come to penetrate the Jewish outlook on the world (particularly among those Jews living in Europe itself). As part of the attempt towards an assimilation into wider European society and a broad acceptance of its social ideals, Jews have increasingly been taking a critical look at the ideological basis of their identity and questioning the received ideas. What has come about as a result has been a massive disintegration and rejection of the traditional consensus. Some Jews—probably the majority, in fact—have reached the point not only that they now regard the tradition as out of date, or out of touch with reality, but also that they see the need to base their own Jewish identity specifically on contemporary, modern preoccupations (Zionism, or the need to fight antisemitism, for example). To be sure, pockets of traditionalists are also ubiquitous in the Jewish world today—those who continue to espouse a feeling of religious self-identification with the Mosaic lawgiver or the greatest of the talmudic or medieval sages. But to speak about modernists as forming a majority conceals other realities. Traditional religious observance has certainly largely collapsed, along with traditional Jewish learning, as the principal Jewish ideal today; and yet the classical ideal has found newer contexts for its self-expression. Zionism restated the ancient Hebrew attachment to the homeland in Palestine—albeit in the modernist terms of national self-determination—and it also brought about the resurrection of the ancient Hebrew tongue as a modern spoken language. Moreover, the very survival of the Jews as an identifiable group, whether in the State of Israel or in the diaspora, also leans on an ancient Jewish concept: the idea of Jewish peoplehood, of Jews as a people with its own special destiny that needs to be fought for, or at least struggled with; and that membership of this people by and large rests on an inheritance from a parent, and thereby from a founding ancestor.

In short, it may well be that at a casual glance the Jews of today seem to differ very markedly in their culture and outlook from how they once used to live; but this is, on the other hand, something quite normal where the transmission of identity is concerned, particularly during times of major social change or over long intervals of time. A twentieth-century Englishman might well have difficulty in engaging in casual conversation with a contemporary of Shakespeare; but both of them, while being able to recognize something of a common culture, would also unequivocally claim membership of an English inheritance, that they are both English. The strange thing about a national, cultural, or linguistic identity is that on the surface it does not necessarily transmit very well from generation to generation; but the fact that some of the manifestations of that identity have become garbled or unrecognizable does not mean that the basic identity has ceased to exist in the popular imagination. On the contrary, what usually happens is that although many of the outward manifestations of identities evolve over time, by being transformed or even totally discarded, ordinary people often tend to pay little attention to the implications of this—much as it is taken for granted that in each generation there will be the need for a fresh, updated edition of the *Oxford English Dictionary*—a succession of dictionaries of the same language, as it is thought. On the other hand, it is also possible that people may finally decide that the language has changed so much that the time has come to give it a new name, and to give themselves a new identity.

The splitting up and disappearance of old identities, and the erection of new boundaries between past identities and new ones, are indeed common pursuits in the history of humanity. In one sense they are simply exercises in futility, since the decision where to make a cut within what is essentially a continuum is purely arbitrary and without any internal justification; in another sense, there may be very good external reasons, based on a variety of political or other circumstances, why the need is felt to rationalize, and to rearrange the world according to contemporary realities.

Whether the Jews of today, then, are the 'same' people as that described in the ancient texts of the Bible is a question that permits no single answer. Jewish identity seen historically reveals both continuity and discontinuity; where the emphasis is to be placed depends on a person's point of view. Traditionalists, in defence of their position, do not need to argue that nothing has changed since the time of Moses, since in any case that would be patently absurd; what they do require, however, is to maintain an attitude towards the past that rests on the assumption that the change that has taken place is of no relevance in defining their present-day identity. It is as if nothing has changed; they are merely (so to speak) rewriting the same old dictionary for today's generation, because the underlying ideology that generated the original identity in the first place is felt to be too important for it to be dispensed with merely because the external circumstances no longer apply. Modernists, however, demand a new appraisal of all the facts and circumstances; for them the very existence of change, even if it is externally derived, is decisive. The 'as if' of the former pattern of Jewish identity constitutes for them a fiction which is neither valid nor desirable.

The critical mode in which identities are fashioned and refashioned thus depends on the degree to which the old assumptions are given precedence over the new evidence, or vice versa. There is a little more to it than that, however. What complicates the picture for those seeking new identities is that their newer identities are seldom based on a total *carte blanche* but in fact rest on assumptions of various kinds inherited from the past (sometimes uncritically) alongside their more rational and up-to-date expositions. The reverse proposition also holds good for those who apparently cling to older styles of identities: they also incorporate into their culture aspects of their contemporary world, even though they may not formally ascribe very much to them by way of ideological significance. The empirical realities, in other words, are highly deceptive. Strictly Orthodox Hasidic Jews, to give a concrete example, may appear by some of their forms of dress to be particularly backward-looking; but they have thrived in the most modern of metropolises such as New York, one reason for which being that they have found excellent ways of adapting to the demands of participating in the economic

structures of modern capitalism.[1] Similarly, secular Jewish Israelis may
appear highly detribalized in terms of their attitudes to their own Jewishness;
and yet (as Eliezer Schweid notes in Chapter 2) they retain a residual historical
consciousness through their attachment to the Hebrew language and a quasi-
biblical mythology regarding their relationship with the land of Israel.

What all this amounts to in effect is that identities do not have an
existence independently of the people who embrace them. Of course the
ideologies that are used to explain and legitimate identities usually put the
emphasis on how very old they are, how very logical and reasonable they are,
how objectively true they are. Identities are treated by peoples as if they
really existed; but in practice identities are constructs that are shaped and
fashioned by the people who rely on them, and they may be full of internal
contradictions of all kinds. Identities may run for centuries without being
substantially tampered with; or they may be totally restructured within the
space of a single generation. At the analytic level, it does not really matter:
after all, identities are not perfectly shaped forms of social consciousness, but
rather are cultural attempts, based on the specific social, political, and
economic circumstances of a particular moment in time, for people to make
sense of the world in which they live in terms of their understanding of their
past and their hopes and expectations for the future. The rhetorical quality
of the way in which identities are often described by those who cleave
strongly to them represents the force of belief rather than of fact empirically
verifiable by the disinterested observer; just as beliefs in general are subject
to change (usually because of changing circumstances or at the behest of
political or religious leaders), so too are the structures of supposed fact that
are employed in the construction of identities that ordinary people normally
believe in. Not that everybody always believes in the packaged forms of
identities that are offered up to them by their parents, their school, their
leaders; on the contrary, group identities do not necessarily always show a
good state of health (to use an image favoured by some social psychologists). Identities can be weak, strong, confused, disordered, or in crisis.
Just as individuals may find their personal identities lost or confused
through amnesia (for example) or through not having come to terms with
their childhood, so too individual societies or minority groups may suffer
identity crises if they have lost hold of their history or sense of roots. One
element in the construction or reconstruction of identity that is critically
important, however, is the attitude of outsiders: being named by others,
being identified by outsiders, may not only 'cure' a group's uncertainty
about itself, it is also an essential part of the group's awareness of its
objective existence. For what good is it having a belief in one's own society's
special history and destiny if others do not recognize this also?

The principle of recognition by outsiders (or the lack thereof) has a special place in the study of modern Jewish identities and forms part of the sociology of antisemitism. But in fact the whole image of Jewish life fundamentally being enacted before an interested wider audience has strong biblical resonances: when the ancient Israelites are threatened by God with extinction because of their sins, Moses pleads for the survival of his people on the grounds that the nations of the world would otherwise form quite the wrong impression of God's power, his promises to the Hebrews, and his love for them (Exod. 32: 12–13; Num. 14: 13–16).

It is not the purpose of this book, however, to trace Jewish identities today specifically along biblical lines, using references and allusions such as these. On the contrary, the broad intellectual assumption that underlies this collection of essays is that classical Jewish identity has in the modern world broken up (if not also broken down) into multiple Jewish identities, some of which indeed trace connections with the more distant past, while others define themselves more directly and explicitly through highly contemporary issues. For no longer is it adequate to describe the meaning and purpose of Jewish identity as once it was; Jewish history, as understood by most Jews themselves today, is no longer tied merely to a constant reworking and remodelling of the ancient vision, narrowly defined. For some Jews, of course, this does indeed remain true; and in a sense (it should be said) they are right—not only on spiritual grounds but also because there is no intrinsic reason why the classical definitions of the Jewish experience cannot still be used to describe what has happened to the Jewish people in the present day. But in practice the Jews now see themselves quite differently— in the mirror of their own experience as citizens of the countries in which they live, using the languages of those countries, as well as their political, cultural, and artistic histories and values. And so what this book seeks to capture is a sense of the different ways in which Jewish identities are today defined and experienced—both how Jews define themselves and how they are defined by others. This is also a very different world from the one occasionally encountered in books and films made by romantics who aim to stress the exotic otherness of certain types of Jews, for example through their possession of a photogenic, ethnically distinctive culture; the Jews of this book are not the quaint exemplars of a remote and strange civilization so beloved of folklorists and certain producers of television documentaries.[2] The Jews as described in this book are portrayed through the categories of the different national and local European societies in which they are to be found—for this is the discourse in which Jews describe themselves today. In some respects it is a discourse in which historically they have been described by others—and it is to this, therefore, that we must now turn.

JEWISH IDENTITIES IN THE EUROPEAN CONTEXT

Jewish identities in Europe today inhabit a substantial range of different environments—different political environments, different religious environments, different cultural environments, different linguistic environments. Jewish communities are to be found in every single country in Europe, with the sole exception of Iceland and perhaps one or two of the smaller principalities such as Liechtenstein and Andorra. But the histories of the Jews in all these different lands is by no means uniform: in some cases Jewish settlement goes back to ancient times (Italy, for example, where Jews first arrived in the second century BC); in some cases it dates back to early medieval times (Poland, for example, where the Jews first settled in the ninth century, although its later history dates from the more substantial immigration of the thirteenth century); in some cases Jewish settlement was originally linked to early modern colonialism (such as Gibraltar, where Jews established a community following the British occupation in 1704); and in some cases the Jewish community is comparatively recent in origin (such as Finland, where Jews were not permitted to settle until 1889 and not granted citizenship rights until 1918).[3] There are countries in which Jews have lived continuously from the time of their first settlement there (Denmark or Greece, for example), and there are countries from which Jews were expelled and then subsequently returned after intervals of varying lengths of time (Spain or England, for example). It follows, therefore, that European Jewish social and political history has varied very greatly from country to country and (before the formation of centralized nation-states) even from town to town. Standing behind the present-day realities of European Jewry, then, is an exceptionally complex history of social relations between Jews and the wider environments in which they have lived and a long series of adjustments Jews have been making over many centuries in terms of their economic, political, linguistic, and cultural roles in a very wide range of different European societies. As far as European Jews are concerned, easy generalizations are hard to come by.

The question that needs to be asked, then, is whether, under these circumstances, European Jews have a common history at all. To what extent does it make sense to push the idea that even though European Jews may (or indeed may not) possess a common sense of a shared identity, they nevertheless have no independent existence or self-contained history but rather an infinitely large set of different histories according to their experience of the various societies they have lived amongst? In one sense, of course, this question is merely a reformulation of the issue discussed above—namely, the answer to it depends on whether one is taking a traditionalist or modernist view of the nature of Jewish identities. (For the sake of the argument I am treating these two extreme positions as mutually exclusive alternatives, although—as explained above—they do in fact interpenetrate, and in reality many Jews would find some accommodation between them.) A traditionalist will say that Jewish identity is fixed across time and space, and even though Jewish communities in their own individual sets of circumstances will necessarily make adjustments according to those circumstances, nevertheless those adjustments possess little if any intrinsic Jewish significance. Once the community has moved on (through migration as a consequence of persecution, for example) the cultural experience of the former place of settlement, even though it may have lasted for centuries, is by and large forgotten from the collective Jewish consciousness. A modernist, on the other hand, will say that the social and political parameters of Jewish community existence are defined within a specific place and time, and that it is pointless to make any attempt to understand Jewish life and culture without treating this as a basic starting-point. The Jews of Ireland have quite a different history from the Jews of Greece or the Jews of Portugal. Since most European Jews today in any case identify with the wider societies and countries in which they live, their own history—as indeed Jewish history in general—cannot by definition be detached from the specific context in which it is enacted.

The purpose of this book is not to persuade the reader of the truth or otherwise of either of these two groups of propositions but rather, on the basis of individual case-studies, to set out the complexity of the relationship between Jews and the highly diverse societies in which they live. Are the Jews a single people, with a common destiny, common identity, and sense of purpose—or are they a series of locally defined peoples? The evidence, in fact, reads both ways. Both points of view have their merit and so at one level should be treated as different perspectives which each offer valuable insights into the functioning of Jewish society in the modern world. Both frames of reference need to be kept in mind and are represented in the essays below. However, the modernist perspective is somewhat more complicated than would appear at first sight. It is not merely that Jewish identity is necessarily located in place and time; rather it is that place and time together form an additional identity which Jews need to adapt to and which in the process necessarily influences the form and content of their own Jewish identity. European Jews today are not only Jews; they are also French, Hungarian, Spanish, and so forth. The Jewish identities of Jews in other words represent only part of who they are—their Jewish identities also coexist with their other national, regional, or local identities. Sociologically speaking, the paradox is that Jews are only partially Jewish (to cite Eliezer Schweid's way of putting it in Chapter 2); or, to put it another way, Jews think of themselves as Jewish in some contexts and as (say) Flemish or Swedish in others. Furthermore, these dual forms of identity are by no means fixed, even (to take an extreme but common example) in the lifetime of a single Jewish individual, let alone in the history of the Jews within a single country. Precisely when Jews think of themselves as Jewish and when they do not is certainly subject to at least some conventional social rules, for example governing the specification of the relevant contexts. But such rules cannot always be relied upon: they may change over time, in line with other changes in the general ethos of Jewish life in a particular country at a particular time; and in any case not all Jews, and not all non-Jews, even within a particular country, would necessarily agree on what those rules actually were. The fit, in other words, between the Jewish world and its non-Jewish environment is not only imperfect; it is also unstable, subject to change, variable from place to place and from one moment in time to another, open to misunderstanding and misinterpretation, and in general cumbersome to describe and communicate to others.

The modernist problem, in short, is that once the narrow, classical definition of Jewish identity is discarded in favour of something ostensibly closer to broader, contemporary social realities, there would appear to be no simple, self-evident, and adequate formula to replace it with. Two of the essays below, those by Konstanty Gebert and András Kovács, carefully sketch out the kinds of identity crises experienced by central and eastern European Jews in dealing with the technical and human difficulties created by this intricate web of social relations governing ordinary Jewish life in modern times. Inevitably, one solution to such crises nowadays has been the return by secularized Jews to some form of traditionalism; but such a step, commoner though it has become in recent years, has been adopted only by a comparatively small minority and in any case does not really tackle the principal underlying issues. For the modernist problem originated in the desire of Jews to assimilate into the majority societies in effect by patterning themselves, their culture and lifestyle, even their forms of social organization, on what they saw as the dominant trends in those majority societies— whilst at the same time believing that their Jewish identity could also be preserved, and indeed would best be preserved, by so doing. At least two factors mitigated against this strategy: nationalist forms of antisemitism that opposed Jewish attempts to disappear into mainstream society (a common phenomenon in Europe in the 1920s and 1930s), and political and cultural change in the majority society (for instance, the transition to Communism) that had the unfortunate result of causing certain previous forms of Jewish cultural assimilation to become rapidly out of date and therefore socially unacceptable. Such developments were by no means universal in modern

European Jewish history; but they give an indication of the potential precariousness of identities structured or patterned on external models.

A good deal of Jewish cultural energy has thus characteristically been spent in modern times in reading the external socio-political environment, given the commitment (whether ideological or merely pragmatic) to adapt Jewish identity to suit the circumstances. The essay below by Max Beloff (Chapter 1) argues very clearly that Jewish identities have always been dependent on the changing political structures and local attitudes of their host society—developments over which Jews have obviously very little control. A good example of this is provided by Shmuel Trigano, who describes in Chapter 14 how the recent evolution of the notion of a Jewish community in France was not at all something that was generated internally, that is, within the Jewish world, but rather must be understood in relation to the evolution of wider political models applicable in France. It was only when earlier, Napoleonic models of socio-political forms of association came to be discredited and finally collapsed, as he argues, that today's French Jews felt themselves able finally to consider the real possibility of establishing a Jewish 'community' on current Anglo-American lines. Trigano's case has important implications for the understanding of contemporary Jewish life, as it points directly to the idea that Jewish life indeed evolves simultaneously with the political culture of the countries in which Jews live. A similar argument appears in the essay by Geoffrey Alderman on the Jews of Britain: Jews have long been thought to be a religious minority community, but recently, with the advent of the notion of Britain as a multicultural society, pressure is growing on Jews to restyle themselves as an ethnic group.

Whether or not Jews are an ethnic group is of more than merely terminological interest, despite popular uncertainty surrounding the precise meaning of the term. Labelling by others, as was noted above, forms a definite part of a group's awareness of itself, and it is unquestionable that the ethnic label in today's multicultural discourse does indeed seem to offer Jews a much greater sense of self-esteem (and scope for assertiveness) in comparison with the former religious label, which in a period when Judaism as a religion was commonly thought to be spiritually inferior to its Christian successor was a category that was in practice often used to legitimate anti-Jewish discrimination and prejudice of various kinds. Whether multiculturalism will in fact represent a significant improvement in the position as far as Jews are concerned—whether for example it is a philosophy of tolerance or rather one of simple moral indifference—is a different matter, however. At any rate, as Alderman notes, British Jews are not united in accepting the new ethnic label, although there are definite political and financial advantages for them in doing so because of the structure and policies of central government funding for the educational and other needs of the country's ethnic groups. Trigano's observations from France suggest that relabelling may have all kinds of unforeseen consequences, notably the ranking of Jews alongside other groups in the new category (in this case immigrant communities) with which the Jews feel they do not at all share a common destiny or identity. The two cases certainly offer good examples of Beloff's argument concerning the influence of external socio-political models on the development of Jewish identities; the latter can never be taken for granted as if they functioned on the basis of an internal dynamic alone.

But the intervention by external agencies of the sort described here poses a new problem for minority groups such as the Jews of Europe, and one which pushes the old Jewish ideologies of assimilation into quite a different perspective. For whereas in the past European Jews may have felt they had a sense of the established culture of the majority society into which they wished to assimilate, in today's new Europe on the other hand the mood is one of change towards a different and better tomorrow (at least as articulated by politicians and journalists). Whereas in the past assimilated Jews occasionally found themselves caught out by major changes in national politics, in today's new Europe the Jews have the opportunity, as do all other European citizens, to participate in the future political and economic reconstruction of the continent—and the question for them is to determine what their own social and political philosophy might be in these new circumstances. How do Jews wish to reconstruct their identities in the new Europe? As Dominique Schnapper points out (Chapter 13), the political agenda for the new Europe—especially when viewed in the context of the history of French Jewry—raises fundamental questions not only about the nature of the nation-state but also the terms under which the Jews originally obtained their political emancipation in each country. What is to be the nature of the future relationship between the nation-state and its minority (or ethnic) groups? What, in effect, will become of Jewish identities in the new Europe?

THE NEW EUROPE IN JEWISH PERSPECTIVE

Heavily promoted by politicians, journalists, publishers, and others, the term 'the new Europe' has gained wide currency in the last few years to convey the sense of the immediacy and urgency of the startling developments witnessed in this continent in recent times. The collapse of Communism in eastern Europe, the disintegration of the Soviet Union into fifteen independent republics, the dismantling of the Berlin Wall and the reunification of Germany, and the consolidation of the Single European Market within the European Community, have together formed a truly remarkable group of events which mark the potential for a complete restructuring of European political, economic, and cultural realities. Among other things, they mark the immense new scope opened up for Europeans slowly to reconsider the logic of their existing national and local identities. As far as Europe's Jews are concerned, or as far as they are accustomed to reading the external sociopolitical environment in order to adapt their own identities accordingly, a situation of this kind is surely an important moment for them to take stock of the new realities.

The immediate question, of course, concerns the problem of interpretation. Is there really a 'new Europe' out there in the making, and in the terms supplied by the politicians and mass media, or is the reference merely to the possibility or potential for change? It certainly remains to be seen how far the concept of a united Europe committed to liberal democracy will indeed fire the enthusiasm of ordinary populations, and how far they will remain indifferent, ambivalent, or perhaps even openly hostile to some of the consequences and implications of the new realities, challenges, and opportunities. For example, many people in western Europe have little idea of what the Single European Market means or ought to mean; while in eastern Europe the adjustment to post-Communist conditions is likely to be slow and painful. 'New' does not always signify better—certainly not better for everyone. The process of acknowledging a situation of change will imply that attitudes to the past will change, as will expectations about the future. The process of change (or the awareness of the possibility of change) will necessarily involve the steady re-examination of many of the old certainties about nations, states, and borders, as well as the linguistic and cultural traditions enclosed within them. This means that the attitude of people to their inherited identities will change, a process which will be followed in due course by change in the actual content and character of the identities themselves.

Change in inherited attitudes to identity, if it takes place gradually and imperceptibly, may signify little more than a fresh edition of the *Oxford English Dictionary*, to cite the image referred to earlier. But if it comes about as a consequence and reflection of political and economic upheaval, people's attitudes to the restructuring of who they are as social beings may well take a far more violent turn. Disorder and crisis in matters of identity constitute a substantial challenge to the established order, a fact which is surprisingly not always taken as seriously as indeed it ought to be. President George Bush, in his 1992 State of the Union address, referred to the events in eastern Europe over the previous two or three years, and the end of the great trauma of totalitarianism there, as 'miracles of biblical proportions'.[4] Perhaps so; but what then happened—in a manner totally unpredicted by the White House—was the disintegration of the former Soviet Union along ethnic lines. No new world order came into being after the fall of the Berlin Wall; on the contrary, as Robert Wistrich describes in his essay (Chapter 18), there came about in Germany an unprecedented rise in violent xenophobia by neo-Nazis claiming 'Germany for the Germans' and a growing rejection by millions of Germans of a multiracial or multicultural society. Communism, as Wistrich puts it, had frozen rather than resolved a host of long-dormant but never-forgotten conflicts, tensions, and territorial issues. Once the iron grip of totalitarianism was unfastened, many of the old problems of national identity resurfaced in Europe, as shown by the horrifying realities in Yugoslavia and by the painful divorce that took place in Czechoslovakia. So much for biblical miracles. The White House had evidently been mesmerized by the existence since 1945 of the Cold War into thinking that the conflict between democracies and Communism was the main issue of world politics. In a recent book the American statesman and scholar Daniel Moynihan has described his frustration over several decades in trying to advise the White House of its mistake in thinking that the end of the Cold War would signify the end of history. Perhaps America's naïvety in underestimating the force of ethnicity in other countries may be attributed to its historical commitment to a melting-pot approach to inter-ethnic relations. Its foreign policy, Moynihan sadly concludes, was for too long based on the simple idea that there is nothing fundamentally wrong with peoples, but only with their governments.[5]

It is useful to recall the American approach to such matters, if only to underline the point that the future form of the new Europe, and the interpretation of current change, is not at all self-evident. Certainly there is a very substantial gap between Europe and the United States as regards the history of the political and cultural status of ethnic or religious minority groups, as David Singer specifies in detail (Chapter 24). But we often forget that an American view will thus be based on totally different assumptions from those considered usual in Europe. Moynihan's remarks come as a warning and a reminder. For the implications, as far as Jews are concerned, are most important. What is it that really characterizes the new Europe? Is it the collapse of Communism and the new scope for the peaceful extension throughout the continent of liberal democracy—a development that Jews would today normally associate with good conditions for their security and well-being? Or is it the explosion of new ethnic and nationalist conflict—a development that Jews would today normally associate with the threat of antisemitism, that is, with very poor conditions for their security and wellbeing? The difference is critical. To quote the question as it is put by Sergio DellaPergola (Chapter 3): what is more typical of today's new Europe—Maastricht or Sarajevo?

Part of the answer to that question depends on what would have been thought typical of the old Europe (with which the new is theoretically in contrast). Within the Jewish world, it is primarily the Zionist ideologues, from the end of the last century onwards, who have emphasized a conflict model of European society: as Daniel Gutwein explains (Chapter 23), the Zionist programme for a Jewish state was based on the assumption that Europe is fundamentally conflict-ridden and endemically antisemitic— which was why Jewish interests would be best served by total physical separation from European society. The view that the non-Jewish world is inherently hostile to the Jews remains an integral element of Israeli Jewish identity; all outbreaks of conflict in Europe, even those today, continue to be seen in Zionist politics as confirming this basic picture. It therefore would not be clear, from such a perspective, whether there really is a new Europe today at all.

In one sense, of course, the White House was correct in postulating that the basic script for European realities prior to 1989 was in fact written in 1945, following a war that was nothing less than the veritable 'unmaking of Europe', to cite the graphic phrase of the historian Michael Howard.[6] For Jews in general, regardless of the appropriateness or otherwise of a conflict model of European society, what it is that unquestionably lies at the centre of any Jewish definition or characterization of contemporary Europe is the Holocaust. In Jewish perspective, it was the Holocaust that constituted the unmaking of Europe; it is this, and virtually only this, that has to be seen as providing the basic script of today's Europe. Prior to the war, Europe for Jews had been steadily declining for some time, in terms of its relative demographic importance as compared with the United States, although the cultural vitality of Europe's Jews was probably unsurpassed elsewhere. The Second World War, however, meant the abrupt and brutal murder of two-thirds of Europe's Jewish population. The sheer size of the catastrophe, as well as the destruction of the greatest centres of Jewish cultural and religious life, effectively marked the end of Europe as the major home for the Jews of the world.

Any Jewish reading of today's new Europe must thus be set against the Holocaust-influenced script of the Europe that has preceded it for the past fifty years—or, to put it another way, reading the external socio-political models alone will in this case not be entirely adequate as a basic pattern for understanding contemporary Jewish life. (This is so on the assumption that the Holocaust was merely an 'internal' Jewish affair, a point of view which is itself problematic and in fact begs a number of questions about the nature of twentieth-century European society in general.) For the Holocaust profoundly affected the entire structure of European Jewry. In ideological terms, the Holocaust unambiguously represents (at least retrospectively) the failure of assimilation as a Jewish social ideal; it put into question the whole viability of modern Jewish hopes and expectations concerning the very basis of Jewish existence in European society and the nature of the relationship between the European nation-state and its Jewish population. Also, and much more obviously, the Holocaust totally changed the demographic spread of Jews across the continent. In 1939, on the eve of the war, Europe's Jewish population numbered nine and a half million; in 1990 it stood at about two million (following DellaPergola's figures in Chapter 3). In 1939, the largest Jewish community in Europe was that of Poland, with three and a quarter million Jews. Today, on the other hand, the largest Jewish community in Europe (outside the former Soviet Union) is that of France, with a size of about half a million. To speak about a transformation in European Jewish identities over the past fifty years would be an absurd understatement; it would be more accurate to say that the entire face of European Jewry has changed: its major centres of population, its longest-established communities and traditions—its identity in the most basic sense.

There are a number of different modes in which European Jewish society today should thus still be characterized as essentially post-Holocaust in outlook and structure. Jews have been living in Europe from the time of the Roman empire. For eight hundred years, down to the latter part of the last century, Europe was undoubtedly the principal centre of Jewish life in the world. In 1860, almost 90 per cent of the world's Jews lived in Europe; today the figure is 17 per cent (DellaPergola's figures), and world Jewry now pivots around two main centres, both culturally and demographically— Israel and the United States. Europe has receded to the margins of the Jewish world, and its former great centres of learning and Jewish civilization have become virtually desolate of Jews. Not all of Europe, of course, was occupied by the Germans during the war, with the consequence that the Jewish populations of those countries who thus escaped deportation and murder correspondingly became very much more visible and more important in intra-European Jewish terms after the war was over. The principal case of this was the United Kingdom, whose Jewish population of about 350,000 in 1946[7] was substantially the largest in the continent at that time, although technically there were other countries in this category, albeit with much smaller Jewish populations: for example, Switzerland, Sweden, Spain, Portugal, and the Republic of Ireland. The Jews of Great Britain and elsewhere who thus remained unaffected in a direct sense by the crude realities of the Holocaust suddenly found themselves after the war projected into the forefront of European Jewish life; but, needless to say, their lack of direct experience of the horrors inflicted on their fellow Jews in occupied Europe also came to reinforce the classic British sense of distance from the affairs of continental Europe. British Jews, it should be said, however, did play an important role in the reconstruction of the community life of the often pathetic remnants of pre-war Jewish communities, notably in the Displaced Persons' camps in Germany (a topic discussed by Julius Carlebach in Chapter 17). For despite the scale of the catastrophe, there were survivors, and many of them lived on after the war in their home countries. Even today, there is not a single European country occupied during the war, and from where Jews were deported and murdered, which does not possess its own Jewish community. These reconstructed communities of Holocaust survivors, with Jewish identities reconstructed out of the wreckage of destruction (psychological as well as demographic) all the way across Europe, thus constitute a category quite different from the sort of Jewish community found in Britain today; moving descriptions and case-studies of the former are to be found in this book in the essays by Konstanty Gebert and András Kovács.

Standing behind present-day European Jewish realities, then, is a tortuous and in many ways tragic human history of accommodations and adaptations of identity that Jews have had to make in a variety of post-Holocaust circumstances. But to define European Jewish communities as constituting just these two post-Holocaust types is, admittedly, a little distant in some respects from the totality of contemporary realities and the events of the years that have intervened since the war: much has happened in Europe in the mean time, notably out-migration (principally to Israel and the United States) but also in-migration (of which the major case, described by Dominique Schnapper in Chapter 13, is the massive influx into France in the 1960s of Jews from North Africa following its decolonization).

But without a doubt the most important post-war Jewish event in Europe, and one which brings us back to a contemporary Jewish definition of the new Europe, is the sudden restoration of full links between Western Jews and the Jews of Russia and the former Soviet Union, following the fall of Communism. One of the major recurring messages of this book is surely the need to re-examine existing assumptions and generalizations about Jewish identity on the basis of the Soviet and post-Soviet Jewish evidence and experience. For the new Europe, in Jewish terms, exists at a variety of levels. In addition to the new Europe proposed by political and economic developments within the European Community, and in addition to the new Europe as symbolized by the dismantling of the Berlin Wall (however that is to be interpreted), Europe for Jews assumed a new shape in the years following

the Holocaust and the massive geographical redistribution of centres of
Jewish population and of creative Jewish cultural energy, especially in
relation to the then newly established State of Israel. Today the new Europe
implies yet another level of significance: the restoration to the Jewish world
of populations of Jewish origin in eastern Europe, particularly the former
Soviet Union, where only now for the first time can the long-term effects of
the Holocaust and of Communist assimilation be faced up to. The statement
made above that the largest Jewish community in Europe is that of France
expresses a perception of reality that for several decades took no note of the
Jews of the Soviet Union. Albeit with certain exceptions, Soviet Jews were
largely thought of in the rest of the Jewish world as remote, assimilated to
Communism, isolated—and, if anything, imprisoned. The fall of Communism opened up a new linkage with a vast and largely unknown Jewish
population; it has opened up an entirely new conception of European
Jewish identity—and with it, a host of new questions.

Perhaps the most critical of these questions, one which Mikhail Chlenov
(Chapter 9) explains at some length, concerns the vexed question of who is a
Jew. Culturally speaking, Jews in the Soviet Union were generally denied
access to Jewish education or other types of Jewish belonging such as
synagogue organizations or community centres; they could not express
themselves as Jews. But the system (and certain types of local antisemitism)
prevented them from completely assimilating into Soviet society; and so
Jews they remained, with perhaps only a faded memory of a partial Jewish
ancestry that could confirm their membership of the Jewish people. Who is a
Jew is in any case not at all clear-cut from a formal point of view. There are
many competing definitions that are known from the contemporary European experience, including the classical rabbinic definition (descent from a
Jewish mother, or via conversion from an Orthodox court of rabbis), modern
Progressive rabbinic definitions (descent from a Jewish mother or father, or
via conversion from a Progressive court of rabbis), Nazi definitions (a given
number of Jewish grandparents, regardless of the individual's personal
religious or communal affiliations or identity), and modern personal *ad hoc*
definitions (self-identification with the Jewish people, for whatever reason,
such as being married or related to a Jew; or being labelled by others as
Jewish). The formation of identity, and patterns of self-identification, are
certainly subject to a considerable degree of flexibility and adjustment
according to the circumstances, as was discussed above, and in the Jewish
case there has been a surprising degree of variation (especially given the
popularity of non-Jewish beliefs in the monolithic quality of the Jewish
people); but the definition of who is a Jew in the Soviet Union was stretched
even further by the development of other criteria, including one that rests on

a popular Soviet misinterpretation of Israeli definitions of Jewishness for the purpose of Jewish repatriation to the Jewish state.

The implications of all this are serious: it means that very large numbers of former Soviet Jews are not technically Jewish at all (on the classic rabbinic definition), or at least are Jewish in terms of local definitions not easily exportable or communicable elsewhere—not an insignificant problem, given the fact that such 'Jews' have emigrated in their masses over the past few years to Israel, the United States, Germany, and elsewhere. They are what a social anthropologist might call classificatory Jews—classified as Jews, regardless of their formal legal or religious status as Jews, or of their knowledge of traditional Jewish culture. The result will be a painful identity crisis, a subject addressed in the essay by Eliezer Schweid (Chapter 2), which includes a detailed and sensitive investigation of the cultural consequences, particularly for Israel. Western rabbinic agencies, both Orthodox and Reform, have quickly responded to the powerful need in Russia and Ukraine for Jewish education and have tried to sort out the complex technical issues surrounding personal Jewish status among Soviet Jewish *émigrés* in Germany; but as Jonathan Magonet reports (Chapter 8), the scale of the need far outweighs the relatively small numbers of individuals that can be cared for. Perhaps the situation of Jews in the former Soviet Union today can be compared in a sense with the reconstruction of Jewish life that was undertaken in Germany after 1945, although on this occasion the task is very much larger. Today's psychology and sociology of peace is in some ways more difficult, more elusive, than the former Soviet psychology and sociology of fear or of bureaucratic antisemitic prejudice. It places great strain on the individual, given the need to develop moral options towards a Jewish identity that has in fact lain dormant for generations—especially in the local absence of role models and established patterns of tradition such as ritual observances or knowledge of the Hebrew language. For some Jews, in Russia and elsewhere (such as the small group in Warsaw described by Gebert), the new Europe means that they can finally return to their roots because they now have the freedom and opportunity to do so—because they can do so, not because they must do so.

It should of course also be noted that measuring the Jewish population of the former Soviet Union is not an easy task: there is no single answer to the question 'How many Jews are there in the former Soviet Union?', because it depends on the criterion being used to determine the Jewish identity of the people being counted; Mikhail Chlenov quotes a figure of one and a half million, as reported in the census of 1989, based on a definition of self-identification.

This Jewish view of the new Europe, then, completely replaces the earlier

Jewish image of a Europe where France, with its population of half a million Jews, was the principal Jewish centre. Suddenly the weight has shifted to the east, as 'Europe' itself takes on a new geographical definition in the public mind (an issue not without its own problems, but that is another story). DellaPergola's figures reveal an interesting twist, however. Theoretically, the weight of Europe's Jewish population has for a very long time remained in the east, even after the end of the war (it was simply that the existence of the Iron Curtain did not permit a pan-European perception of this fact); in 1945, 75 per cent of Europe's Jews were in the east. By 1990, Europe's Jews numbered two million, of whom almost exactly half were in the European Community and half in the seven European countries of the former Soviet Union. But there has been an important development *since* 1990, namely the exodus in 1990–2 from the former Soviet Union of half a million classificatory Jews, including twenty thousand to Germany alone. We thus arrive at a demographic definition of the new Europe: simultaneously with the dawning of a new western awareness of the eastern Jews (and their very different identity problems), there has come for the first time in the modern period an ironic demographic shift from east back to west. This is how the statistician gets the last laugh: in the final analysis, the weight never really shifted to the east at all, even though it was there for most of the time.

The European Jewish demographic realities, in short, are exceptionally unstable. There are no long-term generalizations that can be made across the continent: some communities show stability, some show substantial growth followed by dramatic decline. The chief single factor, DellaPergola concludes, is still the variable intensity of the Holocaust on a country-by-country basis. It is a remarkable, if shocking, conclusion, confirming the argument above that even present-day realities are still sufficiently suffused with the long-term effects of the Holocaust as to render other aspects of change superficial in comparison. But what, then, of the public attention, in western Europe, to the new atmosphere of international collaboration and the loosening of the force of international borders? Is this of any consequence for Jewish identities?

As this book makes clear, there is no single answer, no single Jewish perspective or angle on the nature of the new Europe. At a purely organizational level, the new Europe (as seen from the west) will clearly signify a challenge to Jews to make a more efficient use of their resources on a continent-wide basis. To be sure, there are those authors in this book who unashamedly express considerable anxiety about the future, including Sergio DellaPergola (because of the steady demographic decline of the Jewish population), Robert Wistrich (because of the new scale of antisemitism, now at a height not seen since 1945), and Margaret Brearley (because of the exponential growth in New Age spirituality, an eco-fascist movement deeply opposed to Judaism and committed to a new bio-ethics that is both immoral and cruel). As seen from Israel, today's new Europe can be read both ways, depending on one's point of view: the European Community's self-image as a single political and economic unit contrasts with the rise in ethnic assertiveness and widespread concern about the loss of national sovereignties. Finally, there is one further angle to which some attention is given in this book, an angle which expresses a deep sense of optimism—the blossoming of a new spring in Christian–Jewish relations. Pier Francesco Fumagalli's powerful and unequivocal call for the restoration of reconciliation and respect between the two faith communities (Chapter 21) specifically elaborates how the unification of Europe offers great opportunities (and responsibilities) for Christians and Jews to work together after a centuries-long winter of misunderstanding and persecution. Once again, it will be noted, the Holocaust remains the subtext; and in the essay by Elisabeth Maxwell, who takes up a similar theme in Chapter 20, reference is explicitly made to what will be for many readers a new polarity of symbols: Auschwitz on the one hand, and Vatican II on the other. Maxwell sees the new Europe as fundamentally a post-Auschwitz world, but simultaneously with that perception there has come about the Church's new affirmation of the value of Judaism. The duality of that vision is critical, confronting the Holocaust and transcending it for the greater good. The moral and educational goals of the new Europe are thus clear: the days of bigotry and triumphalism must now be past; let us learn the love of God, the love of one's neighbour, and respect for human life.

JEWISH IDENTITIES AND JEWISH COMMUNITIES

Jewish identities in the new Europe, though considerably influenced by the course of external events, need nevertheless to be read also in the context of the internal dynamics of modern Jewish life. The future of the Jewish people, Julius Carlebach writes (Chapter 17), is in its history; that is why, he says, it is especially difficult to forecast its progress in line with the movements of other nations and peoples. Although it is common enough nowadays to analyse the history of the persecution of the Jews, for example, in terms of the wider economic, political, and theological environment, it is worth recalling that traditional Jewish explanations of antisemitism place the blame squarely on *Jewish behaviour*. In this view, as derived from the Hebrew Bible, most of what happens to the Jews is explicable ultimately only as a consequence of Jewish relations with God. Very roughly, it is a theory of reward and punishment: if Jews do well, they are being blessed by God; if they suffer, it is because of their sins. There is no real need to fear the outsider as such, because in some existential sense the outsider enemies are not inherently dangerous, they are only agents sent by God.

Modern Jewish society has certainly become highly secularized and would rarely ascribe to itself a divine relationship to explain its contemporary history, whatever the theological refinements that might be proposed to a crude theory of reward and punishment. But at the same time it does continue to look inwards as much as it purports to look outwards; in a manner similar to the behaviour of members of many other social groups, Jews often explain who they are on the basis of making distinctions between themselves and their fellow Jews. Jewish identities, in other words, are nowadays as much fashioned on the basis of internal Jewish distinctions as they are on the basis of adaptations to the outside world.

Once again, it could be said that there is excellent biblical precedent for this, inasmuch as the 'children of Israel' (as they are referred to) were from the outset divided into twelve named tribes, each with a specific spiritual and material inheritance; and in pre-modern times the Jewish world was divided into a number of established identities, including Ashkenazim (meaning, roughly, Jews of German or east European origin) and Sefardim (Jews of Spanish origin), to cite only two of these distinctions. The distinction between Ashkenazi and Sefardi Jewish identities still exists today, but the ideology of the differences between them has largely given way to many other kinds of sub-divisions that more closely reflect current Jewish pre-occupations. The typical classification used today is based on a set of rough-and-ready categories that notionally describe the level or type of personal religious observance; thus Jews today divide themselves into Orthodox, Reform, Progressive, Conservative, Liberal—and secular. These modern labels (for they are quite recent in origin) take their meanings from being relative to each other, rather than referring to anything that remains per-manently and objectively definable. For example, not all 'Orthodox' Jews are 'Orthodox' (but merely members of an 'Orthodox' synagogue, for example); Stephen Miller's essay (Chapter 16) supplies a very useful description of the details. The idea of Jews dividing themselves up according to their (notional) degree or style of religious observance is a modern innovation that might seem strange to an outside observer. Certainly it has occurred far more typically in Europe than elsewhere (among Jews in the Muslim world, for example), and it could be said that in effect it reveals the absence of a unanimity of response to the many conflicting pressures placed on Jews in a rapidly modernizing environment. Indeed, the process of Jewish adaptation to the modern world has been marked by communal splits of all kinds, notably including a series of institutionalized ideological differences and a history of internal controversy regarding the contemporary appropriateness or otherwise of many of the details of Jewish religious ritual. In that sense the basis of the diversity in these modern Jewish identities is thoroughly traditional, given the emphasis in the ancient texts and later commentaries on the need for Jewish identity to be firmly rooted in the correct observance of ritual.

There are, however, other styles of internal differentiation among Jews which readers will encounter in this book. The notion of classificatory Jews was suggested above; but of course it is an analytic concept, rather than anything that can be encountered in the street, so to speak. But Mikhail Chlenov's description of the situation in the former Soviet Union leaves no doubt that a set of labels distinguishing at least four different types of Jewish identity (i.e. according to classificatory criteria) is indeed in popular use. Less well known in the street, but of considerable analytic significance, is Sergio DellaPergola's distinction between a 'core' Jewish population (consisting of those who consider themselves Jewish, presumably on any of the criteria discussed above) and an 'enlarged' Jewish population (consisting of those who used to consider themselves Jewish, other people of recent Jewish descent, and non-Jewish members of Jewish households). The need for this distinction between core and enlarged Jewish populations, which as an analytic concept is not intended precisely to fit Mikhail Chlenov's local usages, arises from the blur around Jewish identities caused by the total lack of consensus nowadays regarding the actual content and practice of Jewishness; it is likely to become standard practice in Jewish demographic research, if indeed it has not done so already. It will probably take some time, however, before people catch up with the fundamental implication that there is no more such a thing as a definite figure for a total Jewish population. Different definitions of Jewishness will lead to different population counts and different assessments of future trends.

At least three authors in this book, Igor Krupnik (Chapter 10), Norman Solomon (Chapter 5), and Konstanty Gebert (Chapter 12), refer to the comparatively little-known problem of the somewhat uneasy social relationship between Jewish 'oldtimers' and more assimilated younger Jews returning to various forms of traditionalism or at least some more open form of Jewish self-identification. In some ways the situation is reminiscent of other classic cases of the sense of distance often expressed by members of an established community towards enthusiastic incomers—for example, wealthy purchasers of second homes in a picturesque but economically depressed village setting, or computer-assisted, highly educated urban freelancers working from home in a remote Hebridean island. Konstanty Gebert describes how his circle of young 'new' Jews in Warsaw, finally trying to make sense of their Jewishness from which they had previously found themselves alienated, were treated by those 'old' Jews who had in some form or another retained at least a partial Jewish identity through the vicissitudes of post-war Polish politics. If the 'new' Jews went to the synagogue or to some other Jewish event, they were made to feel that they did not belong (because indeed they were unfamiliar with the procedures or subject-matter). The 'old' Jews treated them first as a nuisance (perhaps they were too closely associated with the underground), then as a fraud (their Jewishness was not seen as authentic), and then as a mystery (what was the point of taking up such a stigmatized identity?). What indeed did these incomers have in common with those oldtimers who in effect controlled the monopoly of Jewish cultural knowledge? Were they not merely imaginary Jews—people who wanted to imagine themselves as being Jewish?

Despite the highly contextual nature of the problems of these young Polish Jews, the conflicting pressures on their identity formation as Jews is worth meditating on as a paradigm. Norman Solomon, describing a comparable group in Russia, observes that in a sense there is an irreconcilable gap between the incomers and the oldtimers: the incomers in fact have no intention of truly 'becoming' like their grandparents. What they want to do is to reconstruct their identity, and to do so on the basis of properly 'authentic' role models—as if there was an objective reality of a Jewish identity 'out there' waiting for them to seize hold of. This is not a return to 'roots', common though it is for people today to use this phrase to describe their behaviour; both reformists as well as reactionaries claim that they are being objectively faithful to the past. Rather what is at stake here is what one might call an authenticity gap: each side does not quite visualize the other as completely real, completely satisfactory as far as their identity aspirations are concerned. For which the reason is that identity can be pieced together only on the basis of the (perceived) facts and circumstances; the grandparents' generation, or the locals' social environment, is by definition different from that of the incomers. The allegiances of different people can never precisely fit; at best, they merely overlap.

The material presented by Igor Krupnik points to the hopeless position of Jewish incomers in the post-Soviet context. Highly assimilated Russian Jews were among those groups of Russians who were encouraged by Moscow to settle in the various republics across the Soviet Union, as part of the state policy to integrate the empire by russifying it. Such Jews often had little in common with the local oldtimer Jewish populations they encountered, and relations were difficult. For example, the oldtimers they found after the war in the Baltic territories (that had first been annexed by the USSR in 1939–40 following the Molotov–Ribbentrop Pact) consisted of small numbers of

Holocaust survivors whose pre-war Jewish experience had been one of a thriving Jewish community, quite different in other words from those communities that had languished under Communism elsewhere in the USSR since 1917, from where the incomers hailed. Another example concerns the Russian Jews who had settled in the Central Asian republics. When the Soviet Union fell apart, these assimilated Jews were perceived as nothing else but Russian—certainly not as 'locals' nor as Jews—and so fell victim to prejudice and discrimination against the outsider. Was it retrospectively a mistake for them to have too closely identified themselves culturally with the imperial power?

These case-studies provide strong evidence for the important fact that the characteristic units of today's Jewish world may not always be tightly knit 'communities' but aggregates of people whose links with each other are not necessarily self-evident, let alone predictably harmonious. The division between incomers and oldtimers in these east European contexts should not be thought of as extreme, even by contemporary west European standards, and evokes something of the complex social forces that perpetually divide and sub-divide the Jewish people. In western Europe, first-generation Jewish immigrants often found themselves subject to considerable pressure from the local, well-established communities to fuse culturally and so disappear as a separate group—with varying degrees of success; Jonathan Sacks's reference (Chapter 7) to the desire by the Anglo-Jewish establishment to anglicize continental Jewish immigrants in the last century is a good example. Perhaps the contemporary west European equivalent of this category would be the so-called 'unaffiliated' Jews, that is those Jews (probably the great majority of Jews, in fact) whose identity is labelled negatively by the establishment: they are treated terminologically as not belonging ('unaffiliated') because they do not formally belong to a recognized Jewish institution such as a synagogue organization or community centre. In practice, however, many of these unaffiliated Jews might well have a subscription to a Jewish newspaper or magazine, make charitable donations to a Jewish philanthropic cause, or have some other link that would induce Sergio DellaPergola to include them within his 'enlarged' Jewish population.

Nevertheless, it is still the word 'community' that is used (in the English-speaking world, at least) to refer to the Jewish aggregate and thereby define the Jewish identity of individuals through that 'community' they 'belong' to. Strictly speaking, it is probably a case of terminological inertia, as the normal implications such as shared communal values and behaviour would be difficult to demonstrate (as Stephen Miller's study shows in Chapter 16). Certainly the term is used very loosely, to refer variously to the Jews of a particular country ('the Jewish community of France', for example), the Jews of a particular town or even suburb of a town ('the Jewish community of Northwest London'), and the Jews of a particular religious grouping ('the community of Orthodox Jews')—as if these 'communities' were in each case genuinely self-contained entities, possessing comparable organizational structures and histories. Even the Jews of a single country do not all have the same history: Holocaust losses may have been uneven across the country, and the borders of the country may have changed (for a good example, see Igor Krupnik's remarks on the Soviet Union in Chapter 10). It should be said, on the other hand, that the notion of national or local Jewish communities, although often manifestly out of date in certain instances (stereotypes are always slow to be reconciled with the realities), has indeed historically been the mode in which Jews have organized themselves. Right across the Jewish diaspora, over a period of many centuries (and millennia), pockets of Jews associated themselves with a local religious leader and even developed a legal notion of *minhag hamakom* ('local custom') to authenticate their sense of Jewish identity, locally defined. In modern times the pattern was continued, without any conscious break with the past in this respect. Local European Jewish communities, now usually accompanied by a substantial and professional bureaucratic infrastructure and identified at law as institutional or corporate owners of valuable communal property (often in downtown city centres), are thus deemed in many cases to be autonomous entities, with both ecclesiastical bodies and lay representative organizations arranged by city or, at most, by country. In these latter cases there certainly are identifiable Jewish communities in a formal sense—as opposed to those terminological usages (such as 'the Jewish community of Northwest London') which in effect rely on a pre-modern conception of Jewish identity, or perhaps even an imaginary classification. But Jews usually treat these classifications as entirely real—more real, perhaps, than communities formally or legally defined. One important source for the construction and consolidation of such identities is doubtless the local Jewish press. While most European Jewish newspapers and magazines do conventionally attempt to include some Jewish news from foreign countries, the presentation of news (including 'communal' announcements and the personal columns for births, marriages, and deaths), as well as advertisers' announcements, clearly aim at a readership defined locally. The *Jewish Chronicle*, for example, a weekly newspaper published in London, contains a section headed simply 'Community Chronicle': its notion of community, as defined by the nature of its coverage, extends no further than the United Kingdom, and principally refers to London. The *Jewish Chronicle*'s instinct here, to see all the Jews of Britain as essentially belonging to a single 'community' (i.e. whether they are technically affiliated or not), is basically sound: this is indeed typical of how European Jews tend to think of their identity, even though in many cases it could be said that they rest on outdated definitions.

The decentralization of modern Jewish identities (in a sense matching the absence in the diaspora of any universal, central authority) means that in certain contexts even the use of national Jewish identities can occasionally be resisted. There is, for example, an (Orthodox) chief rabbi of the British Commonwealth, a post originally established, with a slightly different name, by Act of Parliament more than a century ago—but there is not really any British Commonwealth Jewish identity, and even within Britain itself those Jews who do not consider themselves 'Orthodox' (and even some who do) would not necessarily concur that the mere existence of such a post should mean that they should submit to his authority.

The partial illusion of 'community' (partial because in practice there are bona fide aspects of Jewish social life covered by the term) raises the question of where in fact the centre of Jewish society is to be found, and where its periphery. What is really 'typical' of contemporary Jewish life, and what is only marginal to it? What does one take as constituting true evidence of the Jewish world, and what does one dismiss as irrelevant? The approach outlined above, and one on which this whole book is based, is to take as broadly inclusive a view as possible, but the reader ought to be aware that such a position is not without its problems.

Some Jews would say that one further element is needed—a theory that distinguishes centre from periphery, a theory which accepts responsibility both for the existing varieties of Jewish identities and also for their relative importance and value. At least two contributors to this book, Jonathan Sacks (Chapter 7) and Norman Lamm (Chapter 6), strongly argue the case for an approach to contemporary Jewish life that would emphasize those parts of it that offer the best long-term chances for Jewish survival, and accordingly treat those parts as normatively central. Thus, Jonathan Sacks identifies the current political ideology of ethnic Jewish survivalism, even though it has successfully energized Jews over the past generation, as in fact defunct, out of touch with contemporary Jewish needs, unlikely to be adequately transmitted to the next generation, and altogether in need of replacement by a renewed Jewish identity more closely committed to a sense of continuity. Norman Lamm similarly identifies grave defects in certain current Jewish trends, notably the increasing polarization between assimilated Jews and traditionalist Jews; he even sees the Jewish world as slowly splitting into two peoples. The point is, from such perspectives, that a *disinterested* inclusive view that makes no attempt to specify the normatively essential within the full range of all that is happening in the Jewish world may well be valid and interesting as an analytic exercise in social description—but perhaps it reflects a certain moral indifference and lack of genuine concern to develop more of a global view of Jewish destiny. After all, even though Jews have always thought of their identities as locally based, and put together some notion of a community in order to give that identity some flesh and bones, nevertheless at the same time there was another idea standing behind it—the concept of *kelal yisrael*, the belief in the ultimate unity of the Jewish people despite all its disparate manifestations in time and space. Without this overriding concept of *kelal yisrael* and a long view of the spiritual requirements of Jewish survival, is there not a danger in seeing the diversity of the contemporary Jewish experience as being little more than of exotic, ethnological, or antiquarian curiosity? All Jews are equal, it could be said; but some, in the final analysis, are perhaps more equal, more central, than others.

But who, in fact, are those 'some'? It often turns out, on a close reading of the material (the press, sermons, quarterly magazines, articles in learned journals, and so forth) that it is the position of the author in question that strangely happens to coincide with the centre of gravity in the Jewish world. There may be lip-service paid to some version of a *kelal yisrael* concept, but in practice Jews often behave as if their local neighbourhood synagogue, their home and its surroundings, represents the only true and reliable Jewish identity. 'Those to the left of me', they might say, 'are Communists, apostates, lost to the Jewish world; those to the right of me are fundamentalists.' The Jewish world today is indeed full of countless different agendas, as Eliezer Schweid (Chapter 2) points out; it is full of particularist leaders, each with their own programme for Jewish survival but who in reality are merely leading their followers towards their own particularist destiny. What most of these groups would seem to have in common is a belief that the current Jewish intellectual, spiritual, cultural, or institutional realities are somehow intrinsically deficient in supplying an assured future for the Jewish people, and that what is required is some new vision or at least reorientation. Perhaps what it is that generates all this diversity is a fundamental lack of agreement across today's Jewish world about what constitutes the basis of Jewish community existence—is it a shared set of rituals, a shared set of values, a shared culture, a shared cultural knowledge, a shared collective fate, or perhaps membership of the same institutions? The adoption of any one or more of these definitions or emphases as basic or central will clearly yield very different results with regard to an attitude to the rest of the Jewish world.

For some Jews, Jewish community existence is threatened by one key contemporary phenomenon—intermarriage, now thought to be approaching 50 per cent of marriages contracted by Jews and thus of crisis proportions.

Although partly mitigated in some instances by the conversion to Judaism of the non-Jewish partner (a trend not without its own series of implications), it implies that a huge sector of the population is simply walking out on its Jewishness, reluctant to transmit a normative Jewish identity of some kind to the next generation. Intermarriage is today such an established pattern that many Jewish families may treat it as entirely normal, or at least without further significant consequences; they learn to adapt and cope with it (despite the considerable shock it engendered when it first began to happen). Intermarriage should of course also be seen as a symptom of a wider Jewish cultural, spiritual, or demographic malaise. Sergio DellaPergola (Chapter 3) connects it with the decline of the Jewish family more generally: alongside later marriage, lower marital stability and fertility, and the reduced propensity to marry at all, the high intermarriage rate is perhaps merely the most culturally visible symbol of the dramatic erosion of the Jewish population across Europe—not only in eastern Europe but also in the more affluent and stable west. Furthermore, intermarriage contributes to a shrinkage of the fertile segment of the age pyramid, which is another way of saying that the population is ageing (a long-term consequence also of the Holocaust, during which period the Jewish birth-rate was very low).

Some Jews would either dispute the figures or prefer to look the other way, placing their confidence in Jewish communal survival elsewhere. It is true, for example, that the Hasidic communities, together with other Jews (principally Ashkenazi) who think of themselves as 'strictly Orthodox' or *haredi*, have greatly increased in absolute numbers in western Europe since the Holocaust (contrary to the expectations of many), and are consequently increasingly more visible versus the assimilated majority of the Jewish world. Although they are not quite as isolated from modern trends as is commonly supposed (a topic discussed by Norman Lamm and Norman Solomon), they do nevertheless more closely fit a clear-cut concept of 'community' than the relatively diffuse memberships typical elsewhere. Needless to say, from a 'strictly Orthodox' perspective (a label, incidentally, that has recently come to replace the earlier 'ultra-Orthodox' appellation), there can be only one definition of the centre of the Jewish world—their own. Strict adherence to tradition, especially in the face of the assimilatory challenges of the modern world, is for them the only possible basis for a normative definition of Jewish identity (even though in practice it also remains endlessly subdivided into competing factions, often associated with the influence of charismatic religious leaders). Their comparatively small size (conventionally estimated at 10–15 per cent of the Jewish world) makes no difference to this belief; on the contrary, small is beautiful, and a guarantee of the assumed purity of the community. The rest of the Jewish world is seen as either dying or indeed already dead—a view which has led some of these groups, most notably the Lubavitch Hasidim, led by an elderly, saintly figure living in Brooklyn, to engage in sustained outreach activities to bring about the return of secular, assimilated Jews to a traditional identity, from which (in this view) they have become unnecessarily alienated. Semi-religious Jews, including those who nowadays style themselves as 'modern Orthodox', are also in some sense alienated from their roots—as witnessed for example in their remarkable recent abandonment in the synagogue of traditional Ashkenazi pronunciations of liturgical Hebrew, in favour of a pronunciation deemed to be closer to Israeli forms. Such a development is virtually unknown in *haredi* communities. From their angle, the true crisis of modern Judaism lies in the widespread shift from a consistent and regular association with Jewishness to something far more inconsistent and intermittent—the shift, for example, from daily prayer to weekly prayer on the sabbath, or from total observance of the dietary rules to a new division between the home (where the rules may be observed in some form) and outside the home (where they may be observed to a much lesser extent, if at all). Modern Judaism, for them, is peripheral, having developed a remoteness from the classical heartland: it relies on a poorly remembered and fundamentally uneducated knowledge of the traditions, uninformed by a literate understanding of the classical talmudic sources and their commentaries. Are such communities—often known in the Jewish world also as 'nominally Orthodox'—properly investing adequate energy in transmitting their Jewish identity to the next generation? What kind of schooling is available for the children? Is the educational syllabus limited to a children's Sunday-school knowledge of Judaism, or is it geared to a truly adult cultural knowledge sufficient to sustain the community indefinitely? The evidence from many Jewish 'communities' across Europe today would suggest, in the light of the *haredi* critique, that there is slow but widespread cultural death.

The severity of such a critique has certainly become an element of today's collective Jewish consciousness, even though most Jews would naturally resist it. They would prefer to take a more inclusive view, though not necessarily a disinterested one: for example, Shmuel Trigano's vision in Chapter 14 of a house whose windows are open to the outside world, but one which equally is open to many different kinds of Jews to enter and live, is not at all disinterested. It is the ideology of the centre. As Norman Lamm writes (Chapter 6), the Jewish centre often lacks passion and is easily intimidated by critiques deriving from Jewish traditionalism on the one side, and Western culture on the other. Of course, it is in one sense yet one more Jewish agenda, yet another particularist programme to deal with the issue of Jewish survival. But perhaps it is only through a vision as supplied by the centre (as defined in this way) that the problematic relationship between centre and periphery in today's Jewish world, between Jewish communities and Jewish identities, can somehow be reconciled. If the centre is large enough, generous enough, then the periphery ceases to be a periphery but instead becomes an integral element of the whole. Is such a vision viable? Norman Lamm certainly thinks so, but he admits that it is not without its difficulties. As he puts it, his view is not one of an optimist—rather that of a worried optimist.

CONCLUSION

Any argument about where the Jewish centre of Europe is located—whether in the strictly Orthodox Hasidic communities of Antwerp, the massive newly rediscovered Jewish populations of the former Soviet Union, the concentration of North African Jews of France, or among the Jews of Britain unaffected by the devastation of the Holocaust—is ultimately a sterile one unless it is accompanied by some sort of broader theory or overview that attempts to make sense of the remarkable diversity of modern Jewish life. The purpose of this book is both to document this diversity and put forward a variety of frameworks in which it can be adequately conceptualized. At the same time, it should not be forgotten that, in the perspective of many non-European Jews, European Judaism today is collectively provincial and on the periphery of the Jewish world when contrasted with the main Jewish centres of Israel and the United States. The significance and reputation of European Jewry, however, does not derive primarily from its present-day role but rather from its demographic and cultural centrality in pre-war times, at least in terms of the Ashkenazi world. The steady demographic decline of east European Jewry from its majority status even at the end of the Second World War, and its very recent slippage to a point just under 50 per cent of Europe's total Jewish population, certainly forms at least one clear trend. But at the same time the Jews of Russia are now, with Western Jewish help, reconstituting and reinvigorating their lost or faded Jewish identities and will doubtless gradually develop a significant new model of Russian Jewishness that will eventually become a fresh force within the Jewish world. The demographic realities and the cultural realities thus may not always mirror each other; rather the dissonance between them merely adds to the unstructured chaos of competing styles and formulations that constitutes today's Jewish map of Europe.

Some of the contributors to this book have presented broader perspectives that make it easier to understand the general patterns underlying specific cases. One theme that the reader will encounter is the notion that what seems to have characterized Jewish identities in recent times is the constant lurch from identity crisis to identity crisis, triggered usually by external events that thus come to act as benchmarks in modern Jewish history—the law on Jewish status promulgated in Vichy France in 1940, for example, that shattered the Jewish belief in the almost magical nature of their destiny in France (referred to by Dominique Schnapper). What stands behind this lurching from crisis to crisis is the important point that the whole nature of social identities is precisely to retain a sensitivity both to the novelty of external events and processes and also a sense of loyalty to an inherited culture and a past set of traditions. Identities may thus represent the intersection (for the individual and the community) of the new with the old, the working out of a balance between competing perceptions and pressures, the reformulation of received tradition using the cultural materials of the present. There is a whole variety of such materials to choose from in the shaping and reshaping of contemporary Jewish identities, and Norman Solomon in Chapter 5 presents us with a full list: family history, Jewish history, national identities, European culture, moral and ethical values, the Holocaust, Israel, attitudes to Christianity, minority status, and other external factors (such as real or imagined antisemitism). Jews have in effect a substantial range of options; while some opt for prefabricated identities offered up to them by those in positions of authority (something that Norman Solomon suggests ought strongly to be resisted), the truth is that the very malleability of Jewish identity can positively contribute to the evolution of Judaism, as indeed it always has done. There is no 'correct' mix of all these various elements, nor is there any direct, one-to-one causal relationship between any one element and the overall resulting nature of the identity thus formed. And, in any case, people do not necessarily possess just one fixed social identity or one fixed attitude to who they are; they may indeed have several ideas about themselves simultaneously and switch from one to the other according to context or mood (Jewish identity being emphasized only at rites of passage in the life-cycle, for example). It is this, perhaps, which makes the study of identities such a difficult and elusive subject.

An excellent (and final) example is the case of antisemitism, discussed by a number of the contributors. What effect does it have on Jewish identity? It certainly may play a part in keeping Jews Jewish. But on the other hand, the awareness of Jewishness as a stigmatized identity can have the opposite effect—it can simply encourage Jews to try to conceal their Jewishness, and not at all to live as Jewish Jews. Curiously enough, however, the art of concealing Jewishness is something which many Jews have perfected for so long that they actually transmit it to their children as part of their Jewish identity; as András Kovács (Chapter 11) explains it with reference to his studies of Jews in Budapest, antisemitism there has become internalized as part of the normal socialization process of children. It is thus possible to have a belief in a stigmatized identity as a Jew without any necessary reference to the real world, or even to any personal experience of anti-semitism—just as much as it is possible, as Robert Wistrich describes (Chapter 18), to have non-Jews holding antisemitic opinions in countries where there are virtually no Jews. The relationship, then, between empirical realities and the construction of identities is not at all straightforward. Jews often continue to live in countries which other Jews feel may be particularly dangerous because of antisemitism; local Jews, on the other hand, might simply minimize the threat and consider it exaggerated. Mikhail Chlenov makes a point of this kind about the former Soviet Union (Chapter 9); and Dominique Schnapper and Shmuel Trigano similarly say, in effect, that foreign reports of antisemitism in France are often exaggerated. That is not to say, of course, that antisemitism is not real,[8] or that there are no Jews in France or the former Soviet Union who are genuinely concerned about antisemitism and make allowance for it in their attitudes to their Jewish-ness. What it does mean, however, is that there is good evidence from this book in support of the point that there are no a priori assumptions to be made about just how Jewish identities respond to the problem of anti-semitism or about how in general they relate to Jews' experience of the real world.

This book covers many of the most important themes in an understanding of Jewish identities in the new Europe; but it does not pretend to cover them all. There is no essay devoted to Greece, or to Switzerland, Belgium, or Holland, for example, nor on the thriving but tiny Jewish community of Gibraltar. Other aspects that are missing from this book include studies of Jewish youth culture, the *ba'al teshuvah* (Jewish revivalist) movement, the yeshivah world of talmudic seminaries, Jewish fundamentalism, Jewish secularism, the impact of the Lubavitch Hasidim (notably in France), and the Jewish intelligentsia of central and eastern Europe (notably in the former Soviet Union). For most readers, however, the most significant omission is undoubtedly an essay on the role of women in today's Jewish world. It is, regrettably, a long list of topics. But this book was not designed as an encyclopedia, merely an introduction and a modest commentary. As Rabbi Tarfon put it (Mishnah Avot, 2: 20–1): 'The day is short, the task is great, the workmen are lazy, and the Master is insistent ... You are not called upon to complete the work, even though you are not free to evade it altogether.'

Notes

1. A classic description can be found in Solomon Poll, *The Hasidic Community of Williamsburg: A Study in the Sociology of Religion* [1962] (New York, 1969).

2. For a good general discussion of the problem see Sharon Macdonald, 'Identity Complexes in Western Europe: Social Anthropological Perspectives', in Sharon Macdonald (ed.), *Inside European Identities: Ethnography in Western Europe* (Providence, RI, 1993), 1–26. See also Thomas M. Wilson, 'An Anthropology of the European Community', in Thomas M. Wilson and M. Estellie Smith (eds.), *Cultural Change and the New Europe: Perspectives on the European Community* (Boulder, Colo., 1993), 1–23.

3. The *Encyclopedia Judaica* (Jerusalem, 1972) has excellent entries on all European countries; for a convenient handbook see Antony Lerman (ed.), *The Jewish Communities of the World: A Contemporary Guide*, 4th edn. (Basingstoke, 1989).

4. A phrase borrowed from Charles Krauthammer, cited in Daniel Patrick Moynihan, *Pandaemonium: Ethnicity in International Politics* (Oxford, 1993), 15.

5. Ibid., *passim*.

6. Michael Howard, 'War in the Making and Unmaking of Europe', in *The Causes of War and Other Essays* (London: 1983), 151–68, cited in M. L. Smith and Peter M. R. Stirk (eds.), *Making the New Europe: European Unity and the Second World War* (London, 1990), 2.

7. Figure taken from the *American Jewish Yearbook*, cited in *Encyclopedia Judaica*, s.v. 'Europe'.

8. For a useful recent reference-work see Institute for Jewish Affairs, *Antisemitism World Report 1993* (London, 1993).

PART I

A CHANGING EUROPE

CHAPTER ONE

The Jews of Europe in the Age of a New Völkerwanderung

MAX BELOFF

I BEGIN with something of an apology. Although I am Jewish, I am not a specialist on any aspect of Judaism or Jewish affairs, nor an active member of any Jewish communal organization. My contribution, then, to this consideration of Jewish identities in the new Europe can only come from my experience as a historian. But over the more than half a century that I have been a professional historian, Jewish issues have emerged only peripherally in my fields of study—Britain and its former empire, Europe, and North America; not, it might seem, a promising start for talking about Jewish identities in the new Europe. It seems to me, however, that in order to do this in a meaningful way we must nevertheless have some ideas as to what the new Europe is or is likely to become. And that must be my topic. Yet even here I am left in a quandary since I do not believe historians are much good at prophesying the future—and my own record is not better than anyone else's. It is easier to look back.

Let me begin with a platitude. Jewish history can only be understood in terms of preserving something recognized as a Jewish identity. The question I want to consider is to what degree that identity has been dependent upon its external environment, particularly its political environment. And this goes back to the earliest times. The Jewish polity created by Joshua and his successors was, because of its location in the Fertile Crescent, always likely to be at the mercy of the empires that aspired to control that area as well as of the more local competitors for domination. The Babylonian captivity and the Roman conquest that ousted the Jews from their land were merely the major events in a continuing story of conflict. And when the Jews again laid the foundations of a territorially based existence and identity after nearly two millennia, it came about as the result of the changed relationship between external powers, and remains, as we all know, deeply affected by the changing role of these and other powers in the modern Middle East.

If we look at the Jews of the diaspora, we find the degree of dependence on external decisions even more obvious—and painfully so. For the reasons I have given, I do not propose to venture deeply into the other side of the equation—what is meant by a Jewish identity. But a somewhat simple definition does emerge from the history of these two millennia. Jews are people who share or have shared a common religion together with customs and practices whose primary reason has been to enable them to pursue their commitment to this religious heritage. Since Jewish religious observances are communal as well as individual in character, some form of communal organization has always been necessary if this vocation was to be accomplished. Since at most times and in most places the religious commitment implied endogamy, Jews could also be regarded as what we now call an ethnic group, which is a polite euphemism for a race.

From these simple facts two consequences emerge. In the first place, there must be a modicum of protection by the secular authority, since Jews in the diaspora have rarely or for long been able to provide it themselves: if all the Jews are dead, the question of a Jewish identity does not arise. It also means, and this is much more complicated, that the organization and practices of the host society must be such as to permit the degree of communal organization, including the development of its material underpinnings, that allows the religious commitment to be fulfilled. For repression by the host community can take forms short of physical annihilation that eventually leave a Jewish identity in question. One can have forced conversions to a majority creed, as in the later stages of the Spanish Reconquista, or one can have a secular ideology in command of the state apparatus making it difficult, perhaps virtually impossible, for Jews to possess the minimum required for communal existence. What would Russian Jewry have looked like if Soviet Communism had lasted for another century? A more rare alternative pattern is that of partially secularized societies, where the interpenetration of Jewish and non-Jewish elements has been relatively effortless so that individual Jews and their families disappeared into the mainstream of the host society. In Europe this has never happened to a decisive extent and need not concern us.

The possibility does remind us, however, of the great complexity of what has actually been the case in the Jewish diaspora in Europe. If we contrast that diaspora with the Jewish diaspora of what was the Ottoman Empire in Asia and its offshoots in the Maghreb, or with the Jews of the former Persian Empire, it is clear that for the latter much of what was central to the European debate did not arise. Since religion was the key defining category for all the subjects of these Islamic empires, their minorities—Christians and Jews alike—were organized on communal lines with varying degrees of discrimination applied to them. In medieval Europe, with Judaism being (outside the Iberian peninsula) the only minority religion, its ability to exist in a communal form depended upon the various secular authorities, with all the concomitant dangers of expulsion or annihilation that religious or popular antisemitism might bring down upon the various communities. Given the occupational restrictions imposed by the authorities, Jewish identity in the sense of manifest differences from the host society was hardly ever in question.

The difficulties begin with the Enlightenment and Emancipation and with the reaction to them, modern antisemitism. Communal organization recognized and regulated by the state gave way gradually to the elimination of distinctions in rights and status based upon religion. Jews, particularly in the more western parts of the continent, were left to find their own means of giving expression to their needs for organizations intended to preserve their religious identity. The legal framework and the degree of state intervention, or occasionally assistance, differed from case to case. Today all this is past history, since outside the United Kingdom, France, and Russia the Jewish communities are too small to generalize about in this fashion.

What united the history of the whole of the two millennia in Europe from the Jewish point of view is that, as I have said, Jewish fortunes have varied with the attitude towards them of the peoples and governments of the host societies. And both governments and peoples have changed their stance as circumstances have changed. Only the Vatican and the Greek and Russian Orthodox churches have had a fairly consistent Judaeophobic record.

If we look at the vicissitudes that have befallen Jewish communities, one thing of relevance to our present discussion that does emerge is that what has tended to assist Jewish communal survival, and hence the preservation of a Jewish identity, cultural as well as physical, has been stability. In peacetime, Jewish communities have lived and thrived in many parts of Europe. They have in some cases contributed to the culture of the surrounding society, though care must be taken not to exaggerate the importance of the latter—the record of individual Jews in modern times in, for instance, the natural sciences, or performance on stringed instruments, is not a 'Jewish' contribution, but part of humanity's triumphs.

And that brings me at last to the core of my case. We can say nothing useful about the Jews in the new Europe unless we have some idea of what that new Europe looks like becoming. And no one sees much ground for optimism, despite the presence in almost all European countries of some men of good will. The twentieth century, now approaching its end, has been the worst century in European history since the fourteenth, perhaps since the Dark Ages. Wars and civil wars have been at its heart; massacres of which Jews have been the principal but by no means the only victims have accompanied both the major periods of violence, 1914–21 and 1939–47. The peace that endured between the two world wars as the Jews of central and eastern Europe experienced it was neither stable nor painless. Between 1947 and 1989, Europe seemed to have achieved a new stability based upon the balance of terror. But with the break-up of the Soviet hegemony in eastern Europe and of the Soviet empire itself we have entered upon what seems likely to be an age of new sufferings and new problems to which no current institutions or doctrines or leaders have any obvious answer.

A conspicuous aspect of the current scene is the movement of peoples and the changing ethnic composition of parts of Europe as its consequence. Even more relevant is the fear among some settled populations that they will suffer in economic or social terms from the advent of masses of newcomers. Such movements were not absent in the immediate post-war period. As we know, the bulk of the survivors of the Holocaust found their way to Israel or to the New World. The Germans from the Sudetenland and from parts of Poland's newly acquired territories in the west found refuge in the new German Federal Republic. The changed circumstances in their home countries prevented groups of wartime exiles from returning—Britain's Polish community is one legacy of those events.

During the Cold War period, east–west movement was frozen but there were other changes in population: in Britain there was New Commonwealth immigration, and in France there were movements of more direct Jewish concern—the return of the *pieds noirs* from Algeria, and with them the bulk of Algeria's Jewish community, together with substantial numbers of Jews from Morocco and Tunisia.

With the still incomplete but important relaxation of the control of exits from the countries of the former Soviet Union and central Europe, the east–west movement has once again become considerable and may grow. So far the main beneficiaries have been those population groups with a country willing to take them in: Jews and ethnic Germans. And the experience so far raises some general considerations about the cause of such movements.

The most obvious is fear—fear of harassment or discrimination of an intolerable kind. We have most recently seen the extreme case in the outflow from the former Yugoslavia, where refugees have been deliberately set on the road in order to assure ethnic homogeneity in particular areas. Fear is no doubt playing a part in the further movement of Jews from the depleted communities of eastern Europe as the peoples newly emancipated from

Communism find the traditional scapegoating device of antisemitism useful at a time of difficulty and hardship. Its part in the exodus from the former Soviet Union must be a variable one, but the whole of that subject is too vast to do more than allude to here. Although the official Soviet position towards Jews was a uniform one, the actual position differed in the different parts of the Soviet Union and now differs widely in the republics formed out of what was the Soviet Union. Russia itself, the Ukraine, the Caucasus, and Central Asia all present different pictures. Fear clearly plays a large part in the continued if variably paced exodus to Israel and the Americas. The nationalist reaction in Russia against the collapse of its empire is also exploiting antisemitic themes and this is likely to stimulate further emigration.

The other historic reason for the movement of peoples has been the desire for economic betterment. The land-hunger which propelled large-scale migrations in medieval Europe is less prominent in what are increasingly urban societies. But the richer countries act as a magnet to the populations of the poorer ones, and it is this that explains in part the fear of an unstoppable movement from east to west if the European countries of the former Soviet Union or the countries of central and eastern Europe fail to solve the problems of transition from command to market economies. The attempts of Albanians to reach a haven in Italy is another example.

It also explains the other phenomenon that would appear to be growing, a south–north movement of peoples from North Africa and its hinterland across the Mediterranean into southern Europe. Movement in that direction happened in the past, but it was halted with the check to the Muslim invaders of southern Europe in the early Middle Ages. The impact of the new movement is already perceptible in France, Italy, and Spain.

The reactions of the host populations, there and in other countries of immigration, are what they have always been: a degree of disapproval merging into hostility. The most obvious consequence has been the rise of the radical Right, particularly though not exclusively in France and Germany. Such tensions are unlikely to disappear and may become aggravated. A situation of this kind does not help minorities to take root and build up their communal institutions. While no two cases are identical, it is difficult to see that outside what was the Soviet Union there are communities sufficiently large to lay the foundations of active Jewish identities except in France and the United Kingdom. How much Jewishness will be retained by Jews in the former Soviet Union who decide to remain where they are is impossible to predict.

When we turn from popular reactions to the policies of governments, particularly in respect of the established governments of western and northern Europe, we find two lines of argument being pursued. The first seeks to find means of stemming the movement itself by making staying at home more attractive. This provides a rationale for massive assistance to the countries of central and eastern Europe and those of the former Soviet Union as well as to North Africa. But a mixture of parsimony, protectionism, indifference, and prejudice makes such policies easier to state in general terms than to particularize or implement. The second is to pull up the drawbridge and hope for the best.

Within the European Community, the freeing of international frontiers was a natural objective but it was assumed that people would travel for business or study or pleasure and would not seek to emigrate in large numbers. With the pressure from outside the Community and the porousness of some of its external frontiers, these assumptions no longer hold good. No programmes of trade and aid, whether in respect of eastern Europe and the Soviet Union or of the Maghreb and sub-Saharan Africa are likely of themselves to stem the movement for long. We thus see on all sides a renewed concentration on the nature and purpose and extent of immigration controls, and of attempts on a country-wide or community-wide basis to distinguish in some precise way between 'asylum-seekers' and 'economic migrants'. Jews, with their own history of forced movement, cannot be happy about such distinctions—yet how to ignore them?

Where a change has already occurred as a result of population movements, other consequences for Jewish communities make themselves apparent. The case of France is the most immediately disturbing. In France the Jewish community itself is much changed. The demographic losses incurred through the deportations and mass murders by the Nazis have more than been made up by the influx of North African Jews. The latter paradoxically find themselves rubbing shoulders with their former oppressors, the Arabs of the Maghreb. At the same time, Jews and Arabs alike are lumped together as foreigners by the new French Right with its echoes of Vichy. The terms of political debate in France are changing. Jews, who played an important role as political leaders from the later years of the Third Republic and under the Fourth and early Fifth Republics, are finding their prominence dwindling while their salience increases. The future of French Jewry and the nature of its identity once again depend upon developments in the wider society over which it has little control.

The situation in the United Kingdom is different. The composition of the Jewish element has changed much less, despite some accretion from the Middle East. Its social composition has changed, as has that of the general population; its political representation remains visible, though its position in the party spectrum has shifted from left to right. But the environment has changed even more markedly than in France. Before the Second World War, Britain was a fairly homogeneous society, basically Christian at least in outward form. Jews were the only conspicuous religious minority, and their communal institutions could fairly easily be accommodated into the institutional set-up of the state.

Today, Britain is at least in some urban areas a multicultural society, and the Jews are outnumbered by the Muslims, who are now by far the biggest religious minority. As those familiar with the fate of Jewish societies in institutions of higher education well know, the first result has been the dissemination of antisemitism as Muslim students (including non-British subjects) project their anti-Israeli sentiments on to their Jewish fellow-students.

Ever since the creation of the Yishuv and the establishment of the State of Israel, the problem of a dual allegiance has intermittently haunted those with a Jewish identity. To many Muslims, this problem does not arise since they give religion clear precedence over their political identity. This has been shown both in the Rushdie affair and in the behaviour of the Muslim community at the time of the Gulf War. The retention of Jewish identity through the religious and secular organizations built up in the last century had not involved any challenge to the idea of full and equal citizenship for Jews in a country where disabilities based on religion have been progressively removed. Many Muslims have not come to terms with a similar solution and demand a system in which they can live as a self-isolating community, sojourners in Britain but not part of it. The Islamic Parliament is very unlike the Board of Deputies. If Sikhs and Hindus are impelled in the same direction, further tensions will arise.

How do the Jews fit in? Should they accept multiculturalism as a fact and regard themselves as part of the rainbow coalition against native English and Christian hegemony, or should they demand no more than the minimum guarantees for their own religious and educational purposes? Such dilemmas have been an undercurrent of the educational debate and are not easily resolved. Should Jews press for more assistance to their own schools, knowing that they are setting precedents for Muslim demands which could have effects unfavourable to domestic peace?

I do not know the answers, but I do think it clear that the fate of the Jews of Europe cannot be understood without some reckoning with the characteristics of the present epoch, among them the degree of uprootedness in Europe's population as a whole. That was once a peculiarity of the Jews; it is now a common fate in which Jews too are engulfed.

CHAPTER TWO

Changing Jewish Identities in the New Europe and the Consequences for Israel

ELIEZER SCHWEID

FOLLOWING the collapse of Communism and the Soviet empire, the unification of Germany, and progress in the unification of western Europe, tremendous changes are taking place in Europe. These necessarily involve deep identity crises. The general tendency is to consider these events as an advance towards 'a new Europe', understood as meaning towards a better world-order, but in fact little is known about the real implications. There are certainly hints of latent catastrophic elements not far beneath the surface. At best, everyone will experience some degree of change, and the change will be painful. Moreover, the process of change and the sense of crisis accompanying it will necessarily be enduring, and will have great impact on perceptions of religious and national identities.

It is not only the generation now reaching maturity in Europe that will have to live under the harsh lights and deep shadows of change while preparing itself to assume responsibility for society. Inevitably, it will take at least another generation or two until a certain stabilization and sense of rootedness can be achieved. A new democratic order devoted to realizing a vision of peace and affluence may be grounds for hoping for a better future, but history warns us of the folly of such messianic assumptions. If we want a better future, we would be better advised to consider first the difficulties and great dangers that are inherent in the historical process. We should do our best to confront them well prepared.

Analysing the prospects for the future from the Jewish point of view, let us first remember that the Jewish identity crisis started much before these recent events; one might even say that such a crisis must be inherent in a people founded to bear a religious destiny. Certainly, severe and enduring crises of identity have occurred throughout Jewish history. And if you will forgive me yet another truism, the modern era in Jewish history (that is, since the beginning of the Emancipation in the nineteenth century) has been one in which the very basis of Jewish existence has broken down. The original combination of complementary religious and national identities has broken down into two contradictory types of identities, two different groups of Jews. Even so, it is obvious that neither can survive Jewishly without the other.

The emergence of different national and religious identities within the Jewish people seems to have set off a process of cultural attrition that strangely, obstinately, has endured for several generations. This process has itself taken two forms: assimilation into the surrounding cultural environment, and inner, self-alienating dichotomization. It seems that there is no longer a unifying core but only extremes joined in a state of tension perpetuated by the ongoing struggle.

Every historical turning-point that the Jewish people has faced as a result of economic, social, cultural, and political upheavals has revealed the need for a leadership that could formulate a collective national will. None has emerged. There have been many particularist leaderships, each with its own programme to ensure the survival of the Jewish people. Emancipation was the first such historical turning-point, but since then the Jewish people have confronted at least three more, the last of which was after the tremendous tragedy of the Second World War. On each of these occasions, various Jewish leaders suggested alternative paths for the Jewish people to follow, but in reality each led his own followers towards a particularist realization of a separate destiny. Thus the Jewish people went in all possible directions, and also in some impossible ones.

One may well wonder how Jews still consider themselves as members of one and the same people, or as the continuers of one and the same history. Reality, it seems, should long ago have divided 'the Jewish people' into three religions and four or five peoples. Why has this not happened? Is it the result of an external pressure, namely, of a definition imposed by non-Jewish conceptions of Jewishness and Judaism? Is it the result of a hidden spiritual potential of original Jewishness which has not yet been exhausted? Or is it a miraculous sign of divine providence? Or perhaps a combination of all these? Whatever the reason, the fact is that the Jewish people have stubbornly maintained if not a unifying core then at least a common arena within whose unifying boundary they quarrel over their contradictory demands.

What quarrels and demands are on the agenda now, as Jews are approaching this new turning-point? What are the basic attitudes of the Jewish communities in Israel and the European diaspora as they prepare themselves for the new challenges? In particular, what proposals and what challenges will the new Jewish masses of eastern Europe, endowed with their new, compulsory freedom of choice, have to confront?

From the foundation of the State of Israel until several years ago, the main front in the struggle to define Jewish identity in the post-modern era was over whether that conception was a global one or made up of many parts. This was the front which divided the Israeli Jewish community from the Jewish communities of the diaspora, and particularly from the American Jewish community. The main issue was to arrive at a consensus on the centrality of Israel. It seems to me that a fundamental agreement was reached: that Israel was central in a certain, un-agreed way. I believe that this fundamental agreement still exists, but it has always been utterly unclear what it means, either theoretically or in practice. The diaspora communities continued to maintain their own centrality, and even Zionists refused to accept the Israeli Zionist interpretation of Israel's role as the centre of the Jewish world. They claimed that the continued existence of the diaspora even had its advantages for Israel. Of course, behind this was a conflicting understanding of the meaning of Jewish identity: the one view sees Jewish identity as being a global national identity, the other sees it as being a partial set of ethnic or religious identities and sometimes even a marginal one.

The basic conflict over the nature of Jewish identity is still going on, but recently it has come to have new focuses. The controversy over the centrality of Israel has not been resolved—the coals are still glowing and could catch light again at any time—but for the moment it has lost much of its practical urgency. There is too much else that needs to be done together right now, both for the sake of Israel and for the sake of east European Jewry. At this historical juncture, the significance of Western *aliyah* to Israel, and even of *yeridah* from Israel to the diaspora, has become marginal even from an Israeli Zionist point of view.

The result is that the struggle over conceptions of Jewish identity has been displaced in favour of a tendency, both in Israel and in the diaspora communities, towards a preoccupation with domestic agendas. Each now seems more concerned about the dangers that threaten Jewish unity in its own territory, and with the difficulties of maintaining a meaningful Jewish identity against this background. In consequence, the conflicts within each community are rising to the surface.

This is especially true of Israel—though I would add that such internal conflict is no new phenomenon for Israel. The disagreements over 'Who is a Jew?' and 'What is a Jew?', between religious and non-religious Jews, have been central ever since the State of Israel was established. From the Israeli point of view, these issues were no less engaging than that of Israel's centrality. In the last decade, however, the tensions seem to have become much more acute, and each camp within Israeli society is now striving to achieve a radical solution 'once and for all'. The earlier questions—of the diaspora's expectations from Israel, of the responsibilities associated with Israel's centrality to the Jewish people as a whole—are now almost entirely eclipsed. From the point of view of the problem of identity, Israeli society is now concerned mainly with itself. Israel is trying to decide whether it will in practice continue as a Jewish state, and if so what its image should be.

Let us examine briefly the dynamics of this controversy. In the religious camp, which is still almost wholly Orthodox, there is a movement towards *haredi*-type radicalism. This is manifested in a tendency towards communal self-segregation so as to maintain a 'pure' halakhic lifestyle and to inculcate it successfully into the younger generation. But there is also a tendency for growing *haredi* involvement in national institutional life in an attempt to enforce a halakhic frame on the public domain. In the non-religious camp— or rather the secular camp—there is a parallel movement towards a new 'Israeli' conception of national identity, a concept that in its radical extreme completely rejects Judaism or Jewishness and manifests only a residual consciousness of its historical origins through an attachment to the Hebrew language and to Eretz Yisrael (the Land of Israel).

A paradox emerges from this conflict. Israel projects to the world a global national understanding of Jewish identity based on a common culture, a civilization. It demands that Jewish communities in the diaspora accept this as the normative ideal. But inside Israel two kinds of identities are developing, the one radically assimilationist and the other segregationist. Both identities, it is worth noting, originated in the diaspora.

It is very difficult to foresee how this conflict will be resolved. Will there be a pluralistic compromise that will retain a level of cultural unity, or will there be total estrangement between separate national cultures? My hope is that the first option will win out, but for this to happen those of us who want it must work very hard. It will not be achieved easily. Let me here just mention a theme to which I shall return later: the absorption of the mass immigration of ex-Soviet citizens in Israeli society will surely have a decisive impact on the direction of the solution.

What, then, is on the agenda of diaspora Jewry? I will sum up my views as briefly as I can because obviously they reflect my Israeli bias; a fuller account will have to be given by people closer to the diaspora perspective. But the views of an outsider, coming as they do from a different perspective, must also have their value; as the Hebrew expression has it, *ore'ach lerega ro'eh kol pega*—the visitor sees every flaw.

The dichotomy that we have seen in Israel between the various Orthodox identities, which are ultimately guided by *haredi*-style segregational radicalism, and the non-Orthodox or secular humanist identities is repeated in the diaspora, but here it seems to have acquired an entirely different meaning. Of course, the main non-Orthodox and non-religious movements in the diaspora define and experience their Judaism in terms of their specific sets of ideologies and lifestyles, but this is not the main difference. From an Israeli perspective, the source of these differences is the fact that in the postmodern period, as in the modern period, there is no way to maintain in the diaspora a separate common Jewish public domain. There is no common arena in which all the Jewish movements can confront each other and give expression to their aspirations to dominate the Jewish world. There are of course attempts to institutionalize certain 'ecumenical' Jewish organizations, covering all the communities in one country, and even all communities all over the world, but the pervasiveness of the non-Jewish environment and the lack of Jewish sovereignty do not allow for a real Jewish public domain—at best, only several partial Jewish communal domains.

This means, on the one hand, that the different Jewish movements in the diaspora exist mainly parallel to each other: since they scarcely interact in public, they scarcely clash as movements—a situation that is peaceful in comparison to Israel, but ultimately a situation of alienation. On the other hand, since every kind of Jewish identity in the diaspora is also necessarily and directly rooted in the all-pervasive non-Jewish surroundings, even the aspiration to develop a global Jewish identity lapses: every kind of Jewish identity in the diaspora is necessarily partial. Let me emphasize here that in my opinion this generalization encompasses the *haredim* too. Although their lifestyle is seemingly segregationalist, post-modernity has at last made it possible, and even quite easy, for the *haredi* group to integrate easily with its non-Jewish environment on its own terms. This accounts for its spectacular revival, but the community is hence not as Jewishly self-contained as it seems.

Diaspora Jewish identities are thus always redefining themselves in the context of the all-pervasive and unrestrainable process of assimilation. Indeed, the apparent necessity to constantly reconsider, redefine, and reaffirm Jewish ideologies and Jewish lifestyles reflects the inevitability of this on-going process and the trend towards a final loss of identity, first on the individual level and then on the communal level. This is of course true mainly of the non-Orthodox majority in the diaspora, though I wonder whether the Orthodox and even the *haredi* groups will be able to maintain their impressive stability for much longer. But what captures the eye of an Israeli observer is the fact that the non-Orthodox majority in the diaspora has long ago forsaken the idea of resistance to assimilation. It has adopted instead the contrary strategy of accepting assimilation, not only as an over-whelming reality but also as a positive one. It tries in this way to create a new set of Jewish identities which can partially coexist with assimilation, or at least do not pose obstacles to it. This rather sophisticated strategy is what guides the process of redefining Judaism described above: Jewish indi-viduals, as well as Jewish movements, posit their Jewishness not in terms of obligating norms and principles—which may work against assimilation in the surrounding culture—but in terms of lifestyles: 'This is how we are still Jewish', they say, and explain how they are adapting their Jewishness in the context of their multi-levelled identities as American, French, or English citizens.

The process I am describing has several stages. In the first stage, Jewish identity is strongly partial and segregational. In the second stage it is partial yet not segregational, although being Jewish is still considered a main component of personal identity. This gradually gives way to an indefinably long stage of maintaining an increasingly marginal partial Jewish identity, an identity which continues to fade until the blessed moment where total Jewish amnesia sets in.

One last remark: I believe that this is why the continued existence of Jewish identity of any kind in the diaspora depends on Israel. If Jewish identities relate in any way to a certain comprehensive Jewish existence, or to an 'ecumenical' Jewish public domain—and I believe that this is a *sine qua non* for maintaining the identity of a people—it is only through an attach-ment to Israel, however ambivalent.

Now let us return to the prospects of the forthcoming turning-point. The identity crisis in European societies will clearly have a particularly severe impact on the personal and collective situation of European Jewry and on the awareness of being Jewish as perceived by Jews and others. History, both ancient and modern, teaches us that the lot of Jews in such cases is to experience a double crisis: as participants of the environment in which they are socially, politically, and culturally integrated, and as members of a group distinct from that environment but with a specific identity that they either wish to maintain or are unable to abandon completely. The separate identity of the Jews will be re-emphasized firstly because the crisis in the wider environment is already fanning the endemic antisemitic feelings, and secondly because in the advance towards the new democratic order Jews have already discovered new options both for expressing their separate identity as Jews and for solving their particular problems as Jews. Together with the non-Jewish population around them but in a much more compli-cated and difficult way, Jews will now have to choose between several different options of individual identity and collective belonging and then start the long and painful process of emotional, ideological, and behavioural adaptation necessary for transformation.

This view of the future seems to be true of European Jewry in general. Even the old, well-established communities in France and England will be affected by this process, though to different degrees and in different ways. But the epicentre of the historical earthquake will be in eastern Europe, mainly in Russia and Ukraine. Russia, being the largest and formerly the dominant country in eastern Europe, will suffer the deepest and most extensive crisis of national identity. It also has the largest Jewish population and the most assimilated one. (Ukraine has the second largest.) It is therefore in Russia that the impact of current events on the image and the destiny of the Jewish people will be the widest, the most traumatic, and the most difficult to contain.

A necessary preliminary to understanding the consequences of these developments is to amass precise statistical information about the quantitative dimensions of the problem. This is seemingly a purely technical task, but in fact the attempts to do so immediately expose the painful historical background of a deep and enduring identity crisis. We encounter a phenomenon that seems to be unique in Jewish history: it is impossible to arrive at a definite measurement of the Jewish population in Russia (and other countries which were part of the former Soviet Union), and the reasons for this are not merely technical. It is impossible to measure precisely the Jewish population in these countries since the dimensions of that population increase or decrease significantly according to changing conditions. In other words, in the countries of the former Soviet Union, the number of people identified as Jews is basically a relative quantity that serves as a general measure of inward and outward indecisiveness with regard to identity. There is of course a certain definite, quantifiable population which identifies itself more or less permanently as Jewish. But this population is the minority: the majority consists of those who are only potentially Jewish. This is not the phenomenon of 'marginal Jews' mentioned earlier in the context of western Europe and America, namely, Jews who still retain a certain permanent inner consciousness of being at least partially Jewish. Rather, these are people who are identified as Russians and so on, by themselves and by their environment, even though they still bear in their consciousness a faded memory of having a partial Jewish ancestry. Indeed, in certain conditions, whether negative (antisemitism) or positive (an opportunity to get out of Russia), or more realistically in a combination of both, the bare rediscovery of this ancestry can move such persons to reconstruct a formal, organizational, sense of Jewish belonging.

This unique phenomenon reflects the tragic absurdity of the history of Judaism and Jewishness under the Communist yoke. As is well known, the Jewish population in the Communist countries, especially in Russia, went through a process of a forced yet forcefully restricted assimilation: the expression of its singular identity was forbidden, but full, immediate, and unquestionable integration into the non-Jewish environment was not allowed. Judaism and Jewishness were completely forbidden, but at the same time could not be erased. Jews had always to remain partially Jews, but only in a negative sense—as a consequence of and in perpetuation of hatred.

The phenomenon of a population which is only 'potentially' Jewish as I have described above is the final product of that dark history. But one should be aware that even those Jews who have succeeded in maintaining some form of Jewish identity underwent the same destructive process. The only differences between them and the completely 'Russified' population is that in their case the destructive process was never completed. In other words, wherever individuals may lie on the trajectory, we are basically dealing here with a single ambivalently Jewish population, a population that exhibits in different degrees the strange syndrome of an identity at once denied and enforced.

Three points should be made in connection with this. (*a*) For most of those Jews who retain a consciousness of being Jewish, that consciousness is partial and muted; they have long ago lost the positive drive and the positive substance of knowledge and memories necessary for remaining Jewish, especially for educating their children as Jews. (*b*) The motivation of such Jews to become fully 'Gentile' is generally no different from that which motivates the merely 'potential' Jews. (*c*) The continued adoption of a Jewish identity, and particularly the willingness to transmit it to the next generation, is now dependent mainly on external conditions.

One may add, of course, that here and there one may find singularly stubborn Jews who were sufficiently strong in spirit to maintain a positive Jewish identity, be it religious or ethnic or even cultural. One should also remember that after the establishment of the State of Israel there was an almost miraculous emergence of a small group of young Jewish intellectuals who responded to Communist animosity, rejection, and hatred with a heroic spiritual effort to reconstruct a positive Jewish identity, whether through Zionism or through religion. This last phenomenon is surely a source of hope. It indicates that under conditions of freedom, and through an inspired and sensitive educational process, part of this rootless Jewish population, and particularly the younger generation, may regain a positive Jewish identity. But let us not deceive ourselves as to the magnitude of this phenomenon. The light may be brilliant, but it is still very small.

The Jews who are now finally being given the option—or to be more precise, are being virtually compelled—to choose between their own separate Jewish identity and the nationalist identity of their non-Jewish environment are thus a particular group of Jews with a particular historical background. In opting for a separate, positive Jewish identity, they will also have to choose between the bewildering variety of different forms of Jewish identity—in many ways mutually antagonistic, and in any case problematic in themselves—which have emerged in the free world. This will be a very difficult set of decisions, and the process of adaptation and self-alteration which will begin afterwards will necessarily be a very painful one.

The options available will be the product of and motivated by the newly gained freedom, but in fact the decisions will be made within the narrow limits dictated by powerful internal and external constraints. First, and already fully apparent, are the constraints posed by the non-Jewish environment: antisemitism is flaring up and the prospects for Jews are generally very grim, particularly since they generally belong to the middle class and share its expectations, in terms of career, economic gains, social position, and other aspects of the quality of life. There is also the inner constraint of an attachment to the surrounding cultural environment, an environment that they feel is truly their own—in stark contrast with their deep feeling of estrangement from Jewish culture and the tragic Jewish destiny.

Such constraints are not definitely inclined towards one direction. Antisemitism, for example, may inspire either a wish to emigrate and remain Jewish or a wish to become utterly unrecognizable within non-Jewish society. The natural attachment to the high culture of the surrounding non-Jewish society will in most cases motivate full assimilation, but in rare yet influential cases it may inspire a spiritual need for a return to Jewish origins. However, the nature of the constraints is such that people will need to make a radical choice: in such circumstances there can be no middle way. Jews will feel that they are called upon to decide between the options of full commitment to Jewish belonging and full assimilation. The compromises of partial and synthesized identities with which we are so familiar in the West will appear unrealistic, at least in the first stage of the crisis and for those who decide to remain where they live. The internal and external pressures that such Jews will feel to assimilate will be much stronger than their motivation or their spiritual capability to remain partially Jewish.

But this is not the end of the list of constraints. For those who decide to emigrate, it is only the beginning. They will next have to confront the constraints of their new environment, and there the spiritual conflict will appear even greater. First they will have to give up their east European culture—a culture that they love and that the immigrants' natural nostalgia will surely make much more dear to them. They will then have to adapt to a culture that is initially utterly unknown, strange, superficial, and alienating—or at least perceived as very much less attractive than their own.

A question which may be raised in this context is whether Jews emigrating from eastern Europe will have the motivation and the resources to shape for themselves new collective types of Jewish identity which may be more appropriate for them, given their circumstances. Is there any chance that they will create communities in which they will develop their own east European model of Jewish culture? From what is happening now with Soviet immigrants in Israel, such a development in fact appears almost inevitable. In many cases, the first reaction to Israeli society and its cultural reality, especially in the case of intellectuals (of whom there are many among the Soviet immigrants), is an alarmed refusal to give up their original east European culture. They consider it definitely superior to the new cultural patterns that are offered to them: the religious lifestyle is completely strange to most of them, while Israel's secular lifestyle is considered vulgar and superficial. Still, they know that having come to Israel they have to become Israelis. They must at least learn Hebrew and become acquainted with the economic, political, scientific, and cultural facts of Israeli life. The result is to develop an exile mentality which consists in an attempt to stay apart from the local cultural environment while maintaining the spiritual links with the former cultural centre abroad.

This type of estrangement and separation is unlikely to be more than a passing phase; though it may last longer in the case of creative intellectuals—writers, artists, and so forth—it is not likely to endure among the masses, and especially among the younger generation. On the other hand, east European Jewish immigrants have no religious or other Jewish cultural resources of their own. Therefore, as they begin to feel constrained to be acculturated to a certain positive conception of Judaism, they will have to concede to the existing patterns of Jewishness in their new environments. But one must remember that, even so, the east European immigration will be sufficiently massive in its magnitude, and sufficiently sure in its consciousness of having a superior cultural heritage, to make its own impact on the culture of the absorbing communities. (This will be less true in America or in western Europe than in Israel because in the face of the dominant surrounding non-Jewish culture, the immigrants will in the long run have to give up their east European heritage almost completely.)

One can guess that the change will be felt most strongly in the secular Jewish community in Israel. This is primarily because the majority of the east European immigrants are ideologically secular, and it will thus be within the secular community that they will be absorbed. But because the secular community in Israel is not very sure of its own Jewish identity and therefore has no drive to enforce it on others, it is much more open to the cultural contributions of secular newcomers. The religious community, in contrast, is Jewishly crystallized and very strong-minded. It is ready, even anxiously so, to integrate within itself as many Jews as possible, but on its own terms: it is definitely not prepared to accept any kind of new cultural contributions.

The initial inference from this analysis would appear to be that neither in Israel nor in the diaspora are there grounds for the emergence of new Jewish ideologies, new Jewish lifestyles, or new Jewish movements as a result of the great changes in eastern Europe. The existing religious, religious nationalist, secular nationalist, and humanist trends will remain basically as they are, ideologically and theologically, at least for an initial period. There may be marginal changes as a result of certain cultural imports, but basically the historical consistency will be maintained. Such changes as occur will be due only to the inner sociological and psychological dynamics of these movements and will occur mainly with regard to their original Western background. But there is a second inference that must also be emphasized: the demographic impact of an immigration of such magnitude must be critical in terms of the redistribution of Jewish populations (*a*) throughout the world, and particularly between Israel and the Jewish centres of the diaspora, and (*b*) as between the different movements within each centre. One important consequence will be that Israel will become the leading Jewish community not only in terms of its spiritual centrality in the Jewish world, but also in the demographic sense: it will be where the majority of the Jewish people live. This will have a critical impact on the strength of Israel's claim to lead and represent the Jewish people. At the same time, the secular community in Israel will become numerically dominant, and thus less dependent politically upon the Orthodox religious groups. This is a change which may signify a crucial turning-point in the development of the whole fabric of Israeli Jewish culture, and not only in the political domain.

Thus, contrary to the initial inference, we can in fact expect that more modern movements and patterns of Jewish religiosity will at last gain legitimacy in Israeli society. In fact, it seems likely that a similar change in proportional allegiance to the different Jewish movements will also occur in the diaspora because of the Jewish immigration from the former Soviet Union. This means that at the level of *kelal yisrael*, the level of the collective self-image of the Jewish people, a comprehensive change in the direction of liberal national-centralism and a secular culture is already in the process of realization. This is full of far-reaching implications. Many people consider these prospects as positive developments, but there are several powerful

Jewish movements, both in Israel and in the diaspora, that consider them with alarm. At least in the short run this will increase rather than reduce the deep sense of identity crisis, especially in Israel. The social, political, and cultural consequences are quite apparent.

To prepare properly for the strains and stresses ahead, Jews must accept emotionally and intellectually that the whole Jewish people has already entered a uniquely difficult period. The Jews of eastern Europe are even now undergoing a painful identity crisis. If they decide to regain their Jewish identity, they will be taking upon themselves a doubly painful process of uprooting and rerooting. They will also have to make another decision which will determine whether the ensuing process of readaptation will be positive and creative or negative and destructive: should the change be regarded fatalistically, as a tragedy that reflects the destructive aspects of Jewish destiny in our era, or as a great opportunity to regain a lost authentic identity by contributing creatively to the return of the Jewish people to its full national life in Israel? For it is in Israel, and basically only there, that the life of the Jewish people as such can be renewed.

The Jews of eastern Europe, though deprived of their Jewish memory, are culturally very capable. They are full of creative energies, of cultural talents and spiritual resources. If they so decide, they can contribute a great deal to the cultural revival of the Jewish people. The painful process of change and adaptation can become a source of creativity that will enrich the individuals concerned and the Jewish people as a whole. This will not make the process any lighter or less painful, but the gains will justify the sacrifices. In contrast, adopting an alienated attitude to the process could have tragic consequences both for the individual immigrants and their children and for the whole Jewish community, in Israel and in the diaspora.

The same dilemma faces those who have to carry out the task of absorbing the immigrants, particularly in Israel. Israeli society can either try to force its own patterns of cultural identity, whether religious or secular, upon the east European immigrants, or it can relate to the whole process not as one in which one side actively 'absorbs' while the other side is passively 'absorbed', but as a reciprocal process in which both sides change. Such a strategy will not basically change the characteristics of Jewish identities in Israel, in terms of their singular Jewish or Israeli components, but it can motivate much creative interpretation, improvement, and enrichment.

At the time of the mass immigration from Muslim countries after the establishment of the State, Israeli society adopted the first of these two models of absorption. We now know that this was a gross mistake, even a tragedy; its results are still considered among the great failures of Israeli culture. Israeli society will now be judged by its ability to resist the temptation to dominate, by its capacity to open itself to the newcomers' cultural contributions—to give not only by shaping others but also by accepting them; not only to demand from others but also to show a readiness to be changed by them.

I am sure that a decision by Israeli society, and especially the non-religious trends within it, to accept this new strategy of cultural absorption will contribute to a pluralist solution of the conflict between the religious and the non-religious and thus to the development of a global national Jewish culture. Moreover, I believe that it will establish the centrality of Israel as a unifying centre for the whole Jewish people. One must of course translate such general advice into a pragmatic policy and suggest practical options, but creating the intellectual awareness and motivating the commitment is clearly a necessary prerequisite. This is the task that Jews must now face.

PART II

DEMOGRAPHIC AND
SOCIOLOGICAL
CONSIDERATIONS

CHAPTER THREE

An Overview of the Demographic Trends of European Jewry

SERGIO DELLAPERGOLA

T HE study of European Jewry is reasonably well developed with regard to the history of its Jewish communities, and to a lesser extent also with regard to social patterns at both local and national levels. Attempts to grasp the contemporary Jewish socio-demographic scene in a coherent and integrated continent-wide framework, however, are really in their infancy. This situation is partly a reflection of general difficulties relating to collecting, organizing, and meaningfully analysing a variety of data pertaining to geographically dispersed and quite heterogeneous institutional settings, as is the case when dealing with Europe. However, it also reflects problems that are specific to contemporary Jewish socio-demographic research.

A central problem is that the deepening of processes of integration and assimilation in recent generations has affected the perception and practice of Jewishness, and hence the size, corporate personality, and cultural contents of Jewish communities. The boundaries and definitions of the Jewish collective have tended to become increasingly complex, blurred, and inconsistent. To accommodate this, new concepts have gradually gained a central place in the research vocabulary, such as those of a 'core' and an 'enlarged' Jewish population. The 'core' consists of people who consider themselves Jewish, while the 'enlarged population' includes also people who previously considered themselves Jewish, other persons of recent Jewish descent, and non-Jewish household members associated with any of these categories. Clearly, different definitions of the Jewish collective will lead to different population counts, different assessments of future trends, and different evaluations of

Research for this article was carried out at the Division of Jewish Demography and Statistics at the A. Harman Institute of Contemporary Jewry at the Hebrew University of Jerusalem.

prospects. In this article, all estimates of Jewish population refer to the 'core' population unless otherwise stated.

An additional problem is that since the end of 1989, Jewish migration across international boundaries has reached peak historical levels—a reflection of a continuing crisis at the global level, but especially in Europe, which further complicates the analysis because it distorts the projection of trends. And when the aim is to grasp the complexity of present Jewish realities not just at the local level but at the level of an entire continent—characterized as it is by a larger number of countries showing substantial diversity of historical development and current situations—these factors tend to complicate matters even more.

The difficulties in studying European Jewry actually begin with the problem of defining Europe's geographical boundaries. From the point of view of assessing contemporary and future Jewish social developments, is it more relevant to adopt an inclusive geographical definition, or one which is limited to the twelve member-countries of the European Community? The latter is a highly significant framework for discussion, but the bonds and commonalities of the Jewish experience clearly transcend the narrower institutional definition, which is itself subject to change in the course of time. I shall therefore have to make reference here to different geographical definitions of Europe.

Coherent analysis is also hampered by the lack of sources, and by the fragmentary and disparate nature of such data as are available. In the past, official censuses and demographic statistics in many European countries reported information on Jewish population, but since the Second World War such information has only been available for relatively few countries, and mostly those with small Jewish populations. The main exception was the Soviet Union, where quite a range of official data used to be collected, but the difficulty here (besides the problematic use of the official 'nationality' criterion for defining Jews), was that the publication policy for such data was selective. More information has now become available for past periods, but the prospects for statistical documentation about the Jews in the several successor states of the former Soviet Union are not clear.

Given these circumstances, the main bulk of documentation has in recent years been obtained through Jewish community sources. These include routine compilations of vital statistics (marriages and divorces, male births, and burials), analyses of membership registers in synagogues and other Jewish institutions, and special surveys of representative samples in selected countries or locales. Where such surveys have been conducted, they have provided an integrated view of the demographic, socio-economic, and Jewish behavioural and attitudinal characteristics of the populations surveyed, but the general lack of co-ordination between the various efforts and of systematic updating has hampered meaningful comparisons and syntheses.[1]

In the current context of European integration, the need for a more systematic approach is keenly felt. The ideal instrument through which the different communities in the continent might be assessed would be a European Jewish population survey, based on a common set of questions and definitions. It is to be hoped that this challenge will be soon taken up by the relevant European Jewish institutions, at least those within the European Community.

PATTERNS FROM THE PAST

Historically, the size of the Jewish population and its distribution over the European continent reflected a very complex set of experiences over a number of centuries. Some of these were shaped by constraints imposed from the outside, by the wider non-Jewish society; some reflected patterns and needs emerging from inside the Jewish community itself. Political, economic, and cultural factors determined quite different and changing rates of growth among Jewish populations across the various regions and countries of Europe. Most communities, countrywide and locally, experienced an alternation of periods of sustained growth and sudden collapses, due to large scale in- or out-migration or the physical destruction of communities. In addition, different local trends in marriage, fertility, mortality, and natural increase changed the size and geography of European Jewry. Finally, secession from Jewish communities on religious or ideological grounds generally exceeded accessions, resulting in further net losses to the Jewish population.

Several interesting features emerge from an attempt to reconstruct the Jewish population profile. First, the phenomenon of rapid population growth occurred much earlier among the Jews than in European society in general (see Fig. 1). The number of Jews in Europe grew from an estimated 719,000 in 1700 to approximately 2 million in 1800, 8.8 million in 1900, and 9.5 million in 1939—an increase of over 13 times, while the total population of the continent increased only 4.6 times, from 125 million in 1700 to 575 million in 1939. This early demographic take-off was the crucial element of a transformation of world Jewish population that was overwhelmingly rapid by contemporary standards. In the process, European Jewry came to dominate other sections of the Jewish diaspora both numerically and culturally. Whereas in the early eighteenth century just less than two-thirds of world Jewry lived in Europe, and in earlier centuries an even lower proportion, by 1860 European Jews accounted for approaching 90 per cent of the world's total. Continuing intense Jewish population

Population

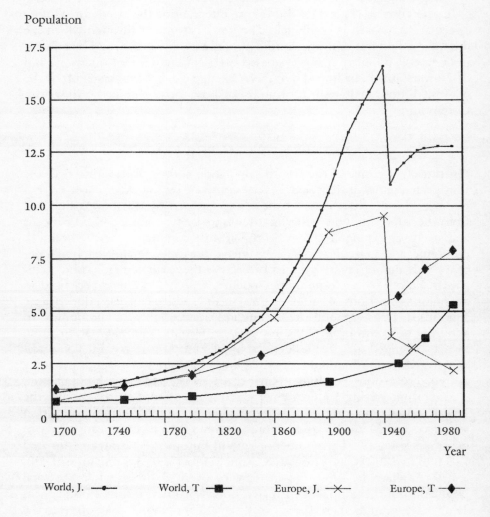

Fig. 1 Total population growth and Jewish population growth, Europe and the world, 1700–1990. Note that the scales of the estimates differ: Jews are shown in millions, the total population of Europe in hundreds of millions, and the total world population in billions. (*Sources:* J. N. Biraben, 'Essai sur l'évolution du nombre des hommes', *Population*, 34: 1 (1979), 13–25; United Nations, *World Population Prospects 1990* (New York, 1991).

growth in Europe led to chronic disequilibrium between the size of the Jewish communities and their economic resources and political security; this in turn led the way to mass migration, the formation of major new Jewish centres outside Europe, and a decline in the share of European Jewry among the world's total.

Between the end of the nineteenth century and the 1930s, the Jews of Europe again preceded the total population in a general lowering of growth rates and a tendency towards zero growth. However, the particular rhythm of Jewish demographic transformation reflected the unique blend of a minority social stratification and its distinctive complex of norms, beliefs, and community institutions. Then, in the 1940s, came the Holocaust and the enormous population losses to European, and world, Jewry—losses that were compounded by the very low birth rate during the war and the consequent ageing of the population. Today's European Jewish population as currently estimated is therefore substantially lower than it was on the eve of the Second World War, and will continue to be so for long into the future.

Significant changes have also occurred in the geographical distribution of the Jewish population within Europe (see Table 1). In the past a Jewish presence, both nationally and locally, was only occasionally related to socio-economic factors in the general sense; more often it reflected the willingness of the authorities or ruling powers to permit Jews at least the minimum legal and economic conditions required for living. Taking a broad view of the changing size of Jewish communities at the country level over the past three centuries according to present political boundaries, three basic profiles emerge: (*a*) relative stability, as in the case of Italy and some smaller communities, such as Switzerland, the Scandinavian countries, and Spain; (*b*) substantial growth followed by dramatic decline, as in most east European and Balkan countries, as well as in The Netherlands, Belgium, Germany, and Austria; and (*c*) growth in more recent generations, such as in the United Kingdom and France.

The past demographic patterns of European Jews can be better understood through the use of sophisticated statistical techniques that permit synthesis of vast masses of detailed data. Country-by-country analysis of Jewish population size and growth rates between 1700 and 1990 (not shown in Table 1) indicates clearly that the chief single factor capable of explaining the variable patterns of three hundred years of Jewish demographic history—stronger than any other geographical, political, or socio-economic criterion—is the intensity of the Holocaust in each country. This is a reminder of the extent of the tragedy that put an end to the rich, creative, and often happy modern history of so many European Jewish communities.

Table 1. Estimated Distribution of the Jewish Population in Europe, 1700–1990 (thousands and percentages)

Country	1700	1800	1860	1900	1939	1945	1960	1990
World total	1,100	2,500	5,300	10,600	16,600	11,000	12,160	12,806
Europe total	719	2,020	4,668	8,766	9,500	3,800	3,241	2,157
European Community[a]	180	357	611	1,051	1,295[e]	842[e]	889	999
Other west Europe[b]	1	6	21	180	130[e]	110[e]	48	44
Former USSR[c]	273	854	2,080	4,084	3,394	1,989	1,970	1,000
Other east Europe[d]	265	803	1,956	3,451	4,681	859	334	114
Europe total (%)	100.0	100.0	100.0	100.0	100.0	100.0	100.0	100.0
European Community[a]	25.0	17.7	13.1	12.0	13.6[e]	22.2[e]	27.4	46.3
Other west Europe[b]	0.1	0.3	0.4	2.0	1.4[e]	2.9[e]	1.5	2.0
Former USSR[c]	38.0	42.3	44.6	46.6	35.7	52.3	60.8	46.4
Other east Europe[d]	36.9	39.7	41.9	39.4	49.3	22.6	10.3	5.3
Jews in Europe as % of world Jewry	65.4	80.8	88.1	82.7	57.2	34.5	26.7	16.8

Note: Boundaries as in 1990.
[a] Belgium, Denmark, France, Germany, Greece, Ireland, Italy, Luxemburg, Netherlands, Portugal, Spain, United Kingdom.
[b] Austria, Finland, Iceland, Norway, Sweden, Switzerland.
[c] Belarus, Estonia, Latvia, Lithuania, Moldova, Russia (including Asiatic Russia), Ukraine.
[d] Albania, Bulgaria, Czechoslovakia, Hungary, Poland, Romania, Turkey (European part only), Yugoslavia (all territory of former federation).
[e] Including refugees in transit.

Source: Compiled and adapted from: S. DellaPergola, 'Recent Demographic Trends among Jews in Western Europe', in E. Stock (ed.), *European Jewry: A Handbook* (Ramat Gan, 1983) p. 22; id., 'Major Demographic Trends of World Jewry: The Last Hundred Years', in B. Bonné-Tamir and A. Adam (eds.), *Genetic Diversity among Jews: Diseases and Markers at the DNA Level* (New York, 1992), 7; J. Lestschinsky, 'Die Umsiedlung und Umschichtung des Judischen Volkes im Laufe des letzten Jahrhunderts', *Weltwirthschaftliches Archiv*, 30 (1929), 132; U. O. Schmelz and S. DellaPergola, 'World Jewish Population, 1990', *American Jewish Year Book*, 92 (1992), 493.

Historically, one of the main characteristics of European Jewish demography has been the distinction between the east and the west of the continent. Jewish population grew faster in eastern Europe, despite the fact that western Europe experienced a decline in the rate of mortality far earlier, and also an influx of Jews from the east. But even so, the population increase among the Jews of eastern Europe was more rapid and more massive. As already noted, one of the consequences of this was large-scale Jewish emigration from eastern Europe from the last quarter of the nineteenth century onwards. Most of the migrants settled in America, but some of this migration was for a few decades to stimulate the growth of the then relatively small communities of western Europe, such as those of the UK and France, as well as of larger communities with a longer and more complex history, such as those of Germany. Many of those who did not emigrate were brutally murdered in the Holocaust, which took a greater toll in eastern Europe than it did in the west. (Although a most significant exception was the Russian republic, whose Jewish population was relatively untouched.)

An important factor in the differentiation between Jewish demographic trends in east and west Europe was that modernity came later to eastern Europe, and the pattern of more frequent and younger marriage, more marriage strictly within the Jewish community, and higher fertility levels continued there for longer, in adherence to the traditional Jewish ideal of demographic and cultural reproduction. These basic east–west Jewish demographic differences to some extent reflected patterns that existed in the surrounding non-Jewish society, but it is notable that in both eastern and western Europe the reduction in mortality and fertility generally occurred first among the Jews. Nearly everywhere, Jews were distinctive in the timing of the initial outset of the transition, its pace, and its eventual completion. The chief factor in this outstanding early Jewish population growth, in the presence of traditional family norms and behaviours, was lower mortality.

Explaining such uniqueness within the larger context of general trends in European population requires careful consideration of the cultural framework of socio-demographic behaviour. Of crucial importance here was the intervention and sometimes mobilization of the Jewish community with regard to individual demographic events. Such involvement tended to reduce disease and mortality levels, enhance family formation, lower divorce rates, and provide support in facing the challenges of family growth. Residential segregation at the regional, municipal, and neighbourhood level reinforced the incidence of distinctive Jewish socio-cultural norms. On the whole, these factors operated more intensively in eastern Europe than in the more urbanized, less traditional communities of western Europe.

The historical distinction between eastern Europe and western Europe in terms of Jewish demography is also shown clearly in Table 1. For most of the historical span considered here, the Jewish population of eastern Europe (shown here as the new independent countries which until 1991 formed part of the Soviet Union, and the other countries in the region) was very much larger than that of western Europe (shown here as the twelve countries belonging to the European Community and the non-member countries). Only after the Second World War did the quantitative centre of gravity of European Jewry start moving to the west; and only since the early 1990s, following the most recent exodus from the former Soviet Union, has the Jewish population of western Europe, for the first time in the modern period, exceeded that of eastern Europe.

THE CONTEMPORARY PERSPECTIVE: THE JEWS OF THE EUROPEAN COMMUNITY

At the end of 1990, the total Jewish population of Europe was estimated at just over 2 million, or 2.8 per 1,000 in the total population of the continent (see Table 2). One million Jews lived in the twelve countries of the European Community, another million in the seven European countries of the former Soviet Union, and smaller numbers elsewhere—44,000 in the non-EC countries of west Europe, and 114,000 in other east European countries and the Balkans. Emigration from the former Soviet Union was contributing to a rapid decline in the Jewish population there: altogether, over half a million people, including non-Jewish family members, left the Soviet Union as part of this wave of emigration between 1990 and 1992, viz. 220,000 in 1990, around 190,000 in 1991, and in 1992 somewhere over 110,000. Most of the emigrants were headed for Israel, or for the United States and

Table 2. Estimated Distribution of the Jewish Population in Europe, 1990

Country	Jewish population	Jews per 1,000 population in country	Accuracy rating and year
Grand total	**2,157,800**	**2.8**	
Total European Community	**999,600**	**2.9**	
Belgium	31,800	3.2	C 1987
Denmark	6,400	1.2	C 1990
France	530,000	9.4	C 1990
Germany	40,000	0.5	C 1990
Greece	4,800	0.5	B 1990
Ireland	1,800	0.5	B 1990
Italy	31,200	0.5	B 1990
Luxemburg	600	1.6	B 1990
Netherlands	25,700	1.7	C 1990
Portugal	300	0.0	B 1986
Spain	12,000	0.3	D
United Kingdom	315,000	5.5	C 1990
Total Other Western Europe	**44,000**	**1.3**	
Austria	7,000	0.9	C 1990
Finland	1,300	0.3	A 1990
Gibraltar	600	20.0	C 1981
Norway	1,000	0.2	B 1987
Sweden	15,000	1.8	C 1990
Switzerland	19,000	2.9	C 1980
Other	100	0.1	D

Table 2. *Continued*

Country	Jewish population	Jews per 1,000 population in country	Accuracy rating and year
Total Former USSR in Europe	**1,000,500**	**4.5**	
Belarus	75,000	7.3	B 1990
Estonia	3,500	2.1	B 1990
Latvia	18,000	6.7	B 1990
Lithuania	9,000	2.4	B 1990
Moldova	50,000	11.4	B 1990
Russia[b]	470,000	3.2	B 1990
Ukraine	375,000	7.2	B 1990
Total Other East Europe and Balkans	**113,700**	**0.6**	
Albania	300	0.1	B 1990
Bulgaria	3,100	0.3	C 1990
Czech Republic	4,800	0.5	D
Hungary	57,000	5.4	D
Poland	3,800	0.1	C 1990
Romania	17,500	0.8	B 1988
Slovakia	3,000	0.6	D
Turkey[b]	19,700	0.4	C 1990
Yugoslavia[c]	4,500	0.2	C 1986

[a]The accuracy rating is as follows: A highly reliable and recent figures; B less recent or accurate data; C partial or indirect evidence; D conjectural. The years reported reflect the most recent data available.
[b]Including territory in Asia.
[c]Including all territory of the former federation.

Source: U. O. Schmelz and S. DellaPergola, 'World Jewish Population 1990', *American Jewish Year Book*, 92 (1992), 484–512.

other overseas countries, but a significant flow, estimated at about 20,000 by the end of 1992, had settled in Germany.

To gain a balanced perspective on the present and on possible future changes, it is important to understand the factors affecting Jewish population distribution both among the individual countries and within them. As I have already noted, the differential impact of the Holocaust on the various countries is still a major factor in determining the size of current Jewish populations, but it is also important to assess the nature of the 'push' and 'pull' factors that have generated voluntary population movements to and from given communities more recently. A further critical element is the ability of a population to reproduce itself demographically, which in the case of Jewish communities may be affected by changing patterns of group identification no less than by the biological facts of birth and death.

First, the countries of Europe and their respective Jewish populations must be perceived as components in the broader socio-economic and political system of nations. The balance of forces operating worldwide tends to attract people towards the 'centre'—the more developed and stable countries—and away from the 'periphery', or less developed and more unstable nations. Jews have tended to respond rationally to those incentives and constraints, unless political barriers prevented them from doing so. Indeed, at the world level, both the size of Jewish populations in individual countries and the percentage of Jews in the total population tend to be highly and positively correlated with major indicators of socio-economic development, industrialization, and political freedom.

In the contemporary period, modernization and affluence have more often than not been positively correlated with liberal public attitudes towards the efforts of Jewish communities to conduct a relatively autonomous and viable community life. Since the Second World War, the countries of western Europe have generally offered Jews both freedom and affluence close to the core of the world system, and have indeed attracted quite substantial immigration from other areas. Until the early 1960s, Britain had the greatest concentration of Jews in western Europe, but since the massive immigration to France following the decolonization of north Africa, France has become the flag-bearer of the Jewish presence in western Europe. The relative decline in the British Jewish community is also connected with the less than brilliant economic situation in the United Kingdom, which has promoted a measurable amount of general emigration, including Jewish emigration, in the last three decades.

The major exception to this schematic view of Jewish population trends in western Europe is Germany, which despite being the leading economic power on the continent has a relatively small Jewish population. The historical record notwithstanding, however, the size of the Jewish population in Germany seems likely to increase, especially in the context of continuing large-scale emigration from eastern Europe. But given that the nature of the interaction between the host society and its Jewish minority is one of the more sensitive factors in the growth or decline of a Jewish community, it seems safer to suspend judgement with regard to the prospect of Jewish demographic growth in present-day Germany.

Reviewing the distribution of European Jewry at a more local level confirms even further that the size of the Jewish presence tends to reflect local socio-economic and socio-cultural conditions. Table 3 compares total and Jewish population distributions *c.*1990 among the sixty-nine major regions of the European Community, based on an analysis in which the regions were ranked from richest to poorest, subdivided into five equal

---

Table 3. Estimated Distribution of the Total Population and Jewish Population in the European Community by Level of Regional Standard of Living, *c.*1990

Standard of living stratum[a]	Total population[b]	Jewish population[c]	Jews per 1,000 population
Total (number)	341,321,000	999,600	—
Total (per cent)	100.0	100.0	2.9
1 (highest)	22.2	59.4	7.9
2	27.2	19.1	2.1
3	19.5	19.0	2.8
4	17.6	1.5	0.2
5 (lowest)	13.5	1.0	0.2

[a]The 69 major statistical regions into which the 12 countries of the European Community are divided were classified by per capita PPS (Purchasing Power Standard = gross domestic product adjusted for market prices). Strata 1–4 include 14 regions each; stratum 5 includes 13 regions.
[b]Source: Eurostat, *Regions: Statistical Yearbook 1989* (Luxemburg, 1990).
[c]Source: author's estimates based on files available at the Division of Jewish Demography and Statistics at the A. Harman Institute of Contemporary Jewry at the Hebrew University of Jerusalem.

---

strata, and the distributions of total and Jewish populations in each stratum compared. The analysis showed that while the total population was distributed fairly evenly among the strata (the range being 13.5–27.2 per cent), the Jewish population was overwhelmingly concentrated in the upper stratum: its fourteen component regions included over 59 per cent of the total Jewish population of the European Community while the two bottom strata together accounted for only 2.5 per cent. Accordingly, the number of Jews per 1,000 of total population declined from nearly 8 in the upper stratum to 2–3 in the next two strata, and to 0.2 in the two lower strata.

These striking patterns will be better understood by considering the correlation which exists between several features of the more developed European regions and the social structure of Jewish populations. In general, there is a strong association between a high standard of living and high population density (as appropriate to large urban areas), heterogeneity of economic activities with an emphasis on services (as contrasted to agriculture and industry), and a richness of educational and cultural opportunities. All this fits well with a number of characteristics typical of the Jewish population structure. These are urbanization and conglomeration (92 per cent of all Jews in the European Community live in cities with 1,000 Jews or more), high educational attainment (over half of the younger adults

generations have at least some university education), and a growing specialization in professional and managerial activities.

Further examination of the detailed data reveals that in the fourteen
European regions comprising the top stratum, the intensity of the Jewish
presence (i.e. the proportion of Jews per 1,000 inhabitants) is quite different. In three regions the proportion is definitely above the average: Greater
Paris, with 305,000 Jews, or 30 per 1,000 population; Great Britain's
south-east, including Greater London, with 232,000 Jews, or 13 per 1,000;
and Greater Brussels, with 15,000 Jews, or 15 per 1,000. Each of these
metropolitan areas fulfils the role of a major world or continental capital
whose influence transcends the boundaries of the country in which it is
located. A moderate Jewish presence (1–3 Jews per 1,000 inhabitants)
appears in six further regions in the top stratum. These are Berlin; Hessen
(main city: Frankfurt); Hamburg; Denmark (Copenhagen); Lombardy
(Milan); and Luxemburg. These are all national or regional capital cities
with wide international connections. Five more regions in the top stratum
have relatively few Jews (less than 1 per 1,000): Noord (Groningen) in The
Netherlands; Bremen and Baden-Württemberg (Stuttgart) in Germany; and
Nord-Ovest (Turin) and Emilia-Romagna (Bologna) in Italy. The scarce
Jewish presence in these latter regions, in spite of their relatively high living
standards, is probably because their socio-economic and cultural facilities are
less complex and sophisticated. However, the relatively high standards of
living available there may serve as a potential factor of attraction for larger
numbers of Jews in the future.

At the same time, it should be noted that historical inertia—namely, the
continued presence of a Jewish community in a certain locale even after the
original reasons for it have ceased to be valid—may play an important role in
determining current Jewish population distribution. Relatively large Jewish
communities are to be found in regions whose current socio-economic
situation is just moderately attractive but which had a thriving Jewish life in
the past. Six regions in the second stratum host a Jewish population which is
greater than 10,000 and represents at least 2 per 1,000 of the total population: the West (main city: Amsterdam) in the Netherlands; Lazio (Rome) in
Italy; Vlaams Gewest (Antwerp) in Belgium; and Centre-Est (Lyons), Est
(Strasburg), and Sud-Ouest (Toulouse) in France. In the third stratum, four
regions meet these same conditions of Jewish population size/density—the
Méditerranée (Marseilles) in France; and Scotland (Glasgow), North-West
(Manchester), and Yorkshire (Leeds) in Great Britain. None meet these
criteria in the two bottom strata. Indeed, the very scant Jewish presence in
some of the more economically depressed regions in the European Community, such as Spain, Portugal, Greece, southern and insular Italy, Ireland,

and the Landers in the former East Germany, supports the general interpretation suggested here.

The correlation between a Jewish presence and the existence of attractive socio-economic conditions calls perhaps for further investigation, but there can be no doubt that these findings hint at possible future trends. This is especially true in view of the new European Single Market regulations in force from 1 January 1993: the greatly enhanced freedom of travel and employment for citizens of the European Community within its boundaries will quite probably increase the correspondence between what a certain place or region has to offer economically and culturally and people's willingness to live there. In the longer run this is likely to affect the general distribution of population in Europe, and there is no reason why Jews would not want to be among those taking advantage of the new opportunities.

Quite apart from these external factors affecting the patterns of the Jewish presence across the continent, Jewish demographic projections are also seriously affected by a factor internal to the Jewish community, which is the problem of demographic continuity. Whereas the Jewish family was once a cornerstone of Jewish continuity, several indicators nowadays point to a process of erosion, especially among the Jews of Europe and other diaspora communities. These indicators include a reduced propensity to marry, later marriages, far lower marital stability, lower marital fertility, higher rates of mixed marriage, and the Jewish socialization of only a minority of the children of mixed marriages. In the past—perhaps as late as the 1920s—more than 95 per cent of the adults in a typical east European Jewish community married, and virtually none married non-Jews. Data from a variety of contemporary Jewish communities in both eastern and western Europe indicate that the proportion of Jews who marry may have dropped to as low as 85 per cent (of whom perhaps 10–15 per cent will be divorced at prime reproductive ages), and that the rate of out-marriages is 50 per cent or more. This implies that considerably less than half the Jewish adults reaching the stage of the life-cycle at which children are most typically raised (roughly, between the ages of 30 and 45) find themselves in what once was the universal Jewish status—married, and with a Jewish spouse.

As a consequence, especially since the late 1960s, there has been a marked drop in the total fertility rate of Jewish women, and even more significantly in the effective Jewish fertility rate, i.e. taking into account that part of the new generation raised Jewishly. In countries as different as France and Russia, current total fertility rates tend to range around 1.5 children per Jewish woman, whereas the level required for the replacement of a generation would be 2.1 children. In other words, there is now an intrinsic demographic shortfall of roughly 25–30 per cent of the size of the present generation, which points unmistakably to a shrinkage in population in the next generation. Similarly erosive demographic patterns, albeit somewhat attenuated, have also appeared among Jews who migrated to Europe in the last few decades from more traditional environments in North Africa and the Middle East.

Low fertility is a powerful determinant of the process of population ageing now visible throughout Europe among Jews and non-Jews alike. Among Jews, the general effects of low fertility are compounded by a weakening of Jewish identity, which leads to more frequent out-marriage and thus to further shrinkage of the youngest segment of the age pyramid. The ultimate consequence is a negative balance between the number of births and deaths in an over-aged Jewish population.

One good example of this is apparent from the statistics collected by the Community Research Unit of the Board of Deputies of British Jews. The average annual excess of Jewish deaths over Jewish births in Great Britain was 1,674 in 1975–9, 1,840 in 1980–4, 1,108 in 1985–9, and 1,519 in 1990. This corresponds to a Jewish population loss of nearly 25,000 over a period of sixteen years, out of a Jewish population estimated in the mid-1970s at 330–340,000. The situation in Great Britain is quite typical of most other Jewish communities across Europe, and is by no means the most extreme on record. Smaller communities in western Europe have been experiencing much sharper variations of the same trend, as have Jewish populations in eastern Europe. Low fertility, assimilation, ageing, and a negative balance of births and deaths are contributing to the erosion of the Jewish population across Europe, despite the positive demographic impact of the high birthrates among the more Orthodox Jews. This is true not only of the crisis-stricken communities in eastern Europe, where emigration is causing precipitous decline, but also of the more affluent and stable communities of the European Community. The reinforcement of such populations through immigration, which is happening in some European countries, can be no more than a temporary palliative unless there is significant change in the complex of identificational and demographic factors which influence Jewish population continuity, while small-scale but selective emigration, to Israel and other countries, drains some of the better intellectual forces away from Europe. All in all, the relative weight of European Jewry is diminishing; worldwide, the Jewish population is increasingly polarized between Israel and the United States. This development parallels the general de-Europeanization of world society, at least in the sense that non-European societies are increasing while the population of Europe is in a state of stagnation or incipient decline.

PROJECTIONS AND IMPLICATIONS

One of the main findings of this overview of socio-demographic trends among European Jewry is that Jewish population processes have converged to a highly consistent model of diminished families and ageing, reflecting to a large extent the current demographic regime of most European societies. The implication of the present and projected pattern of population shrinkage must be seen against the background of the changing norms and aspirations of contemporary young adults in a post-industrial European society that is primarily individualistic and secular in outlook.

In the Jewish sphere, a distinction seems to emerge between a 'community of presence' and a 'community of continuity'. Unquestionably, the Jewish presence in Europe, stimulated by migrations and by more or less favourable societal circumstances, has achieved remarkable socio-economic and cultural success, and public visibility and recognition. To account for this, I would tentatively propose the concept of 'equilibrium': the presence or absence of Jewish communities is significantly associated, if not entirely explained, by socio-economic factors in the wider society with which they interact. Perhaps the most essential prerequisite for a viable Jewish presence is a political culture of democracy, pluralism of expression, and freedom of movement. The problem is that socio-economic and socio-political market forces are mutable by nature, so a Jewish presence that is linked to such factors has an inherent tendency to instability. In the long run, only a 'community of continuity'—a community grounded on solid demographic processes and able to nurture and transmit its cultural identity—will be able to survive. Such communities are those that are relatively insensitive to the forces that operate in society at large, finding their major strength instead in their internal value systems and the institutional web of the community itself. The ability to sustain communities of this kind—an unquestioned fact throughout most of the Jewish historical experience—cannot be taken for granted, however, in the light of recent demographic trends. Erosion of the family, assimilation, and the blurring of group identity make the demographic and cultural reproduction of Jewish communities increasingly uncertain.

But what of the future? How will the trends emerging in the new Europe affect the unfolding of Jewish history? Suggesting a clear and unambiguous connection between the Jewish experience of the recent past and the present and future has never been easy, and is particularly difficult at the time of writing in 1992, when even the immediate future of European societies is not entirely clear. The tremendous fluidity of the international scene and the very ambivalent messages emerging with regard to the real spirit of the new

European experience engenders a sense of bewilderment. Is Europe striving for political integration and economic prosperity, or is it headed for ethnic polarization and conflict? Is it Maastricht or Sarajevo that is more meaningful to an assessment of the contemporary European situation? Which will have proved to be the more congenial to a creative Jewish presence in the long run—Leningrad or St Petersburg? And, most significantly, what kind of German culture will prevail in the reunited Germany? Whatever the answers, it must be assumed that the general thrust of social, economic, cultural, and political change in Europe is bound to affect the profile, in fact the very existence, of Jewish communities on the continent.

If Europe succeeds in moving towards an open, pluralistic, and tolerant society, Jewish communities may well thrive. Where significant concentrations of Jews emerge in consequence, this may also have political significance. An interesting case in point is provided by the result of the vote in France on the Maastricht treaty on 20 September 1992, where there was a scant majority in favour of the treaty: the Jewish preference for stability and prosperity in Europe may well have delivered the decisive one percentage point needed to save European economic integration.

If, on the other hand, Europe moves towards a revival of ethnic tribalism and nationalism, Jews, no less than other minorities, will need to be on the alert. Self-defence mechanisms would have to be developed, down to emigration as a last resort. This would of course be a most disruptive and unfortunate outcome.

In the light of historical and contemporary experience, it would seem to be in the Jewish interest to take a united view of Europe and to cultivate the idea of a European Jewish community. The more that European integration becomes a permanent reality, the better-advised Jews would be to fit into it, making a real effort to bridge provincial or particularist divisions so as to bring to bear the intellectual, socio-economic, and political weight of their combined constituency—one million Jews in the European Community, and substantial though declining numbers elsewhere. And if the current population erosion is to be arrested, greater attention needs to be given to how to reinforce the educational roles of Jewish family, school, and community. Efficient management of resources will also require better integration between communities across Europe. If pragmatic choices must be made, priority should be given to the actual or potential centres of greater vitality rather than to the more dispersed and gradually disintegrating periphery. Finally, the connections between European Jewry and the other major Jewish demographic and cultural poles, i.e. Israel and the United States, should be increased.

However, in order to obtain a truly reliable perspective on the socio-demographic trends discussed here and their interplay with socio-economic, cultural, and institutional variables in the new Europe, a well-thought-out and comprehensive research project must be initiated to examine the unfolding reality of European Jewry within a coherent analytical frame. This may help not only to predict the future course of the Jewish experience in Europe, but also to devise ways of making that experience more Jewishly meaningful and secure.

Note

1. Relevant sources on Jewish socio-demographic trends include D. Bensimon and S. DellaPergola, *La Population juive de France: Socio-demographie et identité* (Jerusalem: The Hebrew University; Paris: Centre National de la Recherche Scientifique, 1984); E. Cohen, *L'Étude et l'éducation juive en France, ou l'avenir d'une communauté* (Paris, 1991); S. DellaPergola, *Anatomia dell'ebraismo italiano: Caratteristiche demografiche, economiche, sociali, religiose e politiche di una minoranza* (Rome, 1976); id., 'Recent Demographic Trends among Jews in Western Europe', in E. Stock (ed.), *European Jewry: A Handbook* (Ramat Gan, 1983), 19–62; id., 'Changing Patterns of Jewish Demography in the Modern World', *Studia Rosenthaliana* (special issue), 23: 2 (1989), 154–74; id., 'Israel and World Jewish Population: A Core–Periphery Perspective', in C. Goldscheider (ed.), *Population and Social Change in Israel* (Boulder, Colo., 1992), 39–63; S. DellaPergola and L. Cohen (eds.), *World Jewish Population: Trends and Policies* (Jerusalem: The Hebrew University, 1992); S. Haberman and M. Schmool, 'Estimates of British Jewish Population' (London, forthcoming); U. O. Schmelz and S. DellaPergola, 'World Jewish Population 1990', *American Jewish Year Book*, 92 (1992), 484–512; M. Tolts, 'The Balance of Births and Deaths among Soviet Jewry', *Jews and Jewish Topics in the Soviet Union and Eastern Europe*, 18 (1992), 13–26; S. Waterman and B. Kosmin, *British Jewry in the Eighties: A Statistical and Geographical Guide* (London: Board of Deputies of British Jews, 1986).

General population trends are discussed in D. A. Coleman, 'European Demographic Systems of the Future: Convergence or Diversity?', paper presented at a conference on 'Human Resources in Europe at the Dawn of the 21st Century', Luxemburg, 1991; Commission des Communautés Européennes, Cellule de prospective, *L'Europe dans le mouvement demographique* (Brussels, 1990).

CHAPTER FOUR

Modern Jewish Identities

JONATHAN WEBBER

RIGHT from its origins in biblical antiquity, Jewish identity has oscillated between two contradictory premisses: an underlying belief in the unity and continuity of the Jewish people, despite an awareness of the existence of considerable ethnographic diversity; and a feeling that the Jewish community of one's own village or town constituted the only true Jewish identity, despite the knowledge that other Jewish communities existed, even in very faraway lands. But the nature of Jewish identity has also been governed by the Jewish image of the outside world, and this has also had two faces: the non-Jewish world, whose ways were (at least in theory) not for imitation; and the world of other Jews, whose ways were different and therefore also not for imitation. These ideas about the outside world have persisted in Jewish society down to our own day, although the realities are more complex. Jews have in fact tended to borrow heavily from both worlds; but whereas in the past this was often done without acknowledgement or conscious decision, there is today a much stronger sense of a global Jewish village that while highly differentiated internally is also deeply assimilated. Throughout Jewish history, however, there has always been a constant redrawing of the cultural boundaries, as a consequence of migrations, persecutions, and other fluctuations in Jewish social and economic fortunes—but an awareness of the outside world, wherever it was, and however it was to be defined, has remained integral to the fashioning by Jews of who they are and who they are not.

Coexisting simultaneously with the underlying belief in one people, Jewish identity in every age has thus in practice been divided up differently, according to the circumstances. A hundred years ago, European Jewish identities were commonly divided up in two ways. One type of identity was geographic, that is, derived from the countries where Jews lived at that time (mainly in central and eastern Europe), or where they came from or how

I am grateful to Margaret Rubel and Connie Wilsack for very helpful comments and editorial advice. An expanded version of this paper appears in the *Journal of Jewish Studies*, 43: 2 (1992), 246–67.

they behaved. Thus there were Yekkes (German Jews), Pollaks (Polish Jews), Litvaks (Lithuanian Jews), Galitzianers (Jews from the Austro-Hungarian province of Galicia), Sefardim (Jews of Spanish origin), and so on. The other type of identity was based on competing types of ideology, outlook, and cultural practice, principally the distinctions (and controversies) between *hasidim*, *misnagdim*, and *maskilim* (which very roughly translate respectively as pietists, formalists, and modernists). In the early part of this century, additional overlapping identities came into use in Europe, notably the developing distinction between religious Jews and secular Jews, or between Bundists (secular Polish Jews attached to a Yiddish-speaking socialism) and Zionists. Later still, after the Holocaust, came the notion of a Holocaust survivor, and then, with the establishment of the State of Israel in 1948, there has arisen a new distinction between the Israeli Jew and the diaspora Jew. All these distinctions are themselves endlessly divided, sub-divided, and nuanced, often on the basis of internal controversy; there are different kinds of Hasidim and different kinds of Zionists, for example, and the concept of a religious Jew means a wide variety of things. But the point about these newer distinctions and newer identities is that they have largely superseded the earlier ones, which in many contexts are quietly fading away from the collective Jewish consciousness nowadays as the circumstances have changed. The distinction between *hasidim* and *misnagdim*, for example, has largely lapsed in favour of the new category of *haredim* ('strictly Orthodox Jews')—presumably because of their shared sense of opposition to secular and Reform Jews. The nineteenth-century geographical identities have largely lapsed also—presumably because of the substantial collapse in their absolute numbers following the migrations out of central and eastern Europe at the turn of the century (principally to western Europe and the United States) and, more recently, the Holocaust.

The criteria, in other words, by which Jews identify themselves—that is, what they identify as the most important social facts about themselves—cover a very wide range, and moreover change over time. What has happened to the overwhelming majority of Jews in the process of adjustment to the circumstances of the modern Western world during the past century is that, among other things, the structure that formerly underpinned their Jewish identities has by and large disintegrated. In other words, the Jewish people has collectively undergone an identity crisis—or, more accurately, a succession of identity crises. Thus it cannot be said that there is a consensus on what constitutes the defining characteristics of distinctively Jewish behaviour and culture—or even on the basic question of 'Who is a Jew?' Modern Jewish identity is so deeply divided ethnographically that it almost looks like a parody of the emphasis placed by modernity on free choice as the hallmark of emancipated rational man. The purpose of this essay is to try to briefly outline some sort of framework that would explain or at least encompass the elements and compounds of the new Jewish identities now operative in the Western world.

THE DISINTEGRATION OF TRADITIONAL JEWISH IDENTITIES

To begin with, one can point to at least five obvious reasons for this disintegration of traditional Jewish identities: the mass migrations, with all the consequent adjustments typical of immigrant communities; the massive population losses (from both the Holocaust and assimilation); the rise of Zionist ideology and the establishment of the State of Israel (offering quite new scope for the enactment of Jewish identity); the collapse, through the Enlightenment, of traditional religion as providing the sole legitimate criterion of Jewish identity, and its displacement by an emphasis on Jewish peoplehood—or Jewish ethnicity, as it has more recently come to be known in the diaspora. Finally, of course, there is the external history of the social and political emancipation of the Jews of Europe, with the very important consequence that outsider definitions of Jewish identity came to be accepted by many Jews as part of their own system of self-definition.

The extraordinary but obviously very influential development connected with this last factor was that Judaism came to be thought of as a 'religion', a private matter for the individual, and hence conceptually separable from Jewish ethnic or minority identity. Membership of the Jewish community now became a voluntary act of the individual rather than being imposed from the outside by the state, as hitherto. The consequences are highly paradoxical: the centrality of the synagogue, rabbi, and talmudic seminary has waned in favour of a whole host of Jewish sporting, recreational, philanthropic, political, and cultural associations and private societies, the principle *raison d'être* of which lies in their creating a social framework exclusively for Jews rather than the pursuit of specifically Jewish aims or cultural goals (as traditionally defined). The modern synagogue is thus often a community centre rather than a building consecrated solely for divine worship or study. Despite, or perhaps because of, the absence of centralized leadership, these new forms of associational behaviour have come to offer a completely new range of contexts for the formulation of group identity; indeed, it is now possible for agnostic and even atheist Jews to be actively identified with Jewish culture or Jewish community life, including religious celebrations, and moreover to see nothing particularly unusual about such participation despite their lack of religious commitment. The basis for the recruitment of members has in effect been considerably broadened.

Jewish society today is thus largely unrecognizable compared with what it looked like a century or so ago. Leaving out certain special cases it can be said that a change in expected forms of behaviour, and with it a change in definition, has come about across the broad range of western diaspora Jewish society at two levels and in two contradictory directions simultaneously. The development of what was broadly seen from the outside as a *religious* community coexisted with the internal trend towards what is now commonly called Jewish ethnicity, and a conscious move *away* from religious belief or practice as the principal defining feature. Religion, so to speak, came to be the façade of the community, whilst its internal activity and preoccupations moved off in rather different directions.

The other side of the picture concerns the nature of the acceptance by Jews of wider social and national identities, in addition to their Jewish identities—how far, in other words, they accept being English, French, Polish, Hungarian, or Slovak, for example, and whether they have done so voluntarily or involuntarily, passively or ideologically. The evidence seems to point to the existence of real divisions amongst Jews with regard to their degree of assimilation to the national cultures in which they have lived over the past hundred years. In the nineteenth century in eastern Europe, Jews often sided themselves culturally and linguistically with the metropolitan rather than the local culture (German rather than Polish, Russian rather than Estonian, for example). This decision, which was based perhaps on a faulty understanding of the wider world in which they lived, was to have tragic consequences following the independence of many of these eastern European states after the First World War. Such Jews had, so to speak, opted for the 'wrong' wider identity, a cultural mistake which repeated itself, with horrifying consequences, immediately before, and during, the Second World War.

Looking at the matter globally over the whole period, what the political emancipation of the Jews eventually came to mean is that Jewishness is now a voluntary act of self-identification, whereas national citizenship or loyalty to the nation is the direct opposite—it is given, imposed from the outside. Traditionally, the case was precisely the reverse: it was Jewishness which was the given, while national citizenship was a voluntary act of self-identification. Obviously, if we are talking about a period in which one is moving from one of these systems to the other, there are going to be a lot of *crises de conscience* about identity and a lot of readjustment to the core concepts: who is a Jew, what is a Jewish community, what is the nature of Jewish identity? Moreover, the transition from one system to the other has not happened uniformly country by country, nor even within a particular country. Hence there has been a lot of time-lag, with certain groups of Jews moving in the same cultural direction as others but at a slower speed. The moment the whole process is framed in terms of multiple discourses being at work within Jewish life it becomes easier to explain and rationalize modern Jewish realities.

Thus far, then, the simple proposal would be that the disintegration of traditional forms of Jewish identity can be explained more or less in terms of (say) five major processes, with the observable lack of uniformity across the board being explained in terms of time-lag. After all, the process of Jewish self-modernization did not all happen at once. This self-modernization (or assimilation, as it is often described) in fact consisted of a whole series of cultural adaptations and adjustments, each of which left its mark on today's realities. European Jewish society began to modernize itself in a pre-migration setting, of which the most important example is pre-Holocaust Poland, where (among other things) secular notions of Jewish culture and Jewish identity came to be highly developed. This legacy of the Jewish intelligentsia of pre-Holocaust central and eastern Europe remains central to a large section of the Jewish world today. But perhaps for the majority of Jews, other assimilatory influences and settings came to supersede it: the experience of migration and immigration, followed by the desire for rapid social mobility locally and the drift into a bourgeois Jewish lifestyle, followed most recently today by a post-modern ethnic Jewish identity. These trends have not, of course, been universal, nor always in chronological order, but they nevertheless give a sense of the basic patterns and influences over the last century or so.

BOURGEOIS AND POST-MODERN JEWISH IDENTITIES

One central preoccupation that originally derived from pre-Holocaust central and eastern Europe is Zionism. It continues to exercise a major influence on diaspora Jews. From the outset, the scope it offered for secularists' concern to move away from religion and instead to stress peoplehood and a national Jewish self-definition made Zionism ideologically the most useful and important subject for the modern Jew to think about. After the establishment of the Jewish state, most religious Jews also slowly turned their attention to Zionism. Thus, today it provides a major context for the expression of a new concept of Jewish peoplehood—for example, the sets of competing local Zionist organizations, the extensive use of fund-raising events and other visible types of philanthropic or militant activity on behalf of Israel, the treatment of Israeli tourist souvenirs as quasi-religious artefacts, the learning of modern spoken Israeli Hebrew as a new cultural goal, the accepted desirability for Jews of spending holidays in Israel. All of these suggest a new context for the articulation of areas of identity that otherwise might have remained unmobilized.

Similarly, there is a series of features of modern Jewish life that are attributable to the immigrant phase and are therefore comparable to the experience of other immigrant groups. These include substantial changes in the sociology of the family, including the decline of arranged marriages and of the importance of the extended family; the tortuous linguistic and cultural assimilation of the first generation of immigrants; difficulties in distinguishing those elements of the tradition that needed to be safeguarded from those that could reasonably be dispensed with; the considerable cultural energies expended on debating such issues; and the division and sub-division of communities based on the choice of different cultural solutions in these matters. There is much to be said for treating the variations in contemporary identities from their starting-points during the period of migration: for example, migrants' different origins (e.g. rural or urban), different motives and circumstances, as well as different social and cultural experiences on arrival. Nor, of course, should it be forgotten that there are some local Jewish communities, in London and New York for example, that have still not moved out of the old inner-city ghetto and thus remind us that the immigrant phase, and the existence of a Jewish ethnoclass consisting of poor Jews who remained behind in the inner city, needs in any case to be part of the overall model of contemporary Jewish life.

The dominant mode in western Europe and the United States has for the last two generations been the widespread *embourgeoisement* of Jewish society and its adaptation to middle-class values and behaviour. There are quite a number of features of contemporary Jewish life that can be included under this rubric—for instance the widespread redesigning of synagogue services, wherein the worshipper is now more of a spectator rather than a participant; a lowering of the birth-rate; the rise of salaried professionals to take on various types of ritual specialization that formerly were usually left to volunteers, such as the preparation of corpses for funerals; the rise of fashionable social clubs and community centres that promote leisure activities, rather than cultural or religious activities, and the growth of fashionable synagogues as well; the encouragement of entry into the liberal professions, such as medicine, accountancy, or the law, and in general the abandonment of the traditional Jewish attitude that had accorded status to individuals irrespective of their occupation; the display of wealth, in particular through philanthropy for Jewish causes such as the State of Israel, as a major arena for the expression of identity and group or sub-group loyalty; and so on.

Perhaps one can place Jewish political liberalism under this heading. In practice, of course, *embourgeoisement* means the movement out of the inner-city ghetto to the more affluent suburbs, and the decline that followed, virtually automatically, of the immigrants' *landsmanshaft* organizations—certainly there was no desire on the part of the upwardly mobile to continue institutionalizing what they regarded as the memory of humble origins in the villages of eastern Europe. Note the selectivity of Jewish memory.

Perhaps the main ideological legacy of *embourgeoisement* is the name of the religion nominally underpinning the new identity, viz. 'Jewishness'. This is not of course the same thing as 'Judaism', which has a rather different history and set of meanings. The concept of Jewishness is in effect a product of the redefinition of Jewish identity as Jewish ethnicity, which is itself a by-product of the immigrant experience and the abandonment of traditional religious practices in response to the need to accumulate capital in the new bourgeois social environment. Is the new post-modern religious ethnicity of the 1980s and 1990s a reaction against this bourgeois Judaism, or is it rather a thinking through and further development of it in consequence of the accumulation of leisure?

In fact, today's post-modern Jewish ethnicity is principally concerned with what has come to be regarded as the revival or reconstruction of authentic traditions. This has taken a number of forms, but central to its outlook is the notion of an idealized past which thus presents the modern Western Jew with a new, nostalgic type of identity reconstructed from the presentation of an extraordinarily rich, diverse history of a peoplehood (not always of a religion as such) that unfolded itself in many lands, continents, and epochs. It is as if the contemporary state of plural Jewish identities is being projected back into the past so as to arrive at a picture of successive Jewish identities, all equally 'valid', as a characterization not just of Jewish history but of its meaning or relevance. It goes without saying that it is now Jewish history, usually taught in an entirely secular manner, that in the last few years has become the central subject for Jewish adult education programmes, Jewish publishing, and the new university courses in Jewish studies that are mushrooming in many countries. Jews are now assiduously tracing their origins (now called 'roots') in as literal and empirical a manner as they can. Visits to the actual village of origin, particularly in eastern Europe, or guided tours of long-forgotten Jewish monuments, have become extremely fashionable in recent years, as has an awareness of the impoverished Jewish ethnoclass still lingering, as if time-warped, in the inner cities of London and New York. The colour supplements of the glossy Jewish magazines portray the new category of 'exotic' Jews, which means the now shrunken Jewish communities of such places as Morocco or India; Jewish visitors turn up at the synagogue in Tokyo hoping to find Jews who have Oriental features and speak Japanese.

There is now quite a range of new rituals that promote the new ethnicity, such as conferences, weekend retreats, interfaith services, music festivals, and so on. Collectively, they suggest the attempt to provide a cognitive framework for a set of newly perceived authenticities, on the model of culturally reconstructed ethnic revivals of 'ethnic' or 'minority' identities found elsewhere in wider society, and they provide the sense of an objective basis for a post-modern identity of Jewishness.

For those now involved in the new religions outreach programmes (most notably the Lubavitch Hasidim), and indeed among post-modern groups more generally, authenticity is the key concept. The word comes up time and again in their literature. Whereas both immigrant Judaism and bourgeois Jewishness had abandoned vast areas of traditional Jewish ritual, in order to accommodate other preoccupations and other definitions of a Jewish lifestyle, post-modern Jewish identity presupposes a return to the observance of many rituals of traditional Judaism on the grounds that they are 'authentically Jewish'.

This notion of authentic Judaism applies far more widely than just to ritual behaviour. The Jewish Vegetarian Society, for example, is not simply a society that caters for Jews who happen to be vegetarians, but claims, rather, on the basis of a close reading of selected passages from the Hebrew Bible, that vegetarianism is authentically Jewish—a claim that is of course by no means a reflection of actual Jewish behaviour now or in the past. Similarly, Jews who used to support the Campaign for Nuclear Disarmament chose to use the acronym JONAH ('Jews Organized for a Nuclear Arms Halt')— again, in order to demonstrate that the concept of nuclear disarmament was identifiable as authentically Jewish. From these and other examples, such as Jewish groups concerned with medical ethics, ecology, or feminism, it would appear that the attempt is both to lambast the secularism of bourgeois Judaism and also to cultivate a Jewish angle on issues of the day that derive from the wider secular environment.

One telling area of concern for post-modernist Jewish ethnicity, however, is its interest in the Holocaust. On the one hand, such an interest displays a predictable fascination with roots and origins, as well as representing a confrontation with the silence on this subject with which bourgeois Judaism has, over the past forty-five years, largely avoided coming to terms with the horrors of the Second World War; on the other hand, the uniqueness of the Holocaust makes it difficult to sustain the view that an interest in it forms a part of authentic Judaism. It certainly is not, in the sense that diaspora Judaism has never before had to deal with a set of events or category of this kind or this magnitude, and indeed traditionally Orthodox rabbis today have consistently rejected the demand that commemoration of the Holo-caust somehow be incorporated into the liturgical calendar. It is on this point, perhaps, that post-modern claims to revive an authentic Judaism are (in the eyes of some) most effectively compromised.

THE COMPLEXITIES OF JEWISH IDENTITIES TODAY

In looking over this complex mass of twentieth-century material, the critical point to notice is the remarkable unevenness of contemporary Jewish society in the context of cultural and ideological change. The notion of time-lag, and the idea of a range of assimilation trajectories being followed simulta-neously at different speeds across and through different Jewish communities and sub-communities, may be helpful in offering some sort of historical explanation for this unevenness and for the existence today of countless Jewish social agendas. Each of the phases through which Jewish society has passed over the last century or so has left its mark and provided Jews with new elements and contexts with which to construct their identities along subjective lines. Note that these processes may have little to do with rational planning or the objective demographic realities: they do not necessarily govern how Jews see themselves (even though it is certainly true, of course, that the Holocaust, or movements of Jews through migration, manifestly changed the objective realities, and profoundly so). There is nothing parti-cularly unusual about Jews in this sense. The growth or decline of a popula-tion, although often assumed to be statistically measurable, may equally be located in people's minds. Ethnic minority groups are known suddenly to disappear or suddenly to become visible once again. The reason is that members of minority groups, by definition, can seem as if they belong elsewhere, and in that sense disappear; or alternatively there can be a regrouping of those who were previously thought to be lost, dispersed, or dying out. The dynamics of ethnic identity perpetually rest on the constant reformulation of the ethnic self (which is in part, at least, a response to subjective uncertainty and doubt), a picture that is certainly highly typical of the identity crises that have characterized much of the twentieth-century European Jewish experience.

There is more, then, to contemporary Jewish identities than just time-lag, as if it were merely a question of catching up with the objective realities 'out there'. It is not just the notion of 'authentic Judaism' that can be seen as a construct in response to the circumstances; Jewish identities in general are largely to be understood as constructs in response to the circumstances. Where the complexity of today's Jewish identities derives from is not only the greatly increased number of elements involved in the constructs but also the fact of their coexistence and the resulting simultaneity of internal contradictions and paradoxes.

For example, when British Jews today eat salt-beef sandwiches, or bagels and lox, they would not normally claim that they are eating 'authentic' Jewish food; they just feel that they are eating Jewish food. But that is also an identity construct, though less obviously so. This is because salt-beef sandwiches are by no means a traditional Jewish food; they have, however, most certainly become a modern Jewish food, and as such part of a gastronomic input to modern Jewish identities. New styles of expressing Jewish identity, in other words, coexist with traditional styles. Furthermore, some of the traditional styles have themselves become 'modernized' in the way they find their expression. The word 'kosher', for example, is traditionally a technical term drawn from classical Jewish law; many Jews today, however, have in effect secularized or ethnicized the concept by observing only a small part of the relevant rules (for example, by reducing them down to something like 'Jews do not eat pork'). It is not that Jewish modernity means a total secularization of the culture; for some Jews that would be true, but what is more typical is that the religious and the secular inconsistently intermix. Today's Jewish world thus relies on multiple discourses, in which modern and pre-modern, secular and religious, are by no means rigorously distinct.

A similar simultaneity reappears when considering the analytic problem of disentangling what is authentically Jewish from what Jews have absorbed into their system from the wider societies in which they live. Jews always borrowed cultural traits from other peoples, even in the biblical period, let alone in modern times; but in the past the origins of such traits were either forgotten or else ignored by the system once they had been revalued and incorporated. In modern times the sheer weight of cultural borrowings, and the modernist instinct to be explicit and literal about their existence, has provided fuel for debate and for a self-consciousness about the syncretism embedded in modern Jewish identities. By definition, English, French, or German Jews are today aware of the stereotypes current about Jews in their respective wider societies. Since they participate both in the Jewish world and in the wider society in which they live, they are capable of being both insiders and outsiders to their own Jewishness.

Jewish concern with fighting antisemitism is the key example here. Antisemitism is combated, in the belief that it will somehow or other disappear, even though it is also believed that antisemitism is (notionally) endemic to the non-Jewish world. Jews may feel they have no choice in the matter; but on the other hand it is also true, for secular Jews in particular, that antisemitism reinforces a sense of Jewish identity by confirming that there are boundaries that close them off from the wider society that they otherwise feel a part of. Its existence is in this sense accepted, inasmuch as it explains any difficulties that they encounter in their assimilation trajectories. This is another instance of simultaneity: on the one hand the aim of modern Jews is to assimilate into wider society, on the other to retain their group identity and promote their Jewishness; on the one hand, to create a secular or secularized form of Jewish identity, on the other to cope also with the common view held by outsiders that Jewishness is by definition a form of religion. Once again it is this simultaneous use of multiple definitions, multiple categories, and multiple aims, many of which are in contradiction with each other, that gives rise to some of the ethnographic complexity of modern Jewish identities.

The blanket terms 'assimilation' and 'acculturation', conventional though they are, are thus too broad to convey a sense of the intricacies. For many of the elements of the new Jewish identities are concerned with the small details; as is common with minority groups, it is in the details that there often lurk important matters of principle. The areas in which Jews are capable of making symbolic ethnic differentiation, both between themselves and between them and non-Jews, are of great number: food, dress (the wearing of a *yarmulke* or other headgear, for example), music, issues relating to gender, personal and family names, use of a given language or accent, beards, wigs, type of humour, architectural styles of synagogue buildings, the domestic display of Jewish artefacts, to name but a few. The focus on any combination of these (even simply by way of nostalgia) may provide the motifs for the construction or perception of a Jewish identity; there is no a priori need or even expectation of 'assimilation' in all of them at once. On the contrary, inconsistency is far more typical (and probably always has been so). After all, given that the abandonment of traditional ritual has been not only widespread but considerably uneven, given that during the migration period a good deal became garbled or else lost in the transmission, and given that for many Jews the very feeling of Jewishness is itself not just attenuated but perhaps only intermittent, it is only to be expected that new identities are based on new clusters of Jewish modes of self-identification. Details are selected from the cultural repertoire to shape and fill out the meaning of particular modern identities that are then labelled. Thus for example the term 'Orthodox', which is a newly constructed category; it sounds plausible enough, but it is often used to identify Jews who merely observe the sabbath and kosher foodways—i.e. a selection from the very wide range of ritual forms that are no longer practised by such Jews in their totality. Orthodoxy, like assimilation, may also mean different things in different contexts; indeed, like the expression 'fundamentalist'—a pejorative new term which is used to classify out the threatening, the remote, the unacceptable identities of Jewishness—the labelling of contemporary Jewish identities merely represents the attempt to signpost the way amidst the bewildering confusion of too much meaning being compressed into too small a space.

Some would say that after the Holocaust all those nice distinctions that Jews make in relation to their identities have precious little meaning: *all* kinds of Jews, regardless of their identities and even religions, found themselves in the gas chambers at Auschwitz—and that is the only fixed reality that Jews know or ought to know about themselves. It is true that Auschwitz indeed represented the only place in the diaspora where Jews met each other as one undifferentiated people, yet this very approach is itself part of the ethnography—the Holocaust as the focus of a modern Jewish identity all unto itself. Like many other single-issue identities, it contributes to and partakes of the very substantial internal cultural debate that characterizes modern Jewish society.

It is this willingness to argue, and to make jokes about matters relating to identity, that probably constitutes a Jewish survival strategy in itself in the modern world. It would, I think, be ethnographically wrong to say that the Jewish tradition simply weakened in modern times; it is true that it has weakened, but that is only part of the truth. New solidarities have arisen, new militancies for new identities have taken shape, each of which may present only a fragmentary and parochial view of the Jewish totality, but collectively suggest that it is within a native awareness of the ethnographic complexities themselves that Jewish survival is today being enacted. Diaspora Jews are in any case not comparable with territorially based minority groups, since they lack even a single vernacular language that would unify them; the territory of the Jews in this sense remains what it always has been—a disputatious concern with the fulfilment and meanings of their identities.

CHAPTER FIVE

Judaism in the New Europe: Discovery or Invention?

NORMAN SOLOMON

WHAT IS IDENTITY?

IDENTITY shows in the stories we tell ourselves about ourselves, especially those which relate us to other people. One of the most sensitive indicators of identity is when we use first-person plural pronouns—'we' and 'us'—and when the third person—'they' and 'them'. For example, I am a Welsh Jew, telling my children how the early Britons resisted the Romans. Do I say '*we* resisted' or '*they* resisted'? Note that this is not a question of whether my physical ancestors were involved. If my ancestors had been Angles or Saxons or Vikings I would almost certainly say 'we resisted', though Angles and Saxons and Vikings did not come until the Romans had left.

Clearly, identity with the past is not a matter of physical descent. Is it to do with a metaphysical entity, such as 'soul'? Nowadays, most philosophers would reject the idea of 'soul' or 'self' as a distinct substance. When we ask about people's self-perception, their identity, we are not asking some profound question about a mysterious invisible entity which determines what they are, but about observable things they do and say, and which show how they relate to other people.

As to whether there really is some ultimate soul or self not revealed in the stories and doings of people we may, in the present sociological context, safely remain agnostic.

Agnostic, yes. But we cannot remain indifferent to people who take the hard metaphysical view that the discovery of identity is the discovery of some actual, 'ideal' entity that sets a pattern to which we must conform.

Most Jews deny categorically that there is some objective 'Jewishness' out there which is our 'real' essence, and which we must labour to conform to. We suspect those who adopt such metaphysics of attempting, consciously or not, to impose an identity on us; they are flexing the muscles of their power, not engaging in a scientific investigation. When Ben-Gurion asked 'Who is a Jew?' this was not dispassionate sociological enquiry, but an attempt to secure the ideological foundation for political action.

DISCOVERY OR INVENTION?

I will focus my discussion of Jewish identity on a problem which attracted my attention on a visit to Leningrad (as it was then called) in 1982. By that time, numerous young people were looking for ways to show that they were Jewish; a small number were turning to religion. How could they find out what the Jewish religion required of them? Would they turn to books or to people? If to people, who would provide an appropriate role model?

The group of young Leningrad Jews I met had acquired *tefillin* and were praying regularly. They had received information, presumably from some visiting Orthodox Jew, about correct times of prayer, and were greatly worried to discover that the correct time for morning prayer in the winter was later than the time they were due to commence work. Should they, then, not pray at all before work, or pray without *tefillin*, or were there alternative views as to acceptable times for prayer?

Now, in 1982 there were still a few old Jews in Leningrad who might have given an authentic account of Jewish practice as they knew it before the Second World War; they had lived in a community where people had known the rules and must have reached some *modus vivendi*. Why didn't anybody question them? It wasn't that the young thought ths memories of the old might be confused and unreliable. Rather, the fear was that whatever had been done previously might not be 'authentic', in some sense of 'authentic' which though ill-defined at least carried the message that there was an objective way of determining Jewish standards and that it was possible, even likely, that their grandfathers, however *frum* (religiously observant) they appeared, had failed to comply with those standards. Those of us who came from the West with a knowledge of books such as the *Shulchan arukh*—the main code of Jewish law—were seen as bearers of 'authentic' standards. It was in accordance with this cognitive framework that the new Jewish identity was to be forged, not in terms of a relationship with their grandfathers' generation.

So in what sense were the young Jews of Leningrad returning to their roots? Certainly not in the sense of reclaiming the way of life of their grandparents or great-grandparents. They were not truly rediscovering the Russian Jewish life of the past (or life within the Pale of Settlement), nor even showing any concern with it, except perhaps to give it a decent burial. Rather, they were turning to what they thought was an objectively definable

Torah and working out how to live in accordance with that within Soviet society.

This is a process of invention, rather than of discovery. A Judaism fabricated in this way, and the Jewish identification arising from it in combination with other factors, would be something quite new.

Invention characterizes the *ba'al teshuvah* movement as a whole.[1] While proclaiming itself to be a recovery of the past, in actual fact it generates forms of Jewish life and identification which are quite novel. This is why the 'born religious' find it so hard to get along with the 'reborn', just as the young Leningraders found themselves uncomfortable with the religion of their grandfathers' generation.

Perhaps all movements of religious change, whether reform or reactionary, are inventions, however much they proclaim their return to the past. Indeed, is it not curious that movements of both reform and reaction justify themselves in terms of faithfulness to precisely the same past? This is as true of Orthodox and Progressive Judaism as it is of Roman Catholic and Protestant Christianity. Certainly, Counter-Reformation Catholicism was no more to be equated with the Catholicism of the High Middle Ages than 'Modern Orthodoxy' is with the traditional Judaism of pre-war eastern Europe.

The same phenomenon occurs outside the religious sphere, for instance in defining national identity. Already in 1882, Ernest Renan,[2] commenting on the recently accomplished unifications of Germany and Italy, showed how the concept of the supreme nation-state depended on *l'erreur historique*, the rewriting, indeed the falsification, of history; the nation as a historic entity was the fabrication of the ideologist. 'Ancient' customs are readily instituted to reinforce the fabricated traditions.[3]

The past can never be totally re-created, and that is why 'back to the roots' movements are condemned to the novelty they pretend to shun. The reason the past cannot be restored is that any attempt at restoration depends on resuscitating texts from the past—'texts' here understood as referring not only to literary texts, but to any forms of human activity and communication that can be reproduced. Even if one could perfectly reproduce all the 'texts' of a given epoch of the past, they would no longer be the same texts, no longer communicate the same things, because every text takes part of its meaning from its relationship with other texts, and the context, the 'intertextuality', changes constantly.

In practice things are still worse. 'Texts' get lost or corrupted. Even among the available texts it is difficult or impossible to select those belonging to one particular epoch. Even if it were possible to select texts belonging to a specific epoch, why should that epoch be preferred? If the young Jews of Leningrad are seeking 'authentic' Jewish religion, they are forced not only to make do with imperfect records, but to select which period of history and which Jewish society will be their preferred model. They were apparently under the impression that somewhere 'out there' was a preferred model, an ideal, which could be discovered. In fact, there is no such thing; hence, they are constrained to invent.

Some of my Orthodox colleagues may incline to remind me that there is an ideal Judaism 'out there', the perfect Torah given on Sinai—*torah misinai*. But their reminder is a theological statement, and it cannot be straight-forwardly transposed to the sociological sphere. The *torah misinai* myth is the principal organizing idea of Jewish theology, the story that pulls the whole thing together, that can unify communities and history. Unfortunately, it does not yield an actual perfect Torah, for the 'ideal' Torah it talks about still has to get itself formulated at different times, in different places, among different groups of people. So we end up asking why is such-and-such a formulation preferred, and even when we are satisfied on that score we have to face the reality that if we pick up the formulation now and use it, its meaning will have shifted from what it was in its original context.

The two stages of invention are thus (*a*) the selection of the preferred model of Judaism and (*b*) its modification within its new context. I stress that by 'modification' here I am not referring to deliberate changes of content, for instance a decision that the rules about how to kosher a chicken should be ignored, but about changes of meaning which come about simply because of the different context—koshering of chickens did not convey the same 'message' in the Soviet Union in the 1980s as it did in a Pale of Settlement *shtetl* in the nineteenth century or in fourth-century Babylon. With the demise of Soviet totalitarianism it has changed its meaning yet again (it is no longer an act of defiance against the regime).

Just as the past can never be totally reclaimed, so the new is never totally discontinuous with the past. My 'Leningrad problem' is a specific case-history, illustrating continuity and discontinuity in Jewish self-definition. If I emphasize the role of invention as against that of discovery, it is not to deny continuity but rather to draw attention to the novelty of the forms of Jewish identification which may now be seen all over Europe.

JEWISHNESS AS A SOCIAL CONSTRUCTION

Erik Erikson writes that identity formation

arises from the selective repudiation and mutual assimilation of childhood identifica-tion and their absorption in a new configuration, which, in turn, is dependent on the process by which a society (often through subsocieties) identifies the young indi-vidual, recognizing him as somebody who had to become the way he is and who, being the way he is, is taken for granted. The community, often not without some initial mistrust, gives such recognition with a display of surprise and pleasure in making the acquaintance of a newly emerging individual. For the community in turn feels 'recognized' by the individual who cares to ask for recognition.[4]

This cosy description would pass muster as a barmitzvah sermon but does not explain why a young man or woman in Leningrad in 1982 got uptight about drinking non-kosher milk. Those young persons had neither grown up in nor sought recognition from a society in which the drinking of kosher milk was significant or even meaningful. Mutual recognition with other Jews of Leningrad would have been considerably easier without reference to *kashrut* or times of prayer, or any other religious matters. Clearly, we are not dealing here with the normal process, described by Erikson, of growing up and finding one's place in society, but with an attempt to form a new identification predicated on a new society.

But this raises the problem 'What is a society?' Is it an objective entity, something 'out there' like a horse or a ship, or is 'society' rather a term in the category of 'social artifacts, products of historically situated interchanges among people'.[5] I would certainly opt for the latter view, endorsed with characteristic bluntness by Margaret Thatcher in the words 'There is no such thing as society.' When we try to understand the world about us, and to organize first our observations and then our actions and social relationships, we find it useful to construct general categories. These categories simplify our perception of reality and are basic to our ability to communicate with one another. What actually exists 'out there', however, are particular things. We must not follow the ill-advised path of Plato and subsequent philosophers who maintained that ideas, or 'universals', actually 'existed' in some sense analogous (according to Plato, superior) to that in which physical objects exist.

The term 'society' is a convenient shorthand to refer to a number of individuals who relate to each other in fairly consistent ways different from those in which they relate to outsiders. Typical ways are by using the same language, or at least a distinctive set of words or concepts, following distinctive rules of dress or social interaction, and telling stories about a collective history (itself an artificial construct). There is no reason in principle why an individual cannot belong to many societies simultaneously, and most of us do.

There can be problems in belonging to several societies. If, to take the example of Lilliput and Blefuscu in Swift's *Guilliver's Travels*, the members of one society break their eggs at the large end and the members of the other society break them at the small end, and both societies think this is terribly important, one could be forced to make a choice between the two; or one could simply give up eggs. This doesn't alter the fact that in practice most people have multiple overlapping social allegiances, and on the whole don't find it troublesome.

Now, if societies really were objective entities 'out there', multiple allegiance would not make sense. You would be 'Jewish', or 'Roman', or 'Hindu', 'Lilliputian' or 'Blefuscudian' inescapably, and if you changed you would either be going against your predetermined essence or discovering what it 'really' had been all the time. For centuries you were either a Jew or a Pole, and neither thought you could be both. But it was the structure of society, not predetermined essences, that created the impossibility.

Unfortunately, many people who ought to know better persist in talking as if 'Jewishness' and 'the Jewish people' were objective entities, 'out there'. Martin Buber, for example, in a 1934 address at the Frankfurt Lehrhaus, romanticized about Jewish uniqueness being some extraordinary quality discernible only by the eye of the faith.[6] Others, for instance David Novak, talk of the Jewish people as a 'metaphysical entity',[7] a notion firmly rooted in a rabbinic tradition which can itself be traced through Philo back to Plato; Novak makes this metaphysical entity a party to a covenant with God. A variation on this is the highly racist doctrine of the distinctive Jewish soul, expounded in works such as the *Tanya*; let us charitably assume that its kabbalistic proponents are unaware of its social implications.

Metaphysical notions of what constitutes 'Jewishness' are at best poetry and at worst misleading nonsense. The reason it is difficult to define 'Jewishness' is not that it refers to some profound and mysterious reality but that people have used the term in a variety of ways not always mutually compatible and frequently vague. Complicated mess should not be mistaken for profundity. Nor should one expect to give definitive answers to questions such as 'Is being Jewish an ethnic or a religious matter?' It doesn't particularly have to be either, and there is no mystery behind that observation, merely the prosaic circumstance that people have used and continue to use the term in all sorts of different ways, thereby generating linguistic chaos.

ELEMENTS IN THE IDENTITY OF EUROPEAN JEWS

Thumbnail sketches follow of ten elements which contribute to the identity of the European Jew. The actual mix will vary from individual to individual. Any attempt to lay down a 'correct' mix is likely to be a form of manipulation, and should be resisted.

Note that an individual, even if consciously and contentedly Jewish, may root his or her personal identity far more strongly in family, job, and pastimes than in the specifically Jewish context.

The process is not quite as random as putting just anything you fancy on the smorgasbord. There is, after all, a definite process of transmission of attachments and values from parents, family, teachers, social groups, and events. Nurture, education, and life experience all affect the selection ultimately made.

1. *Family history*. For most people, identity and emotional stability are first established within the 'nuclear' family. The need for a larger social unit in which to find meaning for one's life arises later. But the family already points the way to a broader identity, for its talk, the stories it repeats (when it says 'we' rather than 'they') will relate it to one or several larger collectivities. When, at the Passover Seder, a Jewish family tells how 'we' were saved from Egyptian slavery, it engages in a ritual that binds children, through family, to Jewish 'peoplehood', faith, and history.

2. *Jewish history and culture, including religion*. An individual may find part of his or her identity in terms of history, the large story of which one feels a part. This has little to do with physical descent; as I noted above, the English are happy enough to regard the Ancient Britons as part of their history, even though their own Angle and Saxon ancestors were comparatively recent arrivals on these shores.

There is no difficulty at all—indeed, it is an enrichment of experience—to identify oneself with two or more histories.

Notwithstanding individuals who regard themselves as simultaneously Catholic and Jewish, it is more difficult to identify with two or more religions, at least if we are thinking of Judaism, Christianity, and Islam, because these three religions have traditionally defined themselves in exclusive terms. But if this is true of religious symbols, dogma, and truth claims, it is less true of religious values, where there has been constant interactive flow among religions and societies.

3. *National identities*. Ethnicity has been the major problem in Jewish identity since the Enlightenment. Could Jews be English, French, or Polish? If not, how could they remain citizens? If they developed their own ethnicity, was this to be in the form of a Jewish state (Zionism), or could it be expressed in non-territorial, perhaps religious, terms, so that it did not conflict with local citizenship?[8]

4. *European cultures*. Not only assimilated Jews but also those regarded as 'isolationist' absorb a great deal of general European culture. They listen to the news and read the newspapers; many of them meet non-Jews in the market place or the bus queue. A phenomenon which deserves serious study is the transmission of popular cultural values to their families by Orthodox

women who read secular women's magazines. Sexual attitudes and the bringing up of children have certainly been affected. What happens when the agony aunt's advice runs counter to traditional rabbinic approaches and is apparently more apt? No section of the community is any longer genuinely isolated, and modern communications have stimulated the flow of values and national and local characteristics among people irrespective of community allegiance.

We must be careful not to assume a clear line of division between 'Jewish' and 'European' culture. Jews are not strangers to Europe, but have lived here longer than many of the 'indigenous' ethnic groups, participating in the cultural life of most nations. Europe has been for centuries part of Jewish identity.

In this respect it is anomalous that Oxford University supports only one appointment in Jewish studies—that currently held by Dr Martin Goodman—and that this is placed in the Faculty of Oriental Studies. Undoubtedly, some part of Jewish studies comes under the heading of Oriental Studies, but to omit Jewish studies from elsewhere betrays ignorance or indifference to the fact that for two thousand years Jews and Judaism have been intimately bound up with the history of Europe.[9]

5. *Values*. Jewish identity, even Jewish religious identity, is susceptible to changing moral and ethical values. Religions respond to changing moral perceptions in society either by opposition or by absorption. For instance, Judaism, Christianity, and Islam have all in the past accepted the institution of slavery, yet most adherents of those religions now oppose slavery, basing their opposition on the selective appropriation of those sources that promote the value of individual freedom. Sometimes one sees this process of absorption taking place. For instance, at the time of the American Civil War, Southern priests and rabbis based their acceptance of slavery on biblical texts; their opponents in the North likewise drew on traditional texts, but to reject slavery. Eventually the Northerners won not only the military battle but the battle of the texts, and the newly perceived value of individual freedom was appropriated into religious teaching, so that despite the revolution in practice, Christian or Jewish identity in the form of an evolving hermeneutic of sacred texts could continue.

One cannot tell today which contemporary values are likely to be absorbed in similar fashion into Jewish identity, secular or religious. But it is already clear that liberal democracy, enhanced status for women, and more tolerant attitudes to sexual deviance are being read into sacred texts by Jews as well as Christians. A new hermeneutic arising from these values enables continuity, the preservation of identity.

6. *Holocaust.* For most Jews, especially in Europe, the Holocaust is a significant part of their understanding of who they are. Many families lost someone in the Holocaust, others know someone who did. Some people prefer not to talk about the Holocaust, thereby perhaps indicating how deeply it has affected them.

Yet attitudes vary from country to country. Particularly interesting is Poland, for whereas Jews tend to think of Poles as collaborators with the Nazis in the *Endlösung*—the 'final solution of the Jewish problem'—the Poles see themselves as victims; indeed, it is beyond question that the death camp at Oświęcim (Auschwitz) was originally set up to destroy the Polish intelligentsia (which of course included many Jews). Stanisław Krajewski has written sensitively of the implications of this for his self-perception as a Polish Jew today;[10] his relationship with the Holocaust had to be formed within the framework of a tripartite relationship of German, Polish Catholic, and Polish Jew.

7. *Israel.* Diaspora Jews feel touched more than most people by what happens in Israel. Usually, this manifests itself in terms of support, but the heightened sensitivity also means that Jews become acutely embarrassed if Israel is presented in a bad light—especially if they feel there is some truth in the allegations. Heightened sensitivity is manifested by some in distancing themselves from Israel and its concerns, or in criticizing it. Some find it difficult to form trusting relationships with Arabs, or indeed with Muslims.

Israeli Jews occasionally see 'Jewishness' in negative terms, associating it with messianic politics or religious coercion or the dark side of the diaspora; a fascinating identity problem is faced by *yoredim* who prefer to regard themselves as Israelis temporarily abroad than as 'diaspora Jews'.[11]

8. *Christianity.* Jewish reactions to the Brother Daniel case in Israel, and to the persistent attempts of 'Hebrew Christians' and the like to lay claim to Jewish identity, highlight the broad consensus among Jews that Christians are not Jews.[12] Part of the Jewish sense of identity, within 'Christendom' at least, is that 'we are not Christians'. This sense is so strong that it conflicts with, and even overrides, the basic rabbinic tradition that the child of a Jewish mother is Jewish. It sets one of the sharpest boundaries on Jewish identity. It need not have a theological dimension, but when it does it means that the Jew, however tolerant he or she may be of Christians and Christianity in practice, perceives traditional Christian dogma (such as the virgin birth and the incarnation) as not merely incorrect but as preposterous and irrelevant.

9. *Minority status.* Identifying oneself as a member of a minority leads one to 'look over one's shoulder': 'I mustn't do anything wrong because of what people will say about the Jews.' It leads to the suspicion of being discriminated against, even when this has no basis in fact.

Perceiving oneself as different from the 'norm' may lead to self-hatred. On the other hand, it may lead to a striving to excel, to 'be like others', to 'assimilate'.

10. *External determinants.* Much of the Jewish sense of identity is imposed from without. Prime among the external determinants is antisemitism, real or imagined. Any imposed method of singling out Jews, whether antisemitic or not, heightens the Jewish sense of identity. That Jews in the Soviet Union had 'Jew' stamped on their identity documents was not in itself antisemitic; nevertheless, it had the effect that a generation who knew nothing of their heritage remained conscious of being Jews.

Images of Jews in the ambient culture function as external determinants of Jewish identity. Sometimes they are actually adopted and internalized, more often vigorously resisted and compensated for.

IDENTITY: SOUGHT OR IMPOSED?

People who talk about Jewish identity often fail to distinguish between two radically different questions.

The first concerns individual psychology; it is an empirical question, not a normative one. How do I (or a notional John Cohen or Leah Levi) achieve my own identity? What is the 'social construction' of my person? People trap themselves into the assumption that because I am Jewish my identity can be summed up in terms of 'Jewishness'. Of course it cannot, any more than if I play the piano my identity can be summed up in terms of music. I am a Jew, I am a musician, but I am lots of other things besides, and whatever I am relates me to other people, and all this makes a very grand and complicated mess which I can live with comfortably even though its precise analysis eludes the skill of social psychologists.

Even if I try to define 'my heritage' I must be careful. I am not limited, nowadays, to a small number of classical sources of my own tradition, but have access, if I am prepared to make the effort, to all that has been preserved of other cultures from earlier generations, in whatever language (except for the few that remain undeciphered), as well as to the whole of modern learning. In identifying myself as a Jew I do not mean to relate only to the sources of one tradition. My total heritage is everything now available to me, not excluding other religious traditions. My special relationship with Judaism is to do with which set of people I feel I belong with in family and historical and religious perspectives, and to some extent to do with truth claims; it is not a delineation of the resources available to me for spiritual, intellectual, and social growth.

And in St Petersburg, Warsaw, Birmingham, Berlin, or Tel Aviv today, there is no return to the isolated Jewish tradition of the past, if ever such a thing existed. If Jews, or people from other traditions, isolate themselves today, this is a voluntary act, a wilful rejection of all other sources of knowledge. It is, I believe, an evil and destructive act.

The second question is prescriptive. Somebody—a parent, a rabbi, or a politician—fabricates an identity for me. 'This is not how a Jewish boy behaves', says mother. 'Being Jewish means *abc*', the rabbi tells me, where *abc* might be 'putting on *tefillin* every morning' or 'keeping Shabbat' or 'maintaining a high ethical standard in business'. Rabbi Yochanan (third century) remarks 'A Jew is anyone who rejects idolatry' (Babylonian Talmud, Meg. 13*a*). A politician might say, 'To be a Jew you must support Israel', or 'No Jew will ever forget the Holocaust.' These are not empirical observations: they would not be falsified however many Jews you might list of whom they could not be truthfully asserted. They are disguised demands, telling me that if I want to 'deserve' recognition within the group I had better comply with these requirements.

The speaker is defining me in order to exercise power over me, to modify my behaviour to conform with his or her beliefs and values. The definition has become an instrument of social control. It can be a very potent one indeed. For instance, when Orthodox rabbis lay down that 'one born of a Jewish mother is Jewish', or when American Reform rabbis rule that when either parent is Jewish the child is Jewish, they are exercising a form of control which can deeply affect human lives for generations. It is an awesome power indeed, not subject to democratic process.

OBSERVATIONS AND CONCLUSION

Observations

1. Terms such as 'the Jewish people', 'Jewishness', 'Jewish identity', do not refer to external, metaphysical entities with peculiar or unique qualities. They refer to ill-defined collections of down-to-earth particulars.

2. People who set up definitions of 'Jewishness' must be suspected of attempting by those definitions to manipulate other people into compliance with the behaviour mandated by the definitions. This cunning abuse of power should be resisted.

3. Attempts to 'discover Jewish identity', such as that illustrated by the Leningrad case-history, are endeavours aimed at the creation of a new

collectivity of people whose mutual recognition depends on accepting some form of 'traditional' Jewish discourse as part of their cognitive framework or vocabulary.

4. The Leningraders, and with them other Europeans, east and west, who are 'returning to their roots', are not, and could not be, simply re-creating the lifestyles of one or more Jewish communities of earlier times. They are actually inventing new lifestyles, by selecting one or more past expressions of Judaism, modifying and mixing these with other elements of Soviet, Russian, European, and world culture.

5. The process of 'returning to roots' does not flow from a predefined personal 'essence'. It is a social construct, but since in contemporary society it is one of many available social constructs, there is usually considerable individual freedom as to whether to accept, resist, or ignore it. This freedom has come in the wake of the Enlightenment; society no longer determines individual identity as narrowly as it did prior to the Enlightenment.

Conclusion

The identity of the individual incorporates many elements, and the Jewish elements are never more than part of a whole. European Jews of today face a wide range of options, with which they familiarize themselves by study of the sources and by mixing with other Jewish people. To some extent the options chosen will be influenced by family, community, personal experiences, and the ambient culture. Prominent among the considerations affecting this choice, once the basic knowledge has been acquired, will be the impact of the Holocaust and the significance of the State of Israel. But attitude to modernity will also be of importance; we have not yet fully come to terms with the implications of the Enlightenment.

Predominantly, modern Europe has secular government and plural societies; this model has already been adopted in most of the newly emerging democracies, though not all of them. Wherever it is the norm, Jews have an unprecedented opportunity for development of an individual identity, and should make the most of this by strongly resisting authoritarian definitions of 'Jewishness', including those made by Jewish leaders.

Of course, communities and even larger structures must form 'boundaries', which demands at least a minimum definition of what may or may not be included. Such communities and organizations should seek the maximum latitude in mutual acceptance and recognition. Some will feel insecure if norms are ill defined, but this is a lesser evil than stifling individual freedom and the evolution of Judaism.

When the dust settles on the New Europe, distinctive forms of Judaism and Jewish identity will doubtless emerge. Fools may predict what these Judaisms will be; they may be proved wrong, but there is no great harm in that. Knaves who seek power will try to impose their own patterns on the future; they will probably fail, and will certainly do great damage in the attempt.

Notes

1. For a recent and perceptive account of the *ba'al teshuvah* ('back to the fold') movement, albeit in Israel, see Benjamin Beit-Hallahmi, *Despair and Deliverance* (Albany, NY, 1992), ch. 2.

2. Ernest Renan, 'Qu'est-ce qu'une nation?', in *Œuvres complètes de Ernest Renan*, ed. Henriette Psichari (10 vols.; Paris, 1947–61), i. 887–906.

3. See Eric Hobsbawm and Terence Ranger (eds.), *The Invention of Tradition* (Cambridge, 1983).

4. Erik H. Erikson, *Identity, Youth, and Crisis* (New York, 1968), 159–60, cited in Michael A. Meyer, *Jewish Identity in the Modern World* (Seattle, 1990), 104–5.

5. Kenneth J. Gergen, 'Social Constructionist Inquiry: Context and Implications', in Kenneth J. Gergen and Keith E. Davis (eds.), *The Social Construction of the Person* (New York, 1985), 5.

6. Martin Buber, *Israel and the New World* (New York, 1963), 167.

7. David Novak, *Jewish–Christian Dialogue: A Jewish Justification* (New York, 1989), 7, following Soloveitchik. See my critique in Norman Solomon, 'The Soloveitchik Line on Dialogue', in D. Cohn-Sherbok (ed.), *Problems in Contemporary Jewish Theology* (Lewiston, NY, 1991), 230.

8. On this, see further Meyer, *Jewish Identity*, ch. 1.

9. It should be said, however, that the Oxford Centre for Postgraduate Hebrew Studies makes up much of the deficiency in this regard.

10. Stanisław Krajewski, 'The Controversy over Carmel at Auschwitz', *Christian–Jewish Relations*, 22: 3–4 (1989), 37–54.

11. Meyer, *Jewish Identity*, 78–9.

12. Brother Daniel was born Oswald Rufeisen, the child of Jewish parents, in Poland in 1922. In 1942 he was hidden by nuns in a convent and became a Catholic; in 1945 he entered the Carmelite order. Later, as Brother Daniel, a Carmelite monk, he sought Israeli citizenship under the Law of the Return, on the grounds that he was a Jew. In 1962 the High Court finally rejected his application; Judge Silberg explained that though he might be considered a Jew under rabbinic law, the Law of Return was a secular law and did not regard him as a Jew. See B. S. Jackson, 'Brother Daniel: The Construction of Jewish Identity in the Israel Supreme Court', *International Journal for the Semiotics of Law*, 6: 17 (1993), 115–46.

PART III

HOPES AND UNCERTAINTIES
IN RELIGIOUS TRENDS

CHAPTER SIX

The Jewish Jew and Western Culture: Fallible Predictions for the Turn of the Century

NORMAN LAMM

RATHER than addressing directly and exclusively the theme of Jewish identities in the new Europe, I shall concentrate instead on what I surmise is the future course of those Jews who are intensely committed to Torah and the Jewish tradition, and at the same time do *not* wish to segregate from other Jews, do *not* want to ignore worldly culture, and who *do* believe—as a matter of principle and not merely convenience—that critical engagement with the environing culture and a profound feeling of fraternity with fellow Jews regardless of their own differing convictions is what, to borrow the prophetic style, 'the Lord doth require of us'. My intention is that because such a group undoubtedly exists, in greater or lesser measure, in Europe, my words will be germane to the situation in the new Europe as well, and that my American experience will not prove irrelevant to the subject of this volume.

I speak as one of this self-same group: as a religious, Orthodox Jew, who believes that without Torah there is no future for *am yisrael*, but who wants *all* Jews, no matter what their religious or ideological orientations, to survive and thrive; whose firm commitment to his own vision of Judaism and Jewishness sometimes makes him impatient but never intolerant of competing views; and whose outlook is best summed up in the words *torah umadda*, the integration or confluence of religious commitment and worldly learning. Hence my title: 'The Jewish Jew and Western Culture'.

The subtitle, 'Fallible Predictions for the Turn of the Century', can be explained only on the basis of my outrageous lack of modesty; for the talmudic sages taught that since the destruction of the Temple, the gift of prophecy has been taken from the prophets and given to children and fools...

The polarization of the Jewish community is by now a truism. On the one side, a high mobility rate and the displacements of war have produced a situation whereby, as one scholar estimated a number of years ago, perhaps one in a thousand of us speaks the same language and lives in the same place as did his or her grandparents. Sergio DellaPergola's figures and graphs presented elsewhere in this volume confirm that impression. In the diaspora, assimilation and intermarriage are decimating our communities. Low fertility rates and the ageing of our population confirm the grim impression of where we are heading. The traditional Jewish family structure is crumbling, and the organized Jewish community is uncertain how to react. In the United States, the lack of *adequate* Jewish education and the erosion of Jewish identity are weakening our ties to Israel (and, consequently, all other Jews); witness the relatively narrow base of contributors to the United Jewish Appeal, the declining memberships of Jewish organizations, and the surprisingly small proportion of American Jews who visit Israel.

Fortunately, there is another side to the ledger, though even that does not offer much consolation. The Orthodox community, whose demise Marshall Sklare confidently expected in *Conservative Judaism* several decades ago, has rebounded with renewed strength. The *haredi* (strictly Orthodox) community, especially, has demonstrated great vigour and self-confidence. Indeed, there is a noticeable process of radicalization, and along with it a growing antagonism towards the non-Orthodox (and the Modern or Centrist Orthodox as well).

What does the future hold? As one who is neither a futurologist nor the son of a futurologist, I know, as Alfred North Whitehead has reminded us, that 'it is the business of the future to be dangerous'—especially for overconfident prognosticators. For example, a few years ago, the French political commentator Jean-Paul Revel wrote in his *How Democracies Perish*: 'Democracy may turn out to be a historical accident, a brief parenthesis that is closing before our eyes'—and then came Gorbachev, *perestroika*, the fall of the Berlin Wall, and the collapse of the Communist Empire ...

To illustrate the special danger of prophecy regarding the future of Jewry, recall that but a few years ago Charles Silberman, in his *A Certain People*, offered a Pollyanna-ish and relaxed, happy view of where we are going. Unfortunately, his data were wrong, and his predictions have already been proved false. The pessimists fare no better. Jeremiads about the inevitable decline of the Jewish people usually give rise to naught but a yawn. About three decades ago, *Look* magazine—unaware of the wise insight of the late scholar, Simon Ravidowicz, that Israel is 'an ever-dying people'—published a famous issue on 'The Vanishing Jews of America': we are still alive, but *Look* magazine has vanished.

Given the perils of forecasting about Jews, is there anything we can say with a measure of confidence about the short range—say, the turn of the century?

In general, a sober outlook leads neither to utopia nor to doom. The religious complexion of a community generally responds more to inertia than to revolutionary change. I recommend, therefore, the stance of a 'worried optimist'.

According to this view, polarization will get worse. Those on the fringes will assimilate more rapidly, and those now considered part of the amorphous Left will move to the periphery. An example: a Jewish Telegraphic Agency report of 19 June 1992 informed us that two Jewish women who were candidates for two vacant Senate seats in California appeared before the San Francisco Jewish Democratic Club. 'Neither mentioned the "J word".' *All* were Jews—hosts and candidates alike—yet there was *no* mention of Jews or Judaism or Israel. I take this as both symbolic and symptomatic of where the Jewish community's liberal segment is going.

At the same time, the Right will move ideologically to more extreme positions, if only as a continuing reaction to the deracination of the assimilating segment of the community, which includes much of the Establishment leadership. Thus, right-wing 'Jewish Jews' will be progressively more alienated from Western culture while the less Jewish Jews will absorb that culture to an alarming degree. This is but an intensification of a phenomenon that can already be observed. As a result of this dual movement, the demographics of the Left will continue to plummet while the Right grows, but not enough to make up for the deficit of the disappearing Left. Inevitably, tensions between both groups will increase, so that the spectre of the fragmentation of the world Jewish community into 'two peoples' will represent a credible danger. And for all groups, Jewish education threatens to become less available and certainly more expensive (according to the recent American Jewish Committee report, 'The High Cost of Jewish Living'). Thus, Jewish life in the diaspora will be more tenuous, more difficult, more menacing, even as—especially in the United States—Jews will have less influence on the foreign policy of their respective countries.

And the Modern Orthodox, the subject of this paper, those who are located at the epicentre of this developing earthquake, will be subject to even greater external pressures and internal dissent. I suspect that this will hold true for European Jewry as well as American Jewry, *mutatis mutandis*.

What does this augur for the long-range prospects of the Jewish community? As John F. Kennedy said some thirty years ago, 'Things will get worse before they get better.' The core of nationalist, secularist, cultural Jews will undoubtedly continue as such, but their numbers will certainly be much smaller. Some few will begin to turn inward, for one reason or other, and grow more intensively Jewish. But overall, the non-Orthodox will grow demographically smaller and ideologically more diffident. None of the cultural and political band-aids will be of much use in healing an ailing Jewish identity. Intensive application of the Holocaust to confirm and strengthen Jewish identity will prove a poor palliative. Israel and Zionism are already losing their power to inspire a new generation of Jews who knew neither the horrors of the Second World War nor the drama of the founding of the State of Israel. Jewish philanthropy will likewise not be able to sustain the psychological and spiritual mechanisms that make for a positive Jewish identity. Indeed, in all three cases, the situation is reversed: those who have strong identities as Jews are the ones who are sustaining the memory of the Holocaust, advocating Israel and Zionism, and contributing to Jewish philanthropy!

Certain variables must, of course, be taken into account. Growing anti-semitism, an eventuality that must never be discounted, can draw Jews closer to each other and to Judaism. Equally important, one must never dismiss the possibility of a Jewish religious revival. The emergence of the transcendent and the yearning for it is highly unpredictable; despite all attempts by historians and sociologists to 'explain' their causes, they usually remain at least significantly mysterious and as impervious to our cognitive incursions as is the soul of man himself. But the sad reality remains that non-Orthodox American Jewry is and will for a long time remain in serious trouble.

Meanwhile, at the other end of the spectrum, the move towards the Right in Orthodoxy has probably crested. Even before the Reichmann bankruptcy, there was serious question as to the economic viability of the whole social and educational structure of the *haredi* world. The *kolel* system—whereby young men, including married men with children, continue their talmudic studies into their 30s and 40s thanks to support from the community, but especially from parents and in-laws, requires an ongoing source of wealth, with new infusions every generation, or massive government support as in Israel, two prerequisites on which the *haredim* certainly cannot count indefinitely. Moreover, since it is impossible to survive economically without technology, they will find it impossible to thrive as a cognitive minority that totally spurns Western culture; technology brings along with it a certain amount of intellectual and cultural baggage that simply cannot be ignored. Modernity, if not confronted, has a tendency to come up from behind and pull the hood of contemporary culture over its unsuspecting and reluctant victims—even if they are *haredim*. Hence, one can expect profound changes in the *haredi* world, with militancy increasing as the threats to its integrity increase and as defections to other groups grow.

The centre, the sector most affected by the tension between 'Jewish Jews' and Western culture, is comprised essentially of two groups: the Modern or

Centrist Orthodox, those characterized by a commitment to Torah along with worldly culture (*torah umadda*), and the 'nominal' Orthodox, most of whom used to be known as the 'non-observant Orthodox'. In the United States, this last group is declining, although remnants of it are still visible and viable in many areas. In England, where this group is effectively the Establishment, both assimilation and strict Orthodoxy are increasing at its expense. It is hard to describe, let alone predict, the role of the Modern Orthodox in a community where the leaders of this very group are so intimidated by the Right that they refuse to acknowledge that they do indeed constitute an entity that is effectively functioning as Modern or Centrist Orthodox Jews.

This points to a weakness that is part of the general character of moderate movements: they lack passion and are easily intimidated. Extremists by nature tend to be simplistic and purist in their ideology, and this gives them a sense of certainty and confidence. Moderates, who are aware of the complexities and the greys and uncertainties of life, tend to be demoralized by those on the extremes. In our case, there is a constant fear of delegitimization by the *haredim*. As a consequence, the moderates are beset by internal frictions as they are tugged in opposite directions by competing factions.

Yet the Orthodox centre does possess strengths which must not be overlooked: mostly, it has finally found its voice. At Yeshiva University in New York, the concept of *torah umadda* was once shunned as a topic of research or even conversation, despite the fact that it was a living reality in the lives of faculty, students, and the community behind them; nowadays it is forthrightly discussed. Moreover, it is not confined to rhetoric but is increasingly adopted as a meaningful ideology of Judaism, and is accepted *de jure* and not only *de facto*. It has, thankfully, drawn sufficient attention to itself to become the object of much lively controversy, and is being elaborated and criticized and defended and applied in publications and conferences. Organizationally, the moderate and modernist group in Orthodoxy is getting its act together and beginning to shed its shyness and diffidence.

While one should not expect the spectrum to be abolished, it appears that the centre will gain strength. And if the external world begins to tend towards moderation, away from the militant secularists on the one side and the ayatollahs on the other, the moderates in Orthodoxy will benefit.

My own 'fallible prediction' for *beyond* the turn of the century for the Modern Orthodox community thus includes the following items:

1. The most Left group of Orthodoxy will break off and unite with those 'traditionalists' who recently left the Conservative movement; but they are and will remain few in number and influence.

2. A rather larger number will defect to the Right, thus leaving the centre smaller but more cohesive and less plagued by inner tensions.

3. An increasing number of defections from the Right to the centre will add to the latter's strength.

4. The centre, which now appears rather weak and in disarray, really *does* speak for a silent majority, and that group will be less silent as it recaptures its old self-confidence.

Is that wishful thinking? Perhaps. But experience teaches that optimism and pessimism are not only assessments and projections without practical consequence, but statements of faith or lack of it; and the way we foresee events is often a self-fulfilling prophecy.

I stake my stand on this proposition. I believe that the cause represented by the institution I head and the philosophy I espouse will, ultimately, prevail—in the United States, possibly in the new Europe, and eventually even in Israel—partially *because* I and my colleagues believe it, and despite enormous pressures.

That is why, as I said at outset, I am a 'worried optimist'.

CHAPTER SEVEN

From Integration to Survival to Continuity: The Third Great Era of Modern Jewry

JONATHAN SACKS

M UCH of Judaism is timeless—its beliefs, its values, its way of life. One of its most potent symbols is the *ner tamid*, the everlasting light in the synagogue that can be seen as denoting the unbreakable relationship of the eternal people to the eternal God. The days, the years, the centuries pass, but Judaism and the Jewish people remain.

But there is something else that renders Jews acutely sensitive to time. In one of the classics of modern Jewish scholarship, *Zakhor*, Professor Yosef Hayim Yerushalmi writes: 'It was ancient Israel that first assigned a decisive significance to history and thus forged a new world-view . . . "The heavens", in the words of the psalmist, might still "declare the glory of the Lord", but it was human history that revealed His will and purpose . . . Far from attempting a flight from history, biblical religion allows itself to be saturated by it and is inconceivable apart from it.'

Jews are very aware of the shifting sands of time. Indeed, sensitivity to history yielded a change in the religious personality of the prophet. Unlike Moses, who transmitted laws which were 'everlasting statutes', the later prophets spoke specifically to their generation and its challenges. 'Each generation', said the sages, 'produces its own search and its own leaders.' The prophetic challenge is to identify an age and its problems. In fact, the inner history of Israel could be written solely in terms of what each era saw as its particular challenge and opportunity.

I believe that we are entering a new era in modern Jewish life, one which presents quite different problems from those which have dominated the

This chapter has been adapted from a paper published in June 1993 by the Office of the Chief Rabbi in the Studies in Renewal series.

Jewish agenda hitherto. To fail to see this is to miss the moment and the opportunity. We will find ourselves fighting yesterday's battles instead of today's.

INTEGRATION

What were yesterday's battles? They can be summarized in two words.

From the nineteenth century until 1967, the key word of European and American Jewish life was integration. The secularization of the West and the rise of the nation-state offered Jews the possibility of becoming full participants in the majority society and its culture, something that had been impossible since the age of Constantine in the third century.

Emancipation bestowed on Jews the full range of civic rights. But it carried a price, namely that Jews had to pass through what John Murray Cuddihy has called the 'ordeal of civility' and adapt to the manners and mores of Europe.[1] It meant the end of a certain kind of Jewish apartness and the beginning of a journey 'out of the ghetto'.

Most Jews welcomed the new age, but it quickly proved to be the start of a prolonged crisis of identity that has haunted Western Jewry to this day.

For some Jews, the inner conflict between being an heir to the covenant at Sinai and a citizen of the modern state was simply too great. Some chose modernity and assimilated out of Judaism. Others adapted Judaism to the extent that instead of being the way of life of a particular people, it became the religion of ethical universalism. At the other end of the spectrum, there were those who rejected modern culture and decided that if Jews were to remain Jews they would have to choose not integration but segregation.

In Britain, however, Jews found a society that was both more tolerant and less ideologically driven than elsewhere in Europe. The result was that most found themselves able to reconcile their twin identities. The traditionalism of English life harmonized with the traditionalism of Jewish sentiment and produced, by and large, a happy marriage. Nineteenth-century Anglo-Jews could point to such role-models as Sir Moses Montefiore, who could move with equal ease from the City to the royal family to the synagogue and the Jewish house of study. In Chief Rabbi Nathan Marcus Adler they had a religious leader who combined unbending Orthodoxy with Victorian decorousness. Even Benjamin Disraeli, who had been converted to Christianity as a child, would refer to his Jewish origins with pride. All this was in marked contrast to the tormented inner struggles of central and eastern European Jewry and the reckless abandonment of tradition by the Jews of the United States.

In a sermon delivered in the New West End Synagogue in 1887, Chief

Rabbi Herman Adler spelt out the philosophy of the prevailing Jewish establishment. Their task, he declared, was 'to anglicise, humanise and civilise' the new east European immigrants, and 'to enable them to become absorbed in the intelligent, industrious, independent wage-earning classes of the country'.

Within the terms set for it, the policy worked remarkably well. The story of successive generations of Anglo-Jewish immigrants has been chapter after chapter of rapid transition from poverty to public prominence in the arts and sciences, business and industry, academic and political life. Jews acculturated with astonishing speed and became paradigms of upward mobility. By and large, too, the innate conservatism and tolerance of British society worked to the benefit of Jewish identity. There were moments of awkwardness and occasional outbreaks of antisemitism. But for the most part, Jews were content to remain Jews and join and occasionally attend synagogues. Integration was possible, and few other Jewries achieved it with so little pain and drama.

SURVIVAL

The turning-point, in world Jewish terms, came in 1967. Looking back at that moment some eighteen years later, two American scholars, Steven Cohen and Leonard Fein, described it as the time when the dominant theme of diaspora Jewish life turned 'from integration to survival'.[2]

The cause of this change was Israel, and specifically the threat to its existence in the weeks leading up to the Six-Day War. But its effect was felt no less in American Jewry. It was one of those rare moments, like the Warsaw Ghetto uprising, which can fairly be said to have changed Jewish consciousness and left its permanent mark on the collective Jewish personality. Ironically it was in 1967 that diaspora Jewry finally discovered the Holocaust, which had taken place more than twenty years before. It was as if it took the threat of a second devastation to unlock the floodgates of feeling about the first.

There is a difference between history and memory, especially group memory: between what happened and the way we frame our perceptions of what happened and turn it into a story that explains us to ourselves. Israel's battle for survival in 1967 came to be seen by a whole generation of American Jews as something more than a remarkable military victory, and as something other than a miracle in the traditional sense. It became a symbol, an emblem of a new Jewish identity.

Jews had been sentenced to annihilation in the Nazi Holocaust. In 1967, Israel had come face to face with the spectre of a second holocaust at the hands of its hostile neighbours. But the Jewish people had survived. Indeed that was its fate and destiny. Jews are the people who are threatened but who survive.

The new survivalism was significantly different in mood and attitude from the old integrationism. Israel became far more prominent in diaspora Jewish life. Several commentators were moved to say that Israel had become the religion of American Jews. A new activism began to permeate world Jewry. Jews were to be found less often praying to God than raising funds, mobilizing support, and engaging in political lobbying on behalf of Israel or Soviet Jewry or the fight against antisemitism.

Integrationism had been based on a fundamentally optimistic view of human nature. American Reform rabbis had solemnly declared in 1885: 'We recognize in the modern era of universal culture of heart and intellect the approach of Israel's great Messianic hope for the establishment of the kingdom of truth, justice and peace among all men.' Reason and tolerance would prevail. Prejudice would die. Less than a century later, those hopes were dashed. Accordingly, survivalism took a darker view. The Holocaust had revealed man's persisting capacity for evil in the midst of high civilization. Israel's continuing isolation showed the sheer tenacity of antisemitism, now transmuted into anti-Zionism. For Jews, the modern world had proved to be a dangerous place indeed.

This gave impetus to a new Jewish particularism. Jews found themselves suddenly interested not in what made them the same as everyone else but in what made them different. A generation of young Jews began to search for their roots and lost religious heritage. They took the 'path of return'. Across a wide spectrum of religious affiliation, Jews developed a new interest in ritual—the codes and actions of Jewish difference. They became far readier than any previous generation since the Emancipation to give public expression to their Jewishness. Israel had given them pride. Thoughts of the Holocaust had given them defiance.

There was one other factor in this transformation. It had nothing to do with Israel or indeed with Jewishness as such. The 1960s were also the time when a certain cultural model began to be challenged and overthrown, what was known in America as the 'melting pot' and in Britain as assimilation. This was the idea that a society possessed a single dominant culture into which all minorities must eventually merge. Instead a new model emerged— pluralism, or multiculturalism—which held that society was a mosaic of different groups and their ways of life, none of which held primacy over any other. This change, along with the epic events in Israel, profoundly affected Jews.

To understand why, we must remember the deep effect of secularization on the Jewish community, most notably in America. In the 1960s, Gerhard

Lenski reported in his book *The Religious Factor* that Jews were markedly less 'religious' in their attitudes than either Protestants or Catholics—a finding which remained true in the mid-1980s. Clearly this signalled a crisis for any traditional Jewish identity. To be Jewish, whether in the ancient or the modern world, was primarily to be a member of a people defined by its faith and religious code. But the constellation of forces in the 1960s now made possible quite a different definition. The drama of the Holocaust and the establishment of the State of Israel could be seen less as a chapter in the history of divine providence than as the secular story of a people asserting its will to survive. The pluralism of contemporary American life gave this people its mandate to continue to survive. Jews could now see themselves as something other than a *religious community*. They were, and increasingly saw themselves as, an *ethnic group*.

These changes took place most dramatically in America. But they had an effect on Anglo-Jewry as well. In Britain too, the Holocaust and Israel became touchstones of Jewish identity. Fund-raising and political activism took on a new significance at the heart of Jewish life. At any time prior to 1967 there could be no doubt as to which were the most significant positions of lay leadership within the community: the President of the Board of Deputies and the President of the United Synagogue, the two positions which externally and internally epitomized Anglo-Jewry as a religious community. Today Anglo-Jewish leaders are as likely to be drawn to the secular fields of Israel, welfare, and defence as to the synagogue and representation.

Britain is a less plausible home than America for the idea that Jews are simply an ethnic group. There are fewer Jews in Britain, too few to sustain a viable ethnic subculture. Besides which, pluralism and the associated separation of religion and state never belonged to British values as they did to America, which saw itself as the home of 'huddled masses yearning to breathe free'—Emma Lazarus's words engraved on the Statue of Liberty. None the less, significant numbers of young Jews do now see their identity in essentially ethnic terms. For them, Jewish belonging is a matter of mixing with other Jews, supporting Israel, and fighting antisemitism; it has no especially religious connotation.

THE PASSING OF AN ERA

Just as integration resolved the problem of being Jewish in a modern secular society, so survivalism rallied Jewish energies at a time of flagging commitment. It emphasized the difference the State of Israel has made to Jews worldwide, allowing them to feel more secure and more capable of taking action when particular diaspora communities are under threat of persecution. It played no small part in the worldwide Jewish response to the plight of Soviet and Ethiopian Jewry. Equally importantly, it gave Jews a way of seeing themselves as part of a single people at a time when religious and cultural differences had gone so deep that perhaps nothing else was capable of uniting them. Not all Jews could relate to the idea of being members of the covenant at Sinai. But most could identify with the idea that, but for an accident of history, they might have been victims of Hitler's Final Solution.

The idea of survival energized Jews for a generation. But it can do so no longer. In retrospect we will probably see the publication of the results of the 1990 North American National Jewish Population Survey as the turning-point. This disclosed that the rate of outmarriage among young American Jews had reached 57 per cent. In Britain, Board of Deputies figures have shown for some years that only a third of Jews of marriageable age are marrying in synagogue, and since the 1950s the Jewish population has declined by some 50 per cent.[3] This leads to a most disturbing conclusion: *Jewish commitment to survival has not proved strong enough to ensure that Jews survive*.

During the middle and late 1980s, a school of American Jewish sociologists, known as transformationists, mounted the unprecedented argument that the Jewish community was *not* endangered by high rates of intermarriage. If the non-Jewish partner converted, or if at least half the children of mixed marriages were raised as Jews, there would be no net loss to the community, and perhaps even a gain. Such was the argument of sociologists like Charles Silberman and Calvin Goldscheider.[4] Their optimism has now proved dramatically unfounded. Few non-Jewish partners in mixed marriages convert, and equally few bring up their children as Jews. This is so despite the fact that the liberal Jewish denominations in America have virtually abandoned preconditions for conversion, and have chosen, through the controversial 'patrilineal' ruling of 1983, to recognize the children of Jewish fathers and non-Jewish mothers as Jews. In short, despite every liberal accommodation to mixed marriage, the American Jewish community is losing Jews at a prodigious rate.

Anglo-Jewry is different from America, and no direct comparison can be drawn. On the whole we are more traditional, more affiliated, and more Jewishly educated. Nor have the issues been debated in Britain with the clarity and vigour that they have in America. None the less, the experience of American Jewry in the 1990s allows us to see the deep shortcomings of survivalism as a philosophy of Jewish life. Paradoxically, survivalism fails as a strategy for survival.

It makes sense when what is at stake is physical survival. When lives are at risk or freedoms are in danger, we need no further justification for our concern. Physical survival has dominated modern Jewish concern, and that is why the Holocaust and the State of Israel have been central to Jewish thought. The Holocaust stands as the symbol of the risk Jews face. Israel stands as the guarantor of Jewish lives and liberties worldwide.

But physical survival is not the problem confronting most diaspora Jewries. It is not seriously endangered in either America or Britain. What is at risk is neither life nor liberty but identity. The question is not 'Will we survive?' but '*How* will we survive?' As Jews? Or as something else, whose Jewish content will rapidly diffuse through the generations until nothing of it remains? We should not forget that physically, the lost ten tribes survived. They were merely lost to Jewish history. They chose to live as something other than as members of the people of Israel.

Survivalism answers no questions. It proposes no content for Jewish life other than life itself. In order to sustain even a minimally coherent view of why Jews should remain Jews rather than fade into anonymity it has to postulate the darkest possible view of the human condition, namely (*a*) that Jews are uniquely singled out for persecution; (*b*) that they will remain so even if they marry out and merge into social anonymity; and (*c*) that at times of danger they can rely on no other help than from themselves. For a generation waking to the trauma of the Holocaust at a time when Israel stood embattled and alone, these propositions seemed luminous in their certainty. But it is doubtful in the extreme whether any people can sustain itself on so negative a self-definition.

Each year, on the festival of Pesach, Jews solemnly affirm that 'It was not one alone who stood against us to destroy us; in every generation there have been those who stood against us to destroy us.' Collective Jewish memory begins in the book of Exodus with slavery and the threat of genocide. But what follows is not survivalism but a declaration of faith. The story ends not with endurance but redemption. Liberation from Egypt leads on to holy living, not merely to being alive. 'I will not die' says the psalmist, 'but live'; and the verse continues 'and I will declare the works of God'.

What would Pesach be without its intimate connection with Shavuot? In other words, what would Israelite freedom be without the further festival of revelation? What would Jewish life have been without some content to inspire pride and purpose? Imagine the Bible as a narrative of mere survival. We would read about the Israelites becoming slaves in Egypt. We would thrill to the story of how they were led to freedom and a land of their own. And then we would read about how they mingled and married with the local population and became as dead to the pages of world history as the ancient Jebusites and Perrizites. Could that conceivably be a story to inspire identification or belonging?

Survivalism has had its day. At a certain point in the evolution of modern Jewish consciousness it played a vital part, rousing Jews throughout the world to a full awareness of the epic nature of the events through which they had lived and in which six million of the Jewish people died. As long as there is a Jewish people, future generations will look back on those days with awe and wonder, reflecting on how close the people of the covenant came to extinction and how, hardened by the fires of hell on earth, they fought back to affirm life.

That era, however, has now passed. It will live on eternally in Jewish memory. But it is not present Jewish reality. Israel is engaged in peace negotiations with its neighbours. The Jews of eastern Europe are now free to rediscover their Jewish identity, and even to emigrate to Israel if they wish. Ethiopian Jewry has been rescued. Predictably there will be moments of crisis in the future. We are not yet living at that time of universal peace for which we daily pray. But the period of high drama, in which the mere physical survival of the Jewish people hung in the balance, is over. Another challenge lies ahead. A new era has already begun. A third word must now enter and dominate the Jewish mind.

FROM SURVIVAL TO CONTINUITY

The word is *continuity*. The issue it signifies is this. Having spent the last quarter of a century devoting their energies to helping Jewries elsewhere to survive, British and American Jews have paused to take a look at their own health and discovered that something is going very badly wrong. Young Jews in large and increasing numbers are choosing not to marry other Jews and have Jewish children.

From a secular and sociological perspective there is nothing surprising about this. It happens to all minority ethnic groups in an open and plural society. But from a Jewish perspective there is something very troubling indeed in such an outcome. For Jews, almost alone among peoples, have survived two thousand years of exile and dispersion. Most remained Jews despite every blandishment or threat, seduction or persecution. Only now, when for the first time in two millennia Jews have their own land and freedom and equality, are they losing the will to live as Jews. Having passed every trial in a long and troubled history—including the Holocaust that was perhaps as great as the binding of Isaac six million times repeated—Jews are now in danger of failing the last trial: *that there are no trials*.

An era can be defined by what we cannot take for granted. A good indicator that times have changed comes when something that was simply not a problem for previous generations becomes urgent and problematic.

The era of integration began when Jews who had hitherto led culturally enclosed lives were suddenly faced with the challenge of becoming part of another social order. The era of survival began when Jews, who had always known sporadic violence, were faced with the threat of cold, systematic annihilation. The era of continuity is about to begin with the realization that the transmission of Jewish identity across the generations has become fragile and altogether fallible.

With this discovery there is no need for panic or despair. If recent Jewish history teaches anything at all, it tells us that once the Jewish people summons up its collective will it can overcome any challenge. There were those who fervently believed that the open society spelled the end of Judaism. There were those who, in the shadow of Auschwitz, looked into the future and saw Jewry as a ghost, a corpse. Their fears were not irrational, but they were wrong, because they underestimated the astonishing—one might almost say miraculous—capacity of Jews to 'renew their days as of old'. Ezekiel's vision of the Jewish people as a valley of dry bones that came to life again has stayed with us, and never before have we had such cause to marvel at the depth of that prophetic intuition.

Nothing less than a massive effort of collective energy will now suffice. The same passion that drove first integration and then survival must now go into continuity.

NEW PRIORITIES

The difference between the three great eras of modern Jewry can be summarized simply. In the first, Jews were challenged to show that they could live as Englishmen or Americans. In the second, the challenge was to show that a Jew can live. Now the challenge is to show that a Jew can live as a Jew.

Continuity places firmly on the table the proposition that being Jewish has a content, a content so precious that, having been handed down from generation to generation, it must now be valued, restored, and lovingly passed on to the next generation.

We know that the Jewish world today is culturally and religiously fragmented, and that that fragmentation consists precisely in an argument about what the content of Jewish life is. But that should not paralyse us as Jews any more than we have been paralysed by the dozen different interpretations of the meaning and significance of the State of Israel. Israel means different things to different Jews, but we are united in a total commitment to its welfare. Judaism and Jewishness mean different things to different Jews. But that will not stop us affirming our shared commitment to their continuation.

The move from survival to continuity will mean a massive shift in communal priorities. It will mean that as well as devoting our energies to saving Jewries abroad we will have to take on board the huge task of saving Jewry at home. It will mean that instead of taking Jewish identity for granted we will have to take it as something to be created. It will mean, in short, a momentous decision to engage in education and outreach in all its many forms and contexts on a scale never before attempted. And this must be done in such a way as to enlist and reach every section of the community.

Within a year of my installation as chief rabbi in 1991, the Chief Rabbi's Office began planning such an initiative. After six months we were able to launch our new programme, Jewish Continuity, which will embrace every activity needed to ensure that we summon the will to have Jewish grandchildren.

There is much that needs urgently to be done by way of consultation, organization, planning, and fund-raising. The process has begun and will gather momentum. But something else has to happen if it is to succeed, namely that we must become conscious of the extraordinary challenge with which we are faced. We need a serious communal debate about continuity, one that shakes us from any possibility of complacency and focuses our minds on what we need to do as Jews for the sake of our children and their children. I hope the debate will be joined by every Jew who cares about the Jewish future.

A new era has arrived, a new phase in the perpetual Jewish calendar, and we must meet the challenges it brings. The Jewish blessing over a new phase in the calendar is 'Blessed are You . . . who has kept us alive and helped us to endure and brought us to this time.' Jewish consciousness of the passage of time is linked to an awareness of Jewish continuity. Physical survival is not enough: we must commit ourselves to the spiritual continuity that is the essence of Judaism.

Notes

1. See John Murray Cuddihy, *The Ordeal of Civility: Freud, Marx, Lévi-Strauss and the Jewish Struggle with Modernity* (Boston, 1987).

2. See Steven M. Cohen and Leonard J. Fein, 'From Integration to Survival: American Jewish Anxieties in Transition', *Annals of the American Academy of Political and Social Science* (July 1985), 175–88.

3. See S. Waterman and B. A. Kosmin, *British Jewry in the Eighties*: *A Statistical and Geographical Guide* (London: Board of Deputies of British Jews, 1986).

4. See e.g. Charles Silberman, *A Certain People: American Jews and Their Lives Today* (New York, 1985), and Calvin Goldscheider, *Jewish Continuity and Change* (Bloomington, Ind., 1986).

CHAPTER EIGHT

The Role of the Rabbi in the New Europe

JONATHAN MAGONET

RABBINIC ROLES

A S the principal of a Progressive rabbinical seminary—the only one operating in western Europe and, with the exception of the Budapest Seminary, the only one available to serve eastern and central Europe—I must inevitably have a very particular view of the significance of the rabbinate in general and the Progressive rabbinate in particular. I find myself torn between two distinct perceptions. On the one hand, it could be argued that the rabbi is an endangered species in Europe today because of the lack of candidates coming forward to take on this role within the Jewish community—and the distressing lack of resources and finances made available to support rabbinic training and the work of rabbis in the field. On the other hand, as I look at the number of requests I receive from different parts of Europe for rabbis, I am deeply concerned at our failure to meet the real spiritual, material, cultural, and intellectual needs of the post-war European Jewish world. It represents at best a long-term impoverishment of Jewish life, at worst a form of slow suicide.

Let me make it clear that I am not qualified to discuss the Orthodox rabbinate as it functions in Europe. Graduates of the Leo Baeck College serve Reform, Liberal, and Conservative congregations in the United Kingdom; Liberal congregations in France, Holland, Switzerland, and Austria; and *Einheitsgemeinde* congregations—the 'united communities' that cater for all religious groupings—in Switzerland and Germany. Whatever the particular designation, they are all congregations that, in choosing one of our graduates, have accepted that the balance between tradition and modernity should be tipped towards the latter. Thus they are variously perceived as being either in some way marginal against a supposedly Orthodox norm, or as pioneering the troubled interfaces between tradition and modernity, between the Jewish community and its host society, between Judaism and the pluralistic religious and secular groupings that make up today's Europe. Another way of expressing the latter view, one that certainly applies to what has been happening in Anglo-Jewry, is that the Progressive rabbinate is trying to provide a Jewish home for the masses of estranged, indifferent, or halakhically problematic Jews that increasingly make up today's Jewish world. Our task is including Jews in, rather than defining Jews out.

In this task, the role of the rabbi is surprisingly ignored. Now all of us know of good and bad rabbis, have our own anecdotes about them, may even belong to a community where we have some idea of the role they might play. However, in terms of the sort of research that interests Jewish sociologists, and compared to the recognition given to other professions within the broad spectrum of the Jewish civil service, the rabbinate is curiously invisible. Though I have not gone hunting for documentation, I can think of few studies on the European rabbinate and its composition, or the roles that rabbis play, their training, the perception of them at large, and so forth. When there are conferences of international Jewish welfare, social, cultural, or political organizations, I doubt that rabbis are considered a class to be included on the mailing list. There are obviously individual exceptions, and as we have a very small rabbinate in Europe few can spare the time for such things. But I am not even sure where I would begin to discover how many rabbis there are, or any other statistics about them. There seems to be a degree of ambivalence about the rabbinate as a whole, and a surprising lack of curiosity about its place within the broader Jewish scene.

In the particular kinds of communities and societies in which Leo Baeck graduates serve, the role of the rabbi could be defined, sociologically, between two important tasks. On the one hand he, or she, is the GP—the general practitioner of the Jewish world, the rabbinical equivalent of the family doctor. That is to say, the rabbi's study, or more often telephone, represents the first port of call for all sorts of Jews in need, in trouble, or in search, from within his or her official congregation, but as often as not, from those with no affiliation whatsoever. Most often they come with problems arising from life-cycle events—happy and tragic ones. However, in the current economic situation, it is often the rabbi who has the closest awareness of the problems confronting individual members of the congregation, who is best placed to bring such things to general attention and help seek appropriate support. The rabbi is in this sense a social engineer, and it is a matter of temperament, training, or interest how far he or she pursues such matters. This is remembered once a year, as the High Holyday appeals come round, or indeed when any Jewish charity or organization asserts that if only the rabbi will speak about their cause from the pulpit, the money will come flooding in. But far too little attention is paid to the reality, or lack of it, behind such assumptions, and the significance of rabbinic leadership at this grass-roots level.

The other task that helps define the status of the rabbi, at least in this limited 'sociological' view, is that of ambassador-at-large to the Jewish world. Again, this is self-evident, but its implications are rarely spelled out. If all Jews in the diaspora find themselves, willingly or unwillingly, called to account for every action of the State of Israel, the rabbi is the figure representing the Jewish community to the public at large. The rabbi is often the one who must interpret Israel to his or her congregation, and at the same time justify its actions to the outside world. Indeed, in the face of insatiable public curiosity about Jews and Judaism—sometimes, but not always, bordering on antisemitism—rabbis have a considerable responsibility as interpreters of Jews to the outside, and sometimes have platforms of considerable importance if they wish to make use of them.

There is a more conventional way of viewing the rabbi within the congregational setting. He or she is the one person particularly concerned with maintaining the values, truths, and insights of Jewish tradition, often epitomized in his or her own person: the Jew for others. That is how we tend to see the classical role of spiritual leader today. However, we must also remember that the rabbi is *par excellence* the interpreter of that tradition to a contemporary generation, not merely an archivist. In that sense, the rabbi is as often as not the one who is the agent of change. Paradoxically, in Progressive Jewish circles, change can mean a move back into tradition in various areas, no less than a move in a more radical direction. But over a period of time, it is astonishing how far the views of a rabbi influence the ethos of the community he or she serves—I say astonishing because most rabbis I know are very doubtful that anything they say is actually heard. But if you consider that a rabbi may serve a congregation ranging from a few hundred to a few thousand people over a period of decades, it is obvious that he or she will have an impact—and yet how little we pay attention to this in considering matters like 'leadership' within European Jewry!

The failure to examine the rabbinate, perhaps because of a general Jewish ambivalence about religion and its accredited representatives, has certain consequences. Put bluntly, we get the religious leadership we deserve—or rather, we are making a serious error if we see the quality of rabbinic leadership as being the responsibility only of those who bother to belong to congregations, because rabbinic influence pervades the whole of Jewish life. I do not express this as some sort of dire warning, but merely to record my puzzlement at the surprising lack of curiosity about the rabbinate. And unfortunately, this lack of curiosity means that the resources for rabbinic

education and in-service training remain inadequate, and the lack of attention to the rabbinate prevents more people considering it as a possible
vocation or profession.

SOME CURRENT RABBINIC CHALLENGES

I would like to turn to some of the broader issues which confront us today in
which the rabbinate has a crucial role to play, or at least is a factor that needs
to be taken into consideration. In this I am taking as read the detailed day-
to-day activities of rabbis in the conventional congregational setting. The
following is a personal and somewhat random list of issues based on concerns that have come my way in recent months.

Firstly, a phone call from a colleague in Germany. Some 600 Russian Jews
have been allocated by the government to be settled in his town, more than
doubling the size of his community. Whereas the material welfare matters
can be taken care of, he is in desperate need of teachers and additional
rabbinic support because these people have virtually no Jewish background.
There is a chance to provide a Jewish education at least for their children,
and if more could also be done for the parents, it would be an incredible
opportunity. The same thing is happening throughout Germany and is
totally changing the Jewish demography. A community that has long been
written off, or even condemned, by the Jewish world is on the verge of a
renaissance. But where do you find rabbis who not only speak German but
are also willing to live and work in that country, given its history and the
highly neurotic and charged situation of Jews and Germans still today?

Germany provides another illustration of the problems that confront
rabbis today. There will be major issues of Jewish status to sort out over the
years with these new Russian immigrants, problems that in fact occur
increasingly throughout Europe as intermarriage increases. In the particular
case of Germany I think it highly unlikely that the German rabbinate, as
presently structured and constituted, will be able to do much with these
issues. They are already faced with the unresolved problem of people who
wish to convert to Judaism, many of whom have shown their loyalty by
becoming involved with their local synagogue for several years. Obviously
there are some cases where there may be highly neurotic problems under the
surface, linked to a post-war German feeling of guilt. But there remain many
sincere people with a serious commitment who are unable to get a sympathetic hearing from the community rabbi. They have no alternative to
the Orthodox framework, unlike in other countries where there is also a
Progressive Jewish option.[1] Some are now beginning to approach the
Reform and Liberal rabbinic bodies in Britain to undergo conversion, even

though this risks estranging them further from the rabbinate in Germany. Since Jewish status is the one area left where rabbis actually have power and sanctions within *halakhah*, it is particularly important that the use of that power becomes the concern of the Jewish world as a whole.

Having mentioned the Russians in Germany, it is obvious that there is a staggeringly great task to be done in the newly emergent states of the former Eastern bloc. Progressive rabbis visited refuseniks in the Soviet Union for twenty years or more, and in recent years have been working with groups of young Jews just beginning to explore their Jewish identity in Hungary and in both parts of the former Czechoslovakia. We are only one group of many, of which the Lubavitch Hasidim have the highest profile, and it is regrettable that we are likely to see a major competition for 'souls' in these new areas. But in fact there is room for many sorts of Judaism, and an unlimited amount of work to be done. In 1993, the World Union for Progressive Judaism identified over thirty small communities in different parts of the former Soviet Union that wish to identify themselves with Progressive Judaism. The Leo Baeck College welcomed its first Russian rabbinic student, from Moscow, in the autumn of 1991, and a second, this time a woman from Kiev, in the autumn of 1992. In fact if the resources could be found we could easily be overwhelmed by the number of young Jews from these countries who wish to study for the rabbinate or to be teachers or community leaders or Jewish scholars. Provided that the whole society does not simply fall apart, there is enormous need for young, open-minded rabbis as a Jewish world tries to recreate itself in this strange new environment.

To turn to a different topic, some months ago I visited the site of Auschwitz–Birkenau as part of a group of Jewish intellectuals looking at the use to which the site is put today and the implications of this for the future. We discussed the Carmelite Convent issue and visited the new Catholic centre in the area which is intended to be a meeting place for the work of reconciliation. In view of the Jewish reactions to the convent, and some aggressive rabbinic ones as well, it seemed to me that there was a responsibility somewhere for a more positive Jewish response to the intentions expressed by the new centre. So I have had a few preliminary discussions about the possibility of organizing a small study meeting for a number of rabbis and Jesuit students and priests at the centre. The aim would be to study together, to create some sort of understanding, and to get beyond the politicization that has been the only Jewish response to the centre to date. I have had some experience of this kind of work in Germany, where I am aware of a similar mixture of curiosity, spiritual hunger, and fascination with Judaism that requires a positive Jewish response—if only, once again, we had the human resources to do it. In one sense, this is rabbinic work on the ambassadorial level, but it goes much deeper in today's post-war Europe. For where are today's religious values being created, and with whom can we explore them?

Where does fresh air come into our Jewish thinking? How do we break out of the spiritual isolation and introversion that has been so characteristic of Jewish religious life in the past forty years? How do we move beyond the question of survival into that of seeking a Jewish religious purpose in this new period? In one way, it must be found in facing the issues we find most difficult, and particularly in accepting the overtures of other religious individuals and groups with whom we actually share so much in common today. The very difficulties of past history force us to go beyond providing mere Jewish 'information' or defensiveness, into a deeper exploration of our own Jewish resources. Here we actually need to develop a religious intuition and imagination—if only to prevent our Jewish creativity and spiritual energy becoming sapped in the internecine struggles that serve only to alienate so many Jews. As is so often the case, in journeying to meet the other we begin to rediscover the value of our own home, and make our own small contribution to a new religious possibility for Europe as a whole.

RABBINIC QUALIFICATIONS

I fear that with these last remarks I have moved beyond my brief as an analyst into that of a preacher—always a risk when you ask a rabbi to present his ideas. So let me return to my task with two final observations.

The first is about the training that is needed for rabbis to enter the fray in this new Europe about which we are talking. Clearly they must have access to the tradition in its fullest form. Here emphases will differ, depending upon the particular grouping to which we belong. In the Progressive world, we try to give our students a grounding in Bible, Mishnah, Talmud, Midrash, and Codes—certainly enough for them to feel comfortable in going to them as primary sources. In addition they study Jewish history, philosophy, and theology as the tools needed to translate these traditional materials into today's realities. Alongside that there is a strong emphasis on practical congregational work, and increasingly an attempt to understand the rabbinic–lay relationship so that we can create 'partners in leadership' (as we call the programme we have been running for some years).[2] All students are also expected to spend a year studying in Israel. But I would note two additional factors that are unique to our own programme at Leo Baeck. Firstly, throughout the five years of the studies, the students undergo a programme in pastoral care that includes external courses in basic counselling skills—for example, in bereavement counselling—and often a period of personal psychotherapy. This has its origins in an awareness by many of our graduates that they were poorly equipped to deal with the sort of problems that people actually brought to them, so that some skills in this area became crucial. But also, given the enormous demands made upon them in their work, the fantasies projected upon them, the constant experience of being on call, the pressure on their families, they needed to gain considerably more insight into their own functioning and limitations, and what support system they themselves needed. But if one looks at the way our Progressive rabbinic bodies examine contemporary issues, they seem to be bringing these new skills to bear. I suspect that the combination of an openness and sympathy for human realities, together with an awareness of their own motivations and, indeed, prejudices, will have a long-term impact on the way decisions are made about a whole variety of community issues. We are possibly seeing a new dimension to the halakhic process in the making.

But I would also like to mention a second aspect of the studies. For almost twenty years, all students have gone each year to a Jewish–Christian–Muslim residential student conference that Leo Baeck College organizes in Germany. That means that at least once during their studies (often twice) students are exposed to a highly intensive interfaith experience, and in particular come to know something at first hand of the Muslim world. This is important because of the growing size of the Muslim community in Europe, and the way in which the Middle East conflict always threatens to spill over into the way our two communities view each other. We have begun to build up a network of young religious and community leaders from the three faiths who know each other and have a totally different experience of each other from previous generations. This is a kind of 'tough' interfaith dialogue. Precisely because we live together for a week, sharing all aspects of the programme, we are forced to go beyond superficial politeness and the recital of things we have in common, to examine the issues that divide us, the prejudices we have about each other, and the fears that keep us apart. It provides a 'safe space' for such an exploration, and apparent ideological differences quickly break down into personal stories and journeys in which we find the common human experience that crosses all denominational boundaries. Dialogue, in this sense, is ideologically close to the counselling ethic and training and similarly offers a new dimension to Jewish religious thought which will also have a major long-term impact on our communities.

The final point I wish to address is one that I can already take for granted in a way, but it will clearly need another generation before its full impact can be felt. For more than a decade Leo Baeck College has been ordaining women, and they have already been successfully integrated into the Reform and Liberal movements in the United Kingdom. With the appointment of

Pauline Bébé, one of our graduates, at the Mouvement juif libéral de France in Paris, the first step has been taken on continental Europe as well. I recognize that there are enormous barriers of hostility and anxiety to overcome; this seems to represent a challenge to some of the deepest assumptions, in some case prejudices, in our tradition. The resistance to women rabbis, and to the attempt to introduce new liturgies using inclusive language, are symptomatic of the difficulties throughout Western society as we try to come to terms with this revolution in our thinking and way of being in the world. However, as soon as a woman rabbi *is* appointed, the process of 'normalization' and acceptance is very fast. What is not yet clear is whether women will bring new dimensions to the rabbinate itself, new qualities and insights.

It is almost fifty years since the end of the Second World War. Settled patterns of Jewish life have been established, only to be shaken by the new situation that confronts us. Given the unpredictable nature of Jewish history, it would be absurd to try to predict what will happen. We could see a renewal of communities like those in Germany alongside the newly emergent ones in central and eastern Europe—or we could see the same pattern of assimilation and disappearance that has marked the post-war world. But among the factors that have to be taken into account in this future I would only point out that rabbis represent an intellectual, spiritual, and practical resource, with a five-year professional training behind them. To overlook their actual and potential impact, and to fail to provide the resources to encourage them, would represent a major failure of imagination on the part of Jewish leadership. In Europe today we have a short time in which to build up a new Jewish life, given the human resources now available. The quality of spiritual leadership, in its widest sense, that we offer will determine the future of European Jewry for the next century.

Notes

1. Although there are two graduates of the Leo Baeck College in Germany—in Hanover and Berlin—and theoretically there is a 'liberal' synagogue in Berlin, the latter in fact has to be very conservative and they all have to operate within the Orthodox framework.
2. Leo Baeck College published three pamphlets in 1992 in the Partners in Leadership series that explore this area: Margaret Harris, *Organising Modern Synagogues: A Case of Multiple Models*; Barry Palmer, *Holy People, Holy Place*; and Elizabeth Crossik and Jeffrey Newman, *The Work of the Progressive Rabbi: First Step towards a Post-Graduate Training Programme*. All are obtainable from Leo Baeck College, 80 East End Road, London, N3 2SY.

PART IV

JEWISH COMMUNITIES IN FORMER COMMUNIST COUNTRIES

CHAPTER NINE

Jewish Communities and Jewish Identities in the Former Soviet Union

MIKHAIL A. CHLENOV

A N American colleague who heard me speak about the problems of the Jews of the former Soviet Union said to me: 'Look, we don't have space in our mentality for the image you presented. We see only two scenarios. Either they're hitting you on the head or you're packing your belongings to go to Israel.' Such is the stereotypical image, but as with every stereotype it is far removed from reality.

For more than quarter of a century, Jews in the Soviet Union fought for the right to be 'repatriated'—that is, for free emigration to Israel. Those who were refused permission to leave—the 'refuseniks', as they came to be called—gained worldwide support, and in fact became one of the best-known symbols of the freedom movement in the Soviet Union. Zionism, reviled by the Communist state as a major source of evil in the world, came in this way to constitute a direct challenge to the Soviet regime, even if it did not touch the majority of Soviet Jews.

The Zionist nature of this refusenik movement was beyond any doubt. At the same time it also sparked a genuine revival of interest in Jewish life in the Soviet Union, and attempts to know and understand Jewish behaviour, Jewish culture, Jewish religion. Thus, the seeds of today's interest in Jewish education, Jewish communal life, Jewish culture, and Jewish religious renewal were sown even before *perestroika*; in many respects, the changes that have come about in the character of Jewish life in the former Soviet Union need to be seen against this historical background.

After 1988 the political situation changed radically. People who had waited for years for permission to emigrate finally departed for Israel. Numerous positions of leadership within the Soviet Jewish world were thereby left vacant. In consequence, the rapid new development of the Soviet totalitarian state and its subsequent dramatic decline caused distress and panic among Jews even more than among the rest of the Soviet population.

But the sudden enfeeblement of the unshakable giant caused signs of stress and tension throughout society: the state had always been the source of everything and the ultimate arbiter of everything. The tensions engendered different fears in different factions. There were widespread fears that stores would be plundered, or that civil war would break out. Communists feared that political pogroms and terrorism would be directed against them. For Jews the stress took the form of fear of antisemitism and rumours of forthcoming pogroms. None of these fears, including the fear of a new type of post-*perestroika* antisemitism, should be dismissed as total fantasies. The extent of the fear, however, would certainly seem to have been dispropor-tionate to the real danger, and to have been caused more by a feeling of extreme social distress and perplexity.

The vast majority of ordinary Soviet Jews had not adopted the Zionist ideas of the refuseniks, but even so the build-up of tensions resulted in the emigration of 185,000 Jews to Israel in 1991 alone. It was this situation—the rumours of pogroms and the resulting emigration to Israel—that created the stereotypes mentioned by my American friend. Although this mass *aliyah* was prompted by factors quite different to those that had prompted the *aliyah* of the 1970s and early 1980s, and although the kinds of people interested in emigrating were now also quite different, it was con-strued in the West as a continuation of the earlier waves of migration to Israel, a sign that the Jewish masses were following in the footsteps of their Zionist predecessors.

ANTISEMITISM: REAL OR IMAGINARY?

There were indeed good reasons to fear that the Jews would suddenly fall victim to a new wave of antisemitism. In the West, this new wave of antisemitism was perceived as the re-emergence of a traditionally Russian phenomenon; the reality was not so simple. First of all, the new situation showed that antisemitism is not a characteristic of all ethnic groups; rather, its emergence is dependent on specific political situations. Significantly enough, the first blows to the Soviet empire had come from movements aimed at ethnic self-determination: the Karabakh movement for the reuni-fication of Armenian-populated areas with Armenia proper, the national liberation struggles in the Baltic states, and so on. These and related events between 1989 and 1991 aroused deep sympathy among those members of Soviet society opposed to the suppression imposed by the Communist regime. They were ready to support all kinds of nationalist movements, regarding them as manifestations of justice and freedom. That was the perception of the democratically inclined intelligentsia of the big cities, including the Jews. But it is important to understand that whereas they perceived the nationalist movements as *anti-Soviet*, the nationalists themselves saw their movements as *anti-Russian*.

The reaction of the Russian nationalists was more complicated. Even before *perestroika*, nationalist dissidents had tried to put forward the idea that the Soviet regime represented an alien intrusion imposed by some evil force bent on corrupting the blameless Russian people. This view, shared by different kinds of *pochvenniki* movements and by other descendants of the old Russian Slavophiles, was the reaction of fervent Russian nationalists to the collapse of the Soviet regime. As there were some historical precedents in Russia for identifying this anonymous evil with Jews or Zionists, this nationalist Russian response to the decline of their empire tended to have antisemitic and neo-Nazi overtones. The Russians saw themselves as victims of some mysterious conspiracy organized by the abominable Elders of Zion and supported by various 'citizens of Caucasian nationality', 'cosmopolitans', and other such transcendental 'enemies of the Russian people'.

To date (1993), this new antisemitism has remained a purely Russian phenomenon; it has not emerged in the new republics of Ukraine and Lithuania which were formerly somewhat notorious for their antisemitism. It has become apparent that this radical antisemitism is weak and not influential, and that the rumours of pogroms are an indication of the high level of fear among Jews rather than a tangible and dangerous reality. Even in Russia, where antisemitism did re-emerge, its real incidence has been nothing like as widespread or as intense as the popular stereotype in the West would indicate. This is quite clear from the results of a sociological survey conducted among Jewish activists in Russia in 1992, as indicated in Table 1.

Moreover, such antisemitism as has emerged in Russia in recent years has not been supported by the state, neither before *perestroika* nor following it. Even after the coup in August 1991, Jews had no reason to think that they must start to flee to save their lives. Consequently, after the first panic caused by the demise of the Soviet regime was over, Jewish emigration also started to decrease. In 1992 it had stabilized at some 60,000 emigrants to Israel, and roughly the same number to Western countries, mainly to the United States and Germany. This is undoubtedly quite a high number, but the reasons for emigration are not those popularly perceived in the West. Only 5 per cent of the Jewish activists questioned in the survey cited above considered antisemitism to be the main factor behind the exodus of Jews,

Table 1. Frequency of Antisemitic Incidents Experienced by Jewish Activists, 1992 (percentages)

Circumstance	Frequency		
	Often	Rare	Never
In the street, in public transport, in a queue	11.6	41.9	41.9
While at school	1.7	20.9	61.6
In government offices	3.5	25.6	58.1

Source: V. D. Shapiro and V. Chervyakov, *Results of the Survey among Delegates of the First Congress of the Federation of Jewish Communities and Organizations of Russia (the Va'ad of Russia), April 1992, Nizhniy Novgorod* (Moscow: Jewish Research Centre – Russian Academy of Sciences, 1992), 15.

while 47 per cent cited the economic crisis and the decline in living standards, and 23 per cent cited political instability.

WHO ARE THE POST-SOVIET JEWS?

Since the stereotypes are evidently inadequate to explain current realities in the former Soviet Union, let us now consider the backgrounds and identities of various Soviet Jews: who and what are they, and what makes them feel Jewish?

The last Soviet census, in 1989, recorded a Jewish population of 1,487,000. A Jew, for the purposes of that census, was someone who declared himself or herself as such to the census enumerator. This figure is not necessarily identical with the number of people defined as Jews in their internal passports (a figure that has never been published), but the two numbers are probably close. This 'passport nationality' was acquired in the Soviet Union at the age of 16. If both parents were of the same nationality the child inherited that nationality automatically, but if they were of different nationalities he or she had the opportunity to choose between them. Usually, however, the child would adopt the nationality of the mother.

The 1989 figures indicate that there has been rapid decline in the numerical strength of Soviet Jewry. The reasons usually given for this are the emigration that started in the early 1970s and the low birth-rates associated with city life. However, to understand the real source of this process one has to consider also Sergio DellaPergola's model of 'core' and 'enlarged' Jewry, as explained in Chapter 3 of this volume. The enlarged population is much more numerous than the core, in that it includes not only all those who have some kind of Jewish pedigree, both by descent or by marriage, but also any non-Jews who have been incorporated into a Jewish milieu (for example, through enlarged family or other household connection). The Jewish identity of this enlarged population is thus defined situationally—that is, it is dependent on the political and social context. People whose identification with Jewry is solely within the bounds of this enlarged category and does not touch the core are flexible in their cultural, religious, and social behaviour and tend to blend easily into non-Jewish environments; they would be unlikely to declare themselves as Jews to census enumerators.

One of the most remarkable processes in the contemporary diaspora is the demographic decrease in the number of core Jews. Well established in the developed Western countries, it is even more pronounced in contemporary eastern Europe. An outspoken demographer of Soviet Jewry, Mark Tolts, predicted in 1992 on the basis of census data and other demographic statistics that the Jewish population of the former Soviet Union would completely disappear within twenty to twenty-five years because of such depopulation. But this can be applied only to the core Jewish population as approximately defined by the 1989 census. The size of the enlarged Jewish population in the former Soviet Union is difficult to define (although there are certain indicators that can facilitate estimation), but it is certainly much greater than the core Jewry since it includes all the people who may identify themselves as Jews in certain circumstances.

One reason why estimating the size of this enlarged Jewish population is so difficult, of course, is that 'enlarged Jewry' is not an official entity—although there *are* several legal categories that may be applied to define the Jews of the former Soviet Union. A brief review of these will illustrate the complexity of the situation.

1. *'Census' Jews.* The official definition of a Jew for census purposes, as described above, is useful only for purposes of collective estimation; it cannot be used for identifying individuals since the census is anonymous. Moreover, in using census figures one must remember that when the census was conducted in January 1989, the psychological climate was still very Soviet, in the sense that the majority of Soviet stereotypes, values, fears, and phobias were still firm. Among them was a fear of being Jewish, of belonging to a group that was considered by the authorities as disloyal to the state. It can therefore be taken for granted that the majority of those who could be considered to be in the enlarged category did not at that time identify themselves as Jews. Given that the widespread attitude of the intelligentsia towards the early *perestroika* then in place was a refusal to accept that the regime was capable of reforming itself, the approximately 1.5 million Jews who identified themselves as such in the census were undoubtedly what DellaPergola would consider 'core Jews'.

2. *'Passport' Jews.* Another official way of defining a Jew is by the nationality registered in his or her passport, the criterion for which, as explained above, is socio-biological. There are several problems with this, however. On the one hand, this definition has nothing to do with traditional Jewish standards for affiliation. Second, the possible negative consequences of having a Jewish identity in the Soviet Union must have led many people who were Jewish only in the enlarged sense to avoid official registration as Jews in their passports. Thus, in contrast to the tendency in the wider Soviet society, the offspring of mixed marriages tended overwhelmingly to be registered according to the nationality of their non-Jewish parent, although probably more, up to almost 50 per cent, registered themselves as Jewish in mixed marriages when one of the parents (normally the father) was a Mountain Jew.

The fact that the offspring of mixed marriages disguised their Jewish heritage in this way did not in fact mean that they were invisible as Jews in the Soviet social context. The average Soviet non-Jew considers as Jewish anybody who has some kind of link to Jews or Judaism. The offspring of mixed marriages would thus normally be considered Jewish in the wider society, regardless of what their passport says. The children of a Jewish father would be more visible than those of a Jewish mother because of the patronymic Russian naming model: if a Jewish father called Israel Rabinovich and his non-Jewish wife call their son, in a very non-Jewish way, Ivan or Sergei, the child would be called Ivan (or Sergei) Israelevich Rabinovich; whatever his passport says, everybody would consider him Jewish. Correspondingly, Jewish identity would be less obvious where it is the mother who is Jewish.

Another reason why the passport nationality is not necessarily a reliable ways of identifying Jews is that the offspring of mixed marriages are not the only ones who have tried historically to disguise their Jewish ancestry in the official records: according to unpublished estimates prepared by Mark Kupovetsky, the leading demographer of Soviet Jewry, several hundred biologically 'pure' Jews have succeeded in different ways (war-time confusion, bribery, forgery, etc.) in getting themselves registered as being of a different nationality, which they then transmitted to their descendants.

3. *'Halakhic' Jews.* Another criterion of Jewish identity is that determined by Jewish law, the *halakhah*, which acknowledges as Jewish either a person born of a Jewish mother who has not converted to another religion, or a person converted to Judaism. Until the late 1980s, when the mass *aliyah* made large numbers of former Soviet Jews familiar with the Israeli norms of registering nationality and alerted them to issues of *halakhah*, this definition was virtually unknown in the Soviet Union.

Since matters of *halakhah* were of little concern, marriage patterns among the Ashkenazi Jews who comprised the majority of Soviet Jewry followed the general Soviet secular pattern; various studies have shown that mixed marriages were common among both sexes, with the percentage slightly higher in males. The consequences of this for the Jewish affiliation of any offspring have been discussed above. Among the Oriental Jewish communities of the Bukharan and Mountain Jews (according to my field notes in the mid-1980s), the tendency was to incorporate into the Jewish community just those born of a Jewish father, leaving the offspring of Jewish women married to non-Jewish husbands to other confessions.

The new awareness of *halakhah* that developed in the Soviet Union in the late 1980s led to the creation of a new terminology: *halakhic Jew*, for those people born of a Jewish mother and non-Jewish father; *non-halakhic Jews*, for those born of a Jewish father and a non-Jewish mother; and *full Jew*, for people born of two Jewish parents.

Incidentally, the arrival in Israel of quite a lot of people who were at least potentially acknowledged as Jews in the Soviet Union but not in the Jewish state added to other tensions caused by the hasty absorption of the Soviet Jews in Israel. For example, there arose a problem of where to bury the offspring of Jewish fathers and Gentile mothers—'Jews' by Soviet definition, but not for the religious authorities in Israel. Originally they were sent to Christian (i.e. Arab) cemeteries, until finally the Israeli government allotted a vast piece of ground between Ashdod and Ashkelon for those people, thus creating a new type of cemetery in the Holy Land.

4. *'Law-of-Return' Jews.* Another legal basis for defining a person as a Jew is that embedded in Israel's Law of Return, which gives the right of repatriation to every Jew and his or her family members (Jewish and non-Jewish) in two descending generations. A 'Jew' is defined for this purpose according to the 1970 Amendment to the Law of Return as a person born of a Jewish mother and not confessing another religion, or a person converted to Judaism. Although once in Israel the non-halakhically Jewish relatives of a repatriate are in fact registered as non-Jews, the popular understanding of the law among Soviet Jews inside the former Soviet Union somehow subsumes under the category 'Jew' all those able to claim repatriation to Israel under the Law of Return. This is probably because this definition of 'Jew' practically coincides with the spontaneous definition of 'Jew' in the broader Soviet society. The same understanding was and still is widespread among the Soviet Jews who, being significantly secularized and acculturated, had simply acquired non-Jewish notions of who is a Jew.

SOVIET JEWRY: THE SUB-ETHNIC GROUPS

The nature of Jewish identity in the former Soviet Union is further complicated by the complexities of the sub-ethnic composition of the Jewish population. It comprises an Ashkenazi majority, three sizeable non-Ashkenazi ('Oriental') subgroups and three smaller but none the less identifiable Oriental subgroups.

The Ashkenazim comprise about 90 per cent of all Jews in the former Soviet Union. They form the absolute majority of the Jews in Russia proper, in all the European republics of the former Soviet Union, in Armenia, and in Kyrgyzstan. The common Western stereotypes of Russian Jewry—the *shtetl* culture, the way of behaviour, the *luftmensh* mentality, and so on—all derive from an Ashkenazi frame of reference, and moreover one that is long out of date. In reality, the *shtetls* have long been abandoned for Moscow, St Petersburg, Kiev, and Odessa, all of which had Jewish populations in excess of or close to 100,000 persons until successive waves of emigration began to have their effect. The Ashkenazim are in fact typical city dwellers: highly educated, mostly secularized and acculturated, and with small families (as reflected in the sharp decrease in population). The language of the Ashkenazim is no longer Yiddish, but Russian: in Israel they are normally referred to as *rusim*, in the United States as 'Russians'.

The second largest sub-ethnic group was the Bukharan or Central Asiatic Jews, who numbered about 80,000–90,000 on the eve of the mass *aliyah* of 1989–91. They speak Judaeo-Tajik (a Jewish vernacular of Persian), and to a large extent retain traditional patterns of everyday culture (as do the other Oriental Jewish groups). Their main concentration is in Uzbekistan, where there were historically two main centres of settlement: the Zeravshan oasis, with the cities of Samarkand and Bukhara; and the Ferghana oasis, where the main Jewish centres concentrated in Margelan, Kokand, and Khudzhand. From there the Bukharan Jews migrated to all the adjacent countries: to Kazakhstan (the Tchimkent and Qyzylorda areas), Tajikistan (Dushanbe), Turkmenistan (particularly to the eastern part of the republic), and to a lesser extent to Kyrgyzstan (the Osh–Jalal Abad area). In the *perestroika* and post-*perestroika* eras they have largely resettled in Israel; several thousands have also established themselves in Vienna, and in Queens in New York.

Another major Oriental community are the Mountain Jews (Tats) of the eastern Caucasus, who at the end of the 1980s were around 55,000 strong.

They speak several specific dialects of the Iranian Tati language which together form a Judaeo-Tat dialectal cluster. Their daily behaviour follows religious norms; the synagogue is still the centre of the community. Like the Bukharans they live among Muslims: in Azerbaijan (main centres in Baku and Quba) and in the north Caucasus republics of the Russian Federation (Daghestan, Kabarda, North Ossetia, Chechnya), and in the Caucasian Mineral Water resorts area. Those who lived in Chechnya migrated in 1992, partly to Israel and partly to Nalchik in Kabarda and Pyatigorsk. The contemporary direction of emigration of the Mountain Jews is predominantly to Israel.

The third sizeable Oriental group are the Georgian Jews, who numbered before the mass *aliyah* about 15,000. They speak standard Georgian and share the main cultural traits of their Christian compatriots. Like the other Oriental groups they have retained the external features of Judaism and see their religion as the prime factor distinguishing them from their fellow Georgians. Their main centres now are in the big Georgian cities of Tbilisi and Kutaisi. The small *shtetls* populated mainly by Jews (Kulashi, Oni, and others) ceased to be predominantly Jewish settlements as Jews left the country, mainly for Israel, in the course of the emigration of the 1970s–80s.

There are also three minor Oriental Jewish groups. The Tatar-speaking Krymchaks, who number about 2,000, live dispersed in the cities of Crimea (Simferopol, Yevpatoria), as well as in Novorossiyck, Moscow, St Petersburg, and, until recently, in Sukhumi. The Aramaic-speaking Lakhlukha form part of the Kurdistani Jews; some 1,200 still live in Tbilisi and Alma-Ata in Kazakhstan, to which they were banished by Stalin in the years following the First World War. A small group of Iranian–Afghan Jews from Herat and Mashhad live in south-eastern Turkmenistan in the cities of Bayram-Ali and Iyolotan.

PLURAL JEWISH IDENTITIES

The existence of different backgrounds and ethnic origins among the former Soviet Jews presupposes pluralism in identity. Moreover, the policy of state antisemitism had the effect of reinforcing assimilatory tendencies and Russianization, particularly among the Ashkenazim. This process is now ongoing, and even the abolition of state antisemitism cannot stop it completely. It was formerly to some extent hampered by the passport registration of nationality, but the government of the Russian Federation has now announced its intention to stop registering nationality in its new identity documents. That will in itself have major implications for the existence of a Jewish identity in Russia, which has so far always been non-voluntary (except for children of mixed marriages). It still continues to be so in Israel. Once Jews are not compelled to identify as Jews and there is no state antisemitism to endanger their very existence, there will almost certainly be an erosion in Jewish identity. The consequent uncertainty and arbitrariness in identity, and the multiplicity of ethnic affiliations that will be created where a Jewish identity merges with other cultural and social groupings, will undoubtedly lead to an increase in the number of people who are part of an extended Jewry. Let us remember that current social and demographic trends in the Western diaspora predict the growth of enlarged Jewry at the expense of the core; once the Russian government abandons the passport registration of nationality, as it has proposed, this will certainly stimulate the expansion of this category in Russia too.

The reaction of the various Oriental groups towards state persecution was different from that of the Ashkenazim. Having retained to some extent their communal structure, they reacted as a community rather than as a group of individuals. They tried either to isolate themselves in small, walled settlements, or to persuade the authorities in different ways of their loyalty to the state. Extreme cases of such behaviour were the attempts of the Mountain Jews, the Krymchaks, and the Karaites to proclaim themselves as separate peoples not having any ties with the Jews. Only the Karaites succeeded in this, but in so doing they totally alienated themselves from the rest of Jewry. After *perestroika* the Oriental Jews participated more intensively in migrations than the Ashkenazim, largely because they were living either among Muslims whom they feared or in areas of ethnic unrest and war, like Tajikistan, Abkhazia, and Azerbaijan, where they are endangered as a part of the civil population. Criminal intimidation and threats also combined to push them out from the areas that they had inhabited from time immemorial.

On the other hand there were factors stimulating ethnic consolidation among Jews. The major factor has been that the successor countries of the former Soviet Union are increasingly concerned with ethnicity. The movement for national self-determination of the former Soviet republics that started in 1989 led finally in 1991 to the formation of fourteen 'nation-states' and one multi-ethnic quasi-empire—the Russian Federation. The fourteen states are very different. They represent the whole spectrum of ethnic and nationalistic approaches, from hyperethnic Latvia and Estonia, on the one hand, which have denied some non-aboriginal ethnic groups the right to citizenship, to Ukraine on the other, which is based on a concept of civic nations. But all these countries have a legal notion of 'ethnic/national minority', which at least theoretically presupposes the existence of a locally defined 'ethnic/national majority'. Practically all the new 'national states' not only introduced the concept of a minority but also passed legislation protecting various minority rights. Normally the legislative package includes protection of the national language, certain educational and cultural rights, the possibility of forming ethnic or ethno-confessional communities, and so on. These rights more or less coincide with the Minorities part of the third basket of the agreement reached by the CSCE (Conference on Security and Co-operation in Europe). Nowhere, however, do they include the famous right to political self-determination that served as the pretext for all these countries' liberation.

The Jews, formerly regarded as part of the Russian-speaking majority, suddenly found themselves in the situation of being a minority. This in itself acted as a stimulus to consolidation and community formation. It turned out that an arbitrary plural identity is not a defensive tool in a national state. Jews are faced with the alternative of either 'repatriating' to Israel—where they will again form a part of a minority, the *rusim*—or staying as a minority in their old countries. Both alternatives are attractive to certain groups of Jews. Although there are a considerable number of Jews who seek their way to the non-nationalist West, mainly to the USA, it should not be forgotten that diaspora Jews have typically always identified with the empires in which they lived. They showed their loyalty to the Russian empire by speaking Russian in the Ukraine—just as Jews were loyal to Turkish ways of behaviour in the Balkans in the declining Ottoman empire, and were among the greatest German and French patriots in the nineteenth and twentieth centuries.

Allegiance to the psychology of empire still prevails in the territory of the former Soviet Union within the Russian Federation. First, the Federation remains a multi-ethnic entity, as the Soviet Union was. All the autonomous republics and autonomous regions of the former Soviet Russian Federative Republic except the Jewish autonomous province in Birobidzhan have renamed themselves republics and now also bear the somewhat dubious additional denomination 'subjects of the Federation'. In fact, they resemble very much the former Soviet republics; the threat of dissolution is still present, this time along the borders of the new 'subjects'. Some of these subjects demonstrate separatist strategies: along with the practically independent Chechnya there are the highly separatist Tatarstan, Bashkortostan (former Bashkiria), and Sakha-Yakutia. On the other hand, such republics as Moldova, North Ossetia, Udmurtia, and others remain strongholds of the Communist *nomenklatura*, so that the ethnic factor in their policy is not so much pronounced. Still others, like Kalmykia-Khalmg under its new young president, proclaimed loyalty to the Federation, and at the same time to democracy and to a free market economy. In fact all these 'subjects' are but new 'national states', like the former Soviet republics. The only difference lies in the fact that they are still incorporated in the Federation; the problems they face are more or less similar. They have introduced legal notions of 'aboriginal peoples' and their rights, and other 'minorities'. It is no coincidence that Jewish cultural groups find more protection and support in the 'subjects', such as Kabardino-Balkaria, North Ossetia, Tatarstan, or Yakutia, than in ordinary Russian districts.

But the Federation consists not only of thirty-one national 'subjects' but also of an amorphous bulk of 'Russian' areas, which cover at least half the territory and shelter the major part of the population. In that sense, the Russian Federation again resembles very much the Soviet Union: Russia proper was never politically singled out, and in symbolizing the Union was in fact deprived of its national self-identity. The same situation continues now, confirming the 'empire' nature of the Russian state. Russia has not introduced legal concepts of majority and minority, and Russia is not protecting minorities' rights because of the absence of minorities themselves. Jews are not a minority, but one of the peoples of the Federation. At the same time Russia is not proclaiming itself a national state—that is, it is not a state of the Russians; even to distinguish the ethnic Russians, *Russkiye*, from the Russians as a nation in its civic understanding, a new term has spontaneously come into existence in recent years: *Rossiyane*.

In Russia proper, the Jews are but a part of the *Rossiyane*; hence, their identity remains more amorphous and arbitrary than elsewhere. It does not mean that there is no chance of establishing a proper Jewish community in the Russian Federation. On the contrary, here the Jews are the most numerous, and also the most educated and organized; but on the other hand, the imbalance between the size of the expanded Jewish population and that of the core is also highest here. To strengthen national consolidation among the Russian Jews one would have to transform the very nature of the Russian state. But that in itself would result in the growth of Russian nationalism and antisemitism, with the consequence that Jews would leave the country instead of consolidating.

There are several strategies now open to the Jews in the former Soviet Union, none of them mutually exclusive. 'Repatriation'—*aliyah*—attracts those who find themselves amidst armed conflicts, as well as the elderly, the Zionists, and some Orthodox Jews. A second option, emigration to the Western democracies, is likely to become more restricted in its availability because of fear on the part of the Western countries that accepting economic refugees will undermine the very values they are trying to defend. The third option is for the Jews to stay where they are and to defend themselves by building a communal structure. In the course of history, this alone has proved to be a reliable device for preserving the unique heritage of Jewish civilization.

CHAPTER TEN

Constructing New Identities in the Former Soviet Union: The Challenge for the Jews

IGOR KRUPNIK

THE recent disintegration of the monolithic Soviet state into fifteen independent republics was the most dramatic change in the history of Europe since the Second World War. The consequences of this collapse for the Jews who comprised what was formerly known as 'Soviet Jewry' are still to be analysed, although some public attention has been focused on such urgent issues as inter-ethnic violence, antisemitism, and emigration. My focus here is rather different, for it concerns the nature of the new Jewish communities and Jewish identities in the independent states that are now in the process of being constructed throughout the former Soviet Union.

The key factors influencing that process are the nature of the former 'Soviet' Jewish identity; the differential rates of population loss in the Holocaust, and more recently through emigration, in the various areas; and the social niche that the Jews occupied in the former Soviet republics. As a prelude to addressing the whole question of the challenges that constructing new, post-Soviet identities poses to Jews in the former Soviet Union, I shall consider each of these factors in turn.

JEWISH IDENTITY IN THE FORMER SOVIET UNION

Jewish identity in the former Soviet Union was the product of manipulation and social engineering by the Communist state over many decades. Before the revolution of 1917, the Jewish population of the Russian empire had seen itself as an ethno-religious entity, and the authorities had likewise seen Jews primarily as members of a religious community. Beyond the quotas that had allowed some Jews to enter universities and certain professions, the only official way in which individual Jews could achieve higher social status, unrestricted residence mobility, and greater opportunities was by converting to Christianity.

Under the Soviet state, the virulent antireligious stand of the Communist regime quickly deprived Jews (and other nations) of the religious basis of their identity and sought instead to develop the secular components of that identity. This ethnic and cultural base was first and foremost promoted by recognizing Jews as an ethnic group ('nationality') with an 'ethnic' language of their own, Yiddish. Yiddish-speaking schools received state support, as did various forms of Yiddish cultural activities. The state also tried to manipulate the social structure of the Jewish population through policies aimed at creating a true Jewish proletariat, and even a 'socialist' Jewish peasantry: in the late 1920s and early 1930s the government established five Jewish 'national districts' in the Ukraine and the Crimean peninsula, then part of Russia, to stimulate Jewish agricultural colonization. Even more resources were poured into Jewish agricultural resettlement projects in Birobidzhan in eastern Siberia. In the latter area, a Jewish National Region (*oblast*) was created in 1934 as a major 'ethnic heartland' for Soviet Jews, and a potential Jewish republic.[1] The smaller non-Ashkenazi ('Oriental') Jewish communities in the Caucasus, the Crimean peninsula, and central Asia— Georgian Jews, Mountain Jews, Krymchaks, Bukharan Jews, and others— were also granted for a brief period similar policies of agricultural resettlement, social engineering, and cultural support.[2]

But by the late 1930s the state policy had changed. Most of the state-engineered innovations, including Jewish schools, periodicals, theatres, cultural and academic institutions, and even the local Jewish districts, other than those of the remote Birobidzhan in Siberia, were shut down. All visible manifestations of Jewish culture were effectively destroyed, with the consequence that Soviet Jewish identity was completely deprived of external supporting elements that could reinforce Jewish self-awareness. Jews continued to be registered as such in domestic and official papers, from school and job applications to internal passports, and also in censuses, and in this way they continued to constitute an officially recognized minority. In effect, for the vast majority of Jews in the former Soviet Union the genealogical or racial criterion was the only component of Jewish identity.

The policy of cultural and institutional deprivation had its prime impact in the larger industrial cities of eastern Ukraine and Russia, among the hundreds of thousands of Ashkenazi Jewish migrants from the former Pale of Jewish Settlement who had settled in these areas in the 1920s and 1930s. The situation was somewhat different in the western areas that were annexed by the Soviet Union in 1939–40—the Baltic states, western Ukraine and western Belorussia, Bessarabia, and other territories. Through this annexation the Soviet state received not only about a million new Jewish citizens, but also a well-established network of Jewish religious, educational, and even political institutions, all of which had mushroomed during the inter-war period. The Jews of the western Soviet Union thus had a much stronger cultural basis on which to build their ethnic identity.[3] Some of the non-Ashkenazi groups, particularly the Georgian and Bukharan Jews, were somewhat less subject to government pressure, and were thus also able to maintain the integrity of their communal life more than the Jews of Russia and eastern Ukraine were.

The Jews were not the only ethnic group in the former Soviet Union to face this challenge to their identity in the late 1930s. Mass migration, urbanization, the boom in mixed marriages, and other social processes spurred the rise of a new generation of Soviet citizens. The ethnic identity of millions of individuals of various ethnic origins was gradually weakened as a result of government policies of modernization and of separating people from their cultural legacy and ethnic roots. For the Jews, these processes were compounded by their very high level of urban acculturation, and later by the outcomes of Nazi genocide and by the anti-Jewish Stalinist purges of the 1940s and early 1950s.

Together, these were critical elements in determining the way in which Jewish identity in the Soviet Union would evolve: an ethnicity without an ethnic language (the knowledge of Yiddish and other Jewish languages substantially dwindled); without Judaism as a religion or way of life; without major cultural markers such as rituals, education, and public performances; without community organizations; and even without deep historical roots and memory. The process reached a peak in the 1960s when hundreds of thousands of individuals of the second Soviet-raised Jewish generation came of age and were absorbed into the urbanized, white-collar, Russian-speaking population found throughout the former Soviet Union.

THE DEMOGRAPHIC CONSEQUENCES OF THE HOLOCAUST AND EMIGRATION

An important factor in transforming Jewish identity in the former Soviet Union was the high losses among Soviet Jews as a consequence of Nazi genocide in the Second World War. These losses were not evenly distri-buted, either geographically or in terms of the age-groups that were affected, with the result that the demographic consequences were even more devastat-ing than the figures alone indicate.

Of the 2.5 million Jews who perished within Soviet territory, according to estimates recently prepared by an expert on Soviet Jewish demography,

Mark Kupovetzky, the rate of survival was the lowest in the newly annexed areas along the western border of the country (with the exception of Moldova and Estonia): 92 per cent of the Jews in Latvia were murdered, as were 88 per cent in Lithuania, and about 90 per cent in western Ukraine. Further east, the rate of survival was much higher. About one-half of the pre-war Jewish population of Ukraine (as defined by its 1939 boundaries) and of the western provinces of Russia occupied by the Nazis survived the Holocaust, whether by escaping as refugees, by being evacuated, or through military service.[4]

After the war, the Jewish population of the western areas of the Soviet Union was partly replenished by Jewish refugees returning from the east and by returning survivors, but neither the numerical strength of the pre-war Jewish communities nor their former composition was ever fully regained. Simply stated, the bulk of the original Yiddish-speaking residents had been murdered. Those who had managed to survive by escaping the ghettos and Nazi round-ups were barely representative of the former whole. First, except for Red Army soldiers and a few partisans, those who survived were predominantly young people, teenagers, and children, and particularly those who were less easily identified as Jewish—those with blond hair who were fluent in local dialects and had non-Jewish names—and who had found it easier to pass as Slavs and take refuge among the local population. Girls generally had better chances of survival than boys.[5] The elderly were mostly doomed.

The Jewish population of the western part of the Soviet Union after the war therefore comprised two main components. A minority were indigenous Jews—a few evacuees, some former soldiers, and the younger and more assimilated members of the original local communities who had succeeded in surviving the war. The bulk comprised Jews from elsewhere in Russia and southern and eastern Ukraine who had moved west in consequence of the Soviet policy in the 1940s and 1950s of establishing industries and institutions in these newly annexed areas. The newcomers were highly acculturated and predominantly Russian-speaking. They rarely formed any community bonds with the local Jews, with whom they in fact had hardly anything in common. Post-war census figures relating to the 'Jewish population' in the Baltic republics or in western Ukraine are thus greatly misleading: as much as 80 or 90 per cent were not local Jews at all but newcomers, mostly of east Ukrainian or east Belorussian origin.

This post-war transformation of the Soviet Jewish communities was intensified by the decades of emigration that followed. The local Jews of the western territories were more eager to leave than the assimilated newcomers were, and they formed a disproportionately high share of those who fled the country, especially in the 1970s. Even though they had been through the Soviet school system and were fully socialized in Soviet society, the generation of 'western Jews' born after the war still had greater Jewish knowledge and consciousness than their counterparts in eastern Ukraine or the Russian Federative Republic. The same was true of the smaller central Asian communities—the Georgian, Bukharan, and Mountain Jews—whose numbers also dwindled in the 1970s due to emigration.

The Jews who survived the Holocaust and those who preferred to stay rather than to emigrate thus both demonstrate greater acculturation and integration into mainstream Soviet life than those who perished or left. The fact that the terms 'Russian' and 'Soviet' Jewry have often been used as synonyms is actually not that misleading: by the 1970s, more than 80 per cent of 'Soviet Jewry' was the product of a Russian-focused Soviet culture.[6]

THE SOCIAL NICHES OF SOVIET JEWS

It is widely recognized that Jews have a higher level of general education than any other Soviet ethnic population, and have proportionately the highest share of graduate professional and white-collar workers. Data from the 1989 census show that among able-bodied Jews, the ratio of college graduates is 35–50 per cent, and in Moscow and some other urban areas as much as 65 per cent. Graduate professionals (academics, technicians, and so on) and white-collar workers comprise up to 60 per cent of the Jewish labour force, and in Moscow even up to 85 per cent.[7] Soviet Jewry was highly successful in utilizing the Soviet education system to achieve social mobility otherwise controlled and limited by the state.

What is rarely commented on in this highly impressive picture of Soviet Jewry (which is as well-educated and professionally skilled as American Jews are and shows much better educational performance than the bulk of the Israeli population), is the extent to which it depended upon involvement in the Russian-speaking educational system at every stage. Jewish parents all over the country constantly sought better high-schools for their children, and in the former Soviet Union these were predominantly institutions whose teaching was in Russian. There was likewise a disproportionately high percentage of Jews among students at colleges and universities with Russian-based programmes. The consequent Jewish input to Russian-speaking society was especially noticeable in the provincial Russian cities and in the national republics, where there were Jewish professors and teachers of everything from nuclear physics to violin—but first and foremost of Russian language, literature, and history. And almost always they taught in Russian rather than in local languages.

The factors listed above act as major indicators of present Jewish realities in the former Soviet Union. In general terms, the 'divorce' turned out surprisingly well. The independent republics have proved, with a few exceptions, to be viable political entities, even though their economies and political systems are in turmoil. Russia, on the other hand, whether due to its economic problems or the wisdom of its current leadership, does not seek actively to reintegrate its former empire. This has given the fifteen ex-partners in the Soviet divorce process the opportunity to distance themselves from each other.

This last factor is important because an essential part of the process of making this political divorce irreversible is for each state to construct its own new identity. This includes the construction of symbols that can communicate this identity powerfully to its citizens: national militaries, ministries, academic and scientific institutions, currencies, and so on. In addition, building the markers of independent statehood requires the recruitment of an enormous new national bureaucracy so as to overturn the Russian-dominated power pyramid of the Soviet period. In the process there are winners and losers; and everywhere it is Russians and other so-called 'Russian-speakers' who are the losers.

Although the Jews were never fully associated with the former power structures, they are also among the losers. First, as their former social niche mostly kept them out of military and government positions, their network of contacts in this field is too small to allow them now significantly to penetrate it. Secondly, promotion decisions everywhere, except in Russia and Ukraine, are openly based on affirmative policies on behalf of the new majority nations and/or speakers of the native languages. Jews are greatly disadvantaged in this regard due to their previous concentration in the Russian-speaking social and educational systems.

BUILDING THE NEW IDENTITIES

Last, but probably foremost, the general political climate is generated by the new ideology of state-building. In most of the new republics, the population has been divided along the ethnic lines inherited from the former Soviet Union. The dominant ideology of state-building, therefore, is to consider ethnically alien residents as minority communities set apart from the main nation. The role of the new nation-state would then be to provide the minorities with a recognized status in order to promote their cultures and public life, support their native language, and so forth.

There is thus a dramatic gap between the expected status of the native population (the 'state nation') and the 'outsiders' in the very concept of the new identity to be built, and for the most part Jews would be classified as outsiders. The native residents are anxious to build their new nation-states on the basis of 'blood identity', with the status of a few recognized and loyal ethnic minorities constitutionally approved. The local Russians, and more generally those who are identified as 'Russian-speakers', are in favour of a 'territorial' state identity, with the right to citizenship based on residence.[8] These are philosophies of state-building and identity formation that are difficult to reconcile.

Building identities that accord with the newly established nation-state lines is a jerky and disruptive process for every group involved, but especially for minorities. For Jewish communities in some of the new independent republics it is an extremely ambiguous task. For example, the new Jewish communities of Kazakhstan, Kyrgyzstan, or Turkmenistan are highly artificial entities—several hundred tightly knit local Bukharan Jewish families and a far greater number of disparate and highly fragmented outsiders of Russian Jewish origin. The latter are mostly well-educated, Russian-speaking professionals; they have little in common with either the local Jews or the native Muslims and in fact prefer to associate themselves with the 'Europeans'—that is, primarily with local Russians and other Slavs.

In the current political climate, these 'new' Jewries face growing pressure to demonstrate their new loyalties and to organize as defined minorities along the new state lines. Though the same pressure is also placed upon a few other predominantly Russian-speaking minorities in central Asia (such as the Germans, Volga and Crimean Tartars, and so forth), these groups demonstrate a higher level of inner cohesion than the Jews do and greater distance from the local Russians.

While the newly independent states are anxious to build a full set of new ethnic élites and bureaucracies, they are even more anxious to promote their ethnic languages: language was a ground for bitter confrontation from the very start of the Soviet ethnic movements in the 1980s, and the disintegration of the Soviet Union is seen as a victory of native languages over Russian. In all the new republics, the Russian media are shrinking, the official use of Russian is declining, and the educational system is undergoing rapid transition in favour of native languages. School and university curricula are controlled linguistically by government decree, parliamentary bill, or simply by pressure from newly appointed officials. This process threatens the professional niche occupied by the majority of the Russian Jews in the republics, and indeed the very strategy they followed for decades to acquire social mobility. So entrenched was Russian as the language of Soviet Jews that the language of public meetings, press communiqués, and official records of most of the Jewish organizations in the former Soviet Union wherever they are, remains Russian. Local attempts to shift to any other language often engender bitter splits.

The challenge of the present situation is quite obvious: the Soviet Jews can be said retrospectively to have made a 'cultural mistake'. Having allied themselves to the dominant state language as a path to social mobility in a multi-ethnic empire, when that empire began to disintegrate they found themselves in a cultural dead-end—much as the German-speaking Jews found that they had made a similar 'cultural mistake' when the Habsburg empire collapsed.[9] The new post-Soviet 'Jewries' struggling to construct their now-legitimized minority communities along nation-state lines (and sometimes with the full support of the local government) find themselves frustrated because their former affiliation with the Russians does not fit the new situation. In the hectic and fluid politics of the post-Soviet nation-states, the Jews are merely bystanders in the new identity-building process; they certainly are not in a position to influence the direction of change.

In reality, the majority of the Jewish communities of the independent states seem to share the political prospects of the local Russian population. And these are gloomy, at best, especially in central Asia and the Caucasus. Moreover, because of its current economic problems, Russia does not have the resources to accommodate even the smallest proportion of the potential migrants and refugees from these states, far less to support them in their present locations. Quick to recognize this, the new Russian activists and politicians in Moscow quickly narrowed the focus of their political rhetoric regarding the defence of the Russian ethnic minorities in the republics. The truth is that they have virtually abandoned other Russian-speaking communities, including the Ukrainians, Germans, Tartars, and Jews. Whether these people decide to stay or to move, they will have to rely on themselves.

As the former privileged status of the Russian population of the republics was challenged or overturned altogether, they were reduced to even greater frustration and political apathy.[10] In consequence, local democratic groups and sections of the main Russian political parties are both at an all-time low in their popularity. At the same time, the Russian Orthodox Church and the more militant groups stressing local roots, such as the Cossacks, gain growing support. Experts explain the rise of these new powers as the defensive reaction of frustrated Russian communities. As political forces, both the Orthodox Church and Cossack militants are known to be not very sympathetic to the Jews and unlikely to enter into political alliance with them or to grant them any protection.

The situation for the local Jews is even worse in republics like Moldova, Azerbaijan, or Tadjikistan, where hostile civil confrontations have become full-scale military activities. Open military clashes leave no room for neutrality or non-affiliation—always the Jews' preferred strategy. People must either follow the dominant pattern of bitter political confrontations or move out. In such a situation Jews have no option but to emigrate. By the end of 1991, those three republics, together with war-ravaged Armenia, had lost more than half their Jewish population as compared with that recorded in 1989 in the last Soviet census.[11]

THE FUTURE OF THE JEWS IN UKRAINE AND THE RUSSIAN FEDERATION

The prospects for Jews in Russia and Ukraine, the largest new states to have emerged from the former Soviet Union, differ from this general pattern. First, these two countries have the strongest Jewish communities, numbering several hundreds of thousands of people—actually about half a million each. (Even more if one adds people of mixed origin, and those who did not formerly identify themselves as Jews but are now regaining their roots.) As such, they both have enough human resources for political activity, leadership, community-building, and organized response in case of external challenge or political turmoil. Secondly, in both countries the Jews are a well-defined and highly individual ethnic and political entity with prospects of their own and not likely to be confused or lumped together with other minorities— 'Russian-speakers', 'outsiders', and so on—as is the case in many other territories of the former Soviet Union.

In both countries the governments are building new state identities on the basis of 'territorial citizenship' open to all local residents regardless of their ethnic origin. The new Ukrainian regime has a well-balanced minority policy that is specifically sensitive to the anxieties of local Russians and may be considered highly favourable to the Jews. Jewish communal facilities and educational and religious centres are springing up all over the new Ukraine, while Ukrainian leaders and intellectuals court local Jewish activists with appeals for friendship and co-operation.[12] These and other factors give the Jews a good chance of survival as an established national minority in the new Ukrainian state.

But it is Russian Jewry whose prospects for long-term existence are probably best. The transition to a new, post-Soviet identity will theoretically be easiest in Russia because there is little ground to be made up in terms of language and cultural affiliation, and little real transformation to be made in terms of loyalty and identity issues. Despite all the dramatic change that has occurred, the social environment in Russia turns out to be the most stable of all the former Soviet republics, and its long-term historical continuity the least challenged. And though Russia is the only new state where there is open political and grass-roots antisemitism, because it is a multi-ethnic society the Russian Jews can still follow the behavioural patterns and adaptive strategies with which they are familiar through their former Soviet experience. That is why the rate of Jewish emigration in 1989–90 was lower in Russia than in all the other former Soviet republics (with the exception of Georgia and Turkmenistan), and the situation in 1991 changed only slightly. Thus, whereas about 400,000 Jews emigrated to Israel in 1989–91 from the former Soviet Union, or 27.9 per cent of a Jewish population numbering 1.45 million at the time of the last Soviet census (January 1989), the corresponding rate for Russia proper was only 16.8 per cent. Ukraine, in comparison, lost 27.5 per cent, and the Chernobyl-damaged Belarus as much as 43.8 per cent.[13]

The new alignment of post-Soviet Jewish communities presents the same puzzle of political prospects and frustrations as do the other social fragments of the former empire. A truly autonomous and neutral strategy of Jewish survival, free from any local political interference, has not for the time being been realized. Jews are facing the same problems and questioning the same scenarios as most of the other minorities in the independent states, including the Russians in the new republics.

Historically speaking, there is nothing new for the Jews in the present situation. For example, quite a similar set of circumstances presented themselves with the collapse of the Habsburg empire after the First World War: there also, many Jews had made a cultural mistake in affiliating themselves too closely with the dominant language and culture. 'Soviet Jewry', however, is now a figment of history, as is the social system by which it was created. Those of its local fragments that survive the recent landslide will have to recombine in new amalgamations that will comprise new political entities—Russian, Ukrainian, and even Kazakhstan or Kyrgyzstan Jewries. The world will never be the same after the disintegration of the Soviet Union; that final judgement is as valid for the Jews as for everyone else.

Notes

1. See Binyamin Pinkus, 'The Extra-Territorial National Minorities in the Soviet Union, 1917–1939: Jews, Germans, and Poles', in E. Mendelson (ed.), *Jews and Other Ethnic Groups in a Multi-Ethnic World*, Studies in Contemporary Jewry (New York, 1987), 82–3.

2. See Michael Zand, 'Notes on the Culture of the Non-Ashkenazi Jewish Communities Under Soviet Rule', in Yaacov Ro'i and Avi Beker (eds.), *Jewish Culture and Identity in the Soviet Union* (New York, 1991), 391–415.

3. See Zvi Gitelman, *Becoming Israelis: Political Reconciliation of Soviet and American Immigrants* (New York, 1982), 81, 165 ff.

4. These figures are consistent with the population data provided by Sergio Della-Pergola in Ch. 3. According to his estimates, Ukrainian Jewry lost about 51 per cent of its pre-1939 population between 1939 and 1945, while the number of Jews in Russia was reduced from 903,000 to 860,000.

5. I am grateful for this information to Mr Daniel Romanovsky, now in Israel, who interviewed dozens of Holocaust survivors and local Slavic residents from eastern Belorussia in the 1980s.

6. At least, if judged according to the latest Soviet census of 1989, when 83.6 per cent of Soviet Jews declared Russian as their native language (89.1 per cent of the Russian Federation and 93.7 per cent in Moscow); see Mordechai Altshuler, 'Socio-Demographic Profile of Moscow Jews', *Jews and Jewish Topics in the Soviet Union and Eastern Europe*, 3:16 (1991), 34.

7. Mordechai Altshuler, 'Socio-Demographic Profile of Moscow Jews', 37; Viacheslav Konstantinov, 'Jewish Population of the USSR on the Eve of the Great Exodus', *Jews and Jewish Topics in the Soviet Union and Eastern Europe*, 3: 16 (1991), 54; Sergio DellaPergola, 'The Demographic Context of the Soviet Aliyah', ibid. 54.

8. This distinction was first coined by Helen Krag and Nikolai Vakhtin in their 'Report on the Political Situation in the Estonian Republic with regard to the Status of Ethnic Groups', St Petersburg, 1992.

9. I am grateful to Jonathan Webber for introducing me to this parallel. See Jonathan Webber, 'Modern Jewish Identities: The Ethnographic Complexities', *Journal of Jewish Studies*, 43: 2 (1992), 251, and his comments in Ch. 4 above.

10. The following analysis derives from several presentations delivered by academic experts from Russia and other republics at a conference on 'Russian Minorities in the Former Soviet Empire' organized in Washington DC by the Kennan Institute for Advanced Russian Studies in May 1992.

11. Yoel Florsheim, 'Immigration to Israel from the Soviet Union in 1991', *Jews and Jewish Topics in the Soviet Union and Eastern Europe*, 3: 9 (1992), 6.

12. On the new attitude towards Jews in Ukraine see Evgenii Golovakha and Natalia Panina, 'Jewish Cultural Activity in the Ukraine: Public Opinion and the Attitudes of Local Authorities', *Jews and Jewish Topics in the Soviet Union and Eastern Europe*, 2: 18 (1992), 5–12; Vladimir Levin, 'Jewish Topics in Ukrainian Literary Journals', ibid. 3: 19 (1992), 52–61.

13. See Florsheim, 'Immigration to Israel', 6. These figures, however, do not account for the Jews leaving for destinations other than Israel (about 100,000 in three years), nor do they make any distinction between the 'Law of the Return Jews' and the 'census Jews' in the former Soviet Union; see Mikhail Chlenov's article in this volume.

CHAPTER ELEVEN

Changes in Jewish Identity in Modern Hungary

ANDRÁS KOVÁCS

I N Hungary as elsewhere, the emancipation of the Jews at the end of the nineteenth century caused a tempestuous and conflict-ridden transformation of traditional Jewish identity and initiated the establishment of new identities. The old identities did not entirely disappear in this process, but they diversified; new identities appeared alongside the old ones in successive historical periods. In the nineteenth century, this simultaneous existence of different identities was often a source of fertile cultural conflict, inasmuch as it forced the various Jewish groups to continually restate their self-identification.

My intention in this paper is threefold: to outline the four phases of change in modern Jewish identity in Hungary; to describe the results of my field research into Jewish identity in Hungary in the post-war period; and to briefly consider the factors likely to affect modern Jewish identity there in the future.

1867–1918: THE SOCIAL CONTRACT OF ASSIMILATION

The process of Jewish emancipation in Hungary began at the end of the eighteenth century with the reforms of Emperor Joseph II. In 1867, the Hungarian parliament passed the Law of Emancipation, and in 1895 the process was completed with the enactment of a law that officially recognized the 'Israelite denomination' alongside other denominations—the so-called Law of Reception. Like many other advocates of Jewish emancipation in Central Europe, the liberal Hungarian aristocracy that had advocated the emancipation of the Jews, and the nobility more generally, expected that the Jews would rapidly assimilate—in fact, in moral terms they virtually required assimilation as a condition for emancipation. Initially, the Jews seemed inclined to comply with this requirement; Viktor Karady, writing in 1989, called this period the era of a 'social contract of assimilation'. In practice this meant a tacit agreement whereby the liberal Hungarian nobility supported the Jewish middle class in modernizing the economy—something which they were unable to achieve without the Jews' assistance—while arrogating all the political power to themselves. In consequence, the state afforded the Jews protection from the antisemitism elicited by their emancipation, and the Jews in turn afforded the state unconditional loyalty while trying at the same time to achieve total assimilation—which in turn strengthened the position of the Hungarians in the multi-ethnic Hungarian state.

The process of assimilation in this period was unbelievably fast. In 1881, 59 per cent of the Jews living in Hungary considered Hungarian to be their mother tongue; by 1891 the proportion was 75 per cent, and almost 86 per cent among children. According to another source, whereas in 1900 some 71 per cent of Jews were native speakers of Hungarian, and 75.5 per cent by 1910, the equivalent proportion among Catholics was 54.5 per cent. The intensity of assimilation is even better borne out by the fact that in 1900, whereas some 75 per cent of the Jews declaring themselves native speakers of Hungarian could also read and write the language, this was true of only 61 per cent of Catholic native speakers. Knowledge of the language was of course a major factor in accelerating assimilation. Another very important factor was the modernization of religious worship. By the end of the First World War, moderate Reform (the 'Neolog' movement) had replaced Orthodoxy as the dominant trend, and the associated secularization immensely accelerated the assimilation process. The progress of assimilation is also shown by the fact that more and more Jewish children were enrolled into state schools. The strongest indicator, however, of the speed with which assimilation occurred is that once the Law of Reception had been passed in 1895 and Jews and non-Jews were allowed to marry each other without conversion, the number of mixed marriages increased each year.

The progress of emancipation was such that by the end of the First World War, Jews were perceived, by themselves as well as by others, as being different to other Hungarians only in their religious denomination. In consequence, except for those Jews who insisted on maintaining their traditional Jewish identity, the Jews of Hungary became 'Jewish Hungarians', or 'Hungarians of the Mosaic faith', as opposed to 'Hungarian Jews'.

Quite a few great Jewish leaders of the period tried to move their community in this direction. For example, Dr Ferenc Mezey, director of the National Israelite Office, wrote in 1917: 'In our country, as in other countries, the Jews are trying to amalgamate completely into the community of the given nation and wish only to pursue different practices as far as religion is concerned.' And in the same year, Lajos Blau, director of the Franz Joseph

National Rabbinical Seminary in Budapest, declared: 'There is a Jewish problem if the non-Jews want it so, and there isn't one if they don't. The matter depends on them completely, the Jews can do nothing about it. There is no factual basis for it since the Jews are completely assimilated.'

1918–1944: A RETHINKING OF THE ASSIMILATION OPTION

The Jewish identity established during the liberal period was seriously shaken with the collapse of liberalism after the First World War because it had become apparent what the price of the social assimilation contract had actually been. The compromise that the Jews had made with the ruling aristocracy had denied them the political power consistent with their economic position, and furthermore ensured that even if their economic power grew they would not be able to achieve greater political power.

In the age of nationalism after the First World War, only people who were considered legitimate representatives of the nation had any chance of becoming members of the political élite. Thus, what guaranteed the continued political hegemony of the élite that had historically controlled Hungary was that the Jews could never be considered Hungarian, no matter how much they assimilated. This was achieved through an anti-modernist ideology that declared capitalism, liberal Western-type political structures, and the social and cultural consequences of modernization, such as urbanization or the formation of an urban mass culture, to be alien to the Hungarian tradition and mentality.

According to this ideology, the process of modernization that had begun in Hungary in the nineteenth century was not an authentic Hungarian development at all but had been imported by aliens, primarily Jews, and in the long run served their interests exclusively. In this view, Jewish assimilation was either superficial or illusory; the Jews had assumed a Hungarian disguise simply in order to gain more opportunities to repress the historical élite. Real assimilation was an impossibility because Jews and other aliens could not assume the Hungarian national character or mentality.

Thus, after the First World War, Hungarian antisemitism was no longer directed merely against Jewish immigrants who had come from Galicia with beards and caftans and resisted assimilation but against the middle class, 'cosmopolitan' Jewish citizens who had apparently assimilated into Hungarian society; according to the antisemitic rhetoric of the period, their presence caused an internal corrosion of the unified national character that none the less damaged its integrity and brought about its slow disintegration.

Notwithstanding this ideological reversal, the social amalgamation that had characterized the earlier period continued for some time. For example, the number of mixed marriages continued to increase until the enactment of antisemitic laws from 1938 on finally put an end to the process of assimilation. With political antisemitism becoming the prevalent ideology and with the acceptance of the 'ethnic nation' concept, Jews began to realize that assimilation would no longer protect them from discrimination. On the contrary: attempts to assimilate would strengthen those voices which demanded that the 'Jewish problem' should be solved by law and appropriate measures instituted against Jews perceived as overstepping the mark.

Understandably, these developments caused an identity crisis among assimilated Jews. Although by now already alienated from the Jewish tradition, they saw that they were still regarded as Jews. For many, the situation was intolerable. After almost a whole century of efforts to assimilate, very few opted for the psychological burden of resuming old traditions; Zionism (i.e. a modern, secular Jewish identity), which could in principle have offered an alternative, found very little resonance among them. A group of Jewish intellectuals did make some attempts to formulate a kind of organic double identity—'my blood is Jewish, my skin is Hungarian', as Aladár Komlós, a prominent Jewish essayist of the period, wrote. But the majority buried their heads in the sand and desperately tried to prove that their assimilation was genuine, refuting the arguments of their antisemitic protagonists while at the same time covering up their supposed Jewish qualities and habits. Thus, almost imperceptibly, new Jewish modes of behaviour began to emerge and form the basis of a new identity.

The momentum of this process was arrested, however, by the Nazi occupation of Hungary in the Second World War: between April and July 1944, some 490,000 Jews were deported from Hungary to the concentration camps of the Third Reich.

1944–1990: JEWISH IDENTITY IN COMMUNIST POST-WAR HUNGARY

Although many people believed that the assimilatory tendencies of Hungarian Jewry would change as a result of their wartime experiences, this did not in fact happen.

There were two main reasons for this. First, many of those who felt that events had proved the impossibility of assimilation in fact left Hungary after the war, as did those who did not want to settle in their old surroundings after their families had perished: about 25 per cent of the Jews who had survived the war had left Hungary by 1957. Second, the majority of the approximately 191,000 Jews who did remain in Hungary after the war belonged to the most assimilated strata. This was because the Nazi deportations had primarily affected the Jewish communities in the countryside, which were for the most part bastions of orthodoxy. In contrast, the Jews of Budapest, who were in any case more assimilated, were not systematically deported; moreover, in the chaos of a war-torn city, those who had the necessary financial means or better non-Jewish connections had a greater chance of survival. A good indicator of the predominance of assimilated Jews among the survivors is that about one-third of the Jewish population of 1945 had been baptized; among the young this proportion is even somewhat higher.

Several factors contributed to the intensification of assimilation after the war. First, since the greatest losses had been among the men and the young, the propensity to marry outside the Jewish community was extremely strong. Second, the political and social transformation that occurred in post-war Hungary under the Communists encouraged assimilation: the nationalization of property, the abolition of the old political institutions and public administration, and the radical transformation of the social structure following the great industrialization campaigns put an end to the bourgeoisie, the private economy, the system of private employment, and free intellectual careers. These were precisely the branches of the economy in which the Jews had typically worked before the war; many therefore lost their means of existence and had to find a new place in society. On the other hand, Jews were now eligible for positions that had previously been closed to them—for example, in the civil service and the army. A further contributory factor was that whereas there had previously been considerable differences between the Christian middle-class way of life and that of the Jews, the economic and political climate of the 1950s, and later the mass consumerism of the 1960s, led to a considerable extent to the blurring of such differences.

Social assimilation thus became commonplace again in Hungary after the Second World War, but the Jewish attitude to it was now fundamentally different. The Holocaust had forced all Jews into a community of fate, regardless of what group they had belonged to and what level of assimilation they had attained. In consequence, the attitude of the Jews who had survived the Nazi era was completely different from prevalent Jewish attitudes before the First World War or between the wars. The experience of persecution had moulded a new group consciousness.

Although one might have expected that the experiences of 1944 would have brought about wholesale adoption of the modern Jewish national identity advocated by the Zionist movement, this did not in fact happen to any meaningful extent. While Zionism did attain a certain popularity in the years following the war, especially among young people, the majority of those who remained in Hungary still favoured assimilation. However, this did not mean quite the same thing as it had before 1944 because the earlier ideal of assimilation within the Hungarian nation had now lost its credibility.

In consequence of the wartime experience, the more assimilated Jews again experienced an identity crisis. They had formerly considered themselves an integral part of the nation, but in 1944 they had seen how the majority of Hungarians had watched passively what was happening to their Jewish fellow countrymen, and how a minority had even facilitated the deportation and persecution of the Jews. Moreover it was not very difficult to find a link between the antisemitism that they had experienced and the 'ethnic nation' concept that had taken root in Hungary after the 1920s. Those who wanted to abandon their Jewish identity now had to find a new route to assimilation.

The route that some of these assimilationist Jews took was Communism. They believed that it would create a society where there would be no 'Jewish problem' and no antisemitism. Joining the Communist party, they thought, would assure them of an integration into society superior even to that which they had attempted to achieve before the war because the Communist programme sought to change not only the life of the Jews but the entire society. As the Communist Jewish hero of Ervin Gyertyán's novel *Szemüveg a porban* (Spectacles in the dirt), published in 1975 but set in the years after the Second World War, says: 'Jews and non-Jews, we are all the children of a bad and unjust society . . . that left its mark on us. We must all assimilate . . . to the new ideal of man. We must all transform into socialist people.' A great majority of the Jews who joined the Communist party did indeed believe that their new 'faith' would free them of their Jewishness: they held that only antisemites continued to regard them as Jews and they must sooner or later become the subject of the same transformation process.

The majority of Jews in fact never became Communists, but for them too 'integration within the nation' ceased to be the self-evident aim of assimilation: they too had learnt from their wartime experiences that they had remained Jewish in the eyes of the surrounding society not because they had not tried to assimilate but because the norms of society were such that they would never be able to rid themselves of their stigma. The result was that they developed a negative identity based on this stigma: Communist or not, they believed that it was only antisemitism that made them Jewish. And since the majority thought that they could have very little influence on shaping the ideology that defined the norms of assimilation, they adopted forms of behaviour (in part inherited from their parents) that would help them avoid social discrimination—a technique known as stigma management, a term introduced into the sociological literature by Irving Goffman.

There are two basic types of stigma management. If the stigmatizing feature is not known to the other person in a particular interaction, individuals may try to conceal it. If the stigmatizing feature is known, they will try to minimize the unpleasant consequences of the interaction. Both forms of behaviour were found to be characteristic of a group of Hungarian Jews investigated as part of a recent research project.

INVESTIGATING JEWISH IDENTITY IN CONTEMPORARY HUNGARY

Our research on Jewish identity in post-war Hungary, which focused on 117 Jewish families, was very much concerned with the types of stigma management mentioned above.

There are two basic types of stigma management, corresponding to whether the stigmatizing feature is known to others or not. Where the stigma is not known to others, one can try to pass oneself off as possessing a different identity—a technique known in the sociological literature as 'passing'. This may be done by concealing material evidence of the stigmatizing feature (for example, by putting away Jewish symbols or ritual objects before guests are expected) or by concealing discrediting facts of one's life history (for example, by saying that one's parents were persecuted in 1944 for being socialists).

Both techniques of stigma management were widely applied in the families of the 117 people interviewed. Only 43 of the interviewees found it natural to reveal the fact of their being Jewish, completely independent of the circumstances; 20 attempted passing under all circumstances, while 46 evaluated situations carefully before deciding what to do. When asked about members of their parents' generation, it transpired that 63 families had tried as far as possible to conceal their being Jewish, and tried to teach their children to do likewise. Of the full sample, there were 40 families who refrained from following any such strategies after 1945, while 19 families chose an extremely dissimulant behaviour—that is, a total denial of their Jewishness.

A well-documented manifestation of the strategy of passing and information control is the aspiration to eradicate the symbols that convey one's identity as a Jew. For example, all but 36 of the families of the interviewees had changed their Jewish-sounding surnames to Hungarian ones. In 25 cases the change had been made by the family after the Second World War, while in 4 cases it was the interviewee who had changed the family name.

Since the interviews had concentrated on family histories, it is obvious that we could pinpoint the ambition for conscious information control most often in the accounts of family and personal histories. Thus, 31 interviewees had found out that they were Jews not from their immediate family or from relatives but from strangers, or even by a process of deduction from various indicators. Fifty-six respondents had no information whatsoever about the pre-war history of their families, while 42 knew only very little about it. Learning of being Jewish was a stigmatizing experience for 47 interviewees, and the content of the identity of 54 interviewees was innately stigmatic, full of feelings of persecution, defencelessness, and fear. It was hardly surprising, then, to discover that 40 interviewees wished to follow their parents' strategies: 9 did not want to tell their children that they were of Jewish origin, and 31 said that they would do so only if circumstances made it unavoidable.

Two main types of information control relating to family and individual life-histories emerged from our interviews. In the first case, interviewees reported that their parents had practised total passing, to the extent of not even telling them that they were Jewish, and that once the secret had been revealed they were left to establish their own rules for stigma management. In the second case, the parents had made them conscious of their stigmatized situation and had also communicated various forms of stigma management behaviour. In this case, where the fact of being Jewish was an open secret within the family, there was no need for the adults to practise passing within the family as they did in the outside world; in the former case, however, the revelation of being Jewish was a great shock and often led to the break-up of the nuclear family.

From examining the behaviour of this group it became clear that stigmatized behaviour had become part of the socialization process. First, people had learnt the 'normal' point of view, and in consequence became conscious of being 'different' as Jews. Next, they had acquired techniques of dealing with how Jews are treated by society at large. During this process they had realized that not everybody knew of their stigma, and that in consequence there were contexts and opportunities for adjusting their social identity if they could master various forms of passing behaviour. This required identification of social spheres, estimation of the information available to others about them, and establishment of the various forms of information control and situation management behaviour. The most important consequence of stigma management behaviour becoming the norm within the stigmatized group is that Jews can recognize each other because they recognize the behaviour pattern, and indeed non-Jews can recognize it too.

This applied to the group we examined: 'When I went out to work,' said one of our interviewees, 'sooner or later I was made to feel that they knew I was Jewish. It was very interesting because you cannot tell from how I look . . . still, somehow they found out—I can't imagine how.' But similar identification mechanisms function on the other side as well. Several interviewees said that at school they had spontaneously chosen their friends from among the Jews, even though they did not talk about Jewishness and often did not know that they were Jews. One of the interviewees explained the way in which members of the group could identify one another: '[the Jews] have perhaps a metacommunicational ability so that they do not actually need to say all the things . . . these are emotional things, like what I feel and what I don't feel, how I react, or whether my partner can guess how I will react— such things.'

This and other similar accounts cast light on an important development: a negative identity in the second and third generation is not necessarily a reaction to an actual experience of being stigmatized (i.e. of antisemitism); at this point it has become an inherited form of identity and form of conduct that exists independently of any challenge in the real world. Thus, a negative identity is being handed down to future generations as part of the socialization process.

CHANGES IN JEWISH IDENTITY AFTER THE FALL OF COMMUNISM

When the Communist system collapsed in Hungary, the efforts to establish a positive Jewish identity grew more intensive. Of the 117 people interviewed, only 7 had maintained Jewish traditions in the mid-1980s, while 22 said that they had been at the stage of seeking their roots and beginning to take an interest in Jewish history, culture, and religion in one form or another. At the time of our research in the 1990s, many of those we interviewed—members of the 'second generation', and especially their children, the representatives of the 'third generation'—were about to break free of an identity created by a stigma. Obviously, the fact that under the new political circumstances the obstacles to manifesting various identities have disappeared has played an important role in all this, but in fact it seems that the main reason for the change is the reappearance of antisemitism in political and cultural discourse: people who conceive their identity only through the challenges of the outside world are now more frequently obliged to feel Jewish. Thus today, stigma management and information control requires much more effort and constitutes a heavier burden than before, and at the same time the ambition to establish other, positive identities has grown accordingly. But what is the content of this new identity? Some people consider returning to Jewish religious tradition to be the only possible solution, while others strive to form a national or minority identity. A substantial number of those looking for a positive identity, however, define ethnicity as the positive content of their identity.

Indeed, interpreting ethnicity as a modern phenomenon is based on the observation of situations like the ones the Jews in Hungary found themselves in during the last century. In a situation in which different ethnic groups occupy competitive positions, it is in the interest of a dominant ethnic group to define the evaluation of 'normalcy' in such a way that any rival groups should end up with an inferior status. That is what happened in Hungary when the Jews would have been accepted as Hungarians only on ideologically defined conditions which were impossible to meet. However, people who are discriminated against must try to achieve a new definition of norms if they do not want to get stuck in a stigmatized role. They have the best chance of that if they act as a group—that is what makes ethnicity an effective organizational principle. The ethnic group is thus the political organization of an interest group whose cohesion is provided by emotions derived from the ethnic identity of the group members.

In the case of assimilated groups, establishing an ethnic identity is not an easy task. As Ki-Taek Chun showed in his paper 'Ethnicity and Identity', published in a volume edited by T. R. Sarbin and E. Scheibe under the title *Studies in Social Identity* (New York, 1983), if the group is no longer separated from other groups in its environment by its tradition, new and clearly distinguishing identificational markers will need to be found in order to create ethnic identity. Ethnic identity is thus not an automatic product of existing differences between the groups but the result of the mobilization of the differences, or their substitution by symbols if the original group markers have already faded. Consequently, a group with a specific ethnic identity is separated from the other groups by the boundary that divides them, and not necessarily by what the boundary encloses. The differentiation between the boundary and what it encloses is essential. The gradual diminution over time of (ethnic) habits, preferences, and practices is likely to weaken ethnic identity or ethnic self-definition over years and generations, but that identity may later be reawakened or determined by a totally different set of factors.

There is no telling today what elements Hungarian Jews trying to establish an ethnic identity will use to create the boundaries that will establish that identity. There are many possibilities: the peculiar history of Hungarian Jews, the awareness of a common fate, the memory of persecution, the special socializing mechanisms observed in Jewish families, typical life strategies or cultural preferences, the emphatically symbolic manifestation of the Jews' particular relationship with the Jewish state, or perhaps the creation of new identity symbols.

One thing is certain: alongside traditional Orthodox Jewish identity, the identity formed in terms of the liberal, assimilation paradigm of the 'Hungarian of the Mosaic faith', an identity formulated as an organic double loyalty and the post-war identity springing from stigma management, a new and positive form of identity has recently appeared in the Hungarian Jewish community: the modern ethnic identity. This poses a serious challenge to identities forged earlier that are still in existence, and it is the conflicts and interactions between them that will determine the future of Jewish identity in modern Hungary.

CHAPTER TWELVE

Jewish Identities in Poland: New, Old, and Imaginary

KONSTANTY GEBERT

H OW many Jews are there in Poland? This seems a simple and reasonable question, but the answer depends to a great degree on who is asking whom, when, and why. This should not be surprising: in Poland's tortuous post-war history, the Jewish question has been amply used as an instrument of political struggle, usually with total disregard for the attitudes and aspirations of the Jews themselves. The simple statement 'I am a Jew' (or 'I am not a Jew') became thus heavily loaded; the person making it not only declared his or her personal identity, but also by implication took a stance on a number of crucial political issues. The acceptance or rejection of a Jewish identity was thus part of a wider package.

To understand the complexity of the issue, one must appreciate that, before the war, Jews in Poland were perceived as a national minority, not a religious denomination or ethnic group. Most often they perceived themselves that way too. Given that they numbered about 3.5 million, or over 10 per cent of the then population of the country, and that they had a distinct culture, language, and religion that set them apart from others, this is hardly surprising. The intensity and character of this national identity varied with its bearer's political affiliation within the Jewish community, but it was national all the same. This implied an incompatibility in being Polish *and* Jewish.

The spectacular failure of the pre-war assimilationists only stressed this point. Even when they converted—even when they became priests, as in the famous case of Father Puder, a converted Jew who became a priest and in 1938 was slapped in the face at the altar by an enemy—they were still considered nationally alien by most Polish Catholics, and therefore rejected. And this notwithstanding the fact that much of pre-war twentieth-century Polish culture had been produced by assimilated Jews.

The war might have been expected to change all that. The Jewish people had largely been murdered, and one could imagine that whatever the 280,000 survivors did would not be of importance to the Poles. This, however, was not the case.

Those among the survivors who upheld their Jewish identity were a constant provocation to many of their Gentile neighbours. On the one hand, they reminded them of horrors barely past, and of skeletons in cupboards. On the other, they became convenient targets of hatred, as the Communist regime imposed on the country had among its leaders and functionaries a visible percentage of people of Jewish origin. Assuming one's Jewish identity meant, therefore, exposing oneself to hostility and rejection from much of society at large. Due to this, many Jews deemed it necessary to seek the good-will of the new authorities—not an easy task, given the Communists' opposition to 'national separatism' and 'clericalism'.

But the other solution was hardly more promising. Renouncing one's Jewishness to become 'a Pole' did not make one more accepted by the Gentile majority than before the war. Furthermore, as the regime pressed its functionaries of Jewish origin to polonize their names and identities, assimilationists were sometimes accused of being Communist agents trying to infiltrate Polish national society. Finally, the very statement that one can become Polish by choice, that citizenship overrides ethnicity, ran counter to what most of the anti-Communist nationalists believed.

A minority can develop and thrive either within a caste system guaranteeing its autonomy, or within a liberal society. The former existed in Poland almost within living memory, the latter was an as yet unattained goal, already subverted and corrupted by Communist rhetoric. The Jews were caught in between.

Most emigrated, especially those who clung to their Jewishness, in particular after the Kielce pogrom of 1946. Of those who clung to their Jewishness who remained, most tried to adapt to circumstances. Basing themselves, to an extent, on the pre-war culture of the Bund, they produced a secular anti-Zionist Yiddish culture, true to the Stalinist formula of being 'Socialist in content and national in form'. A small minority within the minority tried to maintain a religious presence. Most Jews, however, chose assimilation, out of conviction or convenience, concealing their Jewishness to an extent that almost warranted the use of the term 'new Marranos'.

Neither strategy was successful. In 1956, and even more forcefully in 1968, antisemitism, instrumentally used in inter-party struggles, wrecked the hope that there was a place for Jews—any Jews—in a Communist Poland. In 1968, party hardliners resorted to the mass use of antisemitism in a bid to seize power. A nationwide purge of Jews ensued, both within the party and outside it, eventually causing the emigration of some 20,000 Polish Jews over two years. By the early 1970s, some 10,000–12,000 Jews were thought still to remain in Poland. Today, the total membership of the two Jewish organizations—the religious congregation, and the ex-Communist Socio-Cultural Association—is assessed at 4,000 nationwide. This number gives a first possible answer to the question raised earlier.

They are Poland's 'old' Jews, not only in the sense that the median age of the group approximates 70, but because they are the last living bond between the country's thriving pre-war Jewish community and the Poland of today. Most of them are assimilationists who failed to assimilate—and recognized that failure during the 1968 purges at the latest—though some have heroically maintained a religious life-style and conscious Jewish identity over the years. After all they have gone through, the divisions between them are now unimportant and they just want to be left alone.

But not all Jews left in 1968. Those who stayed did so because to emigrate was to acknowledge defeat, to recognize that entire lives had been based on illusions. More: the option of a return to Jewishness for them did not exist, for their Polish identities had not been adopted under duress but out of free choice, or often had already been those of their parents. To 'become a Jew' now would mean not only adopting an alien identity, but confirming the accusation hurled against them by the antisemites, namely, that they were not 'really' Polish. They could not do it.

But this left their children out on a limb. For them too, 1968 became a watershed year. Confronted as students, their identity still not mature, with the fact of their Jewish origins being 'unmasked', they had no option but to interiorize both the Polishness they got from their homes, and the Jewishness thrust upon them by the outside world. What is more, the latter was often perceived through the categories and values of the former. Hardly surprising that the response of many was a sense of shame, or even self-hatred, a burden they were to live with for years.

However, in the relatively liberal second part of the 1970s, the generation of which they were part—the first generation born and raised under Communism—increasingly started to question official truths and attack hitherto unmentionable taboos. The Jewish question was one such taboo; as their peers started expressing more and more interest in the subject, the Jewish generation that came of age in 1968 could for the first time debate its problems in the freedom of unofficial debating groups. Jewish Culture Weeks organized by dissident Catholic intellectuals, books and articles on Jewish topics, and initiatives such as the Warsaw Jewish Flying University (of which more below) all helped young 'Poles of Jewish origin', as one of their spokesmen labelled them, to make sense of their heritage.

The Flying University was a case in point. Set up by a group of Warsaw intellectuals including myself and attended by Jews and their Gentile friends alike, it became a hot-bed of debate on individual Jewish identities in contemporary Poland. In striking contrast to what had been previously a main trait of Jewish life in Poland, participants did not attempt to elaborate a collective Jewish identity, let alone collective Jewish action. This was not due to hyper-individualism, for most of them were soon to join the Solidarity movement. Rather, it resulted from a realistic (or so it seemed) appreciation that demography, more than politics, precluded any future for organized Jewish life in Poland. What remained was possible individual futures for individual Jews, and these would be as diverse as the individuals involved.

They were Poland's 'new Jews'—several score, possibly several hundred in Warsaw, conceivably several thousand nationwide, although initiatives similar to that of the Flying University did not appear quickly elsewhere. But the Warsaw initiative may be approached as a representative sample of the different identities of that generation.

At first glance, however, the similarities seem more striking than the differences. For all, Jewishness was first and foremost a psychological problem: a stigma of 'alien-ness' and lesser worth, imposed on them through no act of their own and against their will. Second, their homes had typically given them no Jewish background at all, and sometimes had even concealed the truth about their ethnic origin. Thirdly, having lived with their Jewishness for years, they had in a way made their peace with the fact that it had become part of them. What they wanted was to be able to make sense of that experience, to be prepared to cope with the dangers it entailed, and possibly to transform it into something more positive.

The Flying University satisfied these demands to a surprising degree. It was active, on a regular fortnightly basis, for over two years, and discontinued only after the Jaruzelski coup of 1981. The military regime had outlawed all unauthorized meetings, and most Flying University participants had, for their part, joined the underground movement. Most of the sixty-odd people who had participated did not change their identities dramatically: they remained 'Poles of Jewish origin', albeit with much more knowledge of the Jewish element of their identity and a strikingly more positive attitude towards it. Others started experimenting with various forms of non-religious Jewish identity, expressed for example by organizing activities to conserve Poland's Jewish monuments, by learning Yiddish, or by lecturing on Jewish topics to Gentile audiences. A few developed a more nationalist form of Jewishness and started preparing for *aliyah*, but so far they have not left Poland. And a few more—but, characteristically, including the most active organizers—became religious.

The relationship between the 'old' Jews and the 'new' Jews was strained. Those of us who started going to the synagogue or attending Jewish cultural manifestations, felt—and were sometimes made to feel—that we did not belong. Lacking Hebrew or Yiddish, unfamiliar with services and having no role-models, we learned our Jewishness from books—mainly American books. The contrast between the religious lifestyle portrayed in the American books and the reality of run-down buildings and tired, defeated people was difficult to accept.

For many of the 'old' Jews, we were first a nuisance, then a fraud, and finally a mystery. It was obvious that the influx of young people would elicit heightened interest from the all-controlling state authorities, which was the last thing the established community wanted. This was the 1980s: had the old-timers known that many of us were involved in the Solidarity underground, they would have almost certainly considered us an unacceptable risk—the more so as they feared the Catholic and nationalistic aspects of that movement.

Furthermore, our Jewishness, self-made and often contradictory, did not strike them as authentic. Marek Edelman, the last surviving leader of the Warsaw Ghetto uprising, expressed it succinctly when he said to me: 'You guys are a fraud, a literary fiction. The Jewish people is dead, and you have simply thought yourselves up, looking for originality and exoticism. You are not for real.' There was some truth in this, although less and less with the passage of time.

But what puzzled the 'old' Jews most was 'Why?' For what conceivable reason would young people who could well pass as Poles (give or take an unpleasant situation or two) adopt of their own volition and actively pursue a fate they themselves had spent their lives avoiding? This cognitive dissonance had some long-term effects. In retrospect, I believe we have helped to infuse the old-timers' community with some pride and assertiveness, though this was a two-way street: we also learned from the 'old' Jews, and finally gained their acceptance and a sense of belonging.

All this was much easier for those of us who tried to integrate into the religious congregations, the secularist community being overtly hostile to the 'clericalist obscurantism' which, even among the non-religious 'young' Jews, constituted an important element of their identity. As late as the end of the 1980s, a 'new' Jew from Wrocław who asked at a meeting of the local chapter of the Jewish Socio-Cultural Association why Jewish traditions were not being upheld was told that the anniversary of the October Revolution *had* been properly celebrated. And some of us consider it a minor triumph that the Association's summer rest-house has recently stopped serving ham on Friday.

Still, some of us were 'imaginary' Jews, in the sense that the connection with Jewishness was based on nothing more than a vague biographical accident and a social climate in intellectual milieux which supported attempts at root-searching, the almost archaeological excavation of an identity. Under other circumstances, their 'Jewishness' would probably immediately have evaporated, nor did they do much to sustain it as it was. This is not necessarily negative—in a free society everyone is free to mould an identity as he or she sees fit. Given, however, the 'Jewish fashion' that was the rage of the Warsaw intelligentsia at that time, the motivations of some 'root-searchers' seemed somewhat recognition-oriented.

But many more and different imaginary Jews were to appear on the scene. After the breakthrough of 1989 and the downfall of Communism, Solidarity split under the burden of its own victory. In the ensuing struggle for power, antisemitism was again used to besmirch political rivals, and Jewishness became in some circles once again an accusation. The reappearance of anti-semitism was not entirely a surprise, since it had been present on the margins of the Solidarity movement from the very beginning, but the scope of the phenomenon was. In fact, the term 'Jew' was used as a coded label to designate liberals, for in a country which had just won a victory against oppression, it was unthinkable to attack liberalism frontally. Liberal Catholic politicians of purely Polish stock like the prime minister, Tadeusz Mazowiecki, were attacked alongside their political allies—Poles of Jewish origin such as Bronisław Geremek or Adam Michnik.

The issue of 'Who is a Jew?' resurfaced once again, not only in political mud-slinging, but on a deeper level—for us. Accepting the New York Central Synagogue's 'Jew of the Year' award in 1991, Adam Michnik stressed that he is a Pole, though his bonds with Jewishness are twofold. One is the bond with his Jewish ancestors, with their ashes at Auschwitz and Treblinka; the other—solidarity with Jewish suffering. Yet in his own words, he feels no solidarity with the Jewish religion, tradition, culture, history, nation, or state.

Michnik was a leader of the student movement of 1968, a long-time political prisoner, repeatedly denounced as a Jew by the Communist media. Without in any way belittling his personal freedom to choose his identity or his motives in choosing the Polish one, it is permissible to wonder whether the fact that his accepting Jewishness could be construed as a validation of those denunciations did play a role in his final decision.

For me and others like me, solidarity against antisemitism is hardly a basis for a Jewish identity: it is sufficient to be a democrat of whatever ethnic origin to feel that. Nor do we believe that there is a particular reason to feel a special solidarity with Jewish suffering, if there is no accompanying solidarity with anything else Jewish. At such a level of abstraction, this solidarity is simply a case of solidarity with victims of any oppression, commendable in its own right.

Whatever the pattern of the Jewish identity of the 'new' Jews, it *is* built around a solidarity with religion, tradition, culture, history, nation, and state. This also involves an element of pain: to quote Michnik once again, 'one is of the nation one can feel ashamed for'. Our Jewish identities matured at the time of the massacres at Sabra and Shatila—though the element of shame is counterbalanced by our pride in the achievements of our people, in the State of Israel and outside it.

We—the 'new Jews' of fifteen years ago—are gradually approaching middle age. We might have resolved some of our identity problems, but have hardly produced the basis for a revived Jewish communal life. This is why some continue to say that we are Poland's last Jews.

Those who say so are wrong—and not only because they ignore the future of our children. In late 1990, a Jewish kindergarten opened in Warsaw, the only one to operate since the results of the 1968 antisemitic purge had paralysed the functioning of the Jewish community. The breakthrough of 1989 not only liberated antisemitism, but also created the conditions for the return of the next generation of the descendants of Communist Poland's 'Marranos' to Jewishness. Hundreds of teenagers now flock to the different Jewish activities organized by the existing Jewish institutions, as well as by relative newcomers to the Polish scene, such as the US-based Ronald Lauder Foundation which had been sponsoring Jewish education in Poland—from kindergarten to adult education. For these young people, 1989, not 1968, was the watershed year. They turn to their roots because they can, not because they must. And while they share many of our problems, the scope of solutions offered them is much larger. They organize clubs, publish news-letters, and establish close ties with Israel. They are much more community-oriented and nationally inclined than we were or are, though less interested in religion. It is as yet unclear how long their enthusiasm will last, or what its outcome will be. They do, however, have both the drive and the numbers—estimated at some 10,000—to make things happen.

Much of this would not have been possible if not for the activities of the Lauder Foundation. At one of their summer camps, a group of teenage girls kept the visiting American rabbi awake long into the night, firing volleys of questions. Finally, the rabbi, very tired, said that the question period was over, that it was time to go to bed. One of the girls replied: 'But you don't understand! We are the next generation of Jewish mothers in this country! We must know everything!' Whatever one thinks of the conclusion, her premiss might well prove true.

PART V

JEWISH COMMUNITIES IN WESTERN EUROPE

CHAPTER THIRTEEN

Israélites *and* Juifs: *New Jewish Identities in France*

DOMINIQUE SCHNAPPER

UNTIL the Second World War, France's policy towards its cultural and ethnic minorities was one of cultural assimilation. As the nation-state *par excellence*, it refused to take account in the public domain of their specific cultural characteristics. In so far as the national tradition saw political and cultural unity as closely linked, any demonstration of separate identity, whether Breton, Provençal, or Jewish, was considered a threat to national unity. Since the foundation of the state school system in the 1880s, the government has seen to it that all French people share the same language and culture, the same historical and patriotic points of reference.

France's centralized and authoritarian primary and secondary education system is the product of involvement by the state in the task of nation-building since the time of the monarchy, and of the universal citizenship which presided at the birth of modern democracy. This educational system has allowed a single French nation to be forged from populations not only of different regional origins (Corsica, Alsace, Brittany) but also of different national origins—the children of Belgian, Italian, Jewish or Polish immigrants, to mention only the most numerous of these waves. It is important to remember that in terms of the national origins of its citizens, France is unique in Europe: it is the sole country in Europe to have started 'importing' citizens at the beginning of the nineteenth century, at a time when many other European countries were 'exporting' their citizens all over the world.

Among all Europe's Jews, then, it was the French Jews who were the most effectively assimilated. Moreover, the Jews responded enthusiastically to French policy: France was for them 'the land of the Revolution and of Jewish Emancipation'. This view of France as a protector of the Jews is aptly captured in the Yiddish expression 'happy as God in France'. The Jews of

Translated from the French by Penelope Johnstone.

France shared with fervour in the cult of nationhood founded on the values and the myths of the Revolution, for by what must have seemed to them a miracle it enabled them to combine the most intense patriotism with upholding their own religious traditions. As Chief Rabbi Zadoc Kahn (b. 1839) declared, speaking of the Revolution: 'It seemed as though the era predicted by the prophets of Israel had finally begun.' And, even more clearly, Raymond Bloch: 'The time of the Messiah had come with the French Revolution. The time of the Messiah had come with the new society, which substituted for the Old Trinity of the Church that other Trinity whose name can be read on every wall: Liberty, Equality, Fraternity.' The antisemitic campaigns of the 1880s were indeed very violent, but the dramatic events of the Dreyfus Affair eventually ended with Dreyfus himself being proved innocent. The extreme-Right press of the 1930s was no less mean and violent in its attacks on Jews, but it proved unable to prevent Léon Blum from becoming prime minister in 1936.

One has to be familiar with this past in order to understand the extent to which the Vichy government's adoption of an anti-Jewish edict, the Status of the Jews, on 3 October 1940, was traumatic for the Jews of France. This edict excluded Jews from a whole series of social positions and denied the principle of equality of all citizens before the law. The French state that had hitherto always protected Jews if necessary against the antisemitism of civil society now betrayed them, going even beyond the German demands. The French population, stunned by military defeat, showed itself indifferent as the state destroyed the very special relationship that French Jews had enjoyed with France. From then on, Jews understood that even a country that had made public declaration of human rights one of its founding principles was still in danger of betraying them.

The Status of the Jews thus opened a new epoch: it marked the end of the Jews' belief in the magical nature of their destiny in France. This fundamental break has since been compounded by the continuing impact of the two historic events that since the Second World War have defined the awareness of all Jews: the Holocaust and the creation of the State of Israel.

Aliyah from France has never been on a large scale; it has never exceeded several thousand a year—even after the Six-Day War which shook the consciousness of the Jews of France (as of Jews the world over) and led a large number of them to rediscover their identity. It was really only ever considered an option by small groups of intellectuals, such as the Strasbourg school of religiously observant Jews around André Neher, and other religious Jews, often recent immigrants, originating from North African countries. Secular *aliyah* remained marginal. But even those who were too firmly rooted in France to ever consider *aliyah* were forced by the existence of the State of Israel to rethink the terms of their own citizenship and admit that there were indeed specific ties, both objective and symbolic, with Israel. In fact, right through the 1980s the only common denominator uniting French Jews was the various forms of solidarity with Israel.

A second characteristic specific to Jewish life in France was the large-scale migration of Sefardim at the start of the 1960s from the former French colonies in North Africa. Any demographic data relating to religion must be treated with caution in France, since questions about religion are excluded from its censuses and only a very small proportion of French Jews are active in Jewish organizations; but it is estimated that migration from North Africa had quadrupled the number of Jews in France to around 600,000 by 1992, making it the largest Jewish community in western Europe. These Sefardi Jews brought a new vitality to Jewish society in France because they combined a familiarity with French culture (having been part of it for the past two or three generations) with a greater Jewish self-awareness than Jews in metropolitan France had. This latter factor was because they originated from closely linked communities with a strong sense of their Jewish identity and firmly established religious practices. The Sefardi immigration has thus caused a veritable renaissance in Jewish life in southern France: Jewish communities that had disappeared two centuries earlier have been reinaugurated in Carpentras, Nîmes, and Aix-en-Provence, and new communities of Sefardi Jews have been established in Paris, Marseilles, and elsewhere. Sefardim have made their presence felt in all the central organizations—the Consistoire, the Fonds social juif unifié, the Appel unifié juif de France, and the Chief Rabbinate; in fact, the president of the Consistoire, as well as the present chief rabbi and his predecessor, are all of North African origin.

Today, in line with the general trend in French society, Jews no longer follow the old policy of assimilation, nor do they limit their expression of Judaism only to the private and family sphere. Since the 1970s, new forms of Jewish identity have established themselves and found expression in a new religious and cultural life. Enrolment in Jewish primary and secondary schools and in university departments of Jewish studies is steadily increasing. There is similar expansion in intellectual gatherings, in the preparation of university dissertations on Jewish topics, in the publication of religious texts and of books of more general Jewish interest. The sole common denominator among Jews otherwise completely different—whether on account of their national origins, group membership, cultural level, Jewish consciousness, or intensity of religious practice—has for a long time been solidarity with Israel. Until the 1980s, Jews were for the most part what I called in my book *Juifs et Israélites* 'militants': they adopted a primarily historical definition of Judaism, and expressed their Jewish identity chiefly through their links and solidarity with the State of Israel.[1] But over the past ten years there has been a startling return to Judaism as a religion. Thus, whereas in 1979 it was at the behest of secular organizations and under the banner of 'Twelve Hours for Israel' that tens of thousands of people came together at the Porte de Versailles to express their solidarity with Israel, in 1989 it was at the behest of the chief rabbi that thirty thousand people gathered at the Parc des Expositions in Villepointe for a celebration centred on the Torah. Reflecting this trend, the officials of Jewish organizations are themselves now more likely to be 'religious' Jews than 'militants'. At the same time, this reinvigoration of the religious element in community life had by the end of the 1980s engendered a response from secular Jewish intellectuals, in the form of organizations promoting a secular, cultural, and historical view of Judaism.

The return to Judaism in a religious sense takes many different forms, ranging from religious practices within the family to attendance at *yeshivot* or at study circles. The *yeshivot* offer Talmud study under the authority of a rabbi; in conformity with tradition, this study focuses on the knowledge of ethical norms ruling social contacts and the relationship to God. Above all, the *yeshivot* are concerned with reaffirming a form of return to traditional education. The study circles, in contrast, are a more innovative way of raising Jewish consciousness. Scattered in places where neither the Jewish religion nor Jewish communities have traditionally been well established, they attract Jews without much knowledge of Jewish tradition or culture to re-educate themselves together with their relatives or friends, primarily in response to the demands of a personal quest for identity. In this latter case, the concern is rather to situate oneself in a supportive milieu, to rediscover family memories, to reconstruct an identity on the basis of emotion rather than intellect, and to find ways of adapting the strictures of Jewish law to the modern world. At the same time, fundamentalist groups such as the Lubavitch Hasidim have engaged in substantial outreach activity and built up large communities of followers, impressive for their sheer size; the Liberal Jews, who tend to comprise members of the upper classes and intellectuals, have likewise revived their activity. The Consistoire, formally the official body of French Jewry, has no more than a minor regulatory impact on any of these groups.

Thus, the main communal bodies—the central philanthropic, intellectual, and religious Jewish organizations—no longer control the forms in which Jews practise their faith and establish their identity: Orthodox and Liberal, religious and secular, traditional and innovative—the range is today exceedingly wide. To see this, one need only to look at the number of associations whose existence and activity have not only escaped the control of the umbrella organizations but are not even known to them.

This new vitality in the Jewish world, both religious and secular, and its consequent atomization were clearly demonstrated in a recent controversy occasioned by the bicentenary celebrations of the Republic in 1989. A debate arose among Jewish intellectuals regarding a proposal to transfer to the Panthéon the ashes of Abbé Grégoire, who throughout the years of the Revolution had championed the cause of the Jews and in particular their claim to French citizenship. Three different attitudes emerged. The first group reaffirmed the values that Abbé Grégoire had stood for. They reasserted their attachment to the principle of citizenship defined by an abstract body of rights and duties, and their conviction that this in no way conflicted with their attachment to Judaism, defined in moral, intellectual, and religious terms. In their view they could thus remain loyal to a private, religious, intellectual Judaism, while participating actively in public life on an individual basis; for them Judaism is essentially a religion, an intellectual and moral tradition. This is the extension of national integration 'French style'.

The second group criticized not the principle of citizenship, but the particular form that it took in France. In their view, the political tradition, which they consider excessively centralized and culturally unified, has led to the demise of many collective forms of Jewish life. They would like to be granted cultural and social recognition as a 'Jewish community'. In their view, the British or American nation accords greater respect to the tradition of Judaism. This attitude is often found among the officials of secular and Consistoire organizations, for whom the 'community' model, on the pattern of the 'American Jewish community', is an ideal.

The final group want a fundamental redefinition of Jews' relations with French society and citizenship. They want recognition for the Jewish community as such, in the public and political domain—not only the cultural and social domains—as both a religious and a secular entity. They voice a fundamental criticism of the place accorded to Jewish citizens, in that their specific characteristics have never been given recognition. This utopian view of a new relationship between the Jews and the nation—a relationship never yet realized in any country—is often adopted by young Jews of Sefardi origin, whose inner awareness of the tradition of citizenship in the French style is less strongly developed.

Through this debate, it is possible to perceive the new, specifically French form of the problem of Jewish modernity. Until the Revolution ushered in the modern political era in France, Jews were considered a 'nation' in the sense of the old regime, with its twofold national and religious dimension; in giving autonomy to the diverse spheres of existence, and in particular in separating politics from religion, the modern nation obliged Jews to choose between a national self-definition and a religious one. In the traditional nation-state, Judaism could not retain its political dimension: it had to be reinterpreted as a religion. This was the position adopted up to 1940 by the vast majority of French Jews in calling themselves *israélites*. The revelation, comparatively belated, of the specific role of the Vichy government and of the full horror of the Holocaust constituted specifically Jewish events which could not fail to give rise to new reflections on the terms of the contract between Jews and the nation. The creation of the State of Israel represented one more such occasion.

The debate concerning the reinterpretation of the Revolution is part of a wider movement. The fact that French Jews are questioning the mode of their participation in French society is part of a more general discussion among various groups, while the evolving concept of 'Europe' calls into question the basis of the nation-state. Contemporary criticism of the assimilationist policy and recognition of the value of particularism have caused some Jews to question the terms under which Jews received their emancipation, and to weigh anew the contract of citizenship and secularism which governs the relationship between the nation-state and particularist groups. This historical reinterpretation has strong ideological roots, and the questions the Jews are asking find their echo elsewhere in French intellectual and political circles.

The progress made by the National Front since 1983 often gives the impression that antisemitism is growing in French society. There is no doubt that in France, as in all Western countries, the taboo that attached to antisemitism for the thirty years or so following the Holocaust has grown weaker, but it is important to maintain a proper perspective on this. All opinion polls on the subject show the continual decrease of antisemitism and the growing acceptance of Jews by the population as a whole. The number of French people expressing hostility towards Jews has decreased steadily from 33 per cent in 1946 to 2 per cent in the most recent polls. More than 90 per cent state that Jews are no different from other citizens; less than 10 per cent would hesitate to vote for a Jewish candidate for President of the Republic. The vast majority affirm that Jewish practices are not a 'disadvantage'. Polls merely confirm what can be clearly seen in public life: Jews play a full and active role in the collective life of the nation, including its political life. During the most recent European elections, four of the most important lists were headed by Jews, and no one drew attention to the fact. In France, Jews are at the heart of all intellectual activity and cultural life.

At the same time, since 1979 there has been an increase in 'racist' offences, and especially threats (graffiti, pamphlets, anonymous calls). Though these threats are directed primarily against North Africans, Jews have not been spared entirely. Between 1987 and 1989, the number of offences annually rose from 2 to 18, and the number of threats from 57 to 149. Jean-Marie Le Pen is increasingly less concerned to conceal an antisemitism which would be expressed more violently and clearly if it were not proscribed by the law. A small group of Revisionists, though often publicly condemned, continue to make themselves heard.

The action taken by the law in this direction has been very strongly supported by public opinion. After the episode in the Carpentras cemetery in 1990, some 200,000 people, including the President of the Republic, marched through the streets of Paris in response to an appeal by Jewish organizations. Representatives of all religious groups, including the Muslims, expressed their sympathy and solidarity, as did all political leaders except for the National Front. According to opinion polls, this event made an impression on the political consciousness of the French second only to the fall of the Berlin Wall.

Antisemitism is an integral part of Western culture, however, and French culture is no exception to the general rule. Polls regularly show the presence of a small minority keeping up antisemitic prejudices in their most classic form. But the forms, the intensity, and the expressions of this antisemitism vary in accordance with political circumstances. For well-known historical reasons, every incident concerning Jews is accentuated in public life: this was true of the bomb at the synagogue in rue Copernic in 1980, the attack on the Carpentras cemetery, and the emotions raised by the media at the time of Israel's war against Lebanon and the events of Sabra and Shatila. French government policy in the Middle East conflict, seen by Jews as over-preferential towards the Arab countries, often gives rise to disappointment and bitterness, as when Arafat was allowed to visit Paris in the early 1990s. The presence of a large Muslim population in France means that there is always the fear of incidents between Jews and Muslims, although even during the Gulf War no incidents of this kind were reported. It seems clear that despite an upsurge of certain expressions of antisemitism, despite the political tensions (normal in a democracy), despite the frequently disproportionate coverage given to everything concerning Jews and Israelis, which is a fact of life in France—antisemitism has ceased since the war to be a political issue, and Jews have seldom before enjoyed such a favourable situation.

The difference between *juifs* and *israélites* is a symbol of the transformation of Jewish identities in France. Until 1940, the Jews, bourgeois and patriotic and often settled in France for several generations, referred to themselves as *israélites*, thereby distinguishing themselves, culturally, religiously, and socially from the poor Jews, often religious, who sought refuge in France after fleeing from the persecutions they suffered in eastern Europe. But 1940 marked the end of voluntary and enthusiastic Jewish assimilation to the country of the Revolution. After the war, the majority of Jews concluded that the assimilation policy had been a tragic mistake. The term *israélite* was now seen as connoting the illusions of assimilation, and therefore acquired a pejorative meaning. Instead, Jews have now laid claim to the term which had previously designated contempt, persecution, and the Holocaust: they are calling themselves simply *juifs*. This definition of identity, even if the religious and secular forms it takes have burst out in all directions, has been adopted by all. With the adoption of this new common denominator as the basis of identity, Jewish identities in France have thus entered a new era.

Note
1. Published in English as *Jewish Identities in France: An Analysis of Contemporary French Jewry*, trans. Arthur Goldhammer (Chicago, 1983).

CHAPTER FOURTEEN

The Notion of a 'Jewish Community' in France: A Special Case of Jewish Identity

SHMUEL TRIGANO

T HE use of the notion of 'community' to define French Judaism is not
self-evident. On the one hand, if 'community' renders the medieval
kahal, the concept has a long history and has engendered any number of
mythical images: there are therefore reasons for seeing it as a model that
might be found anywhere that Jewish life has developed. But in fact nothing
could be less true of the Jews in France. The idea of a 'Jewish community' in
France was invented only after the Second World War, as a way of
designating the Jewish population as a whole rather than simply the
landsmanschaften of Jewish immigrants of common geographical origin that
had banded together to organize self-help and cultural activities and to
defend their common interests.

Everything in modern French political culture is hostile to the label
'community': the supreme value, embodying the very identity of the nation,
is the state. The state is much more than just a legal authority, and the
integration of nation and citizenship is total. Any 'community' that might
emerge is perceived as a factor weakening the absolute allegiance to the state
that is required of every citizen. A community would represent a secondary
allegiance, an intermediate level between republic and citizen. Some would
see it as a return to the *ancien régime* and its *corporations*. An echo of this was
heard in the debate launched by Charles de Gaulle in 1967 on Jews'
supposed 'dual allegiance', to the State of Israel as well as to France, and
therefore their lesser loyalty to the French nation. The fact that a 'Jewish
community' nevertheless emerged in France must be seen in the context of

Translated from the French by Miriam Kochan.

how the French state itself evolved—just as the way in which individual Jewish identities have evolved cannot be divorced from the changes that have occurred in French society per se.

THE FRENCH RELIGIOUS MODEL: JUDAISM AS A CONFESSION

One of the major consequences of Emancipation—that is to say, Jews' accession to citizenship at the time of the Revolution—was the end of a collective Jewish identity. By doing away with *corporations*, feudal systems, and secondary allegiances, the Constituent Assembly sought to acknowledge only citizens. Jews therefore acceded to citizenship as individuals, not as members of a collectivity. It was hoped that through Emancipation they would be 'regenerated'—acculturated and integrated into the social life of the state and thereby freed from the 'defects' that the ghetto and persecution, even their religion, were assumed to have inculcated. The 'Jewish nation', as such, was to disappear; under the impetus of the Revolution and Emancipation, all Jewish identity, culture, and history—the whole Jewish civil dimension—were destined to fade away. Judaism was to remain merely a religious confession.[1]

The Napoleonic regime did not dismantle the main features of this Revolutionary Jewish model, but it challenged it none the less. By convening a Great Sanhedrin, Napoleon undertook to reorganize the Jewish condition on his own initiative and in terms of the needs of the state. The collectivity would not disappear, but would henceforth be made manifest in the form of a Consistoire: a state agency responsible for governing the life of the Jews, now defined as members of a religious confession, and for supervising their regeneration and patriotism. The status of Judaism was thus aligned with that of other religions.

The Napoleonic model transferred the observance of Judaism entirely to the private sphere. The Jewish condition could no longer be manifested in the civic arena or in public life, but only in religious terms in one's private life. Jews could have no corporate existence beyond that of sharing a religious confession. It was unimaginable at that time that Jews should unite to pursue any broader aims. The best proof of this is that although the Sanhedrin, and later the Consistoire, provided for a strong presence of lay leaders alongside the rabbis, as a body they were limited to expressing themselves only on religious matters.

To understand what implications this had for the Jewish condition, one must consider more closely the debates and resolutions of the Sanhedrin. It was not the differentiation between religion and civil life that was problematic for Jews—Jewish tradition already distinguished religious legal authority (*keter kehunah,* 'the crown of the priesthood') from that of civil authority (*keter malkhut,* 'the crown of the kingdom')—but rather that Jewish civil authority was to disappear and to be entirely replaced by the Napoleonic code. It could be said that Napoleon's empire in this sense came to be thought of as a latter-day replacement for Solomon's kingdom; the new authority of the state was thus seen as messianic. For these new 'French Israelites', Napoleon was a new Cyrus (the king who had allowed the Jews to rebuild the Temple in Jerusalem after its first destruction in 587 BC), or even a new Moses, his Civil Code being the new Tablets of the Law. Accordingly, the Sanhedrin explained that the divine law contained political provisions as well as religious traditions; the political provisions that had governed the people of Israel in Palestine when it had its own kings, elders, and judges were no longer applicable since the people of Israel no longer formed a national body. What was applicable, however, was the religious duty to remain obedient to the laws of the state in civil and political matters—or as the traditional religious codes put it, *dinei damalkhutei dinei* ('the law of the state is the law'). Thus the whole distinction between religion and civil society had long existed in Judaism; what was new here was the removal of a specifically Jewish secular domain. But to make Judaism merely a religion, in the sense of polarization from all things secular, was contrary to its very nature.

The classic model of the Jewish condition in France that in fact evolved (since the Revolutionary period was too short for a model to crystallize) was undoubtedly a retreat from the original plans of the Constituent Assembly, which envisaged the Jews merging totally with the French citizenry and disappearing as a separate identity. The reason for this was that Napoleon had in practice reconstructed a Jewish collectivity. It may have been consigned to the synagogue, but being a collectivity it was in some rudimentary sense a 'nation' all the same, even if it was entirely of a religious nature and cut off from the civil sphere. In one sense, then, Napoleon can be said to have restored the idea of a 'Jewish nation': despite the official recasting of Judaism as merely a confession, in practice the idea of a community was already unofficially written into the Napoleonic model. There was thus a duality of expectations *vis-à-vis* Jews: as individuals they were expected to be citizens like everyone else, but collectively they were established as a 'religious community'. The problem with this was that it laid Jews' loyalty open to question: the idea of a 'Jewish conspiracy' (the accusation that Jews maintained secret international links among themselves that were directed against their fellow citizens) became the basic prism of the antisemitism that emerged, contrary to all expectations, in republican France.

The confessional model gave French Judaism a specific character in the Jewish world because the Judaism of the Consistoire was the only model of Judaism that Jews were allowed. The various ideological religious movements that emerged in German Judaism at the same period, particularly Reform Judaism, were not created in France. Some minor changes were made in ritual, but basically French Judaism remained close to the traditional model. Beyond a shadow of doubt, the obligatory nature of Consistoire Judaism played an important part in maintaining the religious uniformity of Jews in France. Such a universal, centralized Judaism had existed hardly anywhere else in the long history of the diaspora, outside Babylon in the early Middle Ages, medieval Spain, and Poland in the fifteenth to seventeenth centuries. It was a true reflection of the universality of the French state.

THE RESTORATION OF A JEWISH CIVIL SPHERE

The Napoleonic system was subject to unexpected reversals because it was inherently a dialectic system. For Jews, the first change came not in the religious sphere but in the banished civil sphere: the creation of the Alliance Israélite Universelle in 1860 was the reaffirmation of the common destiny of the Jews as a people and of a common identity and sense of purpose beyond that which Napoleon had allowed them. The Napoleonic reforms in the civil field had indeed allowed some assimilation of Jews into the wider civil society, but in practice the degree of assimilation remained moderate in France (unlike in Germany) because contemporary society was strongly polarized between Christianity and anticlerical republicanism. Jews in process of assimilation tended towards the latter, but there was a fundamental contradiction here because anticlericalism, by definition, denied any legitimacy to religion. Deprived in this way of the social value of their identity (the Jewish identity being officially only a religious identity), they sought instead to retrieve their lost secular identity.

Three or possibly four other factors may explain the re-emergence of a Jewish authority in the civil (or secular) sphere. The first factor derives from the decisions of the Sanhedrin, which were tantamount to a Judaic messianization of the realm of the secular. With this messianization, Jews acquired an 'extra soul'; being thus inspired by a mystical excess of republican excellence, they therefore felt themselves to be distinguished from their fellow-citizens. This in turn preserved their sense of separate identity and helped protect them from total assimilation. A related development was the romanticism that blossomed in the nineteenth century: the remnants of ancient Judaism now rose again before the gaze of the Jews and revived long-dormant stirrings.[2] One may also mention in the same context the progressivist idealism of Jews inspired by Saint-Simon, though they were future-oriented rather than past-oriented. A third factor was the reaction to the antisemitism that followed the 1848 revolutions: assimilated Jewish intellectuals, rediscovering that they were Jewish whether they wanted to be or not, set out in quest of the meaning of their forgotten Jewishness. The fourth explanation may be sought in the superficiality of modern institu-tions. The old institutions (in this case, a Jewish civil entity) continued to exist beneath them, and now re-emerged in a new form. This development in the Jewish condition in France also had its parallel in the wider society, with the restoration of the institutions of the *ancien régime*, and particularly the return to strong state centrality and the reconstruction of intermediate orders, both in the political sphere and in the economic.

Somewhat unexpectedly, then, the Napoleonic model for the Jewish condition, which denied Judaism any civil authority, went on to produce a Jewish civil presence in the form of the Alliance Israélite Universelle. Its establishment was due to the initiative of a group of apparently assimilated Jewish intellectuals and politicians, Saint-Simonians who saw it as a global institution that would defend Jews in danger anywhere in the world.[3] It is in fact this aspect of the Alliance that helps to explain its emergence as a Jewish civil institution: its activities were directed beyond France to the world outside. The Jewish population supposed to benefit from its actions was not that of France but Jews of other countries, places where Emancipation had not reached and 'obscurantism' still ruled. Within France itself a Jewish civil authority remained unthinkable, and was in any case considered un-necessary. But abroad was another story: the Alliance aimed to make inter-national contacts at the state level and to develop the capacity for political activity that could save endangered Jews. This was an entirely new form of Jewish institution: Jewish interests had not been internationalized in this way since the Babylonian period when all Jews had lived in the same Muslim empire.

The birth of political Zionism (not for nothing was it conceived in France) must also be viewed from this perspective.[4] Here the civil model departed fairly and squarely from the confessional model, and even from the French national context. Zionism aimed at reconstituting a Jewish civil authority—this time in the form of a state, and by definition outside France.

Thus, the Napoleonic model of the Jewish condition as being a religious confession survived in France, but by the latter half of the nineteenth century Jewish civil organizations had emerged alongside it: although their activities were focused exclusively outside France, they were the first symptom of a crisis in the Napoleonic model. But even so, this model was to persist until the Second World War, when like so much else it was finally shattered.

THE BIRTH OF THE 'COMMUNITY'

The birth of the 'Jewish community' in France is often described as a postwar response to the wartime experience of legalized exclusion under the Vichy regime. The Jews were left feeling naked and exposed; after the war they set to work to clothe themselves, and the garb they adopted was the community. In fact, however, the origins of the community can be dated back to 1944, with the creation of Crif, the Conseil représentatif des institutions juives de France. Crif, created as a resistance movement, was the first Jewish organization created by Jewish initiative to set itself up as a representative body with the general objective of defending Jewish interests. This was something absolutely new: Jewish self-definition in France now went beyond the purely religious field and entered the civil sphere.

At one level, it was the institutional linkage of Crif and the Consistoire that generated the birth of a sense of community immediately after the war. Crif was established as a representative body not of universal suffrage but of institutions. The Consistoire was an integral part of it—indeed, the leading institution, since the president of the Consistoire was the president of Crif. But soon another factor emerged that was to have a decisive effect on the development of the 'community': the Fsju (Fonds social juif unifié). This organization was created in 1950 with the assistance of the American Joint in order to help French Judaism pick itself up from its state of wartime ruin, and it took as its field of action the day-to-day running of social and community affairs. Following the American model of Jewish community organization, a large number of community centres were established all over France to foster a new kind of Jewish life, focusing on cultural and recreational activities within a Jewish framework. Together, these three organizations—the Consistoire, Crif, and the Fsju—comprised an institutional tripod that gave stability to the notion of a French Jewish community. The Alliance, established to solve the problems of a different age and with an orientation towards the rest of the world rather than France itself, became progressively less active. There was thus a total restructuring of Jewish civil society, and French Judaism now began to direct its energies inwards.

In the 1960s and 1970s, the Jewish community concept took strong root in France. Three years were particularly significant in this. In 1962 there was the repatriation of Jews from North Africa, giving the community in France not only increased demographic strength but also a new vigour because of the immigrants' cultural self-confidence as Jews. In 1967 there was massive crystallization of Jewish identity around the threatened State of Israel before the Six-Day War. Then, in 1968, there was the crisis in France that marked the end of the hyper-centralization of French society and political culture so characteristic of the Napoleonic model and opened the way to the recognition of secondary identities for French citizens.

The evolution of the Jewish community in France thus corresponded in large measure to the evolution of the model of political culture in France. The Napoleonic model of French society had abolished the civil component of Jewish life: only when this model was perceived as outmoded for society as a whole was this civil component, now in the form of a fully-fledged 'Jewish community', able to re-emerge.

Thus was born in France a Jewish identity that has no parallel in the Jewish world—just as the character of the French state is unique among states. Whereas the Jewish establishment in the United States is composed of a series of institutionalized ideological movements, operating completely independently in their different domains while nevertheless managing to co-ordinate their efforts within a national framework (such as the Conference of Presidents) on major issues, in France there is one absolute framework that accommodates a diversity of voluntary commitments. It is a little like a block of flats whose tenants share the same address but open their windows to different views of the outside world; in the case of the French Jewish community, the walls of the structure consist of a set of common symbols and representations.

Note that this reintegration of a civil Jewish domain within the French framework seems to have restored two of its earlier features. First, the aspect once symbolized by the Alliance—Judaism as a response to modernity in the civil and secular domains—is now expressed in a 'civic Judaism'. Second, the former crystallization around Zionism has now become 'community Zionism'—an ideology that in France has produced little emigration to Israel but a great deal of collective identification as the community has sought to define itself.[5] In one sense the private Jewish identity, formerly confined to being a religious identity has by virtue of these developments merged with a secular identity which expresses itself in French civic and cultural life.[6] There thus seems to be a superimposition of the public and private domains. However, this merger has not come to represent a true balance because the new civil domain was larger than the old confessional one.

CRISIS OF COMMUNITY

Since the 1980s, the Jewish community seems to have faced new challenges from both the outside and the inside.

The main external factor is linked to the decline of socialism as an ideology. This paradoxical result of the increase in the political power of the French left and its subsequent confrontation with reality has engendered a search for a substitute ideology, and the result has been a return to the great ideals of the *droits de l'homme*, reconstituted today as a concern for human rights. It was also partly a response to the xenophobic tendencies that began to emerge in the 1980s with the 'discovery' of the probably permanent presence in France of a very large immigration of Muslim origin. This provoked anxiety and a reaction of rejection in many sectors of French society, of which the National Front and the policy statements of its leader Jean-Marie Le Pen were only one of the symptoms.

Not surprisingly, this *droits-de-l'hommiste* current evolved in the direction of a pure and hard republicanism: its advocates wanted to see a Jacobinist republic be the sole criterion of the integration of the now variegated populations of a France unsure of its identity and destiny. The celebration of the Bicentenary of the French Revolution in 1989 reinforced this view, but it was the Headscarf Affair that unfolded in the same year that more than anything else crystallized this development. Three young Muslim girls from Creil were barred from school because they refused to take off their Islamic headscarves in class. France was swept by an extraordinarily passionate opposition to the girls' stand, in the name of republican secularism: the voice of the modern and tolerant secularism that had developed since the 1960s had difficulty in making itself heard. This was due to the emergence of a new ideological stance that condemned the existence of communities as well as of the dangerous communitarianism threatening the Republic and battening on religious integration. In the ensuing fray, a distinguished sociologist was heard analysing the 'racist communitarianism of the Jews'. In order to appear unprejudiced, those who advocated such ideas (among them many Jews, including leading figures in some Jewish institutions) put 'the Jewish community' on a par with 'the immigrant community' and 'the Muslim community'. Notably, the Union des étudiants juifs de France helped to create and support the SOS Racism movement by equating the interests of the immigrants with those of the Jews. This altruistic gesture turned out to have unfortunate consequences in some respects, in that by presenting the Jewish community in France as a community of immigration it had the effect of delegitimizing it. More precisely, it made the Jewish community a phenomenon foreign to France. The facts belie this because the emergence of a Jewish community in France after the 1950s was entirely consistent with the evolution of French society at the time; moreover, the great majority of its members had long been French citizens (being Jews from France and Algeria), while even the minority (Tunisians and Moroccans) had already been of French culture before their arrival in France and in any case now had French citizenship. In this context it should also be mentioned that the extent of antisemitism was greatly exaggerated in the discussion of political policy at the time; it is clear that it was primarily against immigrants that racist attacks were directed.

This new development has altered the general climate of the Jewish condition by delegitimizing the category of community in France. The question is, does this represent a new stage in the evolution of the French state, and therefore a reconsideration of the very form of the Jewish condition in France? Before that question can be answered we must also consider developments that have taken place within the Jewish community in recent years, and particularly the polarization that has occurred—once again confirming the principle of simultaneous evolution in the Jewish condition and in that of the wider society. Among the first signs of this new polarization in the French Jewish community was the controversy in 1985 that followed the conversion of a French Rothschild spouse to Judaism in Morocco. The chief rabbi of France, Rabbi Sirat, attacked the conversion, and this led to virulent discussion on the subject of mixed marriages and the difficulties that the Consistoire put in the way of would-be converts. Then, in 1986, as a result of personal differences, the Consistoire withdrew from Crif. (The formal requirement whereby Crif had to be headed by the president of the Consistoire had been abandoned in 1982.) A Jewish secular movement was formed, and this spearheaded the controversy with the powerful Paris Consistoire, where a new and very Jewishly assertive team had meanwhile come to power. Strictly Orthodox values gained increasing importance in the institutions of the Consistoire. At the same time, strictly Orthodox groups, including the Lubavitch movement, which actively proselytized on a very large scale, became much more visible. These movements and values establishing themselves at the core of Jewish life have split the community from within: they do not accept the authority of the Consistoire's *beit din*, regarding it as too lenient in matters of *halakhah*—their spiritual mentors are to be found instead in Brooklyn and Benei Berak—and in general show disdain for the traditional authorities of French Judaism. Their demonstration of halakhic rigour is for them a source of power. So with secular Judaism emerging on the left and an increasingly Orthodox Judaism on the right, it remains to be seen whether in fact separate communities are being formed—just as American Jewry is today organized in isolationist ideological movements. Such a development would clearly mark the end of the unity and universality of the French Jewish 'community'.

The future evolution of the community will depend on the extent to which the major part of French Judaism, the central grouping that is equidistant from the extremes of radical secularism and strict Orthodoxy, will be able to hold its ground. For this to happen, three conditions must be met. First, it must remain confident of its Jewish legitimacy. Second, the concept of a Jewish community must again achieve public legitimacy. And third, it must restore its capacity to accommodate all shades of opinion and unite the Jews of France: it must become again a house whose windows are open to the outside world, where all Jews can enter and find what they want, and where Jews can live together in all their diversity and unity.

Notes

1. I discuss this more fully in *La République et les juifs* (Paris, 1982), and also in my article 'The French Revolution and the Jews', *Modern Judaism*, 10 (1990).

2. The case of Joseph Salvador is a marvellous example of this sort of experience; see Joseph Salvador, *Histoire des institutions de Moïse* (Paris, 1928), and id., *Paris, Rome, et Jerusalem* (Paris, 1860).

3. And also, though this is often forgotten, the Jews as a people and Judaism as a religion; on this see the statement that preceded the *Appel à tous les Israélites* (Paris, 1860), which mentions the 'flag of Israelite monotheism' (p. 10), the 'live forces of Judaism' (p. 13), and the need for a 'solidarity established from country to country, encompassing everything which is Israelite in its vast network' (p. 15)—that is to say, the Jewish *people*.

4. See Annie Kriegel, *Les Juifs et le monde moderne: Essai sur les logiques d'émancipation* (Paris, 1977).

5. See Shmuel Trigano, 'From Individual to Collectivity: The Rebirth of the Jewish Nation in France', in F. Malino and B. Wasserstein (eds.), *The Jews in Modern France* (Hanover, New Brunswick, 1985).

6. A new type of Jewish thought, in dialogue with the traditional texts and contemporary thought, crystallized after the war around the newly opened École des Cadres d'Orsay, led initially by Jacob Gordin and then by Léon Askenazi.

CHAPTER FIFTEEN

British Jewry: Religious Community or Ethnic Minority?

GEOFFREY ALDERMAN

HISTORICALLY British Jews have viewed themselves as nothing more nor less than British citizens dissenting from the established Church, and therefore as differing from the Anglican and Christian majorities merely by virtue of their religious beliefs. This view is neatly summed up in the saying that British Jews are merely Britons of the Jewish persuasion. The attitude that has informed this view has had a profound effect upon the way in which the lay and ecclesiastical leaderships of Anglo-Jewry have viewed the state, and in the way in which the state has approached its relationship with the Jews.

To cite one example, the idea that they were merely Englishmen of the Jewish persuasion exercised a profound influence upon Sir Bernard Waley Cohen and Neville Laski when they were, respectively, vice-president of the United Synagogue and president of the Board of Deputies of British Jews in the 1920s and 1930s. The deep and deeply felt anti-Zionism of both these giants of inter-war Anglo-Jewry stemmed in great measure from this underlying philosophy. To cite another, one (but only one) of the reasons why Jews were not specifically mentioned in the 1976 Race Relations Act was that the state had never conceived of the Jews other than as a religious community; the protection which that Act has fortunately come to confer upon Jews has come indirectly, through the development of case law and the *obiter dicta* of the judiciary.

In reality, Great Britain has for a very long time been a multicultural society. But it is only with the advent of significantly large non-white minorities that the multicultural nature of British society has been recognized by the media, by informed public opinion, and hence, ultimately, by the state. The Race Relations Acts were unfortunately titled, in that they had very little to do with race as biologically defined. What they addressed were problems of discrimination consequent upon the presence in Britain of communities professing cultural (including religious) value systems radically different from those to which the nation had historically been accustomed. For the first time, British society exhibited ethnic diversity through the presence within society of people whose historical and cultural norms of reference were (to put it bluntly) 'foreign'. What is more, these people showed little inclination to cast their ethnic differentiation aside, a procedure made more difficult in any case by the fact of skin pigmentation. A Jew can be a Jew in his home and an Englishman in the street; this type of anonymity is simply not open to an Afro-Caribbean in Brixton or a Muslim in Bradford.

The acceptance of the reality of an ethnic and cultural pluralism in Britain has had profound repercussions. In the arena of anti-discrimination policy, race relations legislation has extended to ethnic minorities a range of protections which were never available to the Jews alone, but from which British Jews have undoubtedly benefited. For example, it has become possible, under the terms of the 1976 Act, to obtain protection against dismissal from employment on the grounds of sabbath observance, and to pursue cases of discrimination arising from the side-effects of the Arab boycott of Israel and of all things remotely Israeli. Recognition of the need for the media to cater for an ethnically diverse population has resulted in the proliferation of minority-oriented radio and television programmes; in London there is a radio station (Spectrum Radio) catering exclusively for the ethnic communities of the capital. Jews and British Jewry have benefited from this recognition. During its last years, the Greater London Council set aside funds for the specific purpose of assisting ethnic minorities; London Jewry benefited as a result. In the inner-London borough of Hackney, the *haredi* (strictly Orthodox) communities continue to derive great financial benefit from ethnically oriented borough council policies.

British Jews have gained in these and other ways, but the gains have more often than not come coincidentally, and almost as an embarrassment. The approach of British Jews to the fact and consequences of their own ethnicity has been anything but positive. There are a number of reasons why this should be so. To begin with, the notion of ethnicity has grown within the British state in a context which has placed ethnic minorities fairly firmly in the camp of the disadvantaged. Modern British Jews do not wish to be thought of as disadvantaged, part of a wider ethnic underclass. Then again, ethnicity is associated with the non-white population. British Jews—even Sefardim of recent oriental provenance—wish to be thought of as white rather than coloured. Thirdly, the notion of ethnicity carries cosmopolitan connotations. British Jews have argued for decades against the charge that they are an international, cosmopolitan intrusion into the British state.

Stemming from this is the most sensitive issue of dual loyalties, which some politicians have raised against the non-white minorities, more especially in the contexts of Islamic fundamentalism and the injection of foreign considerations (e.g. the tensions between Pakistan and Bangladesh) into British domestic politics. Of course British Jews harbour dual loyalties; but they are loath to admit as much in public.

The net result of all these considerations has been that the leaders of Anglo-Jewry have distanced themselves from any close identification with multiculturalism and with what we might term the ethnic dimension in contemporary British life. The Board of Deputies of British Jews has consistently opposed the inclusion of a Jewish category in the question on ethnic origins in the decennial census. Jews are not encouraged to seek redress through the instrumentality of the 1976 Race Relations Act, or to identify themselves as one of those minorities for which the Commission for Racial Equality sees itself as having a special responsibility. From Lord Jakobovits, when chief rabbi of the United Hebrew Congregations, came one of the strongest public denunciations of the multicultural society. In 1986, in his riposte to *Faith in the City*, the report of the Commission on Urban Priority Areas set up by the Archbishop of Canterbury, Robert Runcie, Jakobovits condemned the Blacks for wanting to change the character of British society into 'a multi-ethnic form' (*Jewish Chronicle*, 24 Jan. 1986, pp. 26–8)—as if professing and practising Jews had not already aided and abetted this process by their very presence in Britain.

However, this is not an attitude or a policy pursued by all sections of British Jewry. Partly as a result of the fragmentation of British Jewry over the past quarter-century or so, there is no longer one united community, but rather a series of separate Jewish communities in Britain which overlap to a greater or lesser extent. The *haredim* of Stamford Hill have much more in common with the *haredim* of Antwerp than with the United Synagogue Jews led now by a new chief rabbi, Jonathan Sacks. The integration of European institutions is bound to encourage cross-border co-operation and identification of this sort (for example, in relation to ritual slaughter). Indeed, in Stamford Hill the *haredim* have long ago repositioned themselves, purely for reasons of local politics, alongside other ethnic communities in Hackney, and in so doing have facilitated the receipt of financial assistance from local government.

As the European Community develops policies to address and assist ethnic groups, these sorts of financial inducements and pressures are bound to grow. Meanwhile, on the left of British Jewry (so to speak), outreach programmes designed to assist disadvantaged minority groups are also likely to result in a greater willingness among Jews to identify as an ethnic rather than as simply a religious entity. Self-styled 'secular' Jews have, in effect, adopted a purely ethnic form of identity.

For many British Jews, the transition from a religious to an ethnic status does not and will not come easily. But in the new Europe it is likely to prove an advantageous identity, and one which may be forced upon them in any case by the logic of events and policies beyond their control.

CHAPTER SIXTEEN

Religious Practice and Jewish Identity in a Sample of London Jews

STEPHEN H. MILLER

WITH an estimated Jewish population of around 300,000, the United Kingdom comes considerably behind Russia and France in terms of the size of its Jewish community, but it is arguably more varied in its Jewish lifestyle than any of its European neighbours. Although almost 90 per cent of Anglo-Jewish households are affiliated to a synagogue,[1] there is enormous variation in the religious ethos of British synagogues—from the fervent religious commitment of the right-wing Orthodox *shtiebl*, through the central Orthodox, Conservative, Reform, and Liberal communities, to radical Jewish groups who espouse universalist creeds only loosely associated with Jewish tradition.

This inherent variability in Jewish belief and practice is obscured by the statistics of synagogue membership. The great majority of synagogue members in the United Kingdom—about 70 per cent of them—belong to the central block of Orthodox synagogues that accept the authority of the Chief Rabbi and stand committed to the strict observance of Jewish law (*shabbat*, *kashrut*, etc.). This uniformity is deceptive, however, because only a small proportion of the members of these synagogues are themselves fully observant and committed Jews: the majority are not Orthodox, and they exhibit a wide variety of religious behaviours not dissimilar in scope to those of the rest of the Anglo-Jewish community. The United Kingdom may be unique

This chapter draws on part of a research project funded by the Stanley Kalms Foundation as a contribution to the 1992 review of the United Synagogue published as *A Time for Change: United Synagogue Review* (London, 1992). I am extremely grateful to Stanley Kalms, Simon Kaplan, and all the staff at Traditional Alternatives for their support and co-operation throughout the project. I am also indebted to Marlena Schmool for her invaluable help with the demographic aspects of the survey.

in having such a high proportion of Jews who choose to affiliate to a synagogue movement that does not represent their preferred Jewish life-style even though other synagogues, often located in close proximity, provide a far closer match.

The research reported in this chapter examined the Jewish identity of members of the largest of these central Orthodox groupings—the United Synagogue, a body which comprises more than sixty synagogues in London and surrounding areas of southeast England and has a total membership of just under 40,000—and tried to understand the tension between the religious principles of the institution and the Jewish practice of its members. The research was based on a postal questionnaire distributed to a random sample of 1,500 members and their spouses, and the findings reflect the views of 816 respondents (a 54% response rate). The sampling methodology and demographic characteristics of the sample are described in full in the report itself. The principal aim of the research was to examine patterns of belief, practice, and ethnicity in a central Orthodox community and to look at the relationships between these three aspects of Jewish identity.

RELIGIOUS OBSERVANCE

The survey began by investigating how members described their degree of religious observance. Respondents were asked to characterize their own level of observance by selecting one of five categories to represent 'the way you live in Jewish terms'. The percentage selecting each category is shown in Table 1.

The great majority of the respondents identified themselves as 'traditional' Jews. This represents the central block of nominally Orthodox members who, in their responses to open-ended questions, frequently describe themselves as 'middle of the road' Jews. To their left religiously is a sizeable group of less observant respondents who identified themselves as 'just Jewish',

Table 1. Self-Defined Level of Observance

Category	%
Non-religious (secular) Jew	4
Just Jewish	16
Progressive Jew (e.g. Reform)	3
'Traditional' (not strictly Orthodox)	67
Strictly Orthodox Jew (*shomer shabbat*)	10

'progressive', or 'non-religious'. These three subgroups cannot be distinguished from one another in terms of their responses to items concerned with religious practice and belief (see below), and they have therefore been treated as a single group of 'weak observers'. The remaining 10 per cent of respondents identified themselves as strictly Orthodox. The overall breakdown was therefore as follows: weak observers 23 per cent; traditional 67 per cent; strictly Orthodox 10 per cent.

Age and Observance

The above percentages varied somewhat with age. Older respondents (aged 61 or over) were more likely to be traditional (69 per cent) or weak observers (25 per cent) and far less likely to be strictly Orthodox (5 per cent). The corollary is that a higher proportion of middle-aged and younger respondents identified themselves as Orthodox (13 per cent).

This trend may reflect an increasing tendency among younger Jews to select a synagogue that is seen as being consistent with their Jewish lifestyle. Following the American pattern, non-observant Jews may now be more inclined to join a Progressive synagogue than were their parents;[2] this would leave a higher *proportion* of strictly Orthodox members in the younger age groups of the United Synagogue. Further evidence for this hypothesis is found in the recently observed growth in the membership of Progressive synagogues at the expense of the central Orthodox.[3]

Alternatively, the higher percentage of young Orthodox may be due to differential rates of response, to increased religiosity in the younger age groups, or even to changes in religious practice as people get older.

Patterns of Observance

'Traditional' Jews

As Table 2 shows, the pattern of religious practice among those Jews who categorize themselves as traditional is remarkably consistent.

Following the American pattern, those practices that interfere least with full participation in the wider community (e.g. annual events such as Yom Kippur, the Passover Seder) are the most resistant to erosion, while those that would impact on daily life are more frequently sacrificed. Thus, respondents who describe themselves as traditional are very consistent in their neglect of these 'more demanding' practices: 88 per cent travel by car on the sabbath, and 95 per cent turn on lights on the sabbath.

The only significant source of variation in this group relates to (*a*) the eating of non-kosher meat outside the home and (*b*) attendance at synagogue. Willingness to eat non-kosher meat divides traditional Jews into two

Table 2. Patterns of Observance among Traditional Jews

Religious practice	% observance
Fast on Yom Kippur (or exempt on health grounds)	97
Attend a Passover Seder every year	93
Prefer to stay at home on Friday night	92
Avoid work on Rosh Hashanah	92
Light candles every Friday evening	83
Have a *mezuzah* on all doors	75
Separate milk and meat dishes at home	69

almost equal subgroups (48 per cent do, 52 per cent do not). Similarly, attendance at synagogue is an occasional event for 59 per cent of respondents, but a regular practice (once a month or more often) for the remaining 41 per cent. These practices, together with the items listed above, form the basis of a scale of religious observance which is examined in later sections.

Weak observers

Respondents who classified themselves as either Progressive, secular, or 'just Jewish' had distinctly lower levels of ritual practice than traditional Jews (see Table 3). Like the traditional group, the weak observers fail to keep the more demanding rituals associated with the sabbath, but in addition, the percentage who keep the other key practices is 20–40 per cent lower than in the traditional group.

Further, a weak observer may keep a more demanding practice (e.g. separate dishes) while neglecting a more commonly observed one (e.g. staying at home on Friday night). This is in contrast to the traditional respondents, among whom anybody performing a demanding religious

Table 3. Patterns of Observance among Weak Observers

Religious practice	% observance
Attend a Passover Seder every year	69
Avoid work on Rosh Hashanah	69
Light candles every Friday evening	42
Have a *mezuzah* on all doors	47
Separate milk and meat dishes at home	23

practice will tend to observe all those less demanding (more frequently observed) practices as well. Hence, while the traditional respondents are relatively consistent and individually ordered in their patterns of ritual practice, the weak observers are more variable and idiosyncratic.

The Orthodox

Members of the strictly Orthodox group are, by definition, reliable and consistent in their religious observance. All the respondents who placed themselves in this category claimed to subscribe to the practices expected of religiously observant Jews (for example, avoiding any action rabbinically classified as work on the sabbath), and therefore appear to have used the self-classification scale accurately. No attempt was made to distinguish degrees of orthodoxy within this group.

RELIGIOUS BELIEFS

Measuring Religious Beliefs

The questionnaire incorporated a number of items related to belief in God and other aspects of Jewish faith that have been validated in previous studies. In most cases, respondents were asked to express their level of agreement or disagreement with a statement using a five-point scale, the mid-point representing 'not certain'. Table 4 indicates the percentage agreeing (or strongly agreeing) with a positive item or the percentage disagreeing (or strongly disagreeing) with a negative item.

The responses shown in Table 4, in common with those of previous studies, reveal moderate levels of religious conviction. Broadly speaking,

---

Table 4. Affirmation of Religious Beliefs

Statement	% affirming Jewish view
1. The Jewish people have a special relationship with God	52
2. Praying to God can help to overcome personal problems	52
3. The Torah is the actual (or inspired) word of God	56
4. The universe came about by chance	42 (disagree)
5. Belief in God is not central to being a good Jew	41 (disagree)
6. Judaism has many laws and customs, but they do not help you to become a better person	33 (disagree)

about 50 per cent of the respondents appear to have some degree of faith in God, although the first three items might be seen as reflections of the way individuals respond subjectively to the concept of God rather than judgements of a more existential kind. The fourth item, which calls directly for a view of God's role in human history, elicits weaker support. The last two statements, linking Jewish belief and practice to morality, are still less commonly supported.

Relationship between Belief and Ritual Observance

The levels of belief reported in Table 4 represent aggregate figures for the entire sample. Given that the items reflect quite fundamental elements of Jewish faith, one might have expected the more observant respondents to display substantially stronger levels of belief than the less observant. To some extent this is what happened, but there were some interesting deviations.

Comparing the strictly Orthodox with the rest of the sample there is, as expected, a clear relationship between ritual observance and religious belief. Thus, while less than 40 per cent of traditional and weak observers see belief in God as 'central to being a good Jew', more than 70 per cent of the strictly Orthodox see a connection. Similarly, only 38 per cent of the non-Orthodox reject the idea that 'the universe came about by chance', but among the strictly Orthodox 84 per cent reject it.

However, if the 10 per cent who are strictly Orthodox are excluded from the analysis, the relationship between belief and practice becomes very much weaker, even though there is still a very substantial variation in ritual practice. The range extends from the most observant wing of the traditional group (strict *kashrut*, partial observance of the sabbath, and frequent attendance at synagogue) through to the minimal practices of some weak observers (only occasional attendance at the Passover Seder, a *mezuzah* on the front door but festive decorations at Christmas—the latter reported by 22 per cent of weak observers).

But despite this wide variation, the correlation coefficient between observance and belief among the non-Orthodox is just 0.34—that is, differences in religious belief explain only about 11 per cent of the variation in people's ritual observance. In other words, the large gulf between the religious practices of the traditional Jew and those of the non-observant, secular Jew is not clearly related to fundamental differences in belief. This is in contrast to other religious groups, such as Catholics and Muslims, where variations in observance seem to be driven to a large extent by differences in faith or belief.[4] For our respondents, outside the Orthodox fringe, belief and observance seem to be virtually independent of each other.

ETHNIC IDENTIFICATION

Indicators of Ethnicity

Ethnicity is a difficult concept. An attempt to define an ethnic group objectively may make reference to its distinctive religion, culture, language, or physical appearance, but none of these attributes, nor any permutation of them, can be held to characterize every group that is recognized by scholars as being ethnically distinct. If there is one necessary and sufficient condition for membership of an ethnic group, it is surely a subjective feeling of belonging, of kinship, of a desire for group continuity and a sense of corporate identity. Individual differences in the strength of ethnic identity may therefore be measured by items which assess the degree of affiliation to the group and social interaction with it. Using such measures, and in contrast to the moderate levels of religious belief, the respondents expressed very strong feelings of identity with fellow Jews, most of them agreeing or strongly agreeing with the following statements: 'An unbreakable bond unites Jews all over the world' (88 per cent); 'A Jew should marry someone who is Jewish' (94 per cent); 'It is important that Jews survive as a people' (98 per cent).

Jewish friendship patterns also reflect high levels of in-group preference, with 84 per cent of respondents claiming that 'all' or 'more than half' their close friends were Jewish. And even when Jewishness is pitted against Englishness—as in 'I think of myself more as English than as Jewish'—only 19 per cent give precedence to nationality over ethnicity. But deep down, English Jews are perhaps more English than they claim to be: only 43 per cent of the sample subscribe to the view that 'when it comes to a crisis, Jews can only depend on other Jews'.

Relationships between Ethnic Identification, Belief, and Practice

With agreement to most of the identity statements approaching 100 per cent, there is limited opportunity, statistically speaking, to examine variations in ethnic identity. None the less, there is some evidence of a (predictable) relationship between level of observance and strength of identity. For example, the statement that 'a Jew should marry someone who is Jewish' elicited 96 per cent support among traditional Jews, but only 83 per cent among the weak observers. Similarly, 68 per cent of traditional Jews rejected the notion that they are more English than Jewish, in comparison with only 48 per cent of the weak observers.

The interesting finding is not so much that there should be a relationship between ethnicity and religious observance, but that it should be stronger than the correlation between belief and observance (0.4 *vs.* 0.34)—even though the measures of ethnicity are themselves relatively insensitive. This shows that variations in religious observance have more to do with the intensity of a person's Jewish identity than with his or her beliefs—at least among the non-Orthodox. It is also consistent with qualitative research findings that a feeling of belonging, rather than belief in God, is the driving force behind synagogue attendance and other forms of involvement in synagogue life.

SUMMARY: THE MAIN FEATURES OF JEWISHNESS

In addition to the specific items relating to Jewish practice and belief, respondents were asked to make a forced choice of 'the two most important aspects of being Jewish' from the following list:

- Sense of attachment to Israel
- Jewish home life (food, customs, etc.)
- Links with fellow Jews, Jewish friends
- Jewish culture (art, music, etc.)
- Jewish practices and religion
- Loyalty to the Jewish heritage

The responses to this question can be used to summarize the simple typology of Jewishness described above.

The *strictly Orthodox* have consistent and high ratings on all three dimensions—belief, practice, and ethnic identity. The pattern of responses suggests that fundamental beliefs drive religious practice, rather than a sense of Jewish identity. When forced to select the two most important features of their Jewishness, Orthodox respondents selected, predictably, 'Jewish practices and religion' (77 per cent) followed by 'Jewish home life' (46 per cent). The social, cultural, and Israel-oriented dimensions featured less prominently.

The *traditional* group are very strongly identified in an ethnic sense, observe a common set of key, family-oriented practices (with little variation), but have moderate to low levels of religious belief. In their case, it is the sense of identity, the desire to belong and to support Jewish family life, that seems to influence religious practice. Hence, for traditional Jews, the two most important aspects of being Jewish are 'Jewish home life' (selected by 61 per cent) and 'loyalty to the Jewish heritage' (55 per cent). 'Links with fellow Jews' comes third, with religious, Israel-oriented, and cultural aspects being less salient.

The *weak observers* resemble traditional Jews in having relatively low levels of belief and in being strongly identified in an ethnic sense—though not quite as strongly as the traditional group. They are, however, far less religiously observant, and far more individualistic in their religious practices. For weak observers, as for traditional Jews, observance is more closely related to strength of identity than to belief, but that identity is less family-oriented and more global in nature. Hence weak observers cite the more diffuse category 'loyalty to the Jewish heritage' as the prime aspect of their Jewishness (70 per cent), and 'links with fellow Jews' as the second most salient feature (55 per cent). 'Jewish home life', which is the most important factor for traditional Jews, receives support from only 31 per cent, equal to that accorded to a 'sense of attachment to Israel'.

Weak observers, defining themselves as non-Orthodox or even as secular, are a substantial subgroup (23 per cent) of the United Synagogue membership. It is not difficult to explain why weak observers should retain a few religious practices as a symbolic representation of their ethnic identity, but their decision to express their affiliation via an Orthodox synagogue remains an enigma.

SYNAGOGUE ATTENDANCE

Synagogue attendance is of interest in its own right, and Table 5 summarizes respondents' attendance by gender and religious grouping. In broad terms, it shows the familiar pattern: the majority of respondents are 'three times a year' attenders (or thereabouts), while only 29 per cent attend once a week or more often. However there is evidence of significantly higher levels of attendance than those recorded in previous surveys: in Redbridge in 1983 only 10 per cent of those belonging to Orthodox synagogues were regular weekly attenders,[5] and in Edgware in 1969 only 13.6 per cent came into this category.[6] Even allowing for some response bias and for geographical

Table 5. Synagogue Attendance, by Gender and Religious Grouping (per cent)

	All	Males	Females	Weak observers	Traditional	Orthodox
Not at all	7	6	8	18	4	1
Only Yom Kippur (or only on a few occasions)	53	47	59	67	55	9
About once a month	12	13	11	8	14	4
Most sabbaths (morning only)	20	20	20	5	21	44
More often	9	15	2	2	6	41

variations, it appears that there has been a substantial revival in synagogue attendance rates since these earlier studies. This may mirror the revival in synagogue attendance in third-generation American Jews, which sociologist Steven Cohen sees as part of a move from individual ritual practice to increased involvement in institutional forms of identification.[7]

A more immediate explanation traces the increase in attendance to the disappearance of the gender bias reported in earlier studies. Excluding those who attend several times per week, the proportion of weekly attenders who are female is now 50 per cent, compared to the 40 per cent found in earlier studies.

The variations in attendance across the religious subgroups are not unexpected, but the degree of polarization is worthy of note. In particular, the rate of attendance of respondents who classified themselves as 'just Jewish' or Progressive (a subset of the weak observers) was substantially lower than that of affiliated members of Progressive synagogues in the Redbridge survey. Since the present sample is slightly under-representative of the less involved, the percentage of rare synagogue attenders is probably higher than that suggested in Table 5.

Focusing specifically on regular attenders (those who attend almost every sabbath morning or more often), Table 6 compares how the proportion of regular attenders varies with age in the current United Synagogue survey and in the 1983 survey of the community in Redbridge.

I have already noted that rates of attendance have increased substantially relative to those reported in earlier studies, but Table 6 locates the increase among the younger age groups. Again one has to allow for geographical variations and possible response bias, but there can be little doubt that higher proportions of young people are attending synagogue than in the past.

To summarize: these data point to a growing rate of participation in synagogue services and increased interest among the young and among

Table 6. Regular Synagogue Attendance by Age-Group

Age-group	% of age-group attending synagogue regularly	
	United Synagogue	**Redbridge**
20–40	25	7
41–60	34	9
60+	23	19

female members. The trend has been so marked that gender and age biases in attendance have almost disappeared. Polarization seems to have increased, however, since the proportion of non-attenders is similar to that reported in the Edgware and Redbridge studies even though regular attendance has increased.

Given the parallel erosion in ritual performance among traditional Jews, it is difficult to escape the conclusion that the synagogue has become a major element in maintaining ethnic ties, quite independently of, or even at the expense of, its religious significance. An anecdotal observation which supports this view is the frequency with which regular attenders now openly bring babies' strollers into some United Synagogue premises on the sabbath —a practice that would have been thoroughly discouraged on religious grounds a decade ago.

THE MISMATCH BETWEEN SYNAGOGUE AFFILIATION AND PERSONAL PRACTICE

I began by noting the tension between the Orthodox stance of the United Synagogue and the non-Orthodox practice of the majority of its members. To some extent this inconsistency is resolving itself by a process of realignment; younger members of the traditional (non-Orthodox) Jewish community are joining Progressive synagogues in greater numbers, while the proportion of younger United Synagogue members who are strictly Orthodox is rising. But there remain large numbers of traditional Jews who show no sign of shifting their affiliation and, as noted above, seem to be increasing their involvement in synagogue life.

For these members it would seem that the synagogue is undergoing a transformation in the way it is construed; it is becoming less of a religious institution and more of a focus for the expression of ethnic identification. Given the minimal role of religious belief in the continuation of ritual behaviour, it is not surprising that the synagogue should be seen by some purely as an ethnic club. Once this redefinition occurs, the mismatch between individual practice and the formal position of the synagogue ceases to have any psychological substance.

Here again the United Kingdom is following American trends. The transformation of religious ritual into more loosely defined, ethnically based ceremony is a well-documented feature of American Jewish life and may be seen as a constructive adaptation to modernism.[8] It permits continued engagement in Jewish life and the maintaining of religious distinctiveness without the inconvenience that stems from the precise ritual observance dictated by adherence to religious belief.

There remains, however, a new form of dissonance. If ritual—seen as a link between man and God—is replaced by ceremony—seen as a link between Jew and fellow Jew—what is the essential value and meaning of that ceremony? For some, no doubt, the reinforcement of kinship will be sufficient, but for the more reflective and analytical members of the community, such arbitrary forms may prove unacceptable. This may explain the rapid contraction of the traditional Jewish community through movement in both directions: towards assimilation on the one hand, and to a rediscovered Orthodoxy on the other. Both of these trends may be seen as an attempt to reduce dissonance between the observance of ritual and the erosion of faith.

Notes

1. Steven Haberman, Barry Kosmin, and Caren Levy, 'Mortality Patterns of British Jews', *Journal of the Royal Statistical Society (A)*, 146: 3 (1983), 294–310.
2. Bernard Lazerwitz, 'Basic Characteristics of American Jewish Denominations', *Sociological Papers*, 2: 1 (1993).
3. See Stephen Miller, 'The Impact of Jewish Education on the Religious Behaviour and Attitudes of British Secondary School Pupils', *Studies in Jewish Education*, 3 (1988), 150–65.
4. Elizabeth Weiss Ozorak, 'Social and Cognitive Influences on the Development of Religious Beliefs', *Journal for the Scientific Study of Religion*, 28: 4 (1989), 448–63.
5. Barry Kosmin and Caren Levy, *Jewish Identity in an Anglo-Jewish Community* (Research Unit of the Board of Deputies of British Jews, 1983).
6. Ernest Krausz, 'The Edgware Survey: Factors in Jewish Identification', *Jewish Journal of Sociology*, 11 (1969), 151–63.
7. Steven Cohen, *American Modernity and Jewish Identity* (New York, 1983).
8. Charles Liebman and Steven Cohen, *Two Worlds of Judaism* (New Haven, Conn., 1990).

CHAPTER SEVENTEEN

Jewish Identity in the Germany of a New Europe

JULIUS CARLEBACH

Rabbi Yochanan ben Zakai said:
Woe is me if I should speak
Woe is me if I should not speak!

THE future of the Jewish people is in its history. That is why it is
especially difficult to project it, to forecast progress in line with the
movements of other nations and peoples. And if special difficulties exist in
analysing trends in Jewish life generally, these are exacerbated in any consideration of the situation of the German Jews, by which I mean the Jews
living in Germany today.

Of course, no discussion of the Jews living in Germany today can be
entirely divorced from a consideration of the past. Nowhere in the diaspora
were Jews closer to their host nation than the Jews of Germany were before
the Second World War; no ethnic group has drawn more deeply and more
consistently from the cultural and moral concerns of its neighbours. According to Julius Guttmann, the philosopher of Jewish history, the great heritage
of German Jewry drew heavily on German traditions. First, *religious
orientations*: the various different directions that Jews all over the world
would follow in coming to terms with the secularization of modern life were
developed in Germany: it was the Jews from the land of Martin Luther and
the Reformation who added Reform and Conservative dimensions as well as
a revitalized Orthodoxy to the religious concepts of Judaism. Their second
achievement, according to Guttmann, lay in the creation of a *Wissenschaft des
Judentums*—a science of Judaism that was an explicit attempt to align the
Jewish tradition with the supposedly objective, disinterested values applied
in the scholarly study of the humanities (*Geisteswissenschaften*) which were so
prominent and overpowering in German intellectualism. Thirdly, there was
modern philosophy, a characteristic of German life deeply integrated into the

very soul of Jewish thinkers, from the Hegelianism of Edward Gans to the neo-Kantianism of Hermann Cohen.

If it took more than a century to create this great heritage, it took a mere twelve years to uproot it, to tear it out of that soil which Jews had for a millennium regarded as their own. Instead there was the Holocaust—the murder of the Jews of Europe, beginning with the Jews of Germany: a total rupturing of the course of Jewish history. Never again would Jews be able to rely in the same way on rational discourse, social justice, or the supremacy of law to guarantee them security, harmony, and peace of mind in a non-Jewish environment. Even when Jews today feel safe where they are, they can no longer be sure that this will also apply to their children. If the Jews of yesteryear strove to create a better tomorrow for their children, the Jews of today have not yet succeeded in overcoming their yesterdays. This goes for all Jews, and much more so for Jews who live in Germany. To themselves, no less than to the world at large, they are a puzzle, an astonishment—notwithstanding the fact that there has never been a time when Jews were more welcome, more protected, and better tolerated than they are in that centrepiece of the new Europe—the Federal Republic of Germany.

THE COMPLEXITIES OF THE ISSUE

The complexity of the problem of post-Holocaust German–Jewish relations can be gauged by the differing views that exist on the question of a renewal of Jewish life in Germany. Robert Weltsch, Zionist editor and journalist, writing in 1946, took a very rigorous view: 'Germany is no place for Jews', he stated. Leo Baeck, leader of German Progressive Judaism, also thought that the relationship Jews had cultivated with Germans over a thousand years had ended with National Socialism, never to return. But another contemporary, the founder of the *Allgemeine Jüdische Wochenzeitung*, Karl Marx, regarded the National Socialist period as but an interlude and looked to the time when Jews in a repentant Germany would be a bridge linking past and future.

In fact, time and Jewish need have transformed the perception of continuing and unyielding hostility. Today Germany is once again a land of Jewish immigration: its Jewish population remains small (less than 0.01 per cent of the population), but it is increasing. So we might usefully speculate on the kind of Jewish life likely to develop in Germany, on the determinants in the struggle for a Jewish identity for coming generations who will not have experienced the apocalyptic events that overwhelmed their predecessors.

There are four components that have to be internalized by those who wish to be Jews in Germany: Israel, Germany, the Holocaust, and Jewishness—not necessarily, of course, in that order. It is a circular set of factors in which now one, now the other, dominates the thoughts and feelings of the thinking Jew. All four are, in their own way, problematic.

Regarding Israel, the difficulty lies in the twist that has been engineered to change the world's perception of the Jews of Israel from David to Goliath, from oppressed to oppressor. All the palliative resolutions of the United Nations cannot undo the harm done by fifteen years of its equating Zionism with racism. A whole generation the world over has been tainted by that resolution, and all Jews, more especially those living in Germany, have been disfigured by it. For all that, Israel is and will continue to be a challenge and an inspiration; but it will also be a source of conflict.

Germany itself is problematic because of the affinity that Jews have always felt with German social and cultural aspirations. In the flourishing Germany of today these continue to be seductive and overpowering, so that there is at all times the implicit pressure to assimilate, to merge, to be identified with those whose life-styles and traditions seem so appealing.

It may appear superfluous to comment on the problematics of the Holocaust, but it is necessary because in this respect the burden of the Jew living in Germany is greater and certainly much heavier to bear. Jews in other lands tend to deal with this issue in one of two ways, which tend to be mutually exclusive. Some regard the Holocaust as a Jewish tragedy now belonging to the past—one more episode in the long litany of Jewish suffering. Others present it and its perpetrators as the embodiment of evil: in their deeply ingrained hostility, they reject not only all Germans but also Jews who live in Germany. For the Germans themselves, an accommodation with the appalling past seems to be gaining ground. Germans have all along rejected the notion of collective guilt, but a collective shame is frequently expressed; there is also a nearly obsessive need to restore and reconstruct symbols of the past, a process of memorialization aimed at atonement and the symbolic expression of a sense of remorse.[1] At the same time, there are also, and probably always will be, those whose views are expressed by the destruction of memorials and not by their preservation.

Germans may wish to dissociate themselves from a sense of guilt in connection with the Holocaust, but no Jew living in Germany is able to escape it. Somewhere, somehow, there is a nagging pain in the psyche, a more or less conscious feeling of having betrayed and of continuing to betray the millions of Jews who lie buried in or had their ashes scattered across the fields and plains of eastern Europe. There is no relief from this pain, nor any let-up. The only thing that changes is the way in which it manifests itself. The physical proximity of victim to perpetrators and their respective descendants can distort relationships on both sides; the meaning of a Jewish identity is obscured through the intervention of incomprehensible realities which a Jew outside Germany does not have to face.

Jews who are blessed with a strong Jewish identity perhaps know better how to cope with the knowledge of the Holocaust. They are able to draw on their Jewishness, on their deepest roots, to resolve the conflict, to contain what must be their grief for all time. For those who suffered and died were not only silent witnesses of inhumanity at its worst, they were also bearers and creators of a long and glorious tradition, the link between the present generation and its awe-inspiring ancestors. The greater the distance from the Holocaust, both spatial and temporal, the more Jews will be able to engross themselves in remembering those who lived rather than those who died. But for the new generations of Jews in Germany, the evil is too close for such a perspective to be possible.

I shall demonstrate the problems that surround the development of a Jewish identity in today's Germany by focusing on two issues: the construction of a history of the return of Jewish life to Germany after the Holocaust, and the question of the return of Jewish studies to Germany. Both factors have a part to play in the formation of Jewish identities in the Germany of the twenty-first century and are certainly good indicators of the convoluted realities that Jews in Germany have to unravel.

One must not forget, however, that there is a whole range of other problems with which Jews who live in Germany must come to terms not only in the context of their immediate environment but also in the face of an unsympathetic response from the Jewish world at large. The question of intermarriage, for example, often needs to be considered in a context different from that in which it appears elsewhere because the non-Jewish partner may be the person who saved the Jewish partner's life during the war. Questions of conversion to Judaism may well be much more widespread than many assume and will also often call for halakhic decisions regarding the 'Jewishness' of individuals. Another critical issue is the politically determined lack of religious orientation today: in the birthplace of not only Reform and Conservative Judaism, but also of what is known (albeit incorrectly) as Neo-Orthodoxy, there are now no recognized religious movements except in Berlin. Instead, the spiritual leadership in most communities tends to follow traditional Jewish practice while the great majority of the members remain largely indifferent or tolerantly uninvolved—a consequence of the continued manifestation of the nineteenth-century concept of *Einheitsgemeinde* which is no longer relevant.[2] A closely related problem concerns the development of leadership patterns for communities which have lost their traditional norms and which in some instances have not overcome the suspicions generated by unresolved conflicts over degrees of collaboration with and assistance to totalitarian governments. This brief listing will also make clear that the two topics I have chosen to look at impinge on all the others, and may be expected to influence Jewish identities in Germany.

THE RETURN OF JEWISH LIFE TO GERMANY AFTER THE HOLOCAUST

A question frequently asked is why 'the rabbis' did not place a ban on a return of Jews to Germany after the Holocaust, as had been done in 1492 after the Jews had been expelled from Spain. This seemingly logical question betrays the almost total lack of historical awareness among all but a handful of specialist scholars. The simple answer would be that since Spain forbade the Jews to return, there was no problem for 'the rabbis' to promulgate their own ban without having to worry about enforcing it; but the situation in Germany was quite different.[3] Moreover, the very fact that the question was raised was a manipulation effected both to discredit the Jews who returned to (or remained in) post-war Germany, and to enhance further the already outstanding achievements of Jewish rescue agencies outside Germany.

There is as yet insufficient knowledge about the events in the immediate post-war years in Germany, and indeed in Europe generally. It could be argued that the years from 1945 to 1951—that is, from the end of the Second World War to the declaration by Chancellor Adenauer before the Bundestag acknowledging the responsibility of the German people—can be counted as among the most glorious and most wonderful in the long, mostly bitter, history of the Jews. This is quite apart from the miraculous re-establishment of the Jews as a sovereign people in their ancient homeland in 1948, and apart from the deep satisfaction felt by every Jew who witnessed the downfall and destruction of the most evil opponent the Jews had ever had to face. But in the immediate post-war period, things were much more sombre. When the guns fell silent in all of Europe in 1945, the extent of the disaster that had befallen the Jewish people began slowly to reveal itself. Very few Jews who had lived under German domination had survived. For those who had, the shock of returning to towns and villages now devoid of their Jewish population, compounded in some cases (notably in Poland) by incidents of hatred and violence, caused new traumas that were sufficient to inspire Jews in their thousands to flee west to Germany. Aided by Jewish rescue organizations and especially Zionist organizations, they made their way to the American zone of occupation, to the camps and DP (Displaced

Persons) centres which had been established in Germany to accommodate the massive confusion of peoples of different nations, most of whom had been brought there during the war as slave labourers. Ethnic tensions in these nationally mixed camps, including antisemitism, eventually forced the Allies to separate the different peoples into their national groups, with a separate group and separate camps for the Jews.

By 1946, there were thus a great number of Jews living in Germany. These included Jews in former concentration camps like Bergen-Belsen (the chief camp controlled by the British), which alone had a Jewish population after the war of over 14,000, Jews in urban centres, survivors with non-Jewish partners, as well as the half- and quarter-Jews who had been classified as Jews by the Nazis though they had never identified themselves in that way. All of these survivors—from the refugees from eastern Europe, who brought a great deal of Orthodoxy with them, to those who had never had any contact with Jewish life—were sheltered, supported, healed, trained, and guided by Jewish voluntary agencies, mainly from the United States, such as the 'Joint' (American Joint Distribution Committee) and ORT (Organization for Rehabilitation through Training), both now famous and respected for their work. Help also came from smaller organizations with distinct clienteles, like the Zionist agricultural training centres (*hakhsharot*) for those aiming to live on a kibbutz, and the Va'ad Hatzoloh (rescue committee) of the Agudas Yisroel, which catered for some 40,000 Orthodox Jewish refugees and survivors.

The scale of all these operations, covering more than 200,000 Jews, is too vast to be described here, but a report written by the director of the Va'ad Hatzoloh organization in 1947 gives some idea of the extent of their activities. It was involved in establishing 15 *yeshivot* and 53 Talmud Torah primary schools; publishing over 100,000 prayer-books and providing religious requisites; running 24 kosher kitchens that supplied food to hospitals, as well as to its general clientele; establishing children's homes and old-age homes; and providing a full range of religious services, from the slaughter of kosher meat to ritual baths and circumcision. The various agencies were successful in that they not only cared for needy, hungry, sick, and uprooted human beings but also gave most of the survivors a sense of future, of renewal, of rescue in its broadest sense.

By 1950, though, most of the Jews had left Germany. With them they took their learning, their Jewishness, and their heritage. The few thousand Jews who remained behind were not only bereft of a sense of purpose and community, they were also shunned and despised by Jews outside Germany. Some were people who had returned from Israel, unable to settle there; others were led by strong political convictions to seek a share in rebuilding a new Germany. Some sought pensions and restitution; others were simply too old or too sick to try again. Most suffered the guilt of the survivor.

As the economy in Germany revived and standards of living rose, there came the added guilt of being a Jew in Germany. For many years they consoled and reassured themselves that the temporariness of the DP era still applied. They had a suitcase packed, they were ready to go at any moment; in the meantime they sought solace through generous and devoted support of Israel. In the meantime, too, their children grew up in Germany and were educated in Germany. They were resentful of the ambivalent attitudes towards all things German, contemptuous of the ready-packed suitcase, unwilling to share the parental guilt. Above all, they were angry at being deprived of a place in history: they could identify neither with the distinguished history of pre-Nazi German Jewry nor with the moving Jewish revival in Germany in the period after the Holocaust, a magnificent period in German Jewish history of which no traces remained once the great majority of Jewish survivors had left. It is these people and their children, and those Jews who have come to Germany since the war, who are now in search of a Jewish identity.

THE RETURN OF JEWISH STUDIES TO GERMANY

It is my contention that Jewish studies, whether conducted in the context of a religious Judaism or in a university setting, not only can but must contribute to reinforcing Jewish identities. I am conscious in saying so that I am articulating a personal view which might not be shared by all my colleagues in this field, but this is my proposition and I shall now explore it.

After the war it took a long time before Jewish studies returned to German universities. In 1964 a *Judaistik* post was established in the Free University of Berlin; Cologne followed suit in 1966, and Frankfurt in 1970.[4] By the end of the 1970s there were some thirteen centres, chairs, or institutions devoted to some aspect or several aspects of Jewish studies.[5] Unlike in the pre-war period, all these centres were financed from public funds. Following the traditional pattern from Leopold Zunz to Gershom Scholem and later scholars, they were often engaged in criticism of one another, in disputes which only rarely stemmed from issues in the study of Judaism. But one feature that they shared, quite different from the situation that had obtained in the pre-war period, was that they were all totally divorced from any sectarian purpose and from any association with a living religion. However, the need for an institution where students could be trained to serve Jewish communities while at the same time acquiring a proper university-level education—a need that was most certainly recognized in Germany before the war—remained.

In 1979, in recognition of this need, the Central Committee of the Jews in Germany, supported by the Federal Government and the State of Baden-Württemberg, established the Hochschule für Jüdische Studien (not *Judaistik*, note) in Heidelberg as an institution that could fulfil both functions. It is not actually part of the University of Heidelberg, but it maintains a close association with that institution. Students follow a broadly based programme leading to the award of an MA degree, and funds are available to maintain the six professorial posts needed for the core courses of the programme: a thorough grounding in modern and classical Hebrew to enable students to work with texts in Bible, Talmud, Jewish philosophy, and classical and modern literature. This conception of Jewish studies, which follows the model generally adopted in Israel and English-speaking countries, allows for a broader approach than the *Judaistik* departments of German universities, which have at most two professorial positions. In this respect the Hochschule is privileged, but on the other hand it has the responsibility of dealing with issues that will determine the Jewishness of the institution, and with that its viability.

It would demand too much space to deal with all these issues here, but a brief outline will show how central these concerns are and will be if the Hochschule is to play its intended role in forging the Jewish identities necessary for the reconstruction of Jewish life in Germany.

1. *Relationship with the state*. This is perhaps the simplest issue because there is a constitution that regulates the relationships between the state and all institutions of higher education, and the same principles can be adopted. Continued government support will be crucial in allowing the Hochschule to operate in its dual function and in facilitating the research that is a necessary component of its programme.

2. *The balance between Jews and non-Jews*. At present, some 80 per cent of the student body is not Jewish. Given the small number of Jews in Germany, this disproportion is likely to continue in the foreseeable future. It must also be said that the non-Jewish students have always supported, and for the most part welcomed, the emphasis on Judaism as a living religion in the Hochschule, but it would be irresponsible not to acknowledge that there are deep-seated dilemmas here.

For Jews, it is often a new experience to share their heritage with others, and doing so can be problematic not least because it raises questions of the non-Jewish students' motive and intent. To cite one well-known case, Johann A. Eisenmenger, who studied and taught Hebrew at Heidelberg in the late seventeenth century and spent nineteen years studying rabbinics with Jewish teachers, went on to publish a viciously anti-Jewish text, *Entdecktes Judentum*. On the other hand, Hermann L. Strack (1848–1942) was perhaps the greatest non-Jewish authority on rabbinics in his time—his *Introduction to the Talmud and Midrash* is used to this day—and he was the founder and director of the Berlin-based Institutum Judaicum. He vigorously defended Jews against antisemitic attacks, but was at the same time a forceful missionary.

For the non-Jews, particularly for practising Christians, the experience of learning in such an institution can also be difficult, the more so since acknowledgement of the difficulties tends to be repressed. There have been theology students who have come in search of corroboration of their faith and are resentful if they find instead that the opposite is happening. Others come seeking absolution of their sense of guilt for the Holocaust and are disappointed that none is offered. It must be said that most of the non-Jewish students have a positive attitude to the situation, but the potential for tension demands that the subject must always be open for discussion, and not least because that is the only basis for meaningful dialogue.

3. *Jewish isolationism.* This is the other side of the coin. It is true that forms of withdrawal, of isolation, are deeply embedded in the Jewish tradition, from biblical times (Lev. 20: 26) to the present-day *haredim*. They have their roots in a Jewish theory that assumes that all human beings need a cultural identity before they can identify with the rest of mankind. In traditional Judaism, universalism can only be achieved through particularism. But Jewish isolationism could be misconstrued, and should therefore also always be open to debate.

4. *Scientism.* This is the ultimate weapon used in controlling recalcitrant institutions. Its mystical dimensions, ever present, are incomprehensible because the concept as it is used does not appear to differentiate between scientific process and scientific method. It also seems strange to assign the descriptions scientific/non-scientific to institutions which should properly only be judged by the work they produce.

5. *Jewish studies as a science.* There are two models to choose from here. The first comes from Hermann Cohen and Franz Rosenzwieg, the German Jewish philosophers and pioneers in the scientific study of Judaism who advocated that *Jüdische Wissenschaft* should serve not only the advancement of knowledge but should also be instrumental in revitalizing Jewish life, restoring and enhancing the inner dynamics of Jewish creativity for future generations of Jews. The other approach, perhaps more important because most students of Jewish studies in Germany are today largely not themselves Jewish, is that of Eugen Täubler and Julius Guttmann, whose constant emphases on complete objectivity and scientifically recognized methodologies in the *Wissenschaft des Judentums* were the hallmark of the final, greatest, and most productive period of that movement. Nevertheless, both Taübler and Guttmann also believed that even the most ephemeral enquiry into a Jewish theme will, if conducted with the rigour and precision of a scientific enterprise, ultimately become part of a living, pulsating Jewish world.

6. *Academic and vocational training.* This is a topic very specific to the Hochschule. Coming from a background of British and US universities I find it very difficult to understand why the dual function of the Hochschule as an academic and vocational centre should be so problematic. I think of institutions like Jews' College in London, which offers University of London internal degrees from BA to Ph.D. in Jewish studies while also training rabbis and teachers. Then there is the famous Jewish Theological Seminary in New York, with its formidable reputation both as a centre for research and as a rabbinical seminary; there is Yeshiva University, and the Hebrew Union College in Cincinnati, and many more. In all universities in Israel, the student sitting next to you may very well be a candidate for rabbinical ordination. Yet in the Hochschule the dual function that was originally conceptualized has not yet been achieved. This was partly because Jewish training resources are hard to come by, but mainly because it was felt that the introduction of vocational programmes would somehow dilute the scientific enterprise. But speaking scientifically, it can be said that all the available evidence seems to refute the claim that the two functions cannot be carried out in a single institution.

All these factors will in some way, at some time, exert their influence on Jewish life in Germany. In the meantime, I can summarize all that I have said by quoting Gershom Scholem, the ultimate representative of scholarly method in Judaica: what Jews should talk about is what they have to give, not what they have to give up.

Notes

1. One of my students in Heidelberg wrote an essay on 'Evangelical Theology and Antisemitism in the GRD after 1943' to which he appended the following note: 'I have to mention here briefly that a cousin of my father shot Jews when he was with the SS in the Warsaw ghetto.'
2. An *Einheitsgemeinde* was an officially sanctioned but artificial amalgamation of communities of varying orientations (Orthodox, Reform, etc.) as recipients of taxes paid to the state by Jewish citizens. Samson Rafael Hirsch broke this pattern in 1876 with his Austrittsgemeinde.

3. Nevertheless the World Jewish Congress declared in 1948 that no Jew should ever again set foot on German soil, and the Zionist Organization, after closing its offices in Germany in 1949, stated that 'No law, not Jewish, Zionist, or human, could allow Jews to remain in Germany'; see Monika Richarz, 'Jews in Today's Germanies', *Leo Baeck Institute Year Book*, xxx (1985), 266.

4. Judaistik is a concept specific to German academics interested in the study of classical Jewish literature, modelled on Greek and Roman studies in universities. Its representatives are almost entirely non-Jewish and distance themselves from any identification with a living Jewish world. Jewish Studies as represented uniquely in Heidelberg covers the whole range of Jewish knowledge, from biblical and rabbinic literature to contemporary Jews and Judaism. A full review of *Judaistik* in Germany is provided by Peter Schäfer in 'Judaistik: Jüdische Wissenschaft in Deutschland heute', in *Saculum: Jahrbuch für Universalgeschichte*, 42: 2 (1991), 199–216.

5. The reasons for this growth of interest are not immediately apparent, but three factors certainly played a part. The first was the return to Germany of a handful of young German soldiers, graduates of the Hebrew University conversant with Hebrew and rabbinics, who were eager to establish their new-found discipline in German universities. This coincided with the changing attitudes of German students who for the first time since the war were willing to face the issues of German–Jewish relations. The third, less readily acknowledged factor was the impact of the Six-Day War, and the 're-emergence' of the Jews as a vibrant, living phenomenon.

PART VI

RETHINKING INTERFAITH
RELATIONS IN A
POST-HOLOCAUST WORLD

CHAPTER EIGHTEEN

The Dangers of Antisemitism in the New Europe

ROBERT S. WISTRICH

M OST serious observers agree that in the last three years, since the fall of Communism, there has been a resurgence of the old demons of nationalism and antisemitism on the European continent. This has been particularly evident in central and eastern Europe, which is scarcely surprising for anyone familiar with the history of these areas over the past 150 years. For in this part of the world, problems of national identity have been especially acute ever since the abortive revolutions of 1848. The four decades of Communist rule after the Second World War froze the under-lying conflicts and tensions rather than resolved them. Once this iron grip was unfastened, many of the old problems resurfaced, including the anti-semitism which was traditionally such an integral expression of the struggle for national identity in Poland, Romania, Hungary, and Slovakia between the two world wars. In particular, illiberal, authoritarian, and antidemo-cratic conceptions of the nation have revived, alongside and in opposition to aspirations for national independence based on traditions deriving from the Western Enlightenment. The result, especially in eastern Europe and the former USSR, has been a revival of the 'Jewish question', even if some elements of it have clearly changed since 1945.

On the eve of the Holocaust there were 8.1 million Jews in eastern Europe, the USSR, and the Balkans: (more than 80 per cent of Europe's total Jewish population, and no less than 49 per cent of world Jewry). Today, even if we include the European parts of Russia and also the Ukraine, eastern Europe accounts for not much more than 10 per cent of world Jewry. North America has displaced eastern Europe as the major demographic reservoir of diaspora Jewry, and Israel has taken over the role of being the geopolitical core of Jewish nationhood. The Jewish population of central and eastern Europe (excluding the former USSR) is a decimated, pale shadow of its former self, with only Hungarian Jewry approaching the 100,000 mark (in 1939 there were over 400,000 Hungarian Jews). The great Jewish communities of Poland (3.2 million), Romania (850,000), Germany (over half a million in 1933), Czechoslovakia (357,000), or Austria (200,000), not to mention those in the Balkans and the Baltic states, were almost entirely wiped out by Hitler, and most of their remnants emigrated in the post-war Stalinist aftermath.

Together with them disappeared any 'real' basis for a 'Jewish question' in central and eastern Europe—a question allegedly rooted in socio-economic competition, problems of cultural assimilation and modernization, majority–minority conflicts, and religious differences. Jews were no longer a significant element in the struggle between rival national movements emerging out of the ruins of the multinational empires, as they had been after 1918. They were no longer a force in capitalist modernization, in the urban economy, or in the regeneration of national culture. Nor were there any longer masses of Orthodox Jews, clinging to their particularist life style, to give credence to antisemitic claims of Jewish separatism.

Ironically, the collapse of the Communist regimes has sharpened the nagging old questions of national identity—of what actually constitutes Polishness, Czechness, Hungarianness, or whatever—by removing the totalitarian tissue of illusions, fabrications, and lies woven under Russian domination. Long-dormant but never-forgotten territorial issues have now resurfaced, with the horrifying results we are currently witnessing in Yugoslavia or the Caucasus, and perhaps tomorrow in Moldava, the Ukraine, Hungary, Romania, and the Balkans. Czechs and Slovaks united to overthrow Communism, but subsequently there has been a spectacular revival of militant separatism in Slovakia, leading to its independence. The boiling over of ethnic hatreds in the east European cauldron and the lack of protection for minorities is as potentially dangerous for Jews as it is for society as a whole.

Czechs can at least look back to a functioning inter-war liberal democracy which preceded the Nazi conquest and the later Communist seizure of power. But the newly independent Slovakia can look back only to Mgr. Josef Tiso, the leader of the only separate Slovak state in modern times—a leader who collaborated with the Nazis and bears considerable responsibility for the genocide of Slovak Jews, yet is today admired by many Slovak separatists as a remarkable national politician. Is it any wonder that antisemitic slogans have multiplied on the walls of Bratislava and other Slovak cities? But even the Czechs are not immune to the racial intolerance spreading again across Europe: in Czech areas, there has also been a rise in xenophobic attacks against Gypsies and migrant foreign workers, and a mushrooming of skinhead and neo-Nazi gangs mouthing slogans like 'Czech lands for the Czechs'.

The situation is even more discouraging in Croatia, where the conservative nationalist president, Franjo Tudjman, has proved himself a specialist in rewriting history. In a book published in 1989, Tudjman reduced the number of Jewish victims of the Holocaust to one million and accused Jews of having 'taken the initiative in preparing and provoking not only individual atrocities but also the mass slaughter of non-Jews, Communists, Partisans and Serbs'. According to Tudjman, Jews participated in liquidating Gypsies in the notorious Jasenovic camp—an exact reversal of the historical truth, for thousands of Serbs and innocent Jews were brutally murdered there by the pro-Nazi Croatian Ustashe. In this same work, appropriately entitled *Wastelands of Historical Reality*, Tudjman even labelled Israel a 'Judaeo-Nazi' state. Not a few of his most ardent supporters, it should be noted, are either elderly Croatian Fascists or their offspring. Fortunately for the 2,500 Jews in Croatia, Tudjman's popular support derives not from his antisemitism but from national resistance to Serbian expansionism and aggression. Serbian and Croatian Jews have both aligned with their respective communities in this civil war without, for the moment, suffering specifically as Jews. But that is little consolation in the middle of the 'ethnic cleansing' that is destroying the country.

The elections of 1990 in Hungary, Romania, and Poland, showed that popular antisemitism is still a factor that can be exploited in public life in these countries. In Hungary, the Alliance of Free Democrats (a party generally favoured by Hungarian Jews) was targeted in an antisemitic way by some supporters of the victorious Hungarian Democratic Forum. One of the Forum's spokesmen, the playwright Istvan Curka, scathingly referred to a 'dwarfish minority' (i.e. the Jews) who have made the whole society accept 'that their truth is the only truth', and he openly blamed Jewish Communists for having destroyed the self-esteem of the Hungarian people. This was not merely an isolated example. To a certain extent, the Forum played the card of ethnic nationalism, of 'us' versus the 'strangers' (i.e. Gypsies, Jews, cosmopolitan Budapest intellectuals, Marxists, etc.) in the elections, and they were successful. To balance this it should also be remembered that Prime Minister Antall has vigorously condemned antisemitism, that his government has developed close ties with Israel (as have several other east European countries), and that Jewish life is currently flourishing in Hungary. Moreover, the Hungarian Catholic Church has been more forthright in its recent denunciations of antisemitism than any of its counterparts in eastern Europe, and many of the country's leading writers and intellectuals have similarly spoken out against various manifestations of antisemitism.

This is unfortunately not the case in Romania, where since the coup of December 1989 there has been a steady rise in both xenophobia and anti-semitism even though only about 18,000 Jews remain in the country. A nationalist opposition newspaper like *Romania mare* (with a circulation of over 0.5 million) regularly features antisemitic articles. In April 1991, its editor claimed that too many Jews held key positions in Romania, that 'the heads of TV and radio are all Jews, and in Parliament, it rains Jews by the bucket. It's not their fault—domination has been their style since the dawn of time—but can't they let us breathe a little, instead of trampling on us as they have been doing since 1947?' This charge has been echoed in a number of other newspapers, with Jews frequently being blamed for bringing Communism to Romania. Some members of the Committee for National Salvation, including the former prime minister, Petre Roman, have also been attacked for being of Jewish origin. Antisemitic sentiment was further stirred by the silent tribute in the Romanian parliament in April 1991 to the memory of the country's antisemitic wartime dictator, Marshal Ion Antones-cu, favoured ally of Hitler, and the many long articles that appeared then in the Romanian newspapers praising him as a great patriot—a sign of the aggressively assertive nationalism that characterizes the country. The ex-Communist president, Ion Iliescu, admittedly dissociated himself from these tributes, but he has also accused those who condemn antisemitism in Romania of exaggerating the situation and sullying the country's reputation. Thus, the weakness of the government combined with the economic hard-ships of the population, anger at the slow pace of reform, and the lack of a democratic tradition contribute to keeping antisemitism alive as an outlet for popular frustrations and discontent in Romania. Jews are not necessarily the prime targets—the discrimination and harassment of Gypsies, for example, is far worse—but they remain the oldest and most familiar target of Roma-nian nationalist xenophobia.

This is even more the case in Poland, where the elections of 1990 once again demonstrated the use of antisemitism for political purposes. Anti-Jewish incitement became a central feature of a presidential election campaign in a country where there remain at most 10,000 Jews, even if we include all those who do not publicly identify themselves as such. This is a totally insignificant minority in a population of nearly 40 million, but even so about 30 per cent of Poles, according to recent surveys, hold antisemitic views. This has led, during the past few years, to such grotesque absurdities as the former Catholic prime minister, Tadeusz Mazowiecki, being accused in a whispering campaign of being a 'crypto-Jew' (rumours spread by those campaigning for Lech Wałesa); a prominent Polish bishop even had to demonstrate publicly that over the centuries there had not been a single drop of tainted Jewish blood that could cast suspicion on the ex-premier's claim to be a good Polish Catholic. At the time there was a startling lack of appropriate response from the Catholic Church and other official Polish bodies, a lack which has since been partially rectified. Not surprisingly, in such a climate there was a rash of swastika daubings on Jewish buildings in Warsaw and elsewhere at the end of 1990. Graffiti like 'A good Jew is a dead Jew' ('Dobry Zyd to martwy Zyd') even appeared at the *Umschlagplatz* from which in the summer of 1942 some 300,000 Warsaw Jews had been deported to the Treblinka death camp.

Poland is perhaps the most obvious example that the presence of Jews is not really essential for antisemitism, but it is not the only one. Whether we are dealing with the desecration of Jewish cemeteries, mindless graffiti, pseudo-intellectual theories about a world Jewish conspiracy or the 'hidden' Jews in the government, this type of antisemitism is immune to proof or disproof, to rational argument or refutation, to rules of historical evidence. This is a closed mental system, a language that can perhaps be understood but not translated into anything subject to verification or debate. To borrow a phrase from the British political journalist Neal Ascherson, it is 'irrationality distilled to infinity'.

Those who are surprised or mystified by 'antisemitism without Jews' often forget that Judaeophobia is not a simple cause—effect mechanism based on stimulus and response. Indeed, it is naïve to believe (as some Jews, including not a few Zionist thinkers have held) that antisemites react primarily to a Jewish presence, to the traditions, behaviour, and specific activities of Jews in their midst. Behind most modern forms of antisemitism lies the phantasmagoric assumption that the Jews represent a single, monolithic entity which acts together in mysterious ways as an all-powerful cabal or a sinister conspiratorial group of plotters seeking to take over the world. This may be a paranoid world-view, but it is one that undoubtedly fulfils certain emotional and political needs for those who believe in it, especially if they see their 'national' and 'Christian' values being threatened by anonymous forces of modernity and change which they fear and hate. As I have shown, the actual presence of Jews is scarcely necessary for this kind of free-floating hatred to maintain itself, as we can see in central and eastern Europe today, particularly among those who feel disoriented and abandoned by the drive to greater democracy, individual freedom, and a competitive market economy. For the fear of freedom is real enough when masses of people begin to lose their jobs, the food subsidies on which they rely are removed, and their traditional bulwarks disappear as they are set adrift in open and uncharted seas. The Cold War is over, Communism has collapsed in eastern Europe, but for millions of people the transition is still immensely painful despite the hope and even the euphoria initially unleashed by the revolutions of 1989.

In this context, Germany, for obvious historical reasons, must be a particular cause of concern. Certainly, no serious observer would deny that the reunification of Germany has been an epochal event. The fall of the hated Berlin Wall—a real landmark and a powerful symbol—was a major factor in the downfall of the Soviet Communist empire. The liberation which dismantling the wall brought has been a source of hope, though also of mixed feelings, especially for Jewish people. German unity brought an end to the once seemingly unbridgeable gap between east and west, but there has also been an unprecedented rise in violent xenophobia within the new Germany. Since the winter of 1991, foreigners have been attacked by jack-booted neo-Nazis and skinheads in ever-increasing numbers. Scenes of crowds cheering on these neo-Nazi thugs as they have besieged the hostels sheltering immigrants are not an encouraging omen.

Behind the hostility towards foreigners there has been an all too palpable tinge of racism. Ultra-right groups, here as elsewhere in western Europe, have capitalized on this racial animosity to foreigners, campaigning on the facile but effective slogan 'Germany for the Germans'. At the end of September 1991 the Deutsche Volksunion won 6.2 per cent of the vote in the city-state of Bremen, and recently repeated this performance in Schleswig-Holstein. The radical right-wing Republikaner did even better in Baden-Württemberg in April 1992, winning 11 per cent of the ballots. The German government has consistently underplayed the significance of this extremist protest vote and of neo-Nazi activity in general, ignoring what it signifies—namely, a growing rejection by millions of Germans of the idea of a multiracial or multicultural society. Nor does the government seem able to do anything about the lost generation of the 1990s, especially in east Germany, where the collapse of the industrial and economic infrastructure has engendered a deep cynicism and hopelessness. The combination of social distress, loss of identity, and nihilistic disorientation among the youth has proved a fertile seed-bed for the steady growth of neo-Nazism, with all the attendant warning signals for the Jewish community.

In Austria the radical right has made even more spectacular gains than in Germany. In November 1991, Jorg Haider's Austrian Freedom party won 23 per cent of the vote in Vienna on a xenophobic platform. Though Haider publicly steers clear of the neo-Nazis, some officials in his party are in fact former members of the neo-Nazi National Party of Germany, and one of his closest associates used to publish a magazine that described the Holocaust as 'a lie without end'. Haider himself is on record as having praised the 'orderly employment policy' of the Third Reich and eulogized the Austrian soldiers who fell in the service of the German Wehrmacht, and he never loses an opportunity to warn Austrians about the threat facing them from their 'porous' borders with eastern Europe. Unlike the portly Franz Schonhüber, leader of the Republikaner party in Germany, Haider is no Waffen-SS veteran but a charismatic, boyish 42-year-old who represents the new wave of yuppie-style proto-fascism in central Europe. Though Jews are not usually targeted in his electoral politics, there is no doubt that his Freedom party contains a hard core of unreconstructed antisemites. Since the level of anti-Jewish prejudice in the Alpine republic—as the Waldheim affair vividly demonstrated—has remained remarkably high (often exceeding eastern European levels), a suitably coded populist antisemitism would most likely be no barrier to electability or popularity for a national politician. So Haider's future prospects may well be bright.

In Germany, the situation is admittedly different in this regard, for publicly expressed antisemitism was to a large extent delegitimized in the aftermath of the Holocaust. This may help to explain why opinion surveys consistently show that German parliamentarians and national leaders are far more favourable in their attitudes to Jews and Israel than their counterparts in Austria. But there is a marked gap between the attitude of German élites and the response of the masses, which is disturbing to say the least. A survey taken immediately after German reunification showed that 58 per cent of the population (east and west) believed that 'it is time for Germans to put the Holocaust behind them'; 52 per cent felt that Israel 'should be treated like any other state'; 39 per cent believed that 'Jews exploit the National-Socialist Holocaust for their own purposes', and a similar percentage that 'now as in the past, Jews exert too much influence on world events'. This suggests to me that *Vergangenheitsbewältigung* (overcoming the past) is becoming something of an irrelevance and even an irritation to most ordinary Germans.

In France, too, the dangers of antisemitism have become more evident in recent years as the effect of the Holocaust and the Vichy trauma has begun to erode. Perhaps more than anywhere else in Europe, the combination of high immigration from the Third World (especially from the Maghreb) and economic recession has revived xenophobic reflexes that had long lain dormant in French society. Over the past decade, the radical right in France has ceased to be a marginal phenomenon and has been transformed into a semi-respectable, structured, and well-organized political movement with a mass basis. Jean-Marie Le Pen's Front National has known how to exploit the political vacuum created by deep disillusion with socialist rule, doubts about the new Europe envisaged by Maastricht, fear and anger at being 'swamped' by North African Arabs, national obsessions about French decadence, and anxieties about the loss of French sovereignty.

Even if the main victims of everyday racism in this explosive national-populist cocktail are invariably immigrants from the Maghreb or elsewhere in the Third World, antisemitism remains central to the hard-core of radical right ideology in France. The Jews have traditionally embodied 'the other' (*l'autre*) in French society, and despite their high level of assimilation and integration by the French state, they are still the classic target of the new French right. Moreover, the Jews of France—unlike those of central and eastern Europe—are a successful and highly conspicuous group, with a demographic vitality unmatched elsewhere in Europe as a result of the mass Sefardi influx from North Africa in the 1950s and 1960s. With a population variously estimated at being between 550,000 and 750,000, French Jewry is the only Jewish community in Europe that is considerably larger than it was on the eve of the Holocaust.

The newcomers who replenished the French community after the Holocaust were French by language and culture, and did not initially attract the same kind of racist backlash as the east European Jews who had emigrated to France in the 1930s. But their rapid rise on the social scale, their role in the economy, culture, the media, and politics, has excited the envy and revived the *ressentiment* of antisemites. Alleged Jewish control of the mass media, for example, has become a standard refrain in National Front publications—and this is a movement which represents anything between 14 and 20 per cent of the French electorate.

In recent years, there has been a significant rise in anti-Jewish incidents, including cemetery desecrations, verbal threats, anti-Jewish tracts, and graffiti. The Carpentras affair of May 1990 was particularly disturbing. Though similar acts have taken place elsewhere in Europe (including Britain), the political context is different—partly because of the Le Pen effect, in the sense of creeping antisemitism being symptomatic of a moral destabilization of French society. Though there was an impressive popular mobilization against racism and antisemitism after Carpentras, one in five of the French population surveyed at the time still thought that Jews had too much power in France. This is a sizeable minority and indicative of the persistence of anti-Jewish stereotypes in French society.

Equally troubling for the Jewish community is the importance that Holocaust-denial literature assumes in France, where its high-priest for the past decade and a half has been Professor Robert Faurisson. Holocaust 'revisionism' and antisemitism have become unashamedly linked since the appearance of monthlies like *Révision* in 1989 which fuse motifs drawn from traditional anti-Judaism, from the Protocols of the Elders of Zion, from a virulent anti-Zionism, and an obsession with 'Jewish power'. In France, more than anywhere (except possibly the United States), so-called 'revisionism' has acquired some academic devotees, both on the Right and the extreme Left. This pseudo-scientific school of 'negationism' has thrived on the gradual wearing down of taboos that had previously limited the open expression of antisemitism in post-war France, though these have by no means wholly disappeared. The deeply problematic relationship the French have with their own actions under the Vichy regime highlights the continuing sensitivities to the 'Jewish question' (both positive and negative) that characterize contemporary French society and culture.

It would be too much to say that antisemitism has recovered its pre-war respectability in France or western Europe as a whole, though as the Holocaust recedes in time, and race once more comes to play an important role in politics, this is a real danger. This is the case not only in France, but also in Britain, Germany, Austria, Italy, and Belgium. But it is clear that traditional prejudices and new resentments have emerged against Jews in western Europe, even if they are still expressed more cautiously in these countries than in the post-totalitarian societies of the eastern part of the continent. This background of rising antisemitism inevitably raises the question as to whether Jewish communities have a long-term future in the old–new Europe of the twenty-first century. My prognosis, based on the analysis given here, is not encouraging. Barely fifty years have elapsed since the mass murder of six million Jews in Europe, yet antisemitism is still a significant element in the social and political life of the continent, even if it is not the cataclysmic force it once was. In the east, *glasnost* and democratization have released new anger and frustrations that find open expression in a revived popular antisemitism. Nationalism is on the rise in Germany and eastern Europe, has already brought about the collapse of the Soviet empire, and has torn Yugoslavia apart; in western Europe, racist and neo-fascist trends and movements, though not yet a major threat to the democratic system, are growing in strength. Thus in the 'new' Europe beginning to take shape after the collapse of Communism, there is ample room for concern about antisemitism, which has revived on a scale not seen since 1945.

CHAPTER NINETEEN

The Holocaust as a Factor in Contemporary Jewish Consciousness

EVYATAR FRIESEL

THE intention of this essay is to express concern about some of the ways in which contemporary Jewish society is coping with the Holocaust—to assess what its consequences and significance appear to be for the present generation. Against this background, I shall then try to formulate a more appropriate order of priorities for confronting the results of the disaster that struck the Jewish people some half a century ago, but whose effects are still very apparent.

The present-day preoccupation with the Holocaust falls into two main categories. One is scholarly research in its diverse fields—historical, theological, sociological, cultural, and literary. Another is commemoration of the victims, both on Yom Hashoah (Holocaust Day) and other memorial days, and through institutions that usually combine remembrance, research, and education.

Regarding research, I sometimes wonder whether the historical work being done on the Holocaust is not reaching some sort of limit. In terms of facts and chronology, I wonder if there is still much that is unknown about the Holocaust. The archives now being opened in the countries of the former Communist bloc will certainly provide much new information about the fate of the Jews of those lands in the Second World War, but I doubt if it will change the overall historical picture. It is questionable whether there is another theme in Jewish history that has been as intensively and extensively researched as the Holocaust. Probably no major fact regarding the Holocaust remains unknown, and those aspects about which there is still some obscurity—such as the absence of written orders by Hitler to set in motion the murder of the Jews—are largely likely to remain so. Sometimes one is even tempted to ask whether historians working on the Holocaust are not stretching the bounds of common sense. One example is the debate that took place in 1991 in Frankfurt, where a Study and Documentation Centre is being planned, in which well-known historians participated in a learned discussion on whether the Holocaust had been rational, irrational, or anti-rational. It is true that historical research on the Holocaust is driven by a desire to explain how it could have happened, but the sobering fact is that we are today as far from an answer as we were twenty or thirty years ago. This does not mean that a later generation, looking again at the material accumulated, may not be able to reach wiser or more satisfying conclusions, but for the moment we seem to have reached a saturation point.

MUSEUMANIA

I find the second issue—the way in which Jews are dealing with the memorialization of the Holocaust—a matter of even greater concern. From the late 1980s onwards there has been a rush to build Holocaust museums. Institutions of remembrance and research are, obviously, important and necessary. Yad Vashem, the Holocaust museum in Jerusalem that was established in 1953, has become a shrine for the entire Jewish people. Its research facilities and scholarship are impressive. But what happens when shrines multiply almost uncontrollably, absorbing financial resources running into hundreds of millions of dollars that could well be put to other uses? Moreover, what does it reveal about the spiritual condition of contemporary Jewry?

The most important of the new museums is the one that opened in Washington in April 1993. Plans for such institutions in New York and Los Angeles, and in Frankfurt in Germany, are also in various phases of implementation, and a similar institution is being considered for Berlin.

The Holocaust Museum in Washington is on the Mall, close to the George Washington memorial. Each visitor receives a computer-readable card containing the name of a *Doppelgänger*, an accompanying spirit, a Jew who perished in the Holocaust at the visitor's age; by inserting their cards at appropriate points in the museum's chronologically arranged exhibit, visitors are kept informed of what was happening to their Holocaust counterparts. An audio-visual impression of the Holocaust is conveyed through pictures, films, artefacts, and sounds: scenes of war, the cattle-cars used for transportation, prison walls and ghetto walls and electrified fences, the incinerators used to burn bodies and the dead—many of them. The Museum curators are well aware that some of the pictures and artefacts may overwhelm visitors emotionally, but the intention seems to have been just that: to bring the visitor close to the 'experience' of the Holocaust in every possible way. In the quest to convey the Holocaust experience 'authentically', apparently, half of a barrack that housed Jewish prisoners in Auschwitz II-Birkenau has been obtained from the Auschwitz Museum and reassembled in Washington.

What is happening here? Do we Jews lack appropriate means to express grief—be it private, communal, or national—over the catastrophe that befell the Jews in Europe? Are the Kaddish and El Malé Rachamim prayers, sober and supremely dignified, no longer enough? Is a day of fasting and prayer, as on Tishah Be'av, no longer an answer? Is the old tradition of remembering the departed through a period of study dedicated to their memory no longer a solution? What is the sense of bringing the visitor, together with his or her computer-generated *Doppelgänger*, into concentration camp barracks or cattle-cars to 'share the experience' of the deportees? What else will 'educators' dream up as a way of conveying the experience— perhaps to remind people of the electrified fences by reaching out to them with electrified cattle-prods as they make their way to the exit, or to the cafeteria for a Coca-Cola and a hamburger? Something seems to run amok in our collective psyche when it comes to the remembrance of the destruction of European Jewry. Traditional Jewish ritual in the face of death and sorrow is solemn and restrained. Modern responses to the Holocaust—and not only American Jewish ones—are exactly the opposite. Those mammoth monuments, often vying with each other for recognition as the last word in this or that aspect of memorialization, are unrestrained, even aggressive.

Two possible explanations for this museumania occur to me. One has to do with a distortion that has occurred, particularly in many American universities, where 'Holocaust studies' have multiplied faster than Jewish studies. The result has been that a whole generation of young Jews has been educated about how the Jewish people died, but learnt very little about Jewish life—Jewish history, Jewish culture, Jewish beliefs. The harvest of that unwise seed has now been reaped. One of its products is these Holocaust museums: an hour of staged sorrow, of gimmickry and make-believe, has replaced mourning, remembering, and educating.

Many intellectuals and scholars, observers of the Jewish scene, have felt uneasy for some years now about the situation just described, but they— we—have remained silent. This is another troubling fact. It raises the possibility that we had nothing better to offer. Worse, it raises the possibility that Jews are all suffering from a certain collective disorientation and aimlessness which in itself seems to be one of the consequences of the Holocaust.

In fact, it is becoming increasingly clear that the Holocaust has had some disastrous latter-day consequences whose full significance is emerging only now. The destruction of communities with centuries of Jewish tradition and experience behind them left a void in Jewish life with which Jews seem unable to cope. Jewish life today is characterized by a lack of stability, which can in part be related to the sociological features of modern Jewry but which on a deeper level bears the unequivocal imprint of the Holocaust. Indeed, how can Jews explain to themselves the sense and prospects of Jewish existence if the historical evolution of European Jewry over a thousand years culminated in Auschwitz? The Holocaust wrecked some basic equilibrium in Jewish life in a manner that sometimes appears beyond repair.

It seems to me that Jews are still confronting the Holocaust as a reality of the present, not only a nightmare of the past, and that its acid consequences continue to gnaw away at the foundations of the existence of the Jewish people. To recognize therefore that Jews are still fighting for collective survival is in itself one of the crucial tasks of present-day Jewish intellectual endeavour. It should lead to a re-evaluation of social and spiritual priorities, in the sense that Jews must force themselves to grasp that Jewish life must go on, that the responsibility towards our children and grandchildren must match our sorrow for the dead. The most impressive shrine to the memory of the six million Jews murdered in the Holocaust is not a museum, but a living Jewish people able to carry on the Jewish heritage and transmit its values.

NEW RELATIONSHIPS BETWEEN JEWS AND NON-JEWS

The reconstruction of Jewish life in the second half of the twentieth century obviously has many aspects. Some have implications that relate primarily to issues that may be considered internal to Jewish community life, but some have external implications, for example as regards the relations between Jews and non-Jews. While the first theme is obviously crucial, it is on the second issue that I want here to comment briefly.

One of the cardinal unresolved legacies of the Holocaust is the challenge of developing a more reassuring basis for coexistence between Jews and non-Jews in Europe, and in fact in Western society in general. Responses on that vital issue are so far insufficient. I am not referring to the rather simplistic question of whether the Holocaust can happen again. Of course it can. It is axiomatic that everything that happened once can happen again, and more easily so since there is already a precedent. I do not say this as a prophet of doom, for in my view there seems to be no major catastrophe threatening either Israel or the Jewish communities of the diaspora at this time. What I am referring to is a theoretical question, although for Jews a most significant one. To express it in the contemporary idiom: if a Holocaust 'bomb' is still

stored somewhere in the ideological arsenal of non-Jewish society (and as
long as there is no convincing proof to the contrary, I shall suppose that it
is), what can be done to defuse it?

For those who are Zionists, there was a time when the answer would have
been that the reconcentration of the Jewish people in its historical homeland
would stabilize the Jewish relationship with non-Jews. Almost half a century
after the establishment of the Jewish state, however, many Zionists have
discovered that there are historical characteristics in the Jewish condition
that are very resilient. None seems more resilient than what Leon Pinsker,
over a hundred years ago, called the 'Judaeophobia of the Gentiles'. It is
quite astonishing that more than forty years of Jewish statehood has hardly
changed the basic premisses of the relationship between Jews and non-Jews.
A case in point: even if the attempted delegitimization of Israel is related to
the political tensions of the Middle East, it is none the less also rooted in
traditional negative attitudes towards Jews. As it happens, the brunt of these
negative attitudes is currently borne by Israel. From a broader perspective,
however, they are little more than a particular expression of a general
antagonism. As in the past, non-Jewish society—or more specifically in this
case, the Arabs and those who support their positions—still react to Jews
not as they are, but as they are supposed to be. Something can always be
learnt from past experience, and the Zionist experience teaches that it is not
enough that the Jews change, even radically. To alter a relationship, both
sides, Jews and non-Jews, have to look for new ways and attitudes.

If so, what are the non-Jews doing in this regard? In the case of the
Muslims, the present problems between Judaism and Islam, fed by the
Palestinian issue, represent a pattern of tension that from a historical perspective has little in common with the events that brought about the
Holocaust. However, we should not underestimate its ideological meaning.
Beyond the political controversy surrounding Israel/Palestine, it may well be
that Jews—and probably also the Christian world—are at the beginning of a
new era of tension with a reinvigorated Islam. The possible consequences of
this are still a matter of speculation. It may happen—indeed, it has
happened—that here and there, negative Christian and Muslim attitudes
regarding the Jews converge. Nevertheless, Jews should be clear-minded and
recognize that since the historical circumstances of the two attitudes are
different, they warrant different responses.

The possibility of a new age of tension between the two major historical
civilizations with which Jews have been associated, Christianity and Islam,
might raise the question of who the Jews belong with. For Israelis it could
be a delicate issue, given Israel's geographical position and the ethnic composition of its population. As frequently happens with delicate questions in

public and social life, the more clearly one formulates a stand, the better: Israel belongs to the Western world. I do not see it as an issue of choice, but as a recognition of realities. It is in the Western world that the Jewish people is concentrated. It was from and in Europe that many of the familiar concepts of Jewish life were adopted or developed. Israel, as a state and as a society, has developed on the Western model. True, it was in that same Europe that there was an attempt, only half a century ago, to murder the entire Jewish people. This certainly gives poignancy to the present quest for a *modus vivendi*; there seems to be no other alternative.

What is in fact happening in the Christian West, both ideologically and spiritually, and more especially in Europe, regarding relations between Jews and non-Jews? Both among Protestants and Catholics there is an ongoing redefinition of Christian attitudes towards Jews and Judaism. The general contours are similar: recognition of the common roots of both religions, acceptance that their beliefs are diverse but equally good ways to similar spiritual goals, rejection of antisemitism, recognition of the State of Israel.

The Protestant churches have shown great incisiveness. There have been resolutions by the World Council of Churches. The Dutch churches have issued statements (among which the resolution of the General Synod of the Netherlands Reformed Church of 1970 deserves special attention), as have a long list of American and other churches. The resolution that the Synod of the Evangelical Church of the Rhineland in Germany formulated in 1980, recognizing Christian co-responsibility and guilt for the Holocaust, is very significant. These are important and heartening steps, although the heterogeneity of the Protestant world may limit their actual influence.

The Catholic Church, on the other hand, is centralized, very influential, and relatively monolithic in its thought. It was under its auspices that one of the most important developments in Christian–Jewish relations in the post-Holocaust era began: *Nostra aetate*, the statement issued by Vatican II (the Second Vatican Council) in October 1965, on the relations between the Catholic Church and the non-Christian religions. With respect to the Jews, the draft approved by Vatican II differed from a more incisive earlier draft which had stated emphatically that the Jews were not guilty of killing Jesus Christ—an accusation that had held tragic consequences for the Jews for generations. The draft finally accepted was less emphatic, but even so a Commission for Religious Relations with Judaism approved important new guidelines in December 1974, and again in June 1985. Pope John Paul II's visit to the Great Synagogue of Rome in April 1986 attracted considerable attention.[1] These changes notwithstanding, it is true to say that the Catholic Church has been more hesitant than the Protestant churches. The fact that the Vatican has still not recognized the State of Israel raises questions among most Jews and many non-Jews.

Let me emphasize that what we are considering here is the significance of such religious redefinitions for the attitudes of the Christian churches themselves. Obviously, statements made centuries after an event cannot change deep-seated religious and cultural attitudes overnight, but they are steps in the right direction and they deal with the very roots of the Christian–Jewish problem. Jews can do little but observe such developments, being that they are internal to the churches themselves, but we should certainly not remain indifferent. Too many questions vital to Jewish interests are involved.

CONCLUSIONS

Present-day Jewish attitudes to the Holocaust and its consequences, besides being sometimes of dubious taste and unrewarding content, are very confused about the implications for continuing Jewish life. I consider this a grave mistake. Holocaust museums can be built in stone and marble by Jewish communities around the world, but the existential Jewish questions still remain unresolved. Life goes on. It forces Jews to make hard decisions. Jews, both in the diaspora and in Israel, face key questions regarding Jewish identity, spiritual and social cohesion, and relationships with non-Jews. For better or for worse, and in spite of the Holocaust, it is in the Western world—in America, in Europe—that we Jews have to build a place for ourselves and for Jewish generations to come. It is there that we must seek frameworks of existence and of co-existence that will prove more solid than those of the past.

Note

1. Developments within the Catholic Church in the field of Christian–Jewish relations are described in more detail in Ch. 21.

CHAPTER TWENTY

The Impact of Auschwitz and Vatican II on Christian Perceptions of Jewish Identity

ELISABETH MAXWELL

T HE theme I have chosen for this paper concerns the nature of Jewish identity as viewed by a Christian committed to Jewish–Christian dialogue not only as an attractive concept but as an everyday practicality. I believe it is of the utmost significance for the future of Europe, particularly in the light of the dramatic changes within our continent over the past few years. Under Communist rule, teeming millions of people, especially those living in Belorussia, in Ukraine, in the Baltic states, Romania, and Czechoslovakia, and to a lesser degree in Poland, Hungary, Bulgaria, and Yugoslavia, were formally denied all knowledge of the Holocaust which took place on their own land and were also officially denied worship in the Christian faith. These peoples are now following their nostalgic instincts to return to a Christian past of popes, priests, candles, bells, and incense. But alas, what they are finding in terms of leadership is a cluster of generally ignorant priests, mostly instructed under the Communist regime with bigoted ideas and outmoded Christian theology. They are in consequence largely unaware of two major events of theological significance which have occurred in the past seventy years: Auschwitz, and the Second Vatican Council, which is widely referred to as Vatican II.

The Holocaust was a historical watershed, an event (or rather a process) that damaged the world irretrievably. It is today symbolized all over the globe by the one word 'Auschwitz'. But the significance of Auschwitz is not embedded exclusively in the past. As Jonathan Webber has recently made clear in an excellent article on 'The Future of Auschwitz', it is also a pointer towards the meaning which can and will be attributed to the Holocaust both in the present and in the future.[1] I would recommend that everyone read the paper, for it is an important and positive opening of the debate in a highly problematic area, and it will certainly help to overcome some of the conflicts over Auschwitz.

What is absolutely incontrovertible, however, is the impact of the Holocaust and Auschwitz on twentieth-century Europe and particularly on the Church. More than anything else it was the shock of this catastrophe that forced the Church to look at the Jews with fresh eyes and to ask troubling questions about its own attitudes and behaviour in relation to them.

This in turn is having a fundamental influence on Christian theology. Theological convictions have been overturned by a new understanding of Second Temple Judaism (the background of Jesus and the early Church), by an appreciation of the religious vitality of rabbinic Judaism, and by the encounter with contemporary Jews and their way of life. Christians have been forced to recognize that Jewish faith and religious life as professed and practised still today can greatly help Christians to understand certain aspects of the life of the Church. In consequence the Church has found itself re-examining its own claims concerning Jesus and the significance of the Christ event. All of this profound rethinking occurred as a result of the Holocaust.

The first concrete conclusions of this rethinking resulted in the Second Vatican Council promulgating a document in 1965, called *Nostra aetate* ('In our time').[2] This document, which was produced after some twenty years of study within the Church hierarchy, was a turning-point in the Christian attitude towards Judaism.

Nostra aetate established eight principles that define the Church's attitude to the Jews. Among them it stressed the common spiritual bonds with Judaism, acknowledged the unbroken validity of the promises of the divine covenant with Israel, refuted the accusation of deicide, and rejected all forms of antisemitism. But even more significantly, the publication of *Nostra aetate* did not mark the Church's final statement on the subject. Rather, it proved to be the beginning of a whole series of developments. In 1969, 1975, and again in 1980 and 1982, the original document was reinforced by notes and guidelines for teaching and preaching.[3] *Nostra aetate* is thus a living document, taken seriously by Church leaders.

The positive ecumenical aspect of this must also be stressed. The Pope and his cardinals constantly make statements on the subject. Pope John Paul II has on several occasions referred to the 'unique relations that exist between Christianity and Judaism'. Relations between the two great religions, he has said, were founded on the design of the God of the covenant.[4] Consequently, the Jews and Judaism should occupy an essential and organically integrated place in the catechesis.[5]

This new spirit presupposes repentance. Cardinal Cassidy, President of the Commission of the Holy See for Relations with Judaism, made this clear in his opening address to the Prague conference in September 1990: 'The fact that antisemitism could exist within Christian thought and practice constitutes a call for *teshuvah* (repentance) and reconciliation on our part as we gather together here in this city which bears witness to the fact that in the past we have failed, when we should have demonstrated real and genuine evidence of our faith.'[6]

Although a number of Church leaders had in the past spoken openly or written articles about repentance, the words of Cardinal Cassidy—the Pope's envoy at the conference—constituted the Vatican's first official public act of contrition. There can be no doubt that this statement stimulated thinking and theological research in Christian circles and communities far beyond the Catholic Church itself.

Statements on Jewish–Christian relations from Protestant denominations had preceded *Nostra aetate*, and more followed. Some went much further in their declarations. One of the most hopeful, comprehensive, and courageous statements was made in January 1980, after five years of intense study, by the Protestant Church of the Rhineland. Its Synod adopted by an overwhelming majority a 'Declaration on Renovating the Relationship between Christians and Jews'. This declaration, the most advanced offered at the time by any Christian Church, included a statement of the four factors that led to its adoption:

1. Recognition of Christian co-responsibility and guilt for the Holocaust— the defamation, persecution, and murder of Jews in the Third Reich.

2. New biblical insights concerning the continuing significance of the Jewish people for salvation history.

3. Recognition of the continuing existence of the Jewish people, its return to the Land of Promise, and also the creation of the State of Israel as signs of the faithfulness of God towards God's people.

4. Jewish readiness, in spite of the Holocaust, to engage in common study and co-operation.

In 1988, the World Council of Churches likewise adopted an important resolution.

In July of that same year, the Church of England, meeting at the Lambeth Conference, voted unanimously on the text of a remarkable resolution. This conference, which takes place every ten years, is host to some one thousand bishops and archbishops of the world Anglican communion. Its declarations were very similar in content to that of the World Council of Churches, and its final resolution unequivocally affirmed the existence of the State of Israel and its right to be recognized and to have secure borders. 'Judaism is not only a religion as many Christians understand the word but a people and a civilisation. Jews know and define themselves as Jews even when they do not fully share the religious beliefs of Judaism. It is against this background that the religious importance of the land of Israel to the majority of Jews throughout the world needs to be understood.'[7]

In parallel with these various statements, of which there have been many more than I can refer to in detail, a great deal of research has been undertaken into the early history of Judaism and Christianity, the common bonds between them, and the Jewishness of Jews. In recent years, there has been a marked increase in Christian acknowledgement of the continuing validity of God's covenant with the Jews, as well as enhanced awareness of the Church's intimate connection with this covenant. With this renewed sense of deep and permanent bonding with the Jewish people as a firm theological basis, the Church is now moving towards a positive recognition of its Jewish roots. Many areas of Christian thinking are affected by this change of approach, and I shall simply point out the main ones.

One significant area of change has been the Church's attitude towards and use of the Hebrew scriptures, the First Testament. In the past, the 'Old' Testament served at best as a prelude to New Testament teachings, and at worst as a foil for those teachings. Today, however, the Old Testament is being studied in its own right. Christians are slowly coming to recognize that without a deeper understanding of the spirit of these Hebrew scriptures, they are left with a truncated vision of Jesus' message and hence a watered-down version of Christian spirituality.[8] If the Hebrew scriptures are to continue to grow in significance for the Christian faith, then they must begin to assume the status of primary texts and not merely be regarded as peripheral resources for Christian theological statement. They were, after all, the primary sources on which Jesus, a Jew steeped in the knowledge of the Torah, based his teaching. Their importance must be more fully appreciated in the general theological realms—in systematic theology, ethics, spirituality, and preaching—rather than only in liturgy and sacramental theology.

The Jewishness of Jesus has also been extensively studied in recent years. What is emphasized now is the fact that Jesus can only be fully understood as 'a man of his time and of his environment . . . whose anxieties and hopes he shared'. Jesus taught in the synagogues of his people fully as one of them. His message can be understood *only* as a Jewish message addressed to Jews by a Jew.[9] Any approach which presents Jesus in opposition to the Torah and Judaism will therefore inevitably result in the dilution or even corruption of his essential message.[10] Equally, this is not to deny the unique and personal quality of Jesus' contributions, for the Christian Testament is powerful evidence of the remarkable authority with which Jesus preached.

Jesus' 'Torah of Love' is a prime example of his Jewishness. When asked to give the 'first' or central commandment, he responded by quoting the opening words of the Jewish Shema which come from the Hebrew Bible (Deut. 6: 4–5): 'Hear, O Israel! The Lord our God, the Lord is one! You shall love the Lord with all your heart and with all your soul and with all your might.' Further evidence of Jesus' Jewishness can be found in the Lord's Prayer,[11] derived as it is from the Jewish scriptures[12] and with its striking parallel to Jewish liturgical tradition. Jesus' way of praying finds its original setting and full depth in synagogue prayer, and this is a reality that should moderate the Christian tendency to triumphalism.

A superficial reading of the Gospels can give the impression that Jesus' relations with the Pharisees—indeed, with most of his fellow Jews—were always marked by conflict and polemics. The various Vatican *Notes*, however, together with recent scholarship, should disabuse us of that idea, for they demonstrate clearly that many doctrines crucial to Jesus' teachings have for generations been omitted from Christian instruction and are only now resurfacing. It was the Second Vatican Council, for instance, with its definition of the Church as 'People of God', which led the way in restoring the historical and communal roots of Christianity that had been lost in the original schism with Judaism. Clearly, if the term 'People of God' is to contribute to a constructive re-Judaization of Christianity, it must of necessity be accompanied by the assertion that the Jewish people also remain 'People of God'.

Another major area which Christian teaching chose to neglect was the existence and parallel development of rabbinic Judaism. The fact is that early Christianity developed historically alongside rabbinic Judaism. The Church was originally perceived by the Graeco-Roman world simply as yet another Jewish sect. It is tragic that in claiming its own inheritance, Christianity came to deny that of its sibling; ignoring at its peril Paul's advice against 'boasting', it forgot its own roots. Untold suffering was to ensue from this lapse, as well as an impoverishment of Christianity's self-understanding.[13]

What is clearly highlighted today is the common root, the similarities rather than the differences, for both Christianity and rabbinic Judaism were shaped by their individual responses to the same great crisis of Jewish history, the destruction of the Temple in Jerusalem in the year AD 70. The links between the two faiths are clearly evident, even in specific sacraments such as Baptism, the Eucharist, and the marriage liturgy. Christian teaching has also chosen to conceal the facts concerning the origins of the Gospels, for it is vital to emphasize that the Gospels were actually set down in writing only towards the end of the first century. Thus, they often reflect the contemporary concerns of their authors and communities. The Vatican reminds us that 'many of the Christian Testament references, hostile or less than favourable to the Jews, have their historical contexts in conflicts between the Nascent Church and the Jewish community . . . long after the time of Jesus', even if the evangelists place the references on Jesus' lips.[14]

But what impact does this rediscovery of Jesus' Jewishness really have on the Christian Church? The contemporary dialogue with Jews and Judaism has begun to produce changes in the presentation of the New Testament in Christian circles. We are witnessing a genuine revolution in New Testament scholarship, made possible in part by a much greater understanding of Hebrew and Aramaic and a greater reliance on Jewish materials. In the last decade or so there has been a definite and dramatic shift in New Testament scholarship, ending the dominance of the Hellenistic background of Pauline Christianity and returning Jesus to his Jewish milieu in a central way. Scholars do not completely agree about the precise forms of Judaism that most directly influenced Jesus, but there is none the less a growing consensus which emphasizes the fundamental significance of Judaism.

Such, then, are some of the broad areas of recent scholarship which have led to a reappraisal of Christian teaching, bringing significant progress in analysing the common root and the parting of the ways. What has happened to the Church in the last third of the twentieth century is in every way as momentous as the Reformation in the first third of the sixteenth century. A transformation has been achieved in fundamental Church doctrine—in the traditional position of the Church *vis à vis* the Jewish people and the interpretation of the Hebrew scriptures. And this transformation really began with the Vatican's *Nostra aetate*.

What is the point, it may be asked, of laying such emphasis on the twin symbols of Auschwitz and Vatican II? The answer lies in the rise of antisemitism in the world of today. The euphoria that first greeted the collapse of Communism has been moderated. Ethnic and national divisions have reappeared in bitter forms, minorities are again experiencing harassment and fear. Once again, antisemitism has resurfaced as an ingredient of religious and political action.

We have to face the unpalatable truth that antisemitism has re-emerged on an organized basis throughout Europe. Once again, Jews and Jewish organizations are under physical attack, with press reports of desecration of Jewish graves or daubing of antisemitic slogans becoming ever more commonplace. Just four decades after the end of the Second World War, a war that should have eradicated antisemitism, every Jewish community has to be constantly alert to the danger of assault on its members and institutions. This is part of the reality of being Jewish in Europe today. It is difficult to comprehend that although hardly fifty years have passed since the horrors of the Holocaust shattered the world, we are now witnessing a resurgence of Nazism with overtones so similar to the Hitler Brownshirts that people of my generation feel as if they are reliving 1936.

What we have recently witnessed in east Germany and the Soviet Union follows a similar social pattern, with the collapse of a political regime bringing in its wake materialistic anxieties about the future, unemployment, deprivation, shortages of essential goods, the collapse of currency, widespread black marketeering, xenophobia, racism, and of course antisemitism. Thus the development and increase of organizations such as Pamyat in the former Soviet Union and the skinheads in former East Germany, Poland, and Czechoslovakia are part of the same worldwide neo-Nazi movement, and the targets for their attacks are invariably foreigners, asylum-seekers, and Jews. In east Germany alone, there are estimated to be some 2,000 hard-core activists, with a potential pool of about 15,000 people willing to engage in acts of extreme-right violence; and at the level of general passive support among young people there, a figure of around 50,000 is mooted.

Acts of violence by neo-Nazi groups are on the increase, and the outrages are not confined to eastern Europe. They are also to be found in France, where there have been incidents that highlight the rising support for Le Pen's extreme right-wing Front National. Such, for instance, were the events in Carpentras, a town in southern France where a Jewish cemetery was desecrated and the body of a man recently buried was disinterred and exposed on a spike. As Helmut Kohl has warned us, we can no longer close our eyes to the resurgence in many places of the old demons of nationalism, hostility to foreigners, and antisemitism. The warning signs are plain for all to see.[15]

So there is clearly a great deal of work still to be done in the field of education, and even more so today now that access to the archives of the former Eastern Bloc countries is allowing the full truth of the horrors perpetrated in those countries to emerge. The masses of documents becoming available will allow a more complete picture painfully to be pieced together, especially of Nazi occupation in the more remote areas of the Russian republic, and open up a whole new dimension in Holocaust studies.

Among this new material available to scholars for the first time are records of Nazi army units captured by the Red Army during their rapid advance through the occupied areas in the summer of 1944. Of supreme importance, too, is the vast amount of data collected towards the end of the war by the Soviet Special Commissions for the Investigation of Nazi War Crimes. Kept under lock and key for over forty years, these documents, known collectively as the 'Black Book', were made available to Israeli scholars in 1989. It is a vast collection of personal memoirs, dairies, German documents, testi-monies of survivors, references to local collaborators, and archives of the Jewish Anti-Fascist Committee. What these documents clearly demonstrate is that the Nazis had murdered more Jews in the occupied Soviet territories than had previously been thought (probably about 1.25 million), and with even greater sadism and brutality than had been supposed. Yet while this documentation adds to our knowledge of the Holocaust, that knowledge is still incomplete: until the archives of the Communist Party of the Soviet Union or of the KGB are released, vital information about the Soviet government's response to the implementation of the Final Solution is still lacking.[16]

Clearly, if in the future we are to have any hope of preventing another genocide of the magnitude of the Holocaust, we have to focus on the lessons to be learnt. We have to understand how genocide is set in motion, how people react, and what possible safeguards can be put in place to protect humanity from further tragedy. Education is the key to the future—and especially so for those people in the east who as yet have had so little real information. It is truly imperative that we teach the people of the former Eastern bloc countries what actually happened on their own territory, so that they in turn can understand the urgent need to fight the rising tide of racism and antisemitism. We can no longer be bystanders as history begins to repeat itself: it is a risk which none of us can afford to take. We have to take action, beginning with a programme of information and education which will reach the widest possible audience.

But where should we begin? Auschwitz and Vatican II: these are my twin symbols, and these must be the starting-point of a massive educational effort. The vast progress in scholarship and theology I have outlined above is in itself admirable, but we have to ensure that the message of the new theology filters down from academia to the grass-roots. We have to make lay people more aware of its existence, so that the new spirit of rapprochement becomes a fundamental reality in everyday Christianity.

It is precisely this practical and educational task which we are aiming to tackle at the second *Remembering for the Future* conference, to be held in Berlin in March 1994, at which we hope to gather 800 participants from all over the world. Faced with such an important task we may be hesitant and somewhat daunted, but we have an ideal opportunity to make a start. What we are hoping is that this gathering of scholars, theologians, and researchers will propose practical and positive changes in theological education, and the jettisoning of all false doctrines so that priests being trained in seminaries can finally spread the new spirit of understanding, reconciliation, and mutual respect throughout the Christian community. A definite body of proposals such as this, combined with important media coverage, will, we hope, force the churches to take notice and embolden them to take action.

Our aims in Berlin are reflected in its two main themes. Theme 1 will aim to remind the world of the murder of the Jews of Europe and the obliteration of their civilization. We want to examine the destructive role of the intellectual and leadership groups—the collaborative role of the universities as well as of the medical, legal, scientific, and religious communities. We want to investigate information emerging from the newly accessible archives in central Europe and the former Soviet Union. These elements will all form part of Theme 1.

Under Theme 2, we want to explore the establishment of values for a viable human society, the reconstruction of theology in a post-Holocaust pluralist world. We will be discussing the implications of the Holocaust for political integrity, social structure, and professional ethics, and looking at the integration of ethical values in the teaching of various disciplines in the aftermath of the Holocaust. Finally, we will be examining how knowledge of the Holocaust can be used to prevent inter-ethnic conflicts and the threat of genocide.

The conference is being organized in conjunction with American, English, and German historians, theologians, and philosophers, and scholars of the Holocaust. We have secured the venue and the support of Berlin's Humboldt University. We have the support of the Western world, of Israel, and of our friends all over the world. We know that we cannot allow the Christians of Europe to remain complacent and silent once again about the fate of the Jews in their midst. Those who know must actively educate those who do not know. Those teeming millions now trying to join western Europe must be told that one of the prices they have to pay is to remember what happened under Nazism, Communism, dictatorship, and the spread of idolatry. Nazism itself was nothing more than idolatry of a fake god, leading to false ethics and the subservience of the individual to the so-called greater good of the state, with all its shameful ideology.

If our Berlin conference is to achieve the success it deserves, we need support, both moral and financial, from the world. We can really be a force for good, but we cannot do it without the help of all those who like me remain convinced that only education can stop us from treading the path of destruction again. Indeed, this coming together of Christians and Jews, in profound respect for each other's faith and with genuine curiosity to learn of the richness of the other's tradition, yet without demanding any relinquishing of each other's belief, is the most formidable combination of circumstances for working for peace in our violent and tormented world.

But we live in a pluralist society, and we have to acknowledge that we still have another great task ahead of us; that of entering into dialogue with our Muslim brothers and sisters, in the hope of a similar reconciliation. We have to realize that none of the great religions of the world can claim to be the only way to God, and that if religions could only use their enormous powers to teach what they have in common—the love of God, the love of one's neighbour, and respect for human life—and stop teaching bigotry and triumphalism, we may truly be working for peace in our time.

In the words of Hans Küng's telling conclusion: 'There can be no ongoing human society without a world ethic for the nations. There can be no peace among the nations without peace among the religions. There can be no peace among the religions without dialogue between the religions.'[17]

Notes

1. Jonathan Webber, *The Future of Auschwitz: Some Personal Reflections*. The first Frank Green Lecture (Oxford: Oxford Centre for Postgraduate Hebrew Studies, 1992). Reprinted in *Religion, State and Society*, 20: 1 (1992). The ideas presented there are developed further in Webber's long afterword to the English-language edition of the main documentary photo album of the Auschwitz Museum; see Teresa Świebocka, Jonathan Webber, and Connie Wilsack (eds.), *Auschwitz: A History in Photographs* (Bloomington, Ind., 1993).
2. Helga Croner (compiler), *Stepping Stones to Further Jewish–Christian Relations* (London, 1977).
3. See e.g. John Paul II, *Notes on the Correct Way to Present Jews and Judaism in Preaching and Catechesis in the Roman Catholic Church* (6 Mar. 1982).
4. Ibid.
5. Helga Croner (compiler), *More Stepping Stones to Jewish–Christian Relations* (London, 1985).
6. 'Déclaration du Comité International de Liaison entre Juifs et Catholiques (Prague, 6 Sept. 1990)', *Istina* (1991), 225–30 (my translation).
7. 'Report on Lambeth Conference and Its Resolution', *Ends & Odds Newsletter*, Sept. 1989 (Birmingham: Centre for the Study of Judaism and Jewish–Christian Relations, Selly Oak Colleges).
8. John T. Pawlikowski, 'The Judaising of Christianity, its Impact on the Church and its Implications for the Jewish People', *People, Land and State of Israel: Jewish and Christian Perspectives*, 22–3 (1989). Id., 'On the Relation of the Church to Non-Christian Religions', *After Twenty-Five Years: Jewish–Christian Relations since the Second Vatican Council's Nostra Aetate*. Symposium papers. (OSM, Oct. 8 and 9, 1990).
9. Leon Klenicki and Eugene J. Fisher, *Roots and Branches: Biblical Judaism, Rabbinic Judaism and Early Christianity* (Winona, Minn., 1987), 15. See also Matt. 4: 83, 9: 35; Luke 4: 15–18; John 18: 20.
10. See Mark 12, Luke 10, Matt. 22.
11. See Matt. 6, Luke 11.
12. See Prov. 30: 8–9.
13. Klenicki and Fisher, *Roots and Branches*, 19; see also Rom. 9–11.

14. Ibid. See also Matt. 23.
15. Christopher T. Husbands: 'Neo-Nazis in East Germany: The New Danger?', *Patterns of Prejudice*, 25: 1 (1991), 3.
16. Robert S. Wistrich, 'Recalling Wannsee', *Times Literary Supplement*, 31 Jan. 1992.
17. Hans Küng, *Global Responsibility* (London, 1990); and see also his *Judaism* (London, 1992).

CHAPTER TWENTY-ONE

A New Catholic–Jewish Relationship for Europe

PIER FRANCESCO FUMAGALLI

*W*HEN *the people of God were freed from Pharaoh's bondage and had left Egypt, they seemed at one time on the point of entering the Promised Land. Scouts told them there were huge clusters of grapes and fine pomegranates and figs in it, but that it was also a country of dangerous giants and its cities were fortified up to heaven. The people took fright and most of the scouts, except Caleb and Joshua, discouraged the Israelites, who consequently had to face a long trek in the desert: these, said the Lord, would not 'see the land which I swore to their fathers'* (Num. 14: 23). *Faced with the promises and great changes specific to Europe today, shall we be fearful explorers or shall we encourage our brothers and sisters, as Joshua and Caleb did?*

These words are taken taken from a report on the Fifth Ecumenical Encounter held in November 1991 in Santiago de Compostela.[1] Even today the call for courage that is implicit in this biblical episode can be taken as inspiration to the Church as it reflects on its relationship to the Jewish people in the new Europe.

An important summary of the Church's present view on its relationship with the Jews is given in the Final Declaration of the Special Assembly of the Synod of Bishops for Europe held in Rome in December 1991:

An extremely important factor in the construction of a new order in Europe and in the world is interreligious dialogue, above all with our 'elder brothers' the Jewish people, whose faith and culture are an element of human development in Europe.

After the terrible holocaust of our century, for which the Church feels a profound grief, new attempts have to be made to acknowledge Judaism more profoundly, rejecting all forms of antisemitism as contrary either to the Gospel or to natural law. We commend the suggestions which are according to the mind of the Second Vatican Council, and accordingly promote positive relationships with the Jewish people in the Church's preaching and educational work.

The Church certainly esteems the roots which Christianity and the Hebrew people share: Jesus himself founded his Church in the context of the religion of Israel. Mindful of the spiritual heritage, [and] above all Sacred Scripture, which links it with Judaism, the Church in the current European situation intends to work for the blossoming of a new spring in its mutual relationships. Joint work at various levels between Christians and Jews, taking account of differences and particular doctrines of each religion, could have great significance in Europe's future, civil and religious, and its role in the rest of the world.[2]

The Synod called for 'the blossoming of a new spring' in the Church's relationship with the Jews. In doing so it was making an implicit reference to the recommendations of the Second Vatican Council ('Vatican II'), over the period 1962–5, some thirty years earlier, which were most certainly perceived as the very welcome advent of spring after a centuries-long winter of misunderstanding and persecution, and particularly after the Holocaust. Under the guidance of the Holy Spirit, Vatican II has in fact inspired many new and positive steps over the past thirty years;[3] it represented a fundamental change in the Church's attitude to the Jewish people. Comparing the declaration that the Synod issued with the landmark *Nostra aetate* issued by Vatican II, the basic continuity of the two texts is readily apparent. Why, then, call today for a 'new spring'? In what would the 'newness' consist?

A CALL FOR SPIRITUAL RENEWAL

The 'new spring' that the Church is now envisaging is a call not for a new *attitude* but a new *relationship*—a relationship that will have meaning in the day-to-day life of the two communities and be concretely embodied in structures of dialogue and co-operation as they face together the challenges of history. Achieving this new relationship still requires time, humility, patience, courage, and prayer. Above all else it requires inner change on the Christian side: as Cardinal Edward I. Cassidy said in his address to the International Liaison Committee (ILC) of the Catholic Church and the International Jewish Committee on Interreligious Consultations (IJCIC) in Prague in September 1990, 'that antisemitism has found a place in Christian thought and practice calls for an act of *teshuvah* and of reconciliation'.[4] The call on our part for a new relationship is thus not made in the abstract, but with a deep consciousness of the need for such spiritual renewal.

In recent years there have been several examples of the enduring Catholic commitment to this sort of renewal. One illustration is to be found in the preparatory document issued in connection with the Synod of Bishops for Europe in 1991, which underscores that the Synod was prepared in a spirit of broader dialogue and fraternal co-operation with the Jews; it even incorporated a questionnaire entitled 'How Does Your Church Live Out its Relationship with Judaism?'[5] On the occasion of the Synod, the European Jewish Congress for its part addressed a communiqué to Cardinal Carlo Maria Martini,[6] and notable contributions were made at the Synod itself on the subject of the Church's attitude to the Jews. Particularly noteworthy was Cardinal Cassidy's 'Promouvoir la solidarité avec le peuple juif', which recommended the institution of an annual European day for reflection, prayer, and dialogue on this issue,[7] along the lines of that initiated in Italy by the Italian Bishops' Conference in 1990. Further concrete proposals on co-operation were also made by Cardinal Cassidy at a conference held in Brussels in 1992 on the theme 'My Brother's Keeper: Antisemitism and Prejudice in a Changing World'.[8]

Concern for the ecumenical dimension in Christian–Jewish relations is also expressed by the fact that the Holy See's Commission for Religious Relations with the Jews regularly sends observers to the activities of the World Council of Churches' Consultation on Church and Jewish People,[9] and also to meetings of the International Council of Christians and Jews.

Several specific initiatives on ecumenical co-operation have already taken place in Europe, in addition to the annual day for dialogue, prayer, and co-operation instituted in Italy. An International Council, made up of both Christians and Jews, was established in 1991 for the Centre for Information, Prayer, Dialogue, Meeting, and Education that the Church has set up in Oświęcim, Poland, near the site of the former Auschwitz–Birkenau murder camp. There was formal Christian participation in the commemoration in Spain in 1992 of the 500th anniversary of the expulsion of the Jews, which was given wide publicity in the Church.[10] In the same year, the ILC sent formal delegations to Poland, Czechoslovakia, and Hungary. Finally, a most important step forward was the establishment of a permanent bilateral commission between the Holy See and the State of Israel with a view to normalizing the relations between them.[11]

But let us go back to the two questions I asked earlier: why should the Church be calling now for a 'new spring' in Christian–Jewish relations, and in what should its new elements consist?

For Catholics there are specific spiritual reasons for rectifying the Church's relationship with the Jews, as well as cultural and historical considerations. According to _Lumen gentium_, the Dogmatic Constitution on the Church, issued by Vatican II in 1964, 'from a religious perspective . . . which is the deepest and most mysterious dimension of the human person', we must take our orientation from 'a high sense of the absolute singularity of God's choice of a particular people . . . "His own" people, Israel according to the flesh, already called "God's Church" '. Thus, as _Nostra aetate_ made clear, the Church's reflection on its mission and on its very nature is intrinsically linked to its reflection on the stock of Abraham and on the nature of the Jewish people. The Church is fully aware that the Holy Scriptures bear witness that the Jewish people, as a community of faith and custodian of a tradition thousands of years old, is an intimate part of the mystery of revelation and salvation: Pope John Paul II spoke about this in an address in Rome in December 1990. He then went on to look at the issue from the perspective of the Jewish spiritual position: 'God, his holy Torah, the synagogal liturgy and family traditions, the Land of Holiness, are surely what characterizes your people from the religious point of view. And these are things that constitute the foundation of our dialogue and of our cooperation.'[12] Catholic exegetes and theologians have been working systematically for many years on similar reflections,[13] and analogous trends can be seen in other Christian churches and theological circles.[14] In fact, one of the major requirements for renewing the Christian–Jewish relationship is the further development of these biblical and theological studies, to include such elements as Church history, liturgy, and patristics. This task pertains primarily to Christians, but there is nothing to prevent Jewish scholars and thinkers from offering the fruits of their research, in a spirit of dialogue.

It needs to be said that there is a certain asymmetry in the dialogue, in that for Christians the reference to Jesus Christ is essential. There is no intention of proselytizing, but believers can bring witness only according to their own religious creed—and as *Nostra aetate* reaffirmed, the Church believes that 'by his cross Christ, our peace, reconciled Jew and Gentile, making them both one in himself'. But *Nostra aetate* also stressed another aspect of the Church's relationship with the Jews, recalling that it 'draws sustenance from the root of that good olive tree on to which have been grafted the wild olive branches of the Gentile', and that from the Jewish people sprang the Virgin Mary, her son Jesus—'Christ according to the Flesh' (Rom. 9: 5)—and the apostles. The search for unity through dialogue—in the sense foretold by the prophets, that the day will come when all people will address the Lord in a single voice and 'serve him with one accord'[15]—is a goal awaited by Christians and Jews alike. As the chief rabbi of Milan, Rabbi Joseph Laras, declared in an address in Milan in May 1992, 'Dialogue will help us in coming to that goal of unity that is part of the faith and expectation of both the Christian and Jewish world.'[16]

Another substantial consequence of these principles would be the change in the content and the spirit of Catholic curricula for teaching about Jews and Judaism, as proposed by Remi Hoeckman at the 14th ILC meeting.[17] Hoeckman stressed that co-operation in this task can take place only in the context of an atmosphere of mutual esteem and reciprocal caring. As Pope

John Paul II said, speaking in Rome in 1985, this also implies that Jews must 'try to know the beliefs and practices and spirituality of Christians' as we live today.[18]

DIALOGUE BEYOND THE RELIGIOUS SPHERE

There are other elements in the new Catholic–Jewish relationship that may also have dramatic consequences for today's Europe. This is because the need for dialogue extends far beyond the religious sphere; the new relationship will have cultural, legal, and political implications at both national and international levels.

The interdependence of these dimensions is particularly obvious when one considers the Holocaust—the murder of the Jews of Europe for no other reason than that they were Jews, often referred to by the Hebrew term *shoah*. The act of reflecting on this tragedy may help Catholics to deepen their awareness of a sense of responsibility for developments in Europe—a responsibility on which Cardinal Willebrands, speaking in Philadelphia in November 1990, was quite specific.

As regards the *shoah*, in particular, we have to note—both before and after the *shoah*, and notwithstanding the specific condemnation of racial anti-Semitism by the Catholic hierarchy—the gap or void in Catholic culture that retarded the development of an analysis of the non-religious components of anti-Semitism. Such an analysis could have led to a severe condemnation of this phenomenon on the rational level. As regards the religious level, as also the religious components of anti-Semitism, it has to be borne in mind that the anti-Jewish prejudices deriving from the so-called 'teaching of contempt' also had their effects on the overall atmosphere in Europe.

Before the *shoah*, moreover, Catholic theology failed to elaborate any systematic and positive teaching concerning the contemporary Jewish people in relation to the mystery of salvation.[19]

We must further extend our historical meditation to other similarly murderous strategies—towards Gypsies, homosexuals, the handicapped, the mentally ill, and a generation earlier to the genocide of the Armenians—with an awareness that the shadow of these tragedies has not disappeared from Europe.

The Church is well aware that antisemitism continues to be a problem:

Certain organizations, with branches in many countries, keep alive the anti-Semite racist myth, with the support of networks of publications. Terrorist acts which have Jewish persons or symbols as their target have multiplied in recent years and show the radicalism of such groups. Anti-Zionism—which is not of the same order, since it questions the State of Israel and its policies—serves at time as a screen for anti-Semitism, feeding on it and leading to it.[20]

Even today, we can discern an attempt 'to falsify history to deny the dreadful crimes committed against the Jews in the Shoah', as Cardinal Cassidy pointed out in his address at the Brussels Conference 'My Brother's Keeper: Antisemitism and Prejudice in a Changing World' (cited above). It is a source of much concern that Europe is troubled now by a new nationalism that questions the nature of democracy, the search for solidarity and unity, the pluralism and respect for other identities and minorities in multiracial, multireligious, and multicultural societies.

KEY AREAS FOR CO-OPERATION

At this critical juncture in the development of Europe, the Church sees three key areas in which the new spirit of co-operation between Christians and Jews could be most usefully stimulated: ethical issues; social issues; and political, international, and legal issues.

1. *Ethical issues.* In the biblical revelation, God reveals himself as a universal saviour. Such salvation is intrinsically linked with the human, ethical dimension. The biblical precepts of loving God and loving one's neighbour are inseparable. Close co-operation is therefore appropriate both in theoretical reflection and in creating frameworks for action in such fields as reverence for life, health care, family values, poverty, and the sexual exploitation of women and children.[21]

2. *Social issues.* The broader implications of the above ethical concerns extend to a larger set of problem areas that have global social relevance—for example, the problems of the integrity of creation, addiction, immigration, xenophobia, racism, and antisemitism. Furthermore, the specific call for Christian–Jewish co-operation should be extended to Muslims and members of other religions.[22]

3. *Political, international, and legal issues.* Our common responsibility and commitment extend to all levels of human organization. In general, while we must clearly affirm the Church's respect for the autonomy of each state, we must at the same time work towards 'a communion of convergence, in order to ensure to each human person the fruition of cultural, juridical, social, and political values.[23]

Sometimes the Church must become a critic of the world and of the policies of the nations. The Bishops' Synod for Europe enumerated the areas in which this would be most appropriate as: aid for the south of the planet; staunching the arms trade; developing solutions for international debt; and encouraging the spread of democracy. It further stated specifically that the unification of Europe places 'a huge responsibility' on the churches.[24]

Likewise, the 14th ILC meeting expressed encouragement for a more collaborative engagement within European and other intergovernmental institutions on the regional level, and among non-governmental organizations in general.[25] The ILC has in fact repeatedly affirmed the need to promote appropriate juridical instruments at the national and international level.[26]

In this respect, the Middle East peace process should create new possibilities, especially (but not only) in Israel, to attempt to harmonize the norms, historical rights, and traditions of Jews, Christians, and Muslims.[27] The solutions evolved could provide a paradigm for the complex multicultural and multireligious tensions and conflict situations in Europe that we must try to resolve in peaceful ways.

May the common prayer of the psalms, 'Peace be within your walls' (Ps. 122: 7), become our prayer for the peace of each person in Europe and all the peoples of Europe. May reflection on the spiritual values of Jerusalem for Jews, Christians, and Muslims inspire a relationship open to co-operation with all persons of good will, serving God's dominion of love and justice in our midst.

Notes

1. Dean John Arnold and Cardinal Carlo Maria Martini, ' "At Thy Word": Mission and Evangelization in Europe Today. Report on the Fifth Ecumenical Encounter, Santiago de Compostela, 13–17 Nov. 1991', *Catholic International*, 32: 2 (1992), 93. A report on the special relations existing between Christians and Jews in Europe presented at the encounter was also subsequently published; see Cardinal Johannes Willebrands, 'Jewish Religious and Cultural Contribution to European Civilization', in id., *Church and Jewish People: New Considerations* (New York, 1992), 194–7.

2. The original text was in Latin. The official English translation was published as 'To Be Witnesses of Christ Who Has Set Us Free', *Catholic International*, 3: 5 (1992), 218. A French translation was published in *La Documentation catholique*, 2043 (1992), 129, and translations into other European languages were published in the weekly or monthly editions of *L'Osservatore romano*; a Hungarian translation was made by the Hungarian bishops' conference.

3. See e.g. International Catholic–Jewish Liaison Committee, *Fifteen Years of Dialogue, 1970–1985: Selected Papers* (Vatican City, 1988); also Gerhart M. Riegner's preface to Cardinal Willebrands' *Church and Jewish People*. A summary of the developments, entitled 'Church and Jewish People: Twenty-Five Years after the Second Vatican Council', with an up-to-date bibliography and list of documents, appears in *Sidic* (Service international de documentation judéo-chrétienne), 25: 2 (1992), 18–27.

4. The full text is reproduced in *Information Service*, 75: 4 (1990), 175. On the same theme see 'Après la shoa: Juifs et chrétiens s'interrogent', *Istina*, 36: 3 (1991), 225–352; an issue entirely devoted to this theme.

5. The document and questionnaire are reproduced in *Catholic International*, 2: 15 (1991), 724.

6. See *La Documentation catholique*, 2041 (1992), 37–8.

7. Ibid. 64–6.

8. The proceedings of this conference are in the process of publication.

9. On this theme see the *New Ecumenical Directory*, no. 210, issued on 24 March 1993 by the Pontifical Council for Promoting Christian Unity. (Original French text in *L'Osservatore romano*, suppl. 9 June 1993, i–xvi.)

10. See *L'Osservatore romano*, 1 Apr. 1992, p. 2; *Catholic International*, 3: 10 (1992), 491–2.

11. See *L'Osservatore romano*, 31 July 1992, p. 2; ibid., weekly edn. no. 31 (5 Aug. 1992), p. 8.

12. *Information Service*, 77: 2 (1991), 83.

13. See sources cited in n. 3.

14. See e.g. *Die Kirchen und das Judentum: Dokumente von 1945–1985*, ed. Rolf Rendtorff and Hans Hermann Henrix (Munich, 1989); World Council of Churches, *The Theology of the Churches and the Jewish People* (Geneva, 1988); *Christen und Juden: Eine Studie der Evangelischen Kirchen in Deutschland* (Gütersloh, 1991).

15. Zeph. 3: 9, quoted by Moses Maimonides, *Mishneh torah, Hilkhot melakhim*, xi. 4, and by *Nostra aetate*, 4, and in both texts with deep messianic expectation.

16. See *La Repubblica*, 30 May 1992, p. 20.

17. See Remi Hoeckman, 'The Teaching on Jews and Judaism in Catholic Education', *Seminarium* 346–59; NS 32: 2 (1992); on the results of the 14th ILC meeting, held in Baltimore in 1992, see *Catholic International*, 3: 13 (1992), 606–17 and *La Documentation catholique*, 2052 (1992), 586–94.

18. See United States Catholic Conference, *Pope John Paul II on Jews and Judaism, 1979–1986* (Washington, DC, 1987), 71.

19. Johannes Willebrands, 'The Impact of the *shoah* on Catholic–Jewish Relations', in id., *Church and Jewish People*, 162.

20. Pontifical Commission Iustitia et Pax, *The Church and Racism* (1988), no. 15.

21. See the Final Declaration of the Bishops' Synod for Europe (iii. 9; iv. 10), and the Final Statement of the 14th ILC meeting, as cited above (n. 17).

22. See John Paul II, *Sollicitudo rei socialis* (encyclical letter) (1988), n. 47. *The Church and Racism* (see n. 20 above) comments on the need to promote suitable social structures to prevent discrimination (ibid., at n. 26).

23. Umberto Betti, Rector of the Pontifical Lateran University, in *L'Osservatore romano*, 15–16 June 1992, p. 9.

24. Final Declaration, iv. 11; ibid. iv. 10.

25. *Catholic International*, 3: 13 (1992), 607.

26. See e.g. *The Church and Racism*, no. 26; also the Final Statement of the 13th ILC meeting, reproduced in *Information Service*, 75: 4 (1990), 177, nn. 4-5.
27. See the Pastoral Letter of the Council of Catholic Patriarchs of the East, translated from the original Arabic for publication as 'Présence et témoignage', *La Documentation catholique*, 2052 (1992), 606–8, at nn. 48–51.

CHAPTER TWENTY-TWO

Possible Implications of the New Age Movement for the Jewish People

MARGARET BREARLEY

T HE world is approaching the beginning of the third millennium with a justifiable fear of global destruction and ecological disaster, and hope for a new spiritual and political utopia. These millenarian hopes and fears are embodied in the New Age movement, a movement which teaches that humanity is passing not only from one millennium to another but from one age to another. Its leading architect, the theosophist Alice Bailey, argued that just as the age of Pisces (representing Christianity) had replaced the age of Aries (representing Judaism) in the first century AD, so now the age of Aquarius, the new era of group psychic spirituality, is replacing the age of Christianity. One of the first public statements of this view was in the 1960s' musical *Hair*: 'This is the dawning of the New Age . . . this is the Age of Aquarius.'

THE ORIGINS OF NEW AGE

The two major pioneers of New Age are widely held to have been Helena Blavatsky (1831–91) and Alice Bailey (1880–1948). Their writings are still much quoted and have determined vital strands of New Age ideology. Helena Blavatsky was an occultist and spirit medium; she founded the Theosophical Society in 1875 and wrote two key texts, *Isis Unveiled* (1877) and *The Secret Doctrine* (1888). Alice Bailey was a leading Theosophist who founded influential international New Age organizations, including World Goodwill, after the Second World War. Her works contain 285 passages

For fear of overburdening the reader I have cited sources only for the key concepts I refer to. Other relevant sources are listed in the Supplementary Bibliography.

about New Age; according to a leading New Age promoter, William Bloom, they are held by many both within and outside the movement to be the key inspiration for it.

But New Age gained real popularity partly as a product of the 1960s, when the knowledge that drugs can trigger reactions in the brain which appear to expand consciousness (widely known in other cultures but previously restricted to small circles in the West) became popularized through Allen Ginsberg, Timothy Leary, and the hippy movement. Many who experienced the euphoria of 'trips' on LSD or other drugs, with their distortions of space and time and their sense of heightened reality, then later found that certain techniques of Eastern spirituality, shamanistic religions, or Western occultism could induce similar sensations. The 1970s saw the proliferation of cults and consciousness-raising techniques which produced parallel results: disorientation from previous perceptions and beliefs, and a conviction that one was living on a new plane of reality.

All these strands, originally part of the counter-culture, have now coalesced within mainstream culture as New Age spirituality. New Age is thus intensely eclectic. Predominant features include the practice of Eastern meditation or shamanistic rituals, and belief in astrology, reincarnation, karma, and the monistic 'oneness' of everything. The spirituality is a pot-pourri drawn from Eastern, primal, and esoteric traditions, and embraces techniques as various as crystal-healing, spirit-channelling, TM (transcendental meditation), tai ch'i, EST (Erhard Seminars Training), Raja Yoga, 'rebirthing', ritual drumming, guided visualizations, out-of-the-body experiences, and 'past lives recall'. It possibly represents as major a shift in Western thought and culture as the Renaissance and the Enlightenment: a radical turning away from rationality, from monotheism, materialist humanism, and especially from exoteric Judaeo-Christian traditions.

THE NEW AGE IDEOLOGY

Despite its apparent eclecticism, the core of New Age ideology is consistent. It argues that Judaeo-Christian monotheism is adolescent, egocentric, and defunct, having held the individual in immature reliance on a transcendent deity and enslaved humanity as a whole in 'materialism' (defined as a wrong vision of the world as objective and real rather than as *maya*, an illusion).[1] We have thus been unenlightened and in a state of 'waking sleep', unaware of the 'true Self', of our psychic powers and ability to pierce subjectively the veil of reality.

In the new, adult age of Aquarius, it is argued, humanity is at last evolving to maturity; Peter Russell, New Age scientist and promoter of TM, claims that people who have been transformed by New Age consciousness are becoming fully human, fully conscious, for the first time. They are becoming Self-centred, freed from the shackles of individual ego and personality and from notions of a transcendent God to be feared and loved. New Agers believe in a monistic 'God within' (sometimes called their 'inner divinity', 'true nature', or 'divine Self'), of which they can become aware through private or group meditations, rituals, or experiences in which all sense of space, time, and personal self is lost. David Spangler, occultist, spirit medium, and leading influence on the New Age training centre at Findhorn in Scotland, described this evolution thus: 'Man himself transforms his being into its next stage, which could be called super-man . . . Energies . . . are now entering . . . which demand of man that he become aware of his true nature, which is not an individualized nature but a group nature.'[2]

New Age apologists claim that whereas Judaeo-Christian anthropocentrism led to warfare and destruction of the planet, the Age of Aquarius will lead to global peace, the healing of nature, and the birth of a new human species. (New Age journals now often claim that the dissolution of Communism and the liberation of eastern Europe is a consequence of New Age meditation.) For the first time, humanity will universally adopt what Aldous Huxley called the 'Perennial Philosophy' of transformed consciousness. This is attainable by hallucinogenic drugs, many techniques of meditation, shamanism, or mind-transforming programmes, and, above all, by voluntarily surrendering the individual will to the group will. In the past such techniques were known to only a few, to initiates. It is now a commonplace of New Age belief that as all people are taught how to attain heightened consciousness and transformed values, humanity will be put back in touch with its own psychic powers, in tune with the spirits and energies of earth, moon, and cosmos, and fully conscious at last of its own Godhood. This is heralded as nothing other than the divine evolutionary plan: for the individual to become god is, according to Alice Bailey, 'the next unfolding of divinity'.[3]

THE INFLUENCE OF NEW AGE

The New Age movement represents the world's fastest-growing spirituality. Speaking at a conference at the London School of Economics in 1990, J. Gordon Melton, a leading commentator on cults (new religious movements), stated that over a quarter of American adults adhere to New Age beliefs or practices. In 1980 Marilyn Ferguson argued that there were already 'tens of thousands of entry points to the [Aquarian/New Age] conspiracy'. Throughout the English-speaking world, Europe, and elsewhere, networks of closely interlinked New Age organizations exist at

international, national, and local levels. Conferences, retreat centres, New
Age and esoteric festivals, and training centres like Findhorn in Scotland attract hundreds of thousands of participants annually in Europe and
North America. All are designed to transform minds, attitudes, and values
towards a New Age perspective. In 1988 a British handbook of the New
Age claimed that as many as 1.5–3 million Britons were in some way
affiliated.

Under the New Age umbrella cluster a vast range of specific groups, from
the Unification Church (Moonies), Scientologists—who alone have 8 million members—and Zen Buddhists to 'New Age travellers', modern pagans,
Wiccan witches, 'post-Christian' feminists, and occultists. But New Age
forms of spirituality are now widely practised in the population at large; they
are popularized by publishers such as Thorsons, young people's and
women's magazines, writers such as Shirley MacLaine, and are prevalent
even in children's books and computer games. Reflecting similar trends in
other European countries and the United States, New Age values and beliefs
have begun to figure prominently in the serious British press and on radio
and television, and in areas such as education (especially experiential religious education), ecology, and alternative medicine and therapies. Since the
mid-1980s, New Age spirituality has been at the core of management
courses on personal development adopted by leading companies; it now
extensively influences American and European culture and even finance (the
BCCI bank was imbued with the ethos of New Age).[4] Its recent spread has
been remarkable; promotion of New Age is now multi-billion dollar business world-wide.

One particularly worrying feature of this trend is that New Age is
explicitly the path of non-attachment, of detachment. Rudolf Steiner, a
highly-trained initiate of occultism, argued that occult meditation must
gradually break the bonds between will, thought, and emotion. There is
little doubt that this would lead to detachment both inwardly—from the
personality, memory, conscience—and outwardly—from family and other
relationships. I already know of Jewish marriages that have broken down as
a direct result of New Age practices by one partner. (Breakdown of marriages and long-term relationships became so prevalent at Findhorn that
David Spangler addressed the problem specifically.) It is recognized even
within the movement that opening the seven body *chakras* ('energy points'
supposed to lie within the spine and accessible only through certain psycho-
sexual techniques), raising the *kundalini* (vital sexual force believed to
reside at the base of the spine), and occultism in general can cause psychological harm; a number of occultists, including Dion Fortune, have warned of
this.

THE IMPLICATIONS FOR JEWS

Jews should take the implications of this ideology seriously for several reasons. Firstly, New Age already has major international influence, far beyond Western Europe, the United States, and the English-speaking world. As the ideologies of Communism and capitalist materialism collapse, New Age is increasingly filling the spiritual and intellectual vacuum. The spirituality of New Age is making rapid inroads into the former Soviet Union and eastern Europe, where cults have been gaining hundreds of thousands of adherents since 1989 (TM claimed to have 10,000 members in Prague alone within six months of its arrival). It permeated the two Global Fora of Spiritual and Parliamentary Leaders on Human Survival in Oxford and Moscow, is promoted by some international ecological organizations, including the World-Wide Fund for Nature (WWFN), and influenced some of the alternative events at the 1992 Rio Earth Summit.

Secondly, since a significant number of New Age leaders and their followers are themselves Jewish in origin, it is likely that during the 1990s a new New Age Jewish identity will emerge, particularly among the young, women, the unaffiliated or disaffected, those who have taken hallucinogenic drugs, or who are or have been members of a mind-transforming cult, such as TM, Scientology, or EST. (According to Dr Beit-Hallahmi of Haifa University, a higher proportion of Israel's population has taken EST or TM programmes than of any other country.) In Britain, as elsewhere, there are already increasing numbers of Jews who are seeking spiritual experience from such sources as TM, women's earth rituals, Raja Yoga, Zen, and other practices, as the *Jewish Chronicle* has pointed out (26 June 1992). Rabbi Zalman Schachter-Shalomi, who has a considerable following in the United States, has blended certain aspects of Judaism with New Age spirituality. In Britain, the Jewish New Age group Ruach specifically targets unaffiliated Jews, and the Jewish cultural and listings journal *New Moon* (March 1993) has highlighted the popularity of New Age-orientated events at a major Reform synagogue in London. Internationally, people of Jewish background figure among the leaders of Wiccan witchcraft and New Age occultism, and Kabbalah is widely taught as part of New Age esotericism.

During this and the next decade rabbis will face growing challenges; they will increasingly encounter Jewish casualties of occultism, and will need to give spiritual and psychological counsel. Jewish communities will need to find new ways of reaching out to those who are unaffiliated, disaffected, or lonely. Jewish education will become even more vital than today, particularly for women. It will be necessary to teach authentic Torah-based spirituality and ethics with even more passion and creativity than now to Jews hungry for spiritual experience.

Thirdly, from the perspective of Torah, New Age spirituality represents a widespread and often literal turning to the pagan gods of space, to sun and moon (earth rituals at full moon and solstices are now celebrated in the Anglican church of St James', Piccadilly), to the horned god and Great Goddess (in Wicca). Both the Torah and the biblical prophets condemn outright the ancient psychic and psycho-sexual practices which are at the root of much New Age spirituality. Torah and New Age are thus, in certain crucial ways, polar opposites.

Consequently, from its origins until today, New Age ideology has been anti-Judaic. It derives ultimately from early Gnosticism, a movement explicitly opposed to the Jewish God, to the Jewish Scriptures, and to some of the main tenets of Judaism. Among other roots of New Age thought, the most important is the nineteenth-century discovery of Eastern spirituality, following the eighteenth-century translations of the Upanishads, Vedas, and other Hindu and Buddhist texts. These influenced the German Romantics, and especially the atheist Arthur Schopenhauer, who came to believe that the world was not the work of a benevolent Creator but of a devil. Schopenhauer sought to divorce Western Christian philosophy from Judaism, 'the crudest and worst of all religions'.[5] To achieve the 'end of the nightmare' of Jewish influence in Europe, he tried to reorient Christianity towards Buddhist perceptions: 'the core and essence of Christianity and Brahminism are identical'.[6]

Richard Wagner, a disciple of Schopenhauer and enthusiast of Buddhism, tried even more radically to obliterate Jewish monotheism, both through opera and in his numerous theoretical (and highly antisemitic) writings. He hated Jews and Judaism, seeing the Jewish race as 'the born enemy of pure humanity and everything noble in it'.[7] In the *Ring* he attempted to replace a Judaic world-view and morality with a revival of Germanic paganism, exalting the amoral primacy of nature, man's basic instincts, including lust and cruelty, and a return to 'the unconscious'. In *Parsifal*, he blended racist antisemitism with esoteric Christian symbolism. Like Schopenhauer, he championed what later became key New Age ideas, including reincarnation, the abolition of space and time, and the eradication of the God of Israel. Like Schopenhauer, Wagner envisaged the complete disappearance of all Jewish identity, and through his writings hoped to bring this about.[8]

To clarify the potentially dangerous connotations of the New Age philosophy, I shall briefly explore six areas of concern that are likely to have a specific impact on Jewish identities in the new Europe. It should be noted that, precisely because of the esoteric nature of much New Age teaching, most of its adherents, particularly those who have not read key New Age sources, are unaware of these darker dimensions and are strongly idealistic.

Anti-Jewishness

At a deep, esoteric level, New Age ideology is Aryan and racist. Like earlier Theosophists, Alice Bailey taught that Aryans are the contemporary root-race, embodying the gods of the future. For both Blavatsky and Bailey, Jews were 'a different root-race from Aryans', a defunct form of humanity condemned for 'their ancient sin of non-response to the evolutionary process'.[9] For Alice Bailey, Jews constitute 'a unique and distinctly separated world centre of energy; they represent the energy and the life of the previous solar system'.[10] Jews are characterized by selfishness and worship of a cruel, tribal God, whom Bailey sees as 'the tribal Jehovah, the (rather unpleasant) soul of a nation'.[11] They are full of hatred, aggression, and separativeness, in league with 'the dark forces, the Antichrist governing humanity'.[12] Bailey wished to combine all religions into one single one based on full-moon festivals and nature's rhythms, led by 'highly-evolved men and women'. All traces of Judaism would be removed and Christian symbols would be reinterpreted, the cross becoming the symbol of Aryan development.

Like many occultists, Bailey rejected traditional notions of good and evil, locating evil instead in 'the great sin or heresy of separateness'. She consequently identified the Jews, with their 'sin of separateness', as the world's worst problem, stating *after* the Holocaust: 'There is no other problem like it in the world today.'[13] According to Bailey, the Jewish religion and ethics are obsolete; this has made it possible for the 'forces of separativeness and of hate to use the Jewish race to stir up world difficulty, and thus bring to a crisis the basic human problem of separation. When humanity has solved the Jewish problem, the problem will be rapidly solved and one of the major difficulties will disappear off the face of the earth. Racial fusion will then be possible. Our earth humanity and the group of human beings who are far more ancient in their origin than we are will form one humanity and there will be peace on earth.'[14]

Alice Bailey's writings were intensely antisemitic. In 1947 she described Jews as 'a very cruel and aggressive people.'[15] She condemned Jews for retaining deliberately their racial identity, and argued that the Holocaust was simply the Jewish karma for their 'depths of human evil'.[16] Indeed, she argued that the Second World War had achieved positive results, in that it 'drove back the forces of evil' and released souls into the bliss of death.[17] But although it was in Theosophist circles that *The Protocols of the Elders of Zion* first circulated in Russia, today there is only occasional overt evidence of antisemitism in New Age writings or events. However, such recurrent phrases as 'separative forces', 'men of ill-will', 'selfish entities', 'adolescent' or 'dark' souls are in fact esoteric ways of referring to perceived enemies of the New Age, including observant and Zionist Jews and orthodox Christians.

For many of today's New Age leaders, Bailey's writings represent the unquestioned truth. Her anti-Jewish writings are still reprinted. The Institute of Planetary Synthesis, based in Geneva, recently published a collection of her most antisemitic statements under the title *The Total Challenge of Humanity on Earth: The Jewish Problem*.

Opposition to Zionism

Alice Bailey was opposed to nation-states in general and to Israel in particular, which she saw as dominated by Zionism, 'this evil influence': 'The spirit of totalitarian evil is expressing itself through the Zionist movement which seek[s] to fetter and imprison the spirit of man.'[18] In April 1947 she wrote that through Zionism 'the Jews have partially again opened the door to the Forces of Evil which worked originally through Hitler and his gang. These Forces of Evil work through a triangle of evil, one point of which is to be found in the Zionist movement in the United States, another in central Europe and the third in Palestine. Palestine is no longer a Holy Land and should not be so regarded. [Zionism] marks a point of triumph of the forces of evil.'[19]

One long-term political aim of some New Age leaders (publicly formulated by World Goodwill) is a single world government (governed by psychically guided, 'enlightened' leaders) and the eradication of nation-states in favour of 'bio-regions'. The Middle East would become, therefore, an Arab bio-region; there would be no room for a self-governing Jewish Israel. Strong New Age influence within Green parties in various European countries was one of the reasons why the British Greens nearly adopted in 1989 as part of their official policy the dismantling of the State of Israel. Such proposals may well emerge again.

Judaeo-Christian Monotheism as Scapegoat for Ecological Disasters

In an influential article in *Science* (March 1976), Lynn White argued that Judaism and Christianity are responsible for destroying the planet (although Judaism is in fact one of the most ecologically sensitive religions).[20] Their anthropocentrism led to dominion over and destruction of Mother Earth. This revisionist view of history is now increasingly articulated among New Age feminists such as Merlin Stone: 'Jews killed the mother goddess.' Gore

Vidal, a notoriously anti-Jewish writer, argued on television in 1989 that 'monotheism is the greatest disaster to befall the human race', because worship of 'the totalitarian sky-god' cut Jews and Christians off from nature. Prince Philip, in a speech in 1990 to the National Press Club in Washington, stressed the responsibility of Judaeo-Christian monotheism for ecological destruction and urged a return to the ecological wisdom of pagan/primal religions. Prince Charles, in his foreword to *Save the Earth* (1991), suggested that the Judaeo-Christian heritage had contributed to an overbearing and domineering attitude to creation, and that what is needed is a return to the 'unconscious element' in life. This view has been forcefully supported by other deep ecologists, including Jonathon Porritt, who argues that 'only Buddhism can make any real claim to being permeated through and through with ecological awareness and guidance about "right livelihood"'.[21]

Anti-Judaism

The New Age movement is often openly hostile to Judaism. Paganist journals condemn Judaism, along with Christianity, for having banned the ancient fertility gods and introduced morality. Alice Bailey utterly rejected Judaism as a 'basic evil', its teachings 'obsolete'.[22] New Age journals commonly condemn the Hebrew Scriptures as patriarchal and racist. Judaism was only appropriate for the Age of Aries, and was already obsolete in the Age of Pisces (Christianity), itself now in its death throes. In the Age of Aquarius, the only appropriate paradigm is New Age. Aldous Huxley wrote in *The Perennial Philosophy*: 'There are no chosen people in Nature, no holy lands, no unique historical revelations. Elementary ecology leads to elementary Buddhism.' Gore Vidal argued in the *Observer* (27 Aug. 1989): '[The] single god—Judaic, Christian, Islamic—is one of immaculate evil. It is time for us in the West to look to more subtle religions and ethical systems, particularly those of China and India. Let us give thanks to the Protean Green God!'

There are numerous other ways in which New Age stands in contrast to Judaism. Judaism stresses rationality, objectivity, logical thought, and absolute values and commandments; New Age stresses irrationality, extreme subjectivity, intuition, the dominance of feelings, and a radically relativized morality. While the Torah explicitly condemns worship of other gods and practice of occult techniques, New Age champions both. Since monism can coexist with pantheism or polytheism, within parts of the New Age movement a huge variety of pagan gods are invoked, from Odin and other Nordic and Celtic deities to Ma'at, Astarte (Isis), and the devas or earth spirits. For Blavatsky and Bailey, as for other core New Age leaders such as David Spangler, the ultimate deity is named specifically as Lucifer.[23]

Matthew Fox, a California-based theologian recently expelled from the Dominican order, is now seeking explicitly to take Christianity itself into the New Age. Arguing that only antisemites and fascists would oppose his theology, he claims to be reintroducing Hebrew spirituality. This is highly deceptive. For he in fact rejects the biblical God of Israel as a 'tribal deity', as 'sadistic', 'useless', a 'peeping tom'.[24] He rejects the Jewish Bible as 'man-made word-books' and rejects prayer as 'useless'. Describing our blood as 'divine', Fox argues both that we are God and that 'in some sense God is not born yet'. For Fox there are no evils—except for morality itself, which is 'perverse'. The prime value in Fox's hedonism is ecstasy—in virtually any form. He demands that in the future 'the gay should become leaders of the straight'. The Jewish Jesus must be rejected in favour of the 'Cosmic Christ of sexuality', the 'spirit of Babylon'. Fox's new version of Christianity includes worship of the goddess Gaia, Mother Earth, and a theology based not on God but on Creation. Fox regards the erect phallus as the 'symbol of the god' which must be reaffirmed as sacred. He demands that existing liturgies should be abandoned in favour of creation-centred ones (which can include chanting mantras and OMM). He further demands that each church *and each synagogue* should have a sweat lodge (a dark, steam-filled chamber in which men and women sit naked on hot stones; this practice, drawn from Native American Indian rituals, is said to induce extreme changes of consciousness akin to those associated with drug-use). While Fox retains some Judaeo-Christian vocabulary, it has been given (as in Wagner's *Parsifal*) an essentially pagan content.

Fox's teachings are now highly influential among clergy and laity, theological colleges and retreat centres. In some Catholic and Protestant circles he is increasingly regarded as *the* prophetic voice of the future. Creation-centred, gnostic-influenced liturgies have already been used in several Anglican cathedrals. Fox's Earth-centred spirituality will further alienate many Christians from understanding the Jewish roots of Christianity or observant Jews themselves. Moreover, Fox is preparing the way for Christianity explicitly to blend with goddess religions and implicitly to merge into a future new global religion, as demanded by Alice Bailey and promoted by World Goodwill and other organizations,[25] which will be based on occult full-moon festivals, including a transformed Easter and Wesak (Buddha's birthday). The full moon before the summer solstice is World Invocation Day, when an imminent world leader and New Age Messiah, known as the Christ, Maitreya, Buddha, and the Lord of this World, Lucifer (and, according to Bailey, explicitly *not* Jewish) is already widely invoked. This world religion is intended to utterly oust Judaism (and orthodox Christianity). Alice Bailey wrote: 'Nowhere is the emergence of a new world religion more greatly needed than in the case of the Jew in the modern world.'[26] She stated that one of the three main aims of the New Age is 'the gradual dissolution of the orthodox Jewish faith with its obsolete teaching . . . only when Jews adopt Christ or Buddha consciousness will we form one humanity and then there will be peace on earth'.[27] If New Age ideology continues to gain influence and political power, all Jews wishing to retain Orthodox Judaism, Zionism, or a distinctive Jewish religious, cultural, or political identity are likely in the long term to encounter strong anti-Jewishness.

Anti-Judaic Concept of Humanity

While claiming humanity to be divine, New Age in fact reduces it to be on a par with everything else in creation, even seeing it as a 'damaging virus'. Terms of abuse which were used by Nazi propaganda to denote the Jewish race are now used to denote the entire human race. Peter Russell called it 'a cancer that is ravaging the body of the earth' (*Odyssey*, Oct.–Nov. 1990). Gore Vidal, speaking on television in 1989, termed people 'billions of bacteria'. Some writers distinguish between New Agers, who are potentially divine—in the words of Abraham Maslow, the influential American psychologist, 'self-actualized, holistic and healthy, with no sense of guilt'—and 'average people', whom Maslow describes as 'crippled, stunted, immature and unhealthy specimens'.[28] For David Spangler, only New Age people— often called 'men and women of goodwill'—represent 'a new humanity from which can spring a new heaven and a new earth'.[29] In the Preface to Barry McWaters' *Unconscious Evolution*, Sir George Trevelyan, an influential British New Age leader, wrote of New Agers that 'what is virtually a new human being is emerging . . . directed by consciousness'.

New Age 'Eco-Fascism' and Potential Totalitarianism

In the mid-1980s, some American deep ecologists argued against food aid to Africa—it was in the karma of Africans to starve, and fewer Africans would mean less ecological damage.[30] Traditional, objective humanist ethics are widely rejected or relativized in favour of bio-ethics (good is what is good for the planet) or subjective ethics (good is what is good for me). Some New Age leaders demand radical population reduction; one American writer has called for a reduction of two billion.

Demands for drastic economic change based on the planet's needs and therefore radically lowered consumption could have major political and humanitarian implications. David Spangler, for example, has argued strongly against compassion. An environmental magazine, *Green Line* (Oxford, Sept. 1990) described the New Age futurist agenda as 'the brutal depopulation of vast areas of Africa, Asia and Ibero-America, coupled with a ruthless reduction in the industrialised nations' standard of living'. Even paganists and radical feminists are now expressing fears that totalitarianism may lurk within the New Age agenda: 'We are beginning to hear the crunching of jackboots marching under the new age banner . . . wasn't Hitler elected on a new age ticket?' (*Pagan News*, Leeds, June 1989). Monica Sjoo, an influential feminist and promoter of the Goddess whose *The New Age and Armageddon* was published in 1992, stated in *Green Line* (May 1989): 'What I find most worrying is that some of the thinking of the New Age connects back to some very reactionary and pro-fascist religious views via the Theosophists and the medium Alice Bailey.' James Webb, Nicholas Goodrick-Clarke, and others have indeed shown that Theosophy and its offshoots—Ariosophy, Anthroposophy, and other occult groups—were a major influence within Nazism.

There are indeed direct parallels between public Nazism (as outlined by Richard Grunberger) and private New Age practices and public aims—and all are in contrast to traditional Judaism. Like some New Age cults and groups, Nazism submerged its followers in a collective group identity; the individual must always be sacrificed to the group. Like some New Age cults and groups, Nazism emphasized irrationality and fanatical loyalty to a supernaturally enlightened leader. Other parallels include: the stimulation of emotions to gain a sense of intense living; disregard for the sanctity of life; positivism (the forbidding of negative thought or criticism); the emphasis on will-power; the demotion or celebration of death; blaming the world's ills on one scapegoat; a stress on the role of pain as purifying and transformative; and the revival of pseudo-spiritual rituals and of fertility cults based on the solstices.

New Age does not see all humans as essentially equal; in Spangler's words, 'hierarchy is the governing principle of the universe'.[31] Core texts distinguish four levels of humanity; highest are fully evolved Masters or Adepts, who have attained cosmic consciousness and can transmit their thoughts to initiates. Second in rank is an élite of conscious New Age disciples or initiates, followed by—in the words of Foster Bailey, husband of Alice Bailey—the unevolved 'great emotional mass of men . . . and a group of what are rightly called animal men . . . little more than physical bodies, a dead weight carried by us all'; this is the bulk of the population, who will be involuntarily given 'mass Luciferic initiation'.[32] Lowest are the 'dark souls' who in Rudolf Steiner's words have 'chosen the path of evil',[33] clinging to traditional exoteric Judaism and Christianity and exerting negative, obsolete energies.

These latter people—Jews and Christians—may not survive. Spangler argued in *Revelation: The Birth of a New Age* that opponents of New Age (presumably, Christians and Jews who retain the separatism of orthodox, non-esoteric belief or practice) are ' a corpse . . . a racial thought-form in the process of disintegration'. As the New Age dawns, they will be denied 'access to the etheric planes of power' (i.e. physical existence) and transferred out of 'physical embodiment'. They will experience 'the personal disintegration of millions of personal worlds . . . dying in significantly increasing numbers'. This sounds extreme—but in the logic of reincarnation and karma, mass transference to the next incarnation of those whose karma deserves it and whose separative thoughts have created ecological chaos could theoretically be justified. Spangler has written, channelling the spirit of 'Limitless Love and Truth': 'Understand that you look upon a world of form when you see suffering. Form has little meaning to me . . . If forms must be destroyed . . . then so be it . . . You cannot heal a corpse . . . The old must pass away . . . Do not attempt to save people . . . [Do] not resist if such separation occurs. Release them to me, no matter where their destiny leads them . . . You must not allow your personality to interfere in fear, in anxiety, in pity.'[34]

For the good of Mother Earth, the self-sacrifice—or simply sacrifice—of large numbers of 'unevolved' and therefore 'unfit' humans ('adolescents') whose thought-forms are deemed negative could be demanded by any future world government of 'planetary citizens', and even presented as acceptable. For in Buddhist terms, any suffering and death would be only *maya*, an illusion, and victims would, in Spangler's words, simply go to their proper place. It is worth noting that Matthew Fox's phrase, 'worship without sacrifice is sin', is a key New Age tenet.[35] Many pagan fertility religions, after all, involved restoring energy to the Earth by means of human sacrifice to the gods of nature.

After Auschwitz we cannot afford to be naïve. Hitler's definition of his religion was essentially New Age: 'God in nature, God in our people, God in one's own fate, in one's own blood.'[36] In *Morality after Auschwitz*, Peter Haas has demonstrated how a society that redefines or relocates evil can construct a coherent ethic which permits the most immoral and cruel acts in the name of the good. Spangler's dictum of amorality, that there is 'not good and evil in the New Age',[37] goes hand in hand with the redefinition by Bailey, Fox, and other key New Age thinkers of evil as separateness.

The phrase 'future violent planetary cleansing' of negative forces, often encountered in New Age writings, is sometimes made more explicit. Ruth Montgomery anticipated in 1986 a future global catastrophe to 'cleanse the earth of pollution and evil people'. John Randolph Price stated in 1985: 'Nature will soon enter her cleansing cycle. Those who reject the earth . . . will be removed during the next two decades.' 'The Great Invocation', written by Alice Bailey and distributed by World Goodwill and the Lucis Trust and used as the world-wide New Age prayer, includes the line: 'Seal the door where evil dwells.' The evil to be sealed and the negative forces to be cleansed in the future could well include Zionists and observant Jews, together with orthodox Christians, nationalists, and others defined as dissidents. Sir George Trevelyan has written: 'Those who will not turn to God will be shepherded to some other planetary level while the cleansing operation is completed.'[38] Barbara Marx Hubbard, an American New Age leader, recently wrote: 'All who choose not to evolve will die off; their souls will begin again within a different planetary system which will serve as kindergarten for the transition from self-centred to whole-centred being. The kindergarten class of Earth will be over. Humankind's collective power is too great to be inherited by self-centred, infantile people.'[39] Maharishi Mahesh Yogi, the creator of TM, argued that destruction of the 'unfit' is simply in accordance with nature: 'There has not been and there will not be a place for the unfit . . . Non-existence of the unfit has been a law of nature.'[40] Could the new bio-ethics of a nature-centred New Age potentially lead to another Holocaust? I believe so.

CONCLUSION

The empowerment of the New Age global network may be imminent. I have met international New Age leaders who predict that a global government directed by the New Age movement will be in place by the year 2000. This could prove a crucial factor in determining Jewish experience during the 1990s and beyond. It could determine Christian experience, too. If some areas of Christianity continue to become increasingly paganized through the influence of Fox and revived Earth rituals, some non-Jews may seek out Jewish communities and synagogues in order to retain or relearn biblical ethics and spirituality, and to worship the God of Abraham, Isaac, and Jacob. Jewish leaders will need to respond to this. Far more important, they will need to respond to the internal and external pressures on Jewish communities faced with a repaganized world which condemns all separateness, yet from which they must remain separate in some ways if they wish to be faithful to Torah, to Israel, or simply to Jewish identity.

American New Age futurologists predict a cashless society using microchip implants instead of cheque cards, with travel more restricted than today and curbs on individual freedom. The New Age millennium will not be a golden age of tolerance. A practising psychic, who wishes to remain anonymous, described it at a recent philosophy conference at Cambridge thus: 'New Age means power over other people, a deliberate attempt to influence the way other people think, feel and behave. New Age freedom is slavery of the worst kind, and the creation of an élite. It is the exact opposite of harmony. It is racist, totalitarian, and divisive.'

The new world order in America and Europe could look very bleak for Jews. I believe that the Jewish community must encourage Jewish education, communal unity, and immigration to Israel as a matter of urgency, and that long-term strategies must be sought for survival in what is likely to become an increasingly centralized and hostile world.

The New Age movement is rapidly gaining political power. It has many influential adherents who promote its aims at national and international level. (At the United Nations, for example, long-term supporters of New Age include former UN Assistant Secretary-General, Robert Muller; Norman Cousins; the Brahma Kumaris, who operate the 'spiritual university' of the UN; and its spiritual adviser, Sri Chinmoy.) It appears to aim at ideological and spiritual hegemony. I believe that it could pose as serious a medium- and long-term threat to Jewish identity as Nazism did in the 1920s and 1930s. New Age has some attractive and benevolent features, and its emphasis on ecological preservation cannot be dismissed. But in its innermost core and teaching, it is a deeply anti-Judaic ideology and could eventually lead to the destruction of many Jews and all Jewish identity. For New Age ultimately aims at radically changing human nature—and that, for Hannah Arendt, is the hallmark of totalitarianism: 'What totalitarian ideologies . . . aim at is not the transformation of the outside world or the revolutionising transmutation of society, but the transformation of human nature itself.'[41] Hitler put the totalitarian ideology formulated in *Mein Kampf* into practice when he came to power, with devastating consequences for the Jewish people. If New Age comes to power, its ideology—particularly as embodied in Alice Bailey's writings—could have equally devastating consequences for Jews.

Notes

1. See Alice Bailey, *The Rays and the Initiations* (New York, 1960), 551, 676.

2. David Spangler, *Towards a Planetary Vision*, 2nd edn. (Forres, 1980), 40–1. (All subsequent references are to this edition.)

3. Cf. Spangler, *Planetary Vision*, 75: 'Now comes the time to become the servants of evolution and through our own consciousness . . . to release the light . . . in the occult redemption of the world'; see also ibid. 26–8. For a detailed esoteric outline of 'the Plan for Human Evolution', see Alice Bailey, *Serving Humanity: A Compilation* (New York, 1972), 35–48.

4. Paul Heelas, 'God's Company: New Age Ethics and the Bank of Credit and Commerce International', *Religion Today*, 8: 1 (1992), 1–4. On New Age influence on

wider culture see Russell Chandler, *Understanding the New Age* (Milton Keynes 1989); Marilyn Ferguson, *The Aquarian Conspiracy: Personal and Social Transformation in the 1980s* (London, 1982), esp. chs. 8–10; articles in *The Times* in spring 1992 by Ray Clancy and Brian Appleyard.

5. Arthur Schopenhauer, *Parerga and Paralipomena*, trans. E. F. J. Payne (Oxford, 1974), i. 126.

6. Id., *Auswahl aus seinen Schriften*, ed. S. Friedlaender (Munich, 1962), 217.

7. Letter to Ludwig II, Nov. 1881, cited in Jacob Katz, *The Darker Side of Genius: Richard Wagner's Anti-Semitism* (Waltham, Mass., 1986), 115.

8. See M. Brearley, 'Hitler and Wagner', *Patterns of Prejudice*, 22: 2 (1988), 3–22; id., 'Jewish and Christian Concepts of Time and Modern Anti-Judaism: Ousting the God of Time', *Christianity and Judaism: Studies in Church History*, 29 (Oxford, 1992), 481–93.

9. Helena Blavatsky, *The Secret Doctrine* [1888], 2 vols. (Los Angeles, 1982), ii. 588. Quoted by Bailey in *Rays*, 534.

10. Alice Bailey, *The Externalization of the Hierarchy* (New York, 1957), 76; id. *Rays*, 243. See also Helena Blavatsky, *Isis Unveiled: A Master Key to the Mysteries of Ancient and Modern Science and Technology* [1877], 2 vols. (Covena, Calif., 1950), ii. 302.

11. Alice Bailey, *The Reappearance of the Christ* (New York, 1948), 145.

12. Id., *Rays*, 429–30, 635, 681, 705.

13. Id., *Problems of Humanity* [1947], (New York, 1953), 106, 125.

14. Id., *Externalization*, 79.

15. Id., *Problems*, 122.

16. Id., *Externalization*, 262–5.

17. Alice Bailey and Djwhal Khul, *Ponder on This*, 5th edn. (New York, 1984), 421.

18. Bailey, *Externalization*, 637. She labelled Zionism 'the opposing forces of entrenched evil' (ibid. 616), and said that Zionist leaders were 'contrary to the lasting good of mankind' (*Rays*, 681).

19. Bailey, *Rays*, 429–30, 681.

20. Norman Solomon, 'Judaism and Conservation', *Christian–Jewish Relations*, 22: 2 (1989), 7–25; Aubrey Rose, *Judaism and Ecology* (London, 1992).

21. Jonathon Porritt and David Winner, *The Coming of the Greens* (London, 1988), 246.

22. Bailey, *Externalization*, 551.

23. See David Spangler, *Reflections on the Christ* (Findhorn, 1981), 45.

24. See M. Brearley, 'Matthew Fox: Creation Spirituality for the Aquarian Age', *Christian–Jewish Relations*, 22: 2 (1989), 37–49; id., 'Matthew Fox and the Cosmic Christ', *Anvil*, 9: 1 (1992), 39–54. All quotes come from the following books by Fox: *Whee! We, Wee all the Way Home: A Guide to Sensual, Prophetic Spirituality* [1976] (Santa Fe, New Mexico, 1981); *On Becoming a Musical, Mystical Bear* [1972], (Paulist Press, 1976); *Original Blessing: A Primer in Creation Spirituality* (Santa Fe, 1983); *The Coming of the Cosmic Christ: The Healing of Mother Earth and the Birth of a Global Renaissance* (San Francisco, 1988).

25. See *The New World Religion* (currently distributed by World Goodwill), a 16-page compilation of Bailey's writings from *The Reappearance of the Christ* and *Externalization of the Hierarchy*.

26. Bailey, *Problems*, 122.

27. Id., *Externalization*, 544, 551.

28. Cited in Spangler, *Planetary Vision*, 56–7.

29. Ibid. 59.

30. Porritt and Winner, *Coming of the Greens*, 237.

31. Spangler, *Planetary Vision*, 114.

32. Id., *Reflections on the Christ*, 45.

33. Rudolf Steiner, *Occult Science: An Outline*, trans. G. and M. Adams (London, 1969), 308–13.

34. David Spangler, *Revelation: The Birth of a New Age* (Middleton, Wis., 1976), 141, 139, 143, 74–81. Another leading New Ager, Paul Solomon, wrote recently: 'Know that the time is short. The vibrations of the earth are being raised to such high level that those that are not in tune with God's purposes . . . His message, cannot remain upon that portion of the earth that would be so perfected.'

35. See Annie Besant, *The Ancient Wisdom: An Outline of Theosophical Teachings* (London, 1897), ch. 10, 'The Law of Sacrifice' (pp. 275–90): 'Every religion that springs from the Ancient Wisdom has sacrifice as a central teaching, and some of the profoundest truths of occultism are rooted in the law of sacrifice' (p. 275); 'on that higher plane of Buddha where all selves are felt as one . . . the law of sacrifice [is] felt as a joyful privilege, instead of only recognized intellectually as true and just' (p. 287). The concept of 'willing sacrifice' is important, too, in Wiccan and pagan traditions, and is now championed in feminist literature.

36. Cited by W. Hofer, *Der Nationalsozialismus: Dokumente 1933–1945* (Germany, 1957), 121.

37. Spangler, *Reflections on the Christ*, 45.

38. Sir George Trevelyan, Foreword to David Spangler's *The Rebirth of the Sacred* (London, 1984), p. xii; see also Spangler, *Reflections on the Christ*, 84.

39. Barbara Marx Hubbard, *Happy Birth Day Planet Earth!* (Santa Fe, New Mexico, 1986), 17.

40. Maharishi Mahesh Yogi, *Inauguration of the Dawn of the Age of Enlightenment* (Fairfield, Iowa, 1973), 47.

41. Hannah Arendt, *The Origins of Totalitarianism* (New York, 1951), 432.

Supplementary Bibliography

BAILEY, FOSTER, *Changing Esoteric Values* (Tunbridge Wells, 1955).

BLOOM, WILLIAM, *The New Age: An Anthology of Essential Writings* (London, 1991).

GOODRICK-CLARKE, NICHOLAS, *The Occult Roots of Nazism: The Ariosophists of Austria and Germany, 1890–1935* (Wellingborough, 1985).

GRUNBERGER, RICHARD, *A Social History of the Third Reich* (Harmondsworth, Middx., 1974).

HAAS, PETER J., *Morality after Auschwitz: The Radical Challenge of the Nazi Ethic* (Philadelphia, 1988).

HUXLEY, ALDOUS, *The Perennial Philosophy* (London, 1946).

MCWATERS, BARRY, *Unconscious Evolution: Personal and Planetary Transformation* (Wellingborough, 1983).

MONTGOMERY, RUTH, and GARLAND, J., *Herald of a New Age* (New York, 1986).

PORRITT, JONATHON (ed.), *Save the Earth* (London, 1991).

PRICE, JOHN RANDOLPH, *Practical Spirituality* (Austin, Texas, 1985).

RUSSELL, PETER, *The Awakening Earth: The Global Brain* (London, 1982).

STEINER, RUDOLF, *Initiation and its Results*, trans. Clifford Bax (London, 1910).

STONE, MERLIN, *When God was a Woman* (New York, 1976).

WEBB, JAMES, *The Occult Establishment* (La Salle, Ill., 1976).

WHITE, LYNN, 'The Historical Roots of the Ecological Crisis', *Science*, 155 (10 Mar. 1976).

PART VII

JEWISH EUROPE AS SEEN
FROM WITHOUT

CHAPTER TWENTY-THREE

The New Europe and the Zionist Dilemma

DANIEL GUTWEIN

T HERE are contradictory trends in the new Europe of 1992, and they are forcing the Zionist movement to re-examine some of its fundamental principles and priorities. The two main factors that have to be taken into account in this reassessment are, first, the substantive change that has taken place in the last decade in the nature of international politics; and, second, the ongoing ideological and political struggle within the Zionist movement—that is, regarding the nature of the relationship between the Jewish people and the non-Jewish world, and between Israel and the diaspora.

The world in which the Zionist movement now operates is not that in which it was conceived. The Zionist movement was conceived in the 'old Europe', at a time when international politics was dominated by continual political, social, and economic conflicts. In contrast, the 'new Europe'— which I am defining here as that of the European Community—was to achieve an entirely new world order, in which conflict would give way to stability brought about through international co-operation and agreement. The realization of this vision, however, has been thwarted by the unexpected resurgence of an 'old European' tendency towards conflict—national, political, economic, social, religious, and racial. Although this trend is most apparent in central and eastern Europe (where it has developed primarily as a result of the collapse of the former Soviet bloc) it is also evident in western Europe, albeit in different and less acute forms.

Since the mid-1980s, Europe has been an arena of continuous struggle between two opposing political world orders, one predicated on stability and the other on conflict. The quest for stability is manifest in the end of the Cold War, nuclear and conventional disarmament, and the gradual transformation of the European Community into a single political and economic unit. The tendency towards conflict, on the other hand, is manifest in the Balkanization of the former Eastern bloc and the disintegration of existing states into their ethnic and religious components. Even in the European Community the trend towards conflict is apparent; there is growing opposition to the loss of national sovereignty to the European bureaucrats, and an upsurge in local separatist tendencies, the latter paradoxically encouraged by the existence of pan-European institutions. Similar trends are apparent in the economic sphere: the economic advantages of the Common Market have for the most part increased the affluence of member states, while the countries that emerged from the former Eastern bloc are painfully trying to adapt to a market economy. Without the protection formerly provided by the Communist social security apparatus, they are suffering a chronic economic crisis marked by high unemployment—as indeed are some members of the European Community. All these various economic, social, and ethnic tensions combine to provide fertile soil for the rise of extreme right-wing movements which advance an agenda of placing limitations on civil and human rights. The proponents of stability, on the other hand, seek to lessen ideological tensions and to strengthen democracy and human rights, and indeed to make these policies a pre-condition for membership of the European Community.

The choice between stability and conflict as a way of achieving political ends has been a constant theme of European history throughout the last two centuries, but Europe of 1992 is different in one striking respect. Whereas the old order was clearly dominated by conflict, in 1992 stability became for the first time a tangible reality. The fact that two contradictory world orders now have equal chances of being realized has paradoxically intensified the struggle for dominance and has actually aggravated Europe's political dilemmas.

The struggle between the two world orders has implications for the Jewish communities in the diaspora, for the State of Israel, and for the Zionist movement. Like other players in the international arena, Israel and the Zionist movement must decide which of the two rival options better suits their interests. For example, a stable Europe might facilitate Jewish integration into a multicultural European society, thereby making *aliyah* (emigration to Israel) an option of only secondary importance. A situation of conflict, in contrast, could strengthen antagonism to minorities, thereby making *aliyah* an existential necessity.

Moreover, a Europe caught up in national and social conflicts would have more limited ability to intervene in Middle Eastern politics, and would be likely to have no interest in doing so, whereas a stable Europe would seek actively to protect its geostrategic and economic interests there. The European Community could thus become a powerful factor in Middle East politics and be able to advance solutions that Israel might regard as more favourable to the Arabs, particularly as regards economic development, the settlement of refugees, and the development of water resources, and even to enforce them. As Israel and the Zionist movement face the dilemma posed by the struggle between stability and conflict, they are thus bound to redefine their own interests and priorities with respect to both the Jewish and the non-Jewish world—especially as this process is tied in with a deep, ongoing intra-Zionist debate that the changing ground-rules of Europe 1992 has only exacerbated.

The beginnings of the Zionist movement, it should be recalled, were rooted in turn-of-the-century Europe amidst economic depression, social and political crisis, armed peace, and imperialistic rivalries. Moreover, its major political successes were achieved in the context of a world order of conflict. The Balfour Declaration, which laid the foundations for the Jewish national home, was itself the product of wartime politics and opposing interests that split the Allies. The establishment of the State of Israel was in its turn to some extent a product of the Holocaust and the Cold War. And in its first forty years or so, for various geostrategic and economic reasons, Israel was at the hub of the struggle between the two superpowers for domination of the Middle East, a position which consequently influenced Israeli domestic, foreign, and defence policies.

Given that the history of the Zionist movement is rooted in the old, conflict-dominated European order, it is hardly surprising that its concepts, ideology, and policies are too. Zionism rejected the liberal, emancipationist ideology which, grounded in the concepts of the eighteenth-century Enlightenment movement and the nineteenth-century belief in human progress, had envisioned the political, social, and cultural integration of Jews in European society. Zionism pointed, instead, to the decline of the liberal spirit and the rise of antisemitism and argued that the chances of realizing the liberal, emancipationist vision of Jewish assimilation in *fin-de-siècle* Europe were nil. As Jews increasingly failed to integrate into European society and antisemitism grew, Zionism emerged as a self-declared attempt to find an alternative solution to the Jewish problem. Zionism maintained that antisemitism was not just a relic of medieval bigotry, but an inherent product of the national, political, social, and economic conflicts that dominated modern European life. In the Zionist view, the only solution to the physical and mental threat that modern antisemitism posed to the Jews lay in the Jews' separating themselves from Europe. This separation had two distinct but interdependent dimensions. One was territorial, namely, the concentration of Jews in a land of their own, preferably Israel. The second was political, namely, turning the Jews into a modern political nation that would have, like other nations, the power to determine its own political future. This latter concept was known in Zionist terminology as 'bringing the Jews back into history'.

The interdependence between Zionist interests and the conflict that dominated European foreign and domestic politics went even deeper. An underlying assumption of Zionist politics was that the various European powers would support Zionism as a means in their struggle for influence in the Middle East, and also because Zionism would provide a way of eliminating the domestic instability that antisemitism introduced into European society. Zionist politicians saw the growth of antisemitism as a factor that would not merely encourage European leaders to support Zionism, but also as the factor that would ultimately force the Jews to accept Zionism as the best political programme for their long-term interest.

Seen from the point of view of European politics, therefore, Zionism was an adaptation to the ground rules of a situation of conflict. This conflict stood at the root of Zionist ideology, and was perceived as the starting-point for its realization. Based on the ideology and history of Zionism, then, one might reasonably conclude that when faced with the political choices that Europe of 1992 presents, Zionism would see its interests best served by the perpetuation of conflict.

In reality, though, the relationship today is more complex. Zionism, as well as Europe, has evolved considerably since the turn of the century, and Zionist thinking has become much more ambivalent as to whether conflict will in the long run result in conditions more favourable to Zionism.

In some ways, this is an echo of ongoing ideological divides. The Zionist movement has always been torn between opposing ideological interpretations of its future perspectives and of the nature of the relationship between Jews and the non-Jewish world. One interpretation, originally propounded in the 1880s by Ahad Ha'am and known as 'cultural Zionism', sees the situation in Europe as one of permanent conflict, and similarly views the relationship between Jews and non-Jews as one of latent antagonism; modern antisemitism is just another expression of this. In this view, Zionism is both a metaphorical and a real Jewish retreat from Europe, an expression of a complete lack of confidence both in the will of non-Jewish society to accept Jews as equals and in Jews' capacity to adapt and integrate themselves into those cultures. The other interpretation, whose most prominent exponent was Theodor Herzl, considered Zionism to be an expression of the Jews' lack of confidence in the old European order, but not in the non-Jewish world as such. Its motivation was political rather than cultural. Herzl thus saw modern antisemitism as another expression of the political and social

crises that characterized *fin-de-siècle* Europe. Likewise, the Jews' exodus from
Europe and subsequent territorial concentration in Israel, which would be
achieved in the framework of an international agreement, represents not a
withdrawal from the non-Jewish world but, paradoxically, a way of integrat-
ing within it. Herzl acknowledged the plausibility of a transformation in the
nature of the European world order from one of conflict to one of stability.
As part of such a transformation, which would take place in some distant
future in which Europe would solve its social and political crises—a future
too distant from the point of view of Jewish survival—it would also be
possible to solve the problem of antisemitism. Accordingly, Herzl did not
perceive Zionism to be a consequence of an inherent Jewish antagonism
towards the non-Jewish world. On the contrary, in its deeper sense, Herzl's
Zionism strove to bring about a reconciliation of these worlds. It intended
to integrate the Jewish people into the international community by making
them a nation in the modern political sense and normalizing their economic
and social structure. Thus it can be said that one of the most fundamental
ideological disputes within Zionism—that over the future of the Jews'
relationship with the non-Jewish world—has been conducted along lines
similar to those that divide the new Europe between the opposing orientations of conflict and stability.

Over the years, this ideological rivalry within Zionism has ripened into
two opposing political schools. The 'antagonist' school perceives the conflict
trend as better serving Zionist interests; the 'integrationist' school believes
that Zionist interests are better served by stability. These rival schools
transcend the boundaries of the official political and ideological parties, and
for almost a century they have repeatedly reconstructed themselves as variations on their basic themes as they struggled for domination in Zionist and
Israeli politics. The rivalry between them has influenced the shaping of
Zionist and Israeli identity: more accurately, it has led to the formation of
two opposing identities that contend for dominance of the political and
intellectual life of Zionism and Israel.

Jewish history in the past three generations, which may be broadly characterized by the contradictory experiences of Holocaust and statehood, has
deepened this ideological and political struggle. The establishment of the
State of Israel on the basis of a United Nations resolution might seem to
have confirmed the Herzlian prognosis of integration. Renewed Jewish
sovereignty has given the impression that Jewish history is moving towards
normality, with the Jews becoming a political nation guided by the same
laws that guide the conduct of other nations. Ideologically, however, it is
undoubtedly Ahad Ha'am's perception of antagonism that has prevailed.
Among Zionists and Israelis, the popular interpretation continues to per-

ceive the non-Jewish world as inherently hostile. Moreover, analysis of the
lessons of the Holocaust and the Arab–Israeli conflict from the antagonist
perspective has led, particularly since the Six-Day War of 1967, to a neo-
messianic ideological approach. Classical Jewish messianism envisioned the
renewal of Jewish sovereignty through a miraculous apocalyptic process in
some distant future; the Jewish present was viewed as one of powerlessness.
Neo-messianism, on the other hand advocates almost unlimited use of the
power created by the new Jewish state to reverse the historical experience of
powerlessness.

This rivalry between antagonists and integrationists has manifested itself
in the dynamics through which Zionism will be realized—namely, whether
through Jewish repulsion from the diaspora societies in which they have
lived ('push' factors as they are often known) or through the attraction
exerted by the State of Israel (a 'pull' factor). The 'repulsion' approach links
the relevance of Zionism to the continued hostility of the non-Jewish world:
aliyah will result from Jews being pushed to seek refuge in Israel, not from
Israel's inherent political and social attractiveness. In this view, the fundamental Zionist concept of Israel as a model society is given only secondary
importance. The alternative approach looks forward to the time when the
driving force of Zionist dynamics will no longer be repulsion from the
diaspora, but rather Israel's ability to attract Jews to come and live there
because of the state's own merits. In this view, the creation in Israel of a
model society is perceived not as an idealistic luxury, but as an essential
need—indeed, a precondition—for contemporary Zionism.

In the framework of Zionist ideology and politics, there is thus a clear
correlation between the 'antagonist' and 'repulsion' schools, both of which
believe that the international scene will continue to be dominated by conflict, and between the 'integrationist' and 'attraction' schools, both of which
foresee the probability of stability in international politics. Thus far, it is
undoubtedly the former view that has dominated Zionist ideology and
politics, not least because the historical experiences of the past three generations seemed to validate its assumptions and recommended policies. Indeed,
since the 1930s, most of the people who have emigrated to Israel have
been refugees—victims of rightist or leftist antisemitism, sometimes disguised as anti-Zionism, in Europe, and of anti-Israel trends in the post-1948
Arab world. In consequence, although the desirability of making Israel a
model society has been accepted in principle, commitment to this ideal has
remained superficial.

The belief in the diaspora intrinsically 'repelling' Jews reflects the fact that
Zionist ideology was forged primarily by the Jews of eastern Europe as a
reaction to the conditions in which they found themselves at the end of the

nineteenth century. Historical circumstances have changed, but this approach has not lost its dominant position in Zionist ideology: there has been no adaptation to the radical change that has taken place in the Jewish world and in the international situation since the 1960s. When Jewish immigration from eastern Europe and the Islamic countries became difficult, the mass of Jews who could freely and voluntarily make *aliyah* was to be found in the West. For most of these Jews, living as they did in liberal and affluent countries, 'repulsionist' Zionism had no appeal. Zionist ideology and Israeli politics, however, generally ignored the change, and stuck to the premisses of the repulsion approach. This ideological inertia, which resulted more from Israeli political considerations than from conservatism *per se*, is one of the prime causes of the deepening crisis that Zionism has faced, both in Israel and the diaspora, since the 1960s. As Western Jewry increasingly failed to feel repelled from diaspora society and as Israel failed to present itself as an attractive alternative, Zionism increasingly lost its relevance for them. At the same time, somewhat paradoxically, Israel began to be perceived more and more as a Jewish cultural centre for the diaspora, though even that role is nowadays challenged by the growing popularity, particularly in the United States, of a new 'Jerusalem and Babylon' concept which accords a more equal weighting to the two poles of Jewish community life.

The endurance of the 'repulsion' approach and the concept of Israel as a cultural centre for the Jewish people rather than a territorial one represents a clear victory for Ahad Ha'am's cultural Zionism and for the closely connected view that non-Jewish attitudes to Jews are inherently antagonistic. Thus, all three concepts mutually nourish and sustain one another. If Israel is only a cultural centre, then its political and social profile is of less relevance than the ideology it exports. Accordingly, the more Zionism's role of offering a haven for persecuted diaspora Jews diminishes, the more a consciousness of non-Jewish antagonism towards Jews is cultivated as a compensatory ideological legitimation for Zionism.

At this point, we may now recall that the antagonism–repulsion school of Zionist thought is predicated upon European and international politics being dominated by conflict. Given this dependence, it is likely that the more the new Europe exhibits stability, the more the balance of power in the Zionist movement may shift towards an ideology of integration and attraction. Stability is expected to solve the political, economic, and social contradictions that a century ago generated antisemitism in Europe. *Détente* and *glasnost*—salient manifestations of stability—have opened the gates of the Soviet Union to Jewish emigration, while increased multinational cooperation has facilitated the progress of the Arab–Israeli peace process. Thus, stability actually invalidates the premisses of the antagonism–

repulsion school and strengthens those of the integrationist–attraction school—in theory, at least. In reality, the 'new Europe' is also dominated by growing national, economic, and social conflicts that are a rich seed-bed for the development of various forms of antisemitism—religious, national, racial, and economic. Thus, the antagonists can now validate their ideology by pointing to the danger of pogroms in the various republics of the former Soviet Union no less than to the signs of growing antisemitism, violent xenophobia, and ethnic tensions in western Europe.

As the struggle between the forces of conflict and stability in Europe continues, Zionist antagonists and integrationists alike find justification for their stand. For Zionism as for the rest of the world, 1992 was not the 'end of history' in the Fukayaman sense, and the debate within Zionism will continue along essentially the same lines as before and from the same traditional perspectives. The gradual transformation of the international order to one of stability may indeed shift the balance of power within Zionism towards the integrationist–attraction school, but the new European (and international) order will not be the decisive influence in this respect. Although the changes in the new Europe will make it harder for the antagonists to justify their stand, the struggle between the different Zionist approaches will ultimately be decided by an internal definition of priorities. However, with integration now more possible than ever before because of the general increase in stability, the dilemma becomes much more acute; Israel and the Zionist movement will have to decide whether it would be more in their interests to integrate themselves into a new world order aimed at maintaining stability or to perpetuate a common perception of a situation of conflict.

Select Bibliography

ALMOG, S., *Zionism and History: The Rise of a New Jewish Consciousness* (New York, 1987).

ELIAV, A. L., *The Land of the Hart* (Philadelphia, 1974).

HALPREN, B., *The Idea of the Jewish State* (Cambridge, Mass., 1969).

HERZBERG, A.,*The Zionist Idea: A Historical Analysis and Reader* (New York, 1975).

VITAL, D., *The Origins of Zionism* (Oxford, 1975).

YEHOSHUA, A. B., *Between Right and Right* (New York, 1981).

CHAPTER TWENTY-FOUR

Jewish Renewal in the New Europe: An American Jewish Perspective

DAVID SINGER

THAT European Jewry is now operating in a radically altered landscape is evident. The collapse of Communism in the Soviet empire, the unification of Germany, and the move towards greater co-operation and co-ordination on the European continent have created a dramatic new situation that is bound to alter the manner in which Jewish life is conducted. In thinking through the possibility of Jewish renewal in the new Europe, therefore, attention needs to be given to alternative models of Jewish life which can offer guidance in a situation of sharp flux.

The question I want to raise is this: can the American Jewish experience serve as a model for European Jews in their quest for Jewish renewal? The American Jewish model certainly has much to commend it, since as the writer Charles Silberman has pointed out in *A Certain People*, Jews in the United States 'live in a freer, more open society than that of any Diaspora community in which Jews have ever lived before'. American Jewish life has been an extraordinary success story—in terms of what Jews have achieved and the degree to which Jews have been accepted as full equals by the larger society.

The power and attractiveness of the American Jewish model is evident, but my own view of the matter is that that model is *not* replicable in the European context. This has nothing to do with the nature of Jewish life *per se*, but rather with key structural advantages that the United States enjoys over Europe. In short, what I am arguing for is the uniqueness of the American Jewish experience, which itself is a reflection of the uniqueness of the American situation.

What are the structural advantages of the American situation? I see four in number. The first is that Jews in the United States did not have to be politically emancipated; from the very beginning, they functioned in a post-Emancipation society. Second, the United States, as a nation of immigrants from diverse backgrounds, was strongly pluralist from the start, and this tendency continued to grow over time. Third, the separation of church and state as called for in the United States Constitution freed Jews from the burden of living in an officially Christian society. The public domain in America was, by legal definition, neutral as between Christianity and Judaism. Fourth, as the 'first new nation', the United States lacked a historic culture to which Jews were outsiders at any point. On the contrary, Jews contributed mightily to the creation of an American culture.

Let me now expand on each of these four points, asking indulgence for the fact that in a brief presentation such as this it is necessary to deal in broad generalizations. Clearly, a full-scale analysis of the issues I am discussing would require a much more nuanced presentation.

1. *Jews in the United States, from the very beginning, functioned in a post-Emancipation society.* The key fact that has to be kept in mind here is that everywhere in Europe, prior to the French Revolution, Jews were by legal decree defined as outsiders in society. Jews were considered alien to the body politic, and it took the impact of Enlightenment ideas as carried forward by the French Revolution to bring about a change in the situation whereby Jews could be offered citizenship and be permitted to enter the mainstream of society.

In Europe, the Emancipation appeared to hold out the promise that differences between Jew and non-Jew would be reduced to the private realm of religion. All public relations, in contrast, would be carried on in the neutral areas of citizenship, where Jews were guaranteed equality. Jews assumed that the public realm was identical with the whole sphere of interaction between Jews and non-Jews, and that here they would have full and free contact and equal status with Christians. Sad to say, this assumption proved to be quite wrong. Everywhere in Europe, Jewishness continued to be a barrier and a disability in a wide range of social relations; citizenship opened up far fewer doors than Jews had imagined. In particular, the military, higher government service, the judiciary, and the universities remained largely closed to Jews.

The situation was quite different in the United States. To be sure, American society did not develop in a vacuum. The settlers who came to the American colonies from Europe carried with them attitudes towards Jews that, in many cases, were strongly negative. Jews did encounter hostility in American society. But the fact of the matter is that the Jewish community in the colonial period—the period prior to the American Revolution—was quite small, and that community's legal status as outsiders was never formalized in any significant way. Thus when Enlightenment ideas manifested themselves in American society in the course of the American Revolution, most Americans simply took it for granted that Jews no less than others were entitled to what the Declaration of Independence promised: 'life, liberty, and the pursuit of happiness'. The silence of the Declaration of Independence and the United States Constitution with regard to the status of Jews speaks volumes about what Jews had already achieved on the American scene.

On this point let me quote historian Ben Halpern in *The American Jew*:

Our real history begins *after* the 'solution' in America of the most critical problem that faced other Jewries in modern times, the problem of the emancipation of the Jews. This was the problem that other Jewries had to grapple with when they entered the modern world, and the various solutions that they . . . evolved for it gave them each their individual character. French Jewry dealt with the issues and problems of Emancipation differently from German Jewry, German Jewry differently from Austro-Hungarian or from Russian Jewry; but all of them had to deal with the problem, and there was a continuity and connection between the solution they found. What is characteristic of American Jewry, and what makes us different from all of these together, is that we began our real history as a post-Emancipation Jewry. Emancipation was never an issue among us: we never argued the problems it presented in America, nor did we ever develop rival ideologies about it and build our institutions with reference to them.

It is at this juncture that the issue of modern, political antisemitism needs to be brought into the picture. One has to remember that everywhere in Europe the idea of Jewish emancipation was part and parcel of the agenda of political liberalism—it was the liberals who championed the cause of Jewish emancipation. Conversely, those forces in European society that opposed the larger agenda of political liberalism also opposed the element of Jewish emancipation. The counter-revolutionary thrust in Europe that sought to undo the work of the French Revolution also sought to put the Jews back in their place—i.e. to return to the situation that had existed prior to the Emancipation. Thus one finds in European society in the nineteenth century the development of a powerful form of political antisemitism. Political parties came into existence that had as part of their agenda—sometimes a central part—the turning back of the clock on Jewish emancipation. Whereas conservative antisemitism in an officially liberal society contented itself with excluding Jews from those areas of corporate traditionalism that had not as yet broken down, political antisemitism of the counter-revolutionary type actually sought to reverse the gains that Jews had made under the aegis of liberalism.

Here again the situation in the United States was different. There has, of course, been antisemitism in the United States, and it has sometimes taken a severe form. Still, antisemitism in the American context has run a different course from its European counterpart. The antisemitic movements in France and Germany, Poland and Russia occupied a place in the forefront of the political affairs of their countries. What we have in America, in comparison, is routine hate-mongering. Let me again quote Ben Halpern:

The kind of anti-Semitism common in America is, and always has been, endemic throughout the Diaspora. It may be found in every social condition and in every political persuasion, from extreme right to extreme left. It is an anti-Semitism of impulse: the most characteristic thing about it is that it is not really organized on the basis of a clearly enunciated program providing what ought to be done about the Jews if the anti-Semites had their way. This is something quite different from an anti-Semitism that was primarily political in vision. Modern European anti-Semitism was characterized from the beginning by large and active political aims, and it included, among other far-reaching social revisions proposed in its counter-revolutionary program, precise provisions for making the Jews second class citizens, expelling them, or exterminating them. In comparison with these movements, American anti-Semitism . . . has never reached the level of an historic, politically effective movement. It has remained, so to speak, a merely sociological or 'cultural' phenomenon.

In short, freedom rather than unfreedom has been the norm for Jews in the American context, and this has provided the basis for unprecedented Jewish achievement and unprecedented Jewish acceptance.

2. *The United States, as a nation of immigrants from diverse backgrounds, was strongly pluralist from the start.* The United States is the paradigm of a pluralist society—a society that not only manifests pluralism in its diverse population but also projects pluralism as a social ideal. This respect for diversity is rooted in the American colonial experience, when the foundations were established for broad religious and ethnic tolerance. Unlike the situation in many European countries, where powerful centrifugal forces served to keep diverse groups separate from the main body of the nation, in the United States a powerful centripetal force has drawn the disparate elements of the population into a united national community.

To be sure, religious tolerance did not spring fully blown in American colonial society. Indeed, the colonies were a seething cauldron of religious conflict, and only in the final decades of the eighteenth century was some kind of *modus vivendi* established between the various religious groups. The early settlers were frequently religious zealots rather than advocates of religious liberty. Although many found their way to the New World in quest of greater religious freedom for themselves, they were not inclined to extend that same freedom to others.

Still, there were powerful incentives in the American colonial situation to play down religious antagonism. In many of the colonies, religious struggles displayed a dangerous tendency to divide the polity into 'ins' and 'outs'. Religious conflict added a bitter note to political discourse and in extreme cases threatened the very stability of society. Try as they might, few of the established churches possessed sufficient power to impose their will on the conglomeration of Quakers, Baptists, Catholics, and pietist sects that sought shelter in colonial America. If nothing else, the existence of a vast land space in America made the suppression of religious dissidence extremely difficult.

Ultimately, a formula for religious peace developed in America that stressed a broad, interchangeable religiosity rather than highly particularist religious viewpoints. What ultimately emerged was a 'triple melting-pot', made up of three primary religious groups—Protestants, Catholics, and Jews—with each emphasizing what it held in common with the others. The astonishing thing about the triple melting-pot is that it placed the Jews, a tiny group in American society, and one traditionally conceived of by Christians with the utmost hostility, on an equal footing with the two major Christian groups.

What America's pluralist outlook has meant for Jewish life in the United States has been well expressed by historian Henry Feingold in *Zion in America*:

The religious tolerance ultimately produced in Colonial America was . . . an essential prerequisite for the full development of American Jewry. The Colonial approach to Jews seem[s] all the more exceptional when compared to the practice of the Old World. There history had produced an organic concept of nationhood, which, at best, encouraged the viewing of the Jewish community as a foreign body within the nation, and at worst as a pariah group. America had no such backlog of history to depend on for defining itself. It was an artificial contrivance based on rationalist principles. Rather than being based on the historical experience of one group, the national community could be broken down into a constellation of ethnic and religious and racial groups whose history and interests were often at sharp variance. In order to survive, a formula which allowed the various sub-communities to live in harmony with each other was derived. From the beginning Jews were included in this agreement, which is at the very heart of the American polity. It subsequently became difficult to single Jews out officially as a pariah group without threatening the delicate mechanism which bound this disparate nation together. The development of a pluralistic society in America, in effect, removed the special onus under which Jews had traditionally been compelled to live.

3. *The separation of church and state, as called for in the United States Constitution, freed Jews from the burden of living in an officially Christian society.*

Thus far I have been dealing with pluralism as a social fact and social value in the American context. In turning to the separation of church and state, however, the issue becomes one of pluralism as an established legal fact. (The first amendment to the Constitution states: 'Congress shall make no law respecting an establishment of religion, or prohibiting the free exercise thereof.') It should be evident that in any society in which church and state are united, Jews, to some degree at least, must remain outsiders. It is, of course, possible to have a union of church and state in a particular society and yet have a high degree of tolerance of Jews. But that is just the point: it is tolerance, and tolerance bestowed can easily become tolerance denied. Jews are clearly more secure in a situation in which the public arena is seen as neutral as between Judaism and Christianity.

Here an important qualifier needs to be added. To say that the public domain in the United States is neutral does not mean that it is indifferent to religion, let alone hostile to it. Americans—and there is solid evidence to support this point—are, in fact, an extraordinarily pious people. But the fact that the United States Constitution separates church and state means that the public domain can serve as a common meeting-ground for Jews and Christians, and others as well. This explains why American Jews have always been sensitive to any signs of a breaking down of the 'wall of separation'. To quote from the 1990 Joint Program Plan of the National Jewish Community Relations Advisory Council:

The Jewish community has always been profoundly aware that maintaining a firm line of separation between church and state is essential to religious freedom and the religious voluntarism which fosters the creative and distinctive survival of diverse religious groups, such as our own. There has always been an ebb and flow of attempts to breach the wall of separation between church and state in America. Vigorous efforts to protect the principle of church–state separation continue to be vital.

The separation of church and state in the United States has set the stage for the flowering, on a purely voluntaristic basis, of a vibrant Jewish religious life. As a 1991 American Jewish Committee statement observes:

The beneficent teachings of religion have contributed immeasurably to man's progress from barbarism to civilization. This country particularly, settled in large measure by those seeking freedom of conscience, has been profoundly influenced by religious concepts. With church affiliation in the United States now at an all-time peak, religion is certainly an important factor in our lives.

In the opinion of many, the vitality of American churches and synagogues flows from our unique tradition of separating church and state. This cardinal principle has insured freedom of conscience for all. It has permitted scores of religious sects to flourish without hindrance.

In sum, America's separation of church and state has made Jews full equals in the ongoing American enterprise.

4. *The United States as the 'first new nation' lacked a historic culture to which Jews were outsiders at any point.* Here again a basic distinction between the American and the European situations needs to be pointed out. Everywhere in Europe, even when Jews were awarded citizenship in the context of the Emancipation, they had to cope with the fact that the nation-states to which they now belonged had historic cultures going back many hundreds of years, and that these cultures had been moulded in a Christian context; they were thoroughly permeated with Christian ideas, Christian symbols, and so on. Thus, the burden of proof clearly fell on the newly emancipated Jews to demonstrate that they could meaningfully contribute to the further development of these cultures. Antisemites of every stripe, of course, denied that this was possible. Indeed, one of their main objectives was to bring all culture back into an organic coherence based on national tradition. The participation of Jews in any cultural form was regarded by them as an illegitimate intrusion, or even a plot by the enemies of 'the people' to corrupt the national spirit.

In the United States, the situation was radically different. America was a frontier society, made up of people of diverse backgrounds and cultural traditions. The United States lacked a historical culture at the time of the American Revolution. The development of such a culture was a gradual process, and Jews participated in that process at every stage. In the context of American society it lacked plausibility to suggest that Jews were cultural outsiders. Throughout American history, in fact, Jews made vital contributions towards the development of an American cultural tradition. This process—encompassing such areas as literature, the arts, scholarship, and science—of course continues right down to the present time. As Norman Podhoretz, the editor of *Commentary*, noted with regard to literary expression in *The Bloody Crossroads*:

In the years after World War II Jews—many of them raised in households where Yiddish was still the main tongue spoken—*did* become an extraordinary powerful influence in American fiction, American poetry, American drama, American criticism. And so far as the novel in particular is concerned, the British critic Walter Allen was only echoing a standard view when he said, about ten years ago, that the 'dominance' of the Southern school deriving from Faulkner had now 'largely passed to Jewish writers, through the best of whose work . . . a recognizably new note ha[d] come into American fiction, not the less American for being unmistakably Jewish'.

Even in isolation, any of the four factors that I have discussed would have led the American Jewish experience to diverge significantly from the European pattern. In combination, however, the four have led to a veritable revolution in the Jewish situation, setting the stage for unprecedented Jewish achievement and unprecedented Jewish acceptance in the United States. But the fact remains that the American situation is unique and cannot be replicated in the European context. American Jewry may be the paradigm of a successful diaspora community, but it cannot serve, in a direct fashion, as a model for European Jews in their quest for Jewish renewal. Europe is different, which means that European Jewry will have to find its own path.

Notes on Contributors

Professor Geoffrey Alderman has held appointments at University College London, the University College of Swansea, and the University of Reading. He is currently Professor of Politics and Contemporary History at Royal Holloway and Bedford New College. He has published a number of books, including *The Federation of Synagogues* (1987); *London Jewry and London Politics* (1989); *Britain: A One-Party State?* (1989); and *Modern British Jewry* (1992). He is currently writing a biography of Cecil Roth.

Professor Lord Beloff, FBA, is Emeritus Professor of Government and Public Administration in the University of Oxford and an Emeritus Fellow of All Souls College. A full bibliography of his writings is to be found in his book *An Historian in the Twentieth Century: Chapters in Intellectual Autobiography* (Yale University Press, 1992).

Dr Margaret Brearley is currently Fellow in Jewish–Christian Relations at the Institute of Jewish Affairs, London. She was formerly Lecturer in Mediaeval and Renaissance German Literature at Birmingham University; co-founder and director of the West Midlands Israel Information Centre; and Senior Fellow at the Centre for Judaism and Jewish–Christian Relations, Selly Oak Colleges, Birmingham.

Julius Carlebach is Professor of Jewish History and Rektor of the Hochschule für Jüdische Studien, Heidelberg. He is the author of *Karl Marx and the Radical Critique of Judaism* (London, 1978) and of many essays on German-Jewish and Anglo-Jewish social history. He is a member of the executive committee of the Leo Baeck Institute, London.

Professor Mikhail Chlenov is a Research Fellow of the Institute of Ethnology and Anthropology of the Russian Academy of Sciences (Moscow). Since 1989 he has served as a co-President of the Va'ad, the Confederation of Jewish Organizations and Communities of the ex-USSR, and since 1992 as President of the Jewish Federation of Russia. His academic Jewish interests include, among others, problems of sociopolitical development, communal theory, the social demography of ex-Soviet Jewry, Zionism and other national concepts of Jewry, and Jewish ethnology.

Professor Sergio DellaPergola is currently Head of the Division of Jewish Demography and Statistics at the A. Harman Institute of Contemporary

Jewry, the Hebrew University of Jerusalem. He has been a visiting scholar at the Istituto di Statistica, Università di Pavia, and at the Von Grunebaum Center for Near East Studies at the University of California, Los Angeles. He has published widely in the field of Jewish demography in various parts of the world (including studies on Italy, France, the United States, and Israel). His latest research is a Mexican Jewish population study, for the Hebrew University of Jerusalem and El Colegio de Mexico, which he is undertaking with Susana Lerner.

Professor Evyatar Friesel is Professor of Modern Jewish History at the Hebrew University of Jerusalem. His fields of research are German Jewish history, American Jewish history, and ideological trends in modern Jewry; he has published extensively on these themes.

Mgr Pier Francesco Fumagalli is *doctor* of the Ambriosana Library of Milan. From 1986 to 1993 he served as Secretary to the Holy See's Commission for Religious Relations with the Jews at the Pontifical Council for Promoting Christian Unity.

Mr Konstanty Gebert is a journalist from Warsaw and is the local correspondent of the London *Jewish Chronicle*. Writing under the pen-name Dawid Warszawski that he adopted in the Solidarity underground, he covers, among other things, Polish Jewish issues at *Gazeta Wyborcza*, Poland's main daily. He has been a Jewish activist since the late 1970s.

Dr Daniel Gutwein is a lecturer in Modern Jewish History at the University of Haifa and at the Hebrew University of Jerusalem. He has published articles on Jewish economic and social history and Jewish socialism and nationalism and is the author of *The Divided Elite: Economics, Politics and Anglo-Jewry, 1882–1917* (1992). Currently at the Vidal Sassoon International Center for the Study of Antisemitism, at the Hebrew University of Jerusalem, he is working on the history of antisemitism in Britain before the First World War.

Dr András Kovács is a senior research fellow at the Institute of Sociology, Eötvös Loránd University, Budapest. He specializes in research into problems of ethnicity and ethnic identity, and in particular into antisemitism and Jewish identities in post-war Hungary.

Dr Igor Krupnik is currently a Visiting Scholar in the Department of Anthropology at the Smithsonian Institution, Washington, DC. A cultural anthropologist from Moscow, he has been affiliated for fifteen years to the Institute of Ethnology, presently of the Russian Academy of Sciences. His research interests include ethnicities and ethnic policies in the former

Soviet Union, minority studies, and ecological anthropology. Since the early 1980s Dr Krupnik has been very involved in Jewish cultural activities in Moscow, and he was one of the founders of the Jewish Historical–Ethnographic Commission, an independent academic group which revitalized Jewish anthropological studies in Russia.

Rabbi Dr Norman Lamm is President of Yeshiva University and also the Erna and Jakob Michael Professor of Jewish Philosophy at that institution. His most recent work is *Torah Umadda: The Encounter of Religious Learning and Worldly Knowledge in the Jewish Tradition* (1990).

Rabbi Dr Jonathan Magonet is Principal of the Leo Baeck College, London. For more than twenty years has also organized Jewish–Christian and Jewish–Christian–Muslim annual conferences in Germany. His field is Hebrew Bible and he is the author of *A Rabbi's Bible* (1991), *Bible Lives* (1992), and *A Rabbi Reads the Psalms* (1994). He is also co-editor of the prayer-books of the Reform Synagogues of Great Britain and of the journal *European Judaism*.

Dr Elisabeth Maxwell is the founding chairman of *Remembering for the Future* and lectures widely on the Holocaust and Christian–Jewish relations. She has a doctorate from the University of Oxford, is an Honorary Doctor of Temple University, Philadelphia, and an Honorary Fellow of Tel Aviv University. In 1988 she was awarded the Sir Sigmund Sternberg Annual Award and the Interfaith Medallion, and in 1989 the Anne Frank Institute's Eternal Flame Award. Among her publications are *Silence and Speaking Out* (1990) and *The Righteous Gentiles* (1990).

Dr Stephen Miller is Dean of the School of Social Sciences at the City University, London, and is actively involved in social research on the Anglo-Jewish community. His recent works include a survey of the ethnic identity of South African Jewish *émigrés*, a study of the impact of Jewish education on religious belief and practice, and an ongoing survey of the attitudes of Jewish women to Anglo-Jewish institutions and customs. His particular interest is in the psychological mechanisms underlying the transmission of Jewish identity within families.

Rabbi Dr Jonathan Sacks is Chief Rabbi of the United Hebrew Congregations of the Commonwealth and a former principal of Jews' College, the oldest seat of advanced Jewish learning in Europe. He is a Visiting Professor of the University of Essex, and holds honorary doctorates from the University of Cambridge and Middlesex University. His many books include *One People? Tradition, Modernity, and Jewish Unity* (1993) and *Crisis and*

Covenant (1992), and he is a past editor of *L'Eylah: A Journal of Judaism Today*. In his inaugural address in 1991 he initiated a Decade of Renewal, and is currently involved in the establishment of a programme of Jewish Continuity.

Professor Dominique Schnapper is currently Director of Studies at the École des Hautes Études en Sciences Sociales, where she specializes in sociology. She has published a number of books, including *Juifs et Israélites* (1980; published in 1983 in English as *Jewish Identities in France*), *L'Épreuve du chômage* (1981), *La France de l'intégration: Sociologie de la nation en 1990* (1991), and *L'Europe des immigrés* (1992). She is currently finishing a theoretical work on nationhood.

Professor Eliezer Schweid is Professor of Modern Jewish Thought at the Hebrew University of Jerusalem and is the author of many books and articles in this field. The problem of Jewish identities, especially in Israel, is one of his central themes.

Dr David Singer is Director of Research for the American Jewish Committee and editor of the *American Jewish Year Book*.

Rabbi Dr Norman Solomon is founder and director of the Centre for the Study of Judaism and Jewish–Christian Relations, Birmingham. He is a recognized lecturer of the University of Birmingham and Visiting Lecturer at the Oxford Centre for Postgraduate Hebrew Studies, and has taken an active role in Christian–Jewish dialogue in many countries, including Poland and Czechoslovakia. He is the author of *Judaism and World Religion* (1991) and *The Analytical Movement: Hayyim Soloveitchik and his Circle* (1993).

Dr Shmuel Trigano is currently Professor of Sociology at Paris X–Nanterre University, Director of the Collège des Études Juives at the Alliance Israélite Universelle, and editor of *Pardès*, a journal of Jewish studies. He has published a number of books, including *La Demeure oubliée: Genèse religieuse du politique* (1984) and *Philosophie de la loi: L'Origine de la politique dans la Tora* (1993), and has recently completed editing the fourth and last volume of *La Société juive à travers l'histoire*.

Dr Jonathan Webber is the Frank Green Fellow in Jewish Social Studies at the Oxford Centre for Postgraduate Hebrew Studies, Hebrew Centre Lecturer in Social Anthropology at the University of Oxford, and a Research Fellow at Wolfson College. He co-chairs a weekly seminar series at the University of Oxford on Identity and Ethnicity, and has published on related topics, including Jewish identity, Jewish fundamentalism, the future of Auschwitz, and the mythologization of the Holocaust. Currently, Dr Webber is holder of a research grant funded by the Economic and Social Research Council of the United Kingdom on a project in its East–West programme entitled 'Ethnic Identities in Europe after Auschwitz: The Case of Polish–Jewish Relations'. His most recent publication is *Auschwitz: A History in Photographs*, which he co-edited with Teresa Świebocka and Connie Wilsack.

Professor Robert Wistrich is Professor of Modern Jewish History at the Hebrew University of Jerusalem and is the incumbent of the Jewish Chronicle chair in Jewish History at University College, London. He is the author of a number of distinguished books, including *The Jews of Vienna in the Age of Franz Joseph* (1989) and *Antisemitism: The Longest Hatred* (1991).

Index